Joy Mawby grew up in Camberley, Surrey, became a teacher and later a headteacher.

Throughout her career, she encouraged children with their writing and in the performing arts. She wrote and produced numerous plays for her students.

On retirement, she moved to Anglesey and had time to give to her own writing. She has had plays performed locally and has had two books published, *Footsteps to Freedom* and *Broken Warrior.* Both are true stories of remarkable people she was fortunate enough to meet.

Joy has two children, three very creative grandchildren and two dogs who keep her fit.

www.joymawby.co.uk

John Vesliga's early story is told in this book. He later married and settled in Cheshire where he worked as a technician in the Scientific Services Department of Astra Zenica. There, he was also a leading first aider.

He retired to Anglesey where he engages in DIY, gardening and enjoying the wonderful beaches and countryside. He is still an avid reader.

John has two children and a small grandson.

John Vesligaj and Joy Mawby

THE MAN IN THE NAUTICAL HAT

AUSTIN MACAULEY
PUBLISHERS LTD.

A CIP catalogue record for this title is available from the British Library.

ISBN 978 1 84963 964 4

www.austinmacauley.com

First Published (2014)
Austin Macauley Publishers Ltd.
25 Canada Square
Canary Wharf
London
E14 5LB

Printed and bound in Great Britain

Acknowledgments

We acknowledge our sincere gratitude to:

Ann Donlan for reading the manuscript and giving us great encouragement.

Kay Middlemiss for editing, proof reading and giving constructive criticism on the manuscript.

Geoffrey Lincoln for designing the wonderful cover picture.

Carl Whitfield, of CWW Photography, for supplying the photograph of the beach which appears on the cover (www.photosofcornwall.com)

Dragica Petrak, John's sister for talking over 'old times' with him and for supplying some of the photographs which appear inside the book.

Our many friends who have encouraged us in this endeavour.

Contents

The Story

I met him on the beach, the man with a wide smile, a nautical hat and a black Labrador. As is the way with dog-walkers, we fell into conversation. I couldn't place his accent then he told me he was from Croatia and had lived in Britain for over forty years. His name is John.

Throughout that year I met him walking, often chatting with other dog-owners. Sometimes we'd walk together, sometimes we'd simply exchange greetings.

One day he stopped me and said he'd heard I was a writer. 'I have a story, you know. It's about when I was young,' he said but when I suggested he should write it, he shook his head and asked, 'Would you write it for me?'

So I did.

Once a week, for more than a year, John and I sat in my kitchen and, over coffee, he told me his story and I wrote it down. At last it was finished. As I looked at the pile of typed manuscript I realised that I couldn't let this be the end. I had to visit John's country before I could complete my task.

So I did.

It was then that the story I had recorded came alive for me. Of course times have changed. Of course life has moved on and the country itself has been transformed since John left. But, for me, the towns, cities and countryside of Croatia are now populated with real people, each with his or her unique story to tell.

And this is John's.

Joy Mawby

1962

'How are you doing?' asked Marshal Tito.

'Fine, thank you, sir.'

'Now where did you say you were from? Oh yes, you're from the same part of the country as I am, aren't you?'

'Yes, sir.'

'What does your father do?'

'He was killed in the war, sir.'

'I'm sorry. Which side was he on?'

I hesitated but decided on honesty. 'He was in the German army, sir.'

Tito smiled. 'Well, those were turbulent times. They set brother against brother and son against father.'

I thought of my brothers Milan and Josip. 'Yes, sir,' I said. Then I thought of the turbulent times and of my earliest memory...

Ivica
1944-1949: aged 4-9 years

The beginning

From my safe place under the big oak kitchen table, I see the bright red fireflies hurtling past our window. Suddenly there's a crash against the outside wall. The noise hurts my ears. There's a split second of silence and then our kitchen window crashes inwards on to the floor.

It is 1944, my name is Ivan Vesligaj and I live in Croatia which is part of Yugoslavia. I'm four years old and I will always remember that day. The noise frightens me but I'm curious.

'How can fireflies break the window?' I whisper to one of my bigger brothers, Ignace.

'They're not fireflies, they're pieces of metal called shrapnel,' he says.

Our village is being bombed by the Nazis.

I'm told that, earlier, as we played outside, some Partizans – communists and followers of Josip Broz Tito – came along the path. They were instantly recognisable because each wore a hat, on which there was a red star. The men stopped by our neighbours' door and chalked a number and something else on it and then they walked into our garden and wrote on our door too.

'That number is how many of our loyal fighters you must feed,' said one to my mother and, pointing to the writing, 'this tells you where to take the food.' Later Mama told us that it was the Partizans in and around our village that brought about the Nazi raid. It came as we were all in the garden, enjoying the cool evening. At the first 'boom', Mama grabbed us younger ones and shouted at the others to get inside and under the table. My uncle was not fast enough. A piece of shrapnel sliced off part of his thumb. Mama washed Uncle's hand straight away and carefully bandaged it.

Unfortunately one of my older brothers, Adalbert, and my big sister, Dragica, were some distance from the house at the time of the raid. They decided it would be quicker to dash down the hill to the next village. As they ran, shrapnel hit Adalbert's arm, tearing it open from hand to elbow. Dragica shouted for help and several people appeared and carried our brother into the nearest house. It belonged to a man who was a member of Ustasa, the fascist Croatian army which was fighting with the Nazis. The man, however, immediately snatched my brother up in his arms and ran with him to the German hospital, about an hour away. There, a doctor stitched his arm. When it had healed Adalbert was very proud of his long scar.

The walls of our farmhouse and the adjoining barn were a metre thick but the barn loft, where our grain was stored had wooden walls, lined with dried stalks of corn and the roof was straw. When all the excitement was over, Mama went up into the loft to inspect the damage. She found the walls riddled with holes and the store of corn full of shrapnel. She said it was a miracle that the whole lot hadn't gone up in smoke. Amazingly there were only two fatalities in the village. The bee keeper was killed while trying to ensure the safety of his bees and Franz, a friend of my father's, who lived just above our village, was badly injured. I remember hearing someone call to Mama,

'Hanika, come quickly. Bring sheets and blankets!' She did all she could but Franz died the next day, 25th June.

It's strange that I can actually remember that date. It must be because we were caught up in another adventure. It was a beautiful summer day. I was playing with my brothers outside when we heard planes almost overhead. Peering up, Adalbert said,

'They're British – Wellingtons. I bet they're on their way to bomb the Germans in Hungary.' Almost before he finished speaking we saw two Messerschmitt flying fast and low over the forest which bordered the village. The noise of their engines filled the air as they hurtled between the Wellingtons. They started firing. The British gunners rapidly returned fire. It all happened very quickly. Mama shrieked at us to get inside because bullets were falling all around. Catching her panic, we screamed and made a dash for the door. Once inside, in spite of Mama instructing us to stand back, we crowded to the newly repaired window. For a few breathless moments we watched, spellbound. We saw one of the Wellingtons wobble unsteadily. It had been hit and was starting to fall. Then four shapes, one after the other, fell from it just before the plane itself, now ablaze, dropped to the ground. We saw four white parachutes open and waft down, blown by the wind towards the forest. Two of them disappeared from sight over the trees but two of them hovered for a moment and then seemed to be blown back towards us and, wonder of wonders, they landed in one of our fields.

By now the other planes had gone so we all ran across the rough pasture to find the parachutists. They were unhurt and my mother insisted they should come back to our house.

'You are lucky that there are no Germans around the village today,' she said. 'You can hide here safely.' She spoke in German and acted out her words and they understood.

I remember the shiny fur-topped boots of the airmen. One of them had an impressively big moustache which he wiped with the back of his hand when he'd finished the best part of a bottle of plum brandy. Three Partizans, who had been watching the happenings of the day, came into our house a little later. They talked softly to Mama. When they'd gone she told us that the men would be taken to safety. When we got up the next morning they had gone. One of the airmen left us his parachute from which Mama made underclothes and blouses for herself and my sisters. The white silk blouses were the envy of every woman in the village.

The next day we went to see the wreckage of the Wellington. We weren't allowed to touch it as we were told that one of the crew had died and his body was inside. The remains of the plane are there to this day. They are enclosed by a fence and looked after by the British War Graves Commission.

I was the eighth of ten children. We lived on a farm in Gornja Plemenšćina, a small village sixty kilometres from Zagreb.

Ivan's village

In 1944, there were German soldiers everywhere, even in our unimportant village. These soldiers and the Partizans were locked in an on-going battle. My father and eldest brother, Milan, were in the German army. Another brother, Josip, at fourteen years of age, had run away from home and joined the Partizans. Thus our family was a microcosm of what was happening throughout my country.

I remember, once when my father was home on leave from the army, we all went together to our vineyard which was about a twenty minute walk from home and on the slope of a hillside. Even the youngest of us was expected to help with the harvest. Suddenly we heard the thud of horses' hooves and ran out on to the footpath to see what was happening. Then came firing from St Ann's Church which stood above our land and was held by the Germans. As the horses came into view, we saw they were ridden by Partizans bent on attacking the Germans. Tata and Mama pushed us into the shelter of the vines. Tata sped back to the pathway. He had glimpsed my brother Josip amongst the Partizans. He waited until Josip drew level then he reached up and, somehow, dragged him from the horse. He bundled him into the vineyard and gave him a good hiding. The rest of us watched, open-mouthed. We felt very sorry for our brother but later, when we heard that the group of Partizans had been wiped out by the Germans, we thought our father was a hero.

We were a family of blond, blue eyed children which was important when it came to the 'Race Assessment' carried out by the local German officials. On such occasions, anyone suspected of being a gypsy was singled out and sent away from the village. At that time, none of us knew where they went.

Mama took us to see a wounded German soldier one day. He had escaped from a battle with the Partizans and dragged himself to a nearby farm where he'd crawled into the barn. The farmer had discovered him and was able to communicate with him because he had picked up some German during the First World War. This was the case with many of the older men in the village. The farmer was hurriedly preparing his cow-drawn cart to take the injured man to hospital. I can see that German soldier now, his face ashen against his muddy grey uniform. One leg was badly injured, high up on his thigh and his trouser leg was torn and bloody. He opened his eyes as we gazed at him and whispered, '*Hilfe, Hilfe'*/ 'Help. Help.'

Mama sent us out and re-dressed the man's wound and then made sure that he was as comfortable as possible in the cart. She was always willing to help people in trouble whether they were our neighbours or British or German. It made no difference to her.

Our father was of German descent and my mama of Austrian. German was their mother tongue. Before the war, they had worked hard on our farm where they kept cows, grew corn, potatoes and other vegetables as well as grapes. Once Father had joined the army, Mama kept everything going with the help of my older brothers and sisters. We were fortunate because we were pretty self-sufficient which became vital once *fasung*/weekly rations were imposed. Cows were important to us and we would take them to the local bull when the season was right. Apart from giving us milk, cows pulled our cart which was used as transport for us and the farm produce. Bull calves were kept and fattened for meat or, when old enough, rented to local farmers to serve their cows. There were no cars or even bicycles in our village and, as a rule, we children walked everywhere but we were one of the few families which owned a horse. It had belonged to a German who had moved on with his regiment. I don't know why he left his horse, called Pubi, behind. As a special treat we were sometimes allowed to ride him.

One day the local priest came to the house and, after some discussion with Mama, led Pubi away. I was angry with my mother for giving our horse to the priest but she was short with me. She pulled some money out of the pocket of her overall. 'This money is what the priest paid me for Pubi,' she said. 'It will help me feed and clothe you all.' I didn't say anything else.

My mother was renowned for her cooking and was often called upon to cook for German officers who were stationed in the forest camp near where we lived. They would bring all the ingredients to the house the day before so that the meal was ready when they arrived. We used to sit and watch them enjoying the food while we relished the sugar cubes and chocolate they had brought for us. Later we would curl up in our beds, covered by blankets which they had provided.

On one of these occasions, one of the officers walked across the kitchen to look at the family photos we had on the wall. He pointed to one which showed Milan in his German army uniform and another which showed Josip, wearing his Partizan's hat.

'Who are these?' he asked.

'My eldest sons,' answered Mama.

'Take this one down,' said the officer, pointing to Josip. 'No, on second thoughts, take them both down. It will be safer for you.' Mama did as he said.

She had never complied with the Partizans' requests for food, relying rather on the protection of the Germans who so often ate at our house. I think this was because she felt she had more in common with the Germans. She spoke the same language, to some extent shared their culture and they were always polite while many of the Partizans were rough-mannered and threatening. One day, as I was playing in the garden and Mama was hanging out washing, I heard a man's voice.

'You fascist!' he was shouting. I ran to Mama's side and when I looked to see who had shouted, I saw a tall, thin man, with a red star on his hat, pointing a gun at her. Terrified, I hung on to her skirt. She pushed me behind her then stood quite still. There was a moment of silence and then I heard the quiet calm voice of another man who I could not see.

'No. Put your gun down. That woman has an army of children to feed. What good will it do anyone if you kill her?' Slowly the first man lowered the gun and walked away.

In the autumn of 1944, my father, severely injured, was brought home for Mama to nurse. The path to our village was too narrow for the wagon which had brought him most of the way so soldiers carried him on a stretcher to our house. We stood round as my mother, white-faced, led the men into the bedroom, hastily throwing a clean sheet on to the bed before they put their burden down. Tata's face was wrapped in bloody bandages as was his body and one of his legs. I could only see one of his arms and I began to cry.

'Take the little ones out,' my mother told my sister, Dragica. We were all so shocked that we shivered and held on to each other.

Mama was tireless, feeding Tata, washing and dressing his wounds, hardly ever leaving his side. We crept about the house, looking after ourselves, frightened of what the future might hold. In spite of Mama's best efforts, Tata's condition deteriorated. The doctor came from the next village and said he must go to hospital. Mama went with him in a neighbour's small cart. We were frightened to sleep but exhaustion overcame me and I slept at last. I was woken by unfamiliar noises. My sisters were in the room where I slept with my brothers, and they were crying. Mama came in, looking so sad. We all gathered round her and I could tell, by her face, that something dreadful had happened.

'On the way to the hospital, Tata suddenly became worse,' she said. 'He grabbed my hand and cried out, "Oh my children," then he leant back on the pillow and God took him. His last thoughts were of you all. Now we must be brave and help each other.'

There had been no point in going on to the hospital so the neighbours had carried Tata's body home. Two of them laid wooden planks from headboard to footboard of Mama's big bed and they lifted Tata's body on to these. I had to be lifted up to look at him. He looked as if he were asleep and I thought he would open his eyes at any moment and smile at me.

He lay there for two days and everyone from round about came to pay their respects. Then four men lifted my father's body into a coffin and carried him along the dirt track to St Mirko's Church in the next village. Mama said it took them over an hour to get there. She wouldn't let my little brothers and me go to the funeral, saying we were too young.

I couldn't stop thinking about Tata. I couldn't believe he'd gone for ever. I expected to see him walking along the footpath to our house to spend a few days leave at home. I even looked out for him sometimes until my sisters or Mama gently reminded me that he would not be coming home again.

One night I woke up and was sure I saw him looking at me through the window. I could see him clearly in the moonlight. He waved and I got out of bed and went closer to talk to him. I can't remember what I said but Mama heard my voice and came to investigate.

'Who are you talking to, Ivica?' she asked. I pointed to the window.

'To Tata.'

'Ivica, there's no-one there. Go back to bed. It's the middle of the night.' When I looked again the figure had disappeared. By now the three brothers with whom I shared my bed and even my sisters, who slept with Mama, were awake. When they heard me say I'd seen Tata outside the window, they were all frightened, dashed back to bed and pulled the covers over their heads in case they should see a dead Tata too. The next day Mama told the priest what had happened.

'Innocent children can often see things which we cannot see,' was his response.

Soon after the death of my father, three members of the SS came to our village. One of our neighbours rushed to our house with the news. 'I think they've come to shoot us all, God help us!' he cried.

'Why would they do that?' asked Mama and she went outside to talk to the officers, warning us to stay indoors until she found out what was happening. She came back almost straight away. 'We all have to leave the village,' she said. 'The soldiers say there will be a battle here between Partizans and the German army and we should leave within an hour if we don't want to be caught up in it.'

Just then, another neighbour, Franz, called through the door, 'The soldiers say we should put our own mark on our pigs and let them out to fend for themselves and let the cows and hens out too. They don't think we'll have to be away long. They suggest we all go to Halužini which should be far enough away.'

I remember a scramble to get everything ready then Mama locked the doors of the house and the barn.

'Please God, keep our home safe,' she said. Even I carried a small bundle containing a few clothes. My older brothers and sisters carried more and helped little Lujzek along and Mama carried baby Stjepan.

It was about an hour's walk to Halužini, up a steep slope and through the forest. I was tired long before we arrived. My bundle grew heavier but I didn't complain because everyone else, except the little ones, was carrying much more than I was. We were fortunate to have a family member living in the village – my father's sister had a farm there. She wasn't expecting us but she made us very welcome, accommodating some of us in the house and my big brothers in the barn. We sat round the scrubbed wooden table and had corn bread and soured milk for supper which was absolutely delicious.

I was too young to understand that, in 1945, German rules were replaced by laws laid down by the new communist regime led by Marshal Tito. Mama heard that my brother, Milan, in the German army, had been captured by British paratroopers.

He told us, later, that the paratroopers had taken him and others to the River Drava. There, with about 30,000 other Croatian men, who had been members of the German army, they were handed over to Tito's Forces. They were then marched to the prison at Lepoglava in northern Croatia and many died on the way. In Yugoslavia, this became known as 'The Long March'.

Milan said that every day people were taken out of the prison cells at Lepoglava and shot. After one week, it was the turn of the men in his cell. They were lined up along a wall and an officer ran his eye along them. 'You, you, you and you – come and stand behind me.' He was pulling out the youngest men, those who still looked reasonably fit after their ordeal. Milan was one of the men selected. The rest were shot in front of him. The next day a lorry came for the survivors. They were taken to a naval base and enlisted into what was known as 'Tito's Navy'. It was four more years before Milan saw us all again. He came back to the village, married and had fifteen children.

I remember that it was hard for us after the war. Under communist rule we had to give a third of what we produced on the farm to the local Communist Bureau. As soon as we were old enough, we children had to help in the house and on the farm. However, I remember my childhood as carefree and happy. I was free to roam, to play with my brothers and sisters and to enjoy our stable, happy home. I wouldn't exchange what I had then for a million pounds.

The year 1947, when I was seven, must have been a particularly difficult year for my mother. I was woken by her shouts. We children ran outside into the damp coolness of the early morning and stared, in disbelief at ruined vegetables and, beyond the garden, to our field of flattened corn. A severe hailstorm in the night was to blame. Almost all of our tender vine shoots were destroyed as well. Everyone in the village lost their crops that night and had to fall back on their meagre reserves of cash. At the time, I didn't understand why, but shop keepers were not willing to help my mother out. I know, now, that it was because Mama had chosen to feed German soldiers rather than Partizans.

When my sister, Dragica, took a sack to our local store, hoping to buy corn, the store-keeper refused to serve her. I was frightened when I saw how distressed Mama was when Dragica returned empty-handed. When my brother Josip came in my mother was in tears.

'Whatever's the matter?' he asked. When Mama told him he was furious. 'Come with me,' he said. The next day I heard Mama talking to a neighbour,

'Josip picked up his gun and insisted he would go to the store with me,' she said. 'When we got there, Josip went in, pulled out the gun and pointed it at the store-keeper. He backed away, terrified. I was scared too. I didn't want Josip to do anything silly. He told me to help myself to as much as I could carry. I grabbed what I could and then ran home. At last I could put bread on the table for my children.' Strangely, I don't think there were any repercussions over the incident, presumably because of Josip's erstwhile Partizan connections and membership of the Party.

Just after this, my freedom was curtailed for I had to start school. My teacher, Sajik Fanika, was a young widow. She was slim with curly blond hair but pupils had to earn her wide smile for she was strict and had no time for slackers. I have a lot to thank her for. Not only did she awaken in me a desire to work hard at school and learn more about everything but also I discovered that she cared about all of us, her pupils.

Money was so short at home that we went about barefoot which was fine in the summer but Mama worried about us in winter time. One cold morning, she wrapped my feet carefully in strips of cloth to give some protection against the bitter weather. It took 45 minutes to walk to school and by the time I was half way there, the cloths were becoming uncomfortable. Quickly I stripped them off, put them under a bush to collect on my way home and ran the rest of the way barefoot. As I stood warming my feet by the big stove which stood in the middle of the classroom, the teacher said, 'Where are your shoes, Ivan?'

'I haven't any Miss,' I replied.

'Come with me.'

She took me across the road to the local government social welfare office where an official measured my feet. He pulled out a box of shoes from a cupboard behind him and gave me a strong pair about two sizes too big. This didn't matter because I could share them with my older brother, Martin. I went to the morning sessions of school and he went in the afternoons so we used to meet half way and I'd hand the shoes over to him. A week after the shoe incident Mama received a letter, from the local government bureau, inviting her to take her children to the Red Cross Office. There, we were taken into a room which had lots of shelves on which were piles of clothes. We were given trousers, shirts and jackets by a smiling lady. All this happened because of the intervention of Sajk Fanika.

Things continued difficult into 1948. Those of us who were old enough, got up at 3 am to work on our land before school. After school we tended the animals, chopped wood and did anything else Mama required of us. There was often homework to do after supper and we all went early to bed. When we were hungry we would go to the forest where, in season, wild black cherries and blackberries grew. We gorged on these and if they were maggoty, well, never mind and, in spite of all our work, there was always time to play.

Life, as I had always known it, came to an abrupt end in 1949. Two years earlier, I had been one of about a dozen children attending communion preparation classes in St Ann's Church. These classes were conducted by Father Rukelj Josip. We had to learn the catechism and its history and about the lives of a myriad of saints. I was a fast learner and keen to show off my knowledge at any opportunity. This had brought me to the notice of the priest. He knew what a struggle Mama had to care for us all and one day he called on Mama.

Ivan with his mother – first communion

'Hanika,' he said, 'You have many children to feed and clothe. How would you like me to take one of your boys into my house? I will provide him with clothes and food and I will educate him. In return, he will be my altar boy. What do you say?'

What could she say? Not only was it an honour for the family to be selected by the priest but life was a struggle and to have one of her children secure and with good prospects would be an enormous relief.

'Which of my sons do you want?' she asked.

'Ivek,' he replied.

Background Notes

I am not an historian but alongside writing this story, I felt it incumbent upon me to read something of Yugoslavia's history.

In Ivan's early life, politics and events outside his little world of family, church and school would not have impinged on his consciousness. As I read, however, I could see how from the start these 'outside things' had a bearing on his life – not always directly, of course, but as part of his background.

Thus I have given short historical notes at the end of each section, each stage of Ivan's life. I know I have mentioned only the tiniest fraction of the unfolding history of Yugoslavia but I hope that what I have written will go some way towards putting Ivan's story into context.

1940 – 1949

Ivan was born in Croatia, part of Yugoslavia in 1940, nine months after the outbreak of the Second World War. A year earlier, Britain had supported a coup d'etat in Yugoslavia which had replaced the prince regent, a Nazi supporter, with the young heir to the throne, Petar.

On 6th April 1941 the Germans attacked Belgrade from the air and followed this with an invasion. In spite of a brave defence, Yugoslavia was forced to surrender. Nazi puppet states were set up in Croatia, Montenegro and Serbia. Croatia was re-named 'The Independent State of Croatia'. Prince Petar fled to England and, during June 1941, set up a government-in-exile in London.

The most effective anti-Nazi resistance came from a group known as Partizans, led by Croatian born Josip Broz Tito. One of Ivan's brothers was a member of this movement. In 1943 the Allies recognised the Partizans as the official army of Yugoslavia. Tito became its supreme leader and conferred on himself the title of Marshal. So great was support for him, both at home and abroad – particularly from Stalin, that he was declared head of state. On 29th November 1945 Tito's communist assembly deposed King Petar.

With the end of the war and victory for the Allies, Yugoslavia was re-named 'The Federal Socialist Peoples' Republic of Yugoslavia'. It comprised, six republics; Croatia, Slovenia, Bosnia and Herzegovinia, Serbia (which included Kosovo), Macedonia and Montenegro. National borders took no account of ethnic groupings. Each republic was given the right to secede but, in fact, the Republic would never have allowed a nation to leave the union.

Although Yugoslavia joined 'Comiform', a forum for international co-operation between communist states, Tito was criticised by Stalinists for not adhering strictly to communist principles. A rift started to open between Yugoslavia and the rest of the communist world.

Ivek
1949-1953: aged 9-13 years

Priest's House

On the appointed day, Mama made a little bundle of my clothes and kissed me. 'Be a good boy,' she instructed, handing the bundle to me, with tears in her eyes. 'Behave like a gentleman. Make me proud of you.' By now my sisters were in service, working away from home, but Martin, Lujzek and Stjepan clustered round me, perhaps envious of my good fortune at being chosen. But, at that moment, I would have changed places with any of them. I didn't cry because I was nine years old and I was going to be educated but I felt as if I'd swallowed a walnut, shell and all. I turned my face up to be kissed by Mama and then I walked away from my home.

From the top of the hill, I turned and waved and let the tears run down my cheeks. I dragged my feet through the forest, delaying my arrival, thinking about my brothers playing our favourite hiding game without me. I wondered if I'd be able to learn whatever it was the priest wanted to teach me. The only glimmer in my sadness was that I would soon be seeing Pubi – Pubi, the horse I loved.

Faruh – the priest's house

The door to Faruh

Faruh, the priest's house was in Potkostel, a village close to ours. Of course I had often seen the large grey house with its red tiled roof before but I had never been inside. It was made up of two separate buildings. I knew that three nuns lived in the house and one of them, Sister Kazimira, was looking out for me as I walked up the pathway. She came hurrying round from the back, smiling.

'Welcome Ivek,' she said. 'Come in and make yourself at home.' Much comforted, I followed her round the house to a brown door which had coloured glass in its top half. I learned, later, that the enormous wooden front door I had thought was the main door to the house, led to steps which went down to the cellar. 'Father Josip's bedroom is in the small building over there,' Kazimira said, pointing to the left. 'Your room is in this part of the house where we sisters also sleep.' She took my bundle from me. 'I'll show you where everything is.' I felt afraid that I'd get lost in such a big house and would I ever get used to sleeping upstairs?

Kazimira led me into a hallway. An alien smell filled my nostrils. I was to discover that it was disinfectant. I had never been in such a fine house before and was amazed by the highly polished furniture and by the many rows of books. Sebastijana and Franceska, the other two sisters, came to greet me and all three fussed round me, giving me cake and a mug of milk.

After that Kazimira showed me where Father Josip's study and a conference room were on the ground floor and then we went up to my little bedroom which adjoined the nun's cells. Its walls were painted white and a small white bed stood in the corner. There was a wooden chair behind the door and a cupboard. 'Put your clothes in there,' Kazimira said, 'and then come down to the kitchen.'

I managed to find my way back and, as I went in Sebastijana, the oldest of the sisters said, 'The first thing you need to learn, Ivek, is how to address Father Josip and any other priest or sister you happen to meet and that includes us.' She indicated herself and the other two nuns. 'You must say, "Hvaljem Isus / Blessed be Jesus". Practice saying it now.' When I could say it perfectly, Franceska clapped her hands.

'Well done, Ivek.' Just then Father Josip arrived back from some parish business.

'Ah here you are Ivek,' he said.

Sebastijana nudged me and I stuttered out, *'Hvaljem Isus.'* Father Josip looked pleased and patted my shoulder.

'You've learned that quickly,' he said. 'Now I'm going to take you to Pregrada to buy new clothes. You must look smart if you're to be an altar boy and you need special vestments.' I didn't argue, of course, but I thought it strange because the cassock Father Josip wore was shabby and patched.

We went out into the sunshine and there was Pubi, harnessed to a small trap. I ran to him and stroked his head. He nuzzled against me. I knew he recognised me because he made a little whinnying noise. 'Jump in,' the priest instructed. I obeyed and looked afresh at St Mirko, the church at which I would perform most of my duties as altar boy. To our right, it stood tall and proud. I forgot my earlier sadness and was glad I had been chosen for such an important task.

St Mirko's Church

We visited two places in Pregrada. At the first, I was measured for trousers, shirts and a jacket. At the second, Father bought my new altar boy's clothes. I was to wear a white robe, with red epaulettes. Under that would be a long red skirt which showed below the robe. I was very pleased with the whole outfit. However, when we got back to the priest's house I was alarmed to discover that I was expected to officiate as altar boy the very next morning. 'It's not difficult,' Father Josip said. He explained to me exactly what I had to do and I repeated it back to him. Satisfied, he went on to tell me the words I had to say. They were, of course, in Latin. I felt panic rising. How on earth would I remember this strange language? The kindly nuns drilled me, translating, so that it all made sense and also helped me with the pronunciation.

'Don't worry,' urged Sebastijana. 'We'll be behind you in church. We'll whisper what you have to say if you get stuck.'

'I'll help you as well,' said the priest. 'You'll soon get the hang of it.'

Before I went to bed that night, I had to wash myself, especially my feet. The nuns were very particular about cleanliness. I couldn't help feeling anxious about my duties the next morning but even the anxiety was soon blotted out by my intense loneliness. I had never slept in a bed on my own before. How I missed my brothers. How quiet it was. I felt desolate and cried myself to sleep that first night and on many ensuing nights too.

My comforter, when I was stricken with homesickness, was Pubi. When I was very sad I would go to the stable and stroke him and talk to him. I was delighted to learn that one of my duties was to care for Pubi and even more delighted when I discovered that I would also be required to ride him.

Somehow I got through Mass the next morning and then it was time for school. I had to start at a new one and I never really settled there. There was no-one like Sajk Fanika to take an interest in me and some of the big boys bullied me. I'd been top of the class at my last school but now there was little time to do homework and so I slipped down the ranks. Not only did I have my altar boy duties, I had to collect wood from the forest for the priest, feed and groom Pubi and take him to the river for water, help care for the cows and pigs and do any odd jobs that arose. I also had to study Latin.

One of the few chances I had of seeing my mother was when Father Josip celebrated Mass at St Ann's Church, in my own village. Mama would give me a big hug after the service and ask me if I was well and happy. Sometimes I was allowed to go home with her for a few hours. Then my brothers and I would run up to the forest and play hiding or battles or build a camp. I always had to be back at Faruh before it was dark.

One Sunday, during St Ann's Mass, Mama was gazing proudly at my back view while I knelt at the altar rail when she was horrified to see movement around my collar. I was infested with lice. She hurried me home, venting her anger on the nuns as we went. 'There are three of them. Between them they should be able to keep you clean – they should wash your clothes regularly and make sure you wash every day.'

'They do make me wash and they wash my clothes regularly,' I answered, feeling I must defend my three friends.

'Well, they should inspect you and your clothes more often. And why have they let your hair grow so?' The heads of the boys in the village were generally shaved but I think the nuns liked my blonde wavy hair and had allowed it to grow unusually long.

'I must have picked up the lice at school. Most of the girls there have long hair,' I countered. By now we'd arrived home.

'Strip yourself off,' Mama ordered. She filled a big bowl with cold water and added a little hot from a pan that was always on the stove. 'Wash yourself thoroughly and borrow some clothes from Martin. I'll wash these and dry them quickly in the sun and I shall give you a note to take back to those nuns of yours.'

The nuns were upset and shocked by Mama's letter. 'You picked up those lice at school,' Sebastiajana exclaimed. 'This house is absolutely clean.' After that, one of the sisters inspected my clothes every night and washed them in very hot water and wood ash twice a week.

It wasn't long before my life as an altar boy settled into a routine. I rose at 5 and joined the nuns for prayers. If I wasn't taking communion later, I ate a breakfast of porridge. If I was to take communion, breakfast came after that. One day I was so hungry that I slipped into the garden and ate some fruit. Conscience-stricken, I ran to the church and confessed this misdeed to Father Josip who forgave me because I had been honest but, of course, I couldn't take communion that day.

I had to be in school by 8 am. After school, I groomed, fed and watered Pubi, cleaned out the barn and brought the cows in from pasture as it grew dark.

I usually rode Pubi through the forest to the river for him to drink his fill. On one occasion, I decided to prove my skill as a horseman by riding bareback. The path down to the river was steep, narrow and slippery. I just managed to control the horse although our descent was faster than usual. Suddenly I heard a scream and saw somebody dive out of our way and into a bush. Pubi was going too fast for me to stop him and investigate and soon we reached the river. Immediately Pubi bent his head to drink and, failing to cling on, I slid down his neck, over his head and into the water with an almighty splash. Unhurt but gasping and thoroughly soaked, I emerged from the water and waited for Pubi to finish drinking. I felt relieved that no-one had witnessed my escapade,

Imagine my humiliation when, the next day, my teacher called me forward. 'Ivek, you must be more careful when you ride the horse to the river,' she said. I was dumbfounded. 'It is stupid to ride bareback on such a slope. You have no control over the horse as you found out when you reached the river yesterday.' Here she chuckled.

'But how…?' I began.

'Didn't you wonder who it was on the path? Don't you remember someone jumping into a bush to get out of your way?'

My face flamed red and I never rode the horse bareback to the river again.

After I had finished tending the animals, I would go back to the house, wash and change and then say prayers with the nuns before supper. Afterwards, when I had helped the nuns to clear and wash the dishes, I had to spend time studying Latin.

Each evening Father Josip went to visit his friends. He returned at 9 pm and went to his room. Just before that time, one of the nuns went to prepare the priest's room. Warm water was taken in, the fire tended and a warming pan filled with hot coals was placed in the bed. Franceska told me that when Father returned to his room whichever nun was on duty washed his feet. I noticed that it took Sebastijana only 10-15 minutes to complete her tasks. It took Kazimira a little longer – about half an hour but sometimes it took Franceska almost an hour. I thought this strange because Sebastijana was not as young and energetic as Franceska who, I discovered, was only 18. She was slim and moved swiftly and gracefully. There was always a frosty atmosphere after she had prepared the priest's room and sometimes there were arguments, carried on in Latin so that I couldn't understand. When all was quiet again, Sebastijana would say, 'Time for prayers and you too Ivek.'

One evening Franceska was in the priest's bedroom for over an hour and when she returned to the kitchen the other two nuns turned on her. 'Why have you been so long?' Sebastijana shouted.

'Yes, what kept you?' Kazimira demanded. A very long and loud argument, in Latin, ensued. It was the worst argument I had heard in that house. At times I thought the nuns would come to blows.

Then, quite suddenly it was over and Sebastijana said, 'It's time for prayers and you too Ivek. Franceska, you can lead them.'

The next morning everything appeared normal except that Sebstjana prepared a rota showing whose duty it was, each evening, to tend to the priest's room. She also made a column in which the time taken over this task had to be recorded. A couple of days later, Father Josip called the sisters into his office. I happened to be sweeping the hallway outside and heard an exchange in Latin. Then the nuns went very quiet and the priest's voice rose crossly as he seemed to deliver some sort of lecture. They came out soberly and then, from Sebastijana, came the inevitable, 'Time for prayers. You too Ivek.'

The only house in the village that was larger than Faruh was owned by a Contessa. I was fascinated by the grand old lady who often sat, on a large chair, in her doorway which opened straight on to the road. She always wore a black dress with a white shawl round her shoulders. One day, as I rode Pubi past, she waved to me and, feeling shy, I gave a half wave in her direction.

'She's a widow,' Kazimira said when I asked about the Contessa. 'Her daughter, Mira, works in an office in Pregrada so is out all day. Mira is very musical and plays the organ in church sometimes if I can't be there. The Contessa's son works somewhere far away so can't get here very often. She's got a couple of servants but I think she's quite lonely.'

I was thinking about all this as I passed the Contessa the next day. This time I waved properly and smiled. The day after I said, 'Hello' and on the fourth day, which was a Saturday, she beckoned to me.

I halted Pubi, dismounted and still holding his rein, stood in front of her feeling nervous. But her wrinkled face was kind and she spoke quietly.

'Thank you for stopping to speak to me. What is your name?'

'Ivek, madam.'

'And you live in the priest's house?'

'Yes madam.'

'I was just going to have some coffee and cake, Ivek. Would you like to come in and have some with me?'

I was very surprised. I couldn't understand why she would want to make friends with me and I knew I couldn't accept the invitation without asking Father Josip's permission but I liked the sound of the cake. 'I'm sorry, I have to take the horse back,' I replied, feeling hot with embarrassment.

'Of course you do.' She smiled understandingly. 'Ask Father Josip or one of the sisters if you can come and eat cake with me after you have seen to the horse. I'll be expecting you.'

I met the priest coming out of the church and he laughed when I told him about the Contessa's invitation. 'Rub Pubi down and then have a wash. You need to be clean to eat cake.'

Twenty minutes later I was sitting in the Contessa's big drawing room. It was dim as the rich red velvet curtains were half drawn. The wallpaper was decorated with crimson and gold flowers and a thick patterned carpet covered the floor. The Contessa sat on a deep, soft couch.

She patted it. 'Sit here, next to me.'

I obeyed and looked round at the carved wooden chests and dressers, each covered with china, glass and silver ornaments. I had never seen anything like this room before and I was lost for words.

On a small table, in front of us, was a coffee pot, matching sugar bowl and thin pink china cups, saucers and plates. There was also a large torte, my favourite kind of cake. The Contessa leant forward and poured coffee for us both and then she cut me a generous slice of torte. 'There Ivek, I hope you enjoy it. Now tell me about yourself.'

So I told her about Mama, my home and my family and how I was an altar boy and learning Latin. When I'd finished, she said I should eat the torte and, as I ate, she was quiet.

'Can you read?' she asked suddenly.

'Yes madam,'

'Would you come and read to me sometimes in exchange for coffee and cake?' she asked. 'My sight is very poor and I can't see well enough to read now. What do you say?'

I loved reading. I was surprised by her request but felt excited at the prospect of having access to more books and more cake. 'I'd like to read to you,' I replied, 'as long as Father Josip doesn't mind.'

Father Josip was happy for me to visit the Contessa as long as it didn't interfere with my chores, my homework or my Latin lessons so my sessions at the big house began and I really looked forward to them. The Contessa introduced me to all sorts of books. I remember adventure stories and accounts of travels but the book that stands out in my mind was called, 'Contessa Nera'. Nera was accused of being a witch and was condemned to be burnt at the stake but a gallant captain fell in love with her and was determined to save her. He dressed himself as the Devil, and charged on his horse through the crowd just as Nera was being tied to the stake. He snatched her and carried her off to safety.

I was thrilled with the tale and lay in bed reliving the exciting escape but I knew better than to tell the priest or the sisters about it. They certainly wouldn't have approved.

'Ivek,' Father Josip called one day. 'I want you to come with me to collect some wine for the church. A man who keeps a vineyard in Kostel has promised me some. Saddle up and you can ride behind me.' Sister Kazimira came running out of the house. She handed me a grey goatskin container that I had never seen before. It smelt of warm leather.

'Where does this come from?' I asked.

'From the island of Brač in Dalmatia,' she said. 'From a huge monastery there called Bol. It's where many of our priests are trained.'

Soon Father Josip and I were on our way to the vineyard which was on a hillside. We dismounted near a cottage. 'Hold Pubi, Ivek,' said the priest. A young couple came out to greet us and a few words were exchanged before the man turned back to the house. 'He's too busy to come,' Father Josip explained. 'Madam will come with us to fetch the wine. You can ride with the goatskin. We will walk behind.'

The vineyard was about a kilometre from the cottage. I enjoyed riding through the forest and then past cornfields on my own and felt happy as I heard the priest and Madam chatting and laughing behind me.

When we arrived, Father Josip told me to take Pubi to graze on a patch of pasture. 'Hold on to him,' he instructed. 'Don't let him wander away.'

A long time passed and I was bored and uncomfortable. The long grass was squelchy and soon my sandals and bare legs were covered with mud. I wandered to and fro kicking at the mud. Perhaps something has happened to them, I thought. I mounted Pubi and rode towards the vineyard. I was almost there when the priest and Madam emerged. I couldn't have explained what it was but there was something strange about their attitudes. Father Josip was rather red in the face and Madam seemed to be having some difficulty with her skirt which she kept arranging and re-arranging. On the way back, the priest rode Pubi with the wine held in front of him. Madam and I trailed behind.

The area in which I lived is called *Hrvatsko Zagorje/* Behind the Mountains. The mountains referred to are *Medjevica/* the Zagreb Mountains. There was (and maybe still is) a joke about the area. It goes like this:-

Did you know that every child in Hrvatsko Zagorje is born with a basic education?

No, Why?

Because the father is either a priest or a lord.

Of course, I was totally unaware of all of this at the age of nine.

When we arrived home from the vineyard, I was sent down to the cellar with the goatskin of wine and with the usual warning to 'Mind the well'. I loved the special damp smell of the cold, mysterious and dark cellar. The well was covered and had a pump with a pipe attached which ascended to the kitchen. The priest's house was one of the few in the area with running water. I suppose Father Josip always reminded me to be careful about the well because he knew I had an overriding curiosity about everything, I think he was afraid I'd lift the cover, lean over and fall in.

After I'd placed the goatskin where Father had instructed, I noticed several rows of barrels. Each one had a big cork in its top. I wondered what all these barrels could possibly contain and decided to investigate. With difficulty, I prized out one of the bungs and sniffed the hole. I knew immediately that this was plum brandy. I recognised the glorious smell because Mama made it at home – but in much smaller quantities. Suddenly all the hard work the nuns and

I had put in, gathering plums from the hundred plum tree in the orchard, made sense. True, we'd had plum puddings but I'd wondered what had happened to the rest of the fruit. Now I knew.

My curiosity had recently been satisfied on another matter which had intrigued me since I was small. Why was it that nuns always kept their heads covered? What secrets lay beneath their wimples? It so happened that the sisters had to pass through my bedroom on their way to the toilet each morning. Usually I was still fast asleep and the last one would wake me up on her way back. However, one morning I woke early. As I heard Sebastijana pass through my room, I peeped, through almost closed eyelids, and I saw her secret. What a disappointment it was. I had imagined some grotesque, horrific disfigurement but all I saw was ordinary close-cropped hair. It was the same with Kazimira and Franceska. I felt very let down.

There was great excitement in the village when it was rumoured that something quite magical, called electricity, was coming our way. We knew only candles and paraffin lamps and couldn't think what it would be like to press a sort of button and have light instantly. One day, the electricity company delivered some long wooden poles to Faruh. 'These will be put into the ground so they stand straight up. Wires will be stretched between the poles and it is these which will carry the electricity,' Father Josip told me. I was thrilled and imagined watching this magic stuff as it galloped along high in the air. 'They've asked me to find someone from my flock to coat part of each pole with tar,' he went on. 'Just the part which will be buried underground. Look, they've marked each one.'

I was fascinated with the poles. I stood and stared at them as they lay outside the house. 'Why don't you help Father Josip and start painting them with tar, rather than just looking at them?' suggested Sebastijana. 'Put your oldest clothes on first.' So I did, then I dipped the brush into the heavy black liquid and applied it to the first pole with care. I loved brushing the thick glossy tar on to the wood. I worked steadily until six of the poles were done and I stood back to admire my work. I felt enormous satisfaction, not just with a job well done, but also in knowing I'd played a part in bringing the amazing stuff called electricity to the village.

Delighted with myself, I ran into the kitchen. The three nuns were there and gave a collective gasp when they saw me. I had tar on my hands and arms and running down my legs on to my feet.

'Strip off your clothes at once,' ordered Sebastijana. 'Kazimira, get the bath tub down and put some cold water in it. I'll add some hot.' Then she noticed that I hadn't moved. 'Come on, Ivek, don't hang about. Get those things off now. The water will be ready for you in a couple of minutes.' I felt myself blushing but still I stood still. All the joy of my recent achievement had drained away. I felt hot and embarrassed.

'No Sister, I don't want to undress in front of you. I'll wash myself very thoroughly but I won't do it while you three are here.'

'Good gracious, Ivek, what's brought this on? We won't look. You can cover up what you don't want us to see, if you like,' she said loudly as she tipped hot water into the tub.

'No. I'll wash myself.' Seeing my determination, Sebastijana conceded. She handed me a bottle of spirit and a rag.

'Rub as much of the tar off as you can with this first. Be careful, don't spill it. Then scrub yourself with soap.' She left the homemade carbolic soap, a wash cloth and a towel nearby. 'Come on,' she said to the others with a loud sniff. 'Let's leave him to his privacy.' They trooped out and Sebastijana slammed the door hard behind her.

I was beginning to grow up.

I am not a superstitious man but as I tell of my years at the priest's house, I must relate two singular incidents which are as vivid to me today as they were immediately after they had happened.

Father Josip had impressed on me that I should always be back in the house by 8 pm. A church bell was rung at that time and people in the village crossed themselves as they heard it ring. Early this particular evening, I took the two cows to the pasture land which lay just outside the old graveyard. I'd had a very active and busy day and felt tired. I lay on the grass and must have dozed for I was suddenly woken by the church bell. I crossed myself then thought I'd rest a little longer as I knew the priest would not be home before 9. I dropped off to sleep again but awoke with a start and realised that the cows had wandered through the open gate of the graveyard. I knew I must get them back, shut them in the barn and return to the house as soon as I could.

I ran to the gateway of the graveyard and made as if to walk through but I couldn't. An invisible barrier stopped me. I tried again. Again I failed. Frightened, I raised my eyes to search for the cows and I saw her, a woman clad in white and with a face that could only belong to the Blessed Virgin Mary. She was standing near my father's grave.

Suddenly I felt a hand on my shoulder. I screamed and spun round to see Father Josip. He didn't look at all angry but said quietly, 'Ivek what did you see?' Stumbling over my words, I told him about the woman and the barrier at the gate.

'Hold my hand,' he said. Willingly I obeyed. His hand was warm and reassuring. 'Now squeeze my thumb hard, Ivek.' I didn't question why, I just squeezed as hard as I could. 'Now turn round and tell me what you see.'

I turned, half afraid to look, but there was nothing at all amiss, except the cows, gently munching the long grass of the old graveyard. I didn't need the priest to tell me to obey the 8 o'clock rule in future. I was never late again.

However, I did have one more uncanny experience. This time it was near the new graveyard, a rather dark and forbidding place, a little further away from the house. It overlooked the forest which sloped very steeply away on the opposite side of the road.

Father Josip had been given a bicycle which he gave me permission to use. I was absolutely delighted. It was the first in the village, black and shiny. It fascinated me. One day I borrowed it and, unable yet to ride, I scooted away from the house round a gentle bend and down the hill. All went well until the front wheel suddenly veered away from the new graveyard and off the road. I just managed to save myself from falling down the almost sheer drop, into the forest, by jumping off the bicycle and slowing to a walk. I thought I'd hit a bump so I walked a few metres and then scooted on.

On my return journey, almost exactly the same thing happened except that the front wheel veered the opposite way this time but still away from the graveyard. Again, I just managed to jump clear. Holding on to the bicycle I stared at the road. There were no bumps and I could see no reason for the behaviour of the front wheel. I shivered and thought I felt a strange atmosphere around me. I ran back to the house, pushing the bicycle and was pleased when I reached safety. I could never explain these strange happenings but when I told my Mama about them, she crossed herself and said some prayers. My enthusiasm for the wonderful new machine did not abate, however, and within a day or two I was riding it proudly whenever I could find an excuse.

The village of Potkostel is close to Slovenia. Occasionally we would cross the border to join in special church events. One Friday Edi, a neighbouring farmer, drove up to our front door in his newly acquired jeep. I ran out to look at it and was allowed to sit behind the wheel for a few moments. I felt honoured to sit in such a fine car. Father Josip came out, carrying a suitcase.

'I'm going to Mestinje in Slovenia, Ivek. Edi is kindly taking me. I've been invited to officiate at a special Mass there tomorrow, because it's a Slovenian holy day. You and the sisters will leave here early in the morning to join me.'

The next morning Sebastijana woke me at 5. Immediately I could smell something delicious, meaty and peppery. The nuns were bustling around and said nothing about breakfast.

'Ivek, harness Pubi to the trap and bring him to the door, please,' Sebastijana called.

I did as I was told and Kazimira appeared with an enormous cooking pot. She stowed it carefully in the trap and told me to secure it. When I lifted the lid to peep, the delicious aroma wafted up and made my mouth water. 'Put that lid back on,' ordered Kazimira as the three nuns arrived and climbed on board. 'That paprika goulash is for the priests to eat after Mass.'

By 5.30 am we were on our way, winding through the lanes which ran between hills and over the border into Slovenia. In spite of my enjoyment at being allowed to drive the trap, that tantalising smell tormented me and my empty stomach all the way to Mestinje.

We arrived at about 10 am and already the crowds were surging into the great white church where Mass was to be celebrated at 11. The nuns left me, Kazimira and Franceska managing the big pot between them.

'Stay with Pubi,' instructed Sebastijana. 'Take the trap to the field over there and let him graze.' I found a good patch of pasture and got down to sit on the grass, feeling tired and very hungry. Pubi was munching peacefully and I dozed in the warm sunshine. Suddenly a noise brought me back to my senses. The halter had slipped over Pubi's head. I leapt up and tried to grab him. A young man happened to be passing the field. He saw my predicament and kindly ran to help. Between us we calmed Pubi and re-fixed the halter.

The man had just gone when a young woman came out of a building next to the church. She came over to me. 'You brought the sisters, from Father Josip's house and the food, didn't you?' she asked.

'Yes miss.'

'What's your name?'

'Ivek Vesligaj.'

'Well Ivek, I heard you had a very early start. Have you had any food since you arrived?'

'No,' I said forlornly.

'I won't be long.' A few minutes later she returned bearing a large dish piled with the nuns' goulash and some white bread. I stammered my thanks to her and fell upon the food as if I hadn't eaten for a week. The goulash tasted every bit as good as it smelt.

At 1 pm the nuns appeared, ready to leave. 'Oh Ivek,' Franceska said. 'We've just remembered that we didn't offer you breakfast this morning because we, ourselves, couldn't eat before Mass.'

'Sorry Ivek,' Sebastijana and Kazimira said together and Sebastijana added, hoisting the empty pot on board, 'I'm afraid all the goulash has gone but I'm sure we could find you some bread before we go.'

'No need, thank you,' I laughed. 'I had a big helping of goulash and it was absolutely wonderful.'

The next day was Sunday and after Mass I took Pubi to graze in an enclosed field below the church. It was one of my favourite places. It bordered the forest so had trees for shade and also lush pasture. At the far end of the field, I had made a sort of table and a seat from some fallen branches. Here I settled down to do my school work, spreading the books out in front of me. Suddenly I was startled by a voice from the gate.

'Ivek, I wonder if you can help me.' It was Branko Mežnar, the sexton and gravedigger. He lived in a cottage opposite the field and his son, Stjepan, and I went to the same school. By now the man had come through the gate and closed it behind him.

'Yes of course,' I said.

'Stjepan isn't sure which book he has to buy for mathematics. I wondered if you knew.'

I never had the chance to answer for Pubi tossed his head and charged at the sexton. Fortunately Branko hadn't quite reached me so he was able to turn and sprint towards the gate with Pubi in pursuit. The horse, taking no notice at all of my frantic shouts, had almost caught up with him when I saw something truly amazing. Short, stocky little Branko took a flying leap at the tall five barred gate and cleared it with a bit to spare. Pubi pulled up at the gate and gave an angry snort. The sexton was shaken but unhurt and took it in good part.

'I'll certainly steer clear of your warhorse in future,' he said.

I'd almost forgotten that Pubi was a warhorse, left with Mama by the German officer. I could see how he might have thought I was about to be attacked, I had been sitting on a low seat and Branko had walked swiftly and purposefully towards me, talking loudly.

'Good boy,' I whispered once we were alone. 'I'll always feel safe when I'm with you.'

When I got back to Faruh I told Father Josip what had happened. He wasn't surprised.

'Always remember that he was trained as a cavalry horse,' he said. 'He certainly saved me on one occasion. I'd been to the outskirts of the village to administer the last rights to a parishioner. It was dark by the time I left his house and I had to ride through a bit of scrubby common land to get home. Two men were hiding behind a bush and jumped out as I was passing. I saw that they were carrying knives. They tried to pull me off Pubi. He reared and kicked out, catching one of them on the leg. The man screamed and fell down. I just managed to stay on Pubi's back. The injured man crawled to the side of the path and the other one ran away.'

'So Pubi saved you!' I exclaimed.

'He certainly did. At best I would have been robbed, at worst killed, I have a lot to thank that horse for.'

I was pleased when Father Josip said to me one Saturday morning, 'Prepare the horse and trap, Ivek. We're going shopping in Kumrovec.' I was allowed to drive, which I loved.

Our first stop was to pick up another priest, Father Franz, from Pregrada, about 7 kilometres away. He was carrying a small suitcase and soon he and Father Josip were deep in conversation. The drive took about 2 hours and when we arrived we stopped outside a very large shop which appeared to sell everything you could possibly want – from food to clothes to toys.

As the priests got down from the trap, two boys of about eight and six came running up to Father Franz. I was astonished when they threw themselves on him, hugging him and laughing. He kissed them both on their foreheads. A woman hurried across. She shook the priest's hand and held on to it for a moment. Then she kissed it. I thought she must be a relation of Father Franz.

Father Josip saw me watching and said quickly, 'You stay out here and mind Pubi, Ivan. Give him some oats.' By the time I'd reached for the bag, both priests, the woman and the boys had disappeared into the shop. I noticed that Father Franz had taken the suitcase with him.

After a while, the older boy came out. He walked over to me. 'Please may I stroke the horse?' he said.

'Yes, but be gentle. What's your name?'

'Pepi.'

'Is that lady your mama?'

'Yes.'

'Where's your father? I don't know what made me ask the question. I certainly didn't expect the reply I got.

'There.' He pointed to Father Franz who was just emerging from the shop with the others.

I was astounded. I knew that priests could never marry. If they couldn't marry how could they have children? It was a mystery but I knew instinctively that I couldn't ask Father Josip about it. Father Josip climbed on board and we watched the other priest help Pepi and his mother and brother on to a motor bus. He handed in the suitcase and several bags of shopping and bid the little family a fond farewell. Father Josip said, 'They are his sister and nephews.' Another shock. Priests told lies.

Then as Father Franz joined us, he reinforced this revelation with, 'I love to meet up with my sister and nephews.' I said nothing. I wondered if perhaps it was Pepi who had lied to me or maybe he had misunderstood my question. I decided I'd discuss the whole thing with Mama the next time I went home.

Mama paused for a moment before she answered my question. I think she was trying to decide whether I was old enough to learn the truth. Then she said, 'Pepi was right. Father Franz is his father. The priest had what is called an affair with their mama. She had his babies even though she could never marry him. I'm trusting you by telling you this, Ivek. Please don't repeat the story to anyone. Not many people know.'

'I won't,' I said. Until that day, I had believed that a woman could have a baby only after she was married.

Later I discovered that my sister, Marija, was Father Franz's housekeeper. I'd known she worked for a priest but hadn't known which one. After those priestly lies, I didn't feel quite the same about Father Josip or about any other priest, for that matter.

On our way back from that memorable trip, Father Josip said, 'Tomorrow we are to have an important visitor, Ivek. The Mother Superior of the novice house in Dalmatia is bringing six of her novices to stay with us for four days. I want you to look after them – show them around the village and countryside. Mother Superior and I will have a lot to discuss while she is here.' I was excited by the prospect of some new young faces in the house and, as it was holiday time, I'd have plenty of time to do as Father wished.

They arrived by motor coach the next morning, the stately and formidable Mother Superior and her six young novices. Although the latter wore long blue robes, their heads were not covered and I was immediately attracted by their pretty faces and shining hair. I discovered that they were only about two years older than I. After prayers, we sat down to a special lunch. I was dismayed to find that we were to start with leek soup which I hated. I just couldn't swallow the stringy leeks and I put my spoon down.

'What's wrong, Ivek?' asked Kazimira. 'Why have you left your soup?'

'I can't eat it, Sister. I'm sorry but I don't like it.'

'Don't like it? What nonsense. It's good wholesome soup, made in our own kitchen.'

'Think of all the starving children in the world and be grateful,' said Sebastijan.

'If you don't eat it you'll get nothing else,' Kazimira added. I felt myself blush and stared miserably at my plate of vile, weedy, green soup. As soon as the conversation at the table had resumed, I felt a soft touch on my arm. It was Vilma, the novice sitting next to me.

'Is it the bits of leek you don't like?' she whispered. I nodded. 'Fish them out with you spoon and pass them to me under the table.' She touched my knee to show that her hand was ready to receive the leeks. Within a couple of minutes she had deftly deposited the strings of leek into a bucket filled with water which was on the floor behind her. This was kept for watering the many houseplants in the room. I quickly finished the now clear leek soup.

'There,' said Kazimira triumphantly as she collected the soup bowls, 'I knew you could do it, Ivek.' No-one ever mentioned the vegetable matter in the bucket. I wondered if Franceska, whose job it was to water the plants, noticed it but chose to say nothing.

After breakfast on the following day, Mother Superior came to find me. 'I want you to take my novices out for a walk this morning er...'

'My name's Ivek, Mother,' I said.

'Ah yes. Ivek, take the girls up the mountain, where the sheep are. Show them the ruins of the castle. Will you do that?'

'Of course, Mother.'

Half an hour later, we were on our way. I pointed out the tower of *Stari Grad*/the Castle of the Old Town which perched on a cliff high above the village. I always thought it was keeping guard over us. Today it looked black against a clear bright sky.

'It's a steep climb,' one of the girls said.

'Don't worry, I know a way round which means we won't have to climb the cliff.' Proudly, I led them through the village and up a winding dusty track, through the forest, to the castle. Behind me, the girls sang snatches of religious songs, talked and giggled. They needed a rest when we reached the short grass at the top. Now the castle gleamed silver and grey in the sunshine. Crumbling walls stretched away from the tower. I showed my new friends black holes which, I'd been told by Father Josip, led to tunnels and dungeons under the castle. It was possible to make out the remains of rooms and passage ways too.

'Be careful of snakes,' I called after them when they wandered away to explore. 'Some of them are poisonous.'

When everyone was tired, we gathered in the shade of the castle wall and, to my surprise, Vilma produced a picnic from a bag she was carrying. Some of the girls had brought blankets which we spread out to sit on. We ate bread and cake and grapes. Someone had brought a bottle of water which we passed between us. We laughed and joked and sang songs and I couldn't remember having such a good time since I'd left home.

Too soon we had to return to Faruh. We walked home more slowly although it was downhill. When we got back, the novices crowded round me, hugged me and thanked me for giving them a lovely day, before they went to report to Mother Superior.

'We'd like to thank you too, Ivek,' said Kazimira. 'You took the girls off our hands and they really seem to have enjoyed the trip.' I smiled at her but said nothing. There was nothing to say – it had been a golden day.

A few days after the sad departure of the novices, I helped Father Josip move some timber in the forest. Pubi wore a special harness for the task with towing chains which could be attached to the sledge on which we carried the wood. It was a beautiful summer day. The air was warm and full of the scents of the trees and wild flowers as I rode home. Pubi was pleased to be going downhill. We'd spent several hours in the forest and we were both tired.

As I came close to the barn at Faruh, I saw Kazimira. 'Please would you open the door for me,' I called, 'to save me getting down.'

Kazimira did as I asked and, ducking my head under the door lintel, I entered the dim coolness of the sweet-smelling barn. I turned Pubi to face the manger and, as I started to dismount, my left foot, which I'd been resting on the chain, slipped and slid between the harness and the horse's body. I grabbed Pubi's mane and let out a cry which startled him. He backed off and moved sharply in a circle. In his panic, he circled again and again. I hung on as tightly as possible but I could feel myself slipping about on the horse's back yet my foot was trapped. I screamed. I was sure this was the end of me. My leg would be ripped from its socket and I would crash to the ground with my leg still trapped under Pubi's harness. Kazimira ran in and with great presence of mind and considerable bravery, she flung herself in front of the horse. He pulled up short and she was able to grab his reins. Franceska heard the commotion and arrived, breathless. Seeing the problem immediately and without asking questions, she pulled my foot clear of the harness and helped me down. I was shaking and sobbing with shock. Franceska gave me a big hug and whispered.

'Thank God you're all right. May He bless you.'

When I'd recovered my composure, I led the sweating Pubi to his food and spoke softly to him. It wasn't his fault. I knew the accident had been caused by my riding bareback but I also knew that this wasn't the last time I would do so. It was well worth a few grazes and bruises. However I would be much more careful about where I placed my feet in future. Even the stern Sebastijana patted my head when I limped into the kitchen. My left ankle was raw and my ribs bruised but otherwise I was unhurt. It was only much later that I realised that I probably owed my life to the prompt action of Kazimira.

Father Josip had been invited to a wedding feast. Ruza, a close friend of my mother's was marrying her childhood sweetheart, Joza. The feast was at Mama's house because she was cooking the food and was also to be Ruza's matron of honour. Father said I could accompany him to the party and I was very excited. I scrubbed myself until I shone and put on my smartest clothes but I noticed that Father Josip was informally dressed. I rode Pubi behind him.

The feast was just getting underway as we arrived, spilling from the inside of the house to several large tables outside. I ran indoors to hug Mama who looked beautiful in her fine blue dress. I greeted my relatives and Mama's friends and then went in search of the other children. We sat together and stuffed ourselves with cakes of all kinds. My favourite, of course, was the tall torte with five or six layers. Between each layer there was a delicious filling. When we'd eaten as much as we could, we watched the couples dancing to the music of a small band. We made jokes about some of them and admired others.

Mama came outside and I walked over to join her. Father Josip was enjoying the dancing and I saw him grab one of the local beauties and hold her very close for a slow dance. When it was over, I overheard a conversation between one of the guests and the priest.

'Father,' the woman said boldly, 'you shouldn't join in the dancing. It's not right for a priest to hold a lady so close.'

I saw Father Josip flush angrily. There was a pause in the music, and he clapped his hands for silence. 'Ladies and Gentlemen, there is something I want to explain to you.' There was absolute silence. 'When I am dressed as a priest, when I have my priestly collar on – then I am a priest. When I take that priestly collar off – then I am an ordinary man just like the rest of you men here. Then I behave like a man and not like a priest. Please remember that.' He sat down. There was a stunned silence and then the music started again.

At 10 pm, Father Josip, who was still being an ordinary man, called across to me. 'It's time for you to go back to Faruh now, Ivek.' Reluctantly I said goodbye to Mama, the family and to my friends. It took me half an hour to walk back and the sisters greeted me eagerly.

'Tell us all about it, Ivek,' they said. 'What was the bride wearing? What was your Mama wearing? What did you have to eat?'

'How many people were there?'

'Did Father Josip enjoy himself?' I told them as much as I could before going wearily to bed. However I didn't mention the priest's dancing or the little speech he had made. I had a feeling that they wouldn't want to hear about that.

A few days after the wedding, I arrived home from school to find Father Josip's study door ajar. He came out as I passed and I realised he'd been waiting for me.

'Come in please, Ivek,' he said. I was alarmed to see the three nuns already in the room, looking solemn. I rapidly searched my mind for any recent wrong-doing. Had they heard about my argument with one of the big boys at school? Was I to be sent home in disgrace? 'Sit down,' said Father. He turned to Kazimira. 'You explain things to him, Sister. You ask him.' Kazimira smiled and I relaxed. The trouble couldn't be all that bad. Kazimira moved to my side, and looking intently at me, placed her hand on my shoulder.

'I have something very serious to ask you, Ivek. Will you promise to tell me the truth?'

'Of course, Sister.'

'The question is this. Would you like to study to be a priest?'

I knew this had always been a possibility. Mama had spoken about it several times. Father Josip had also mentioned it but I wasn't sure how I felt about it. The one thing I was sure of was that I desperately wanted to continue with my studies. There was so much to learn and I wanted to know it all. I took a deep breath to give myself thinking time and said, 'You mean be a priest like Father Josip?'

'No, not quite like Father Josip. You'd wear different clothes from the ones he wears and although you would do a priest's duties, you'd do lots of other very clever things too.' Father Josip handed Kazimira a book with a marker in it. She opened it and placed it on my knee. I saw a picture of a tall man, dressed in a long hooded robe with what looked like a narrow white towel running down the front of the robe. I knew at once what he was.

'But he's a monk,' I said.

'That's right,' said Kazimira. 'He's a monk and a priest. A very holy man.'

I didn't say anything for a moment. I knew a monk didn't live in a village like Father Josip. How would I like living in a monastery with lots of other men?

How would I feel being far away from Mama and the family? I looked again at the picture. The monk looked smart and had a kind face. I tried to imagine myself wearing this uniform. I thought it would suit me.

'Ivek, this is a wonderful opportunity for you,' said Father Josip. 'You are a bright boy and if you take up this offer, some of the cleverest men in the Church will be your teachers. You will learn Latin, Greek, mathematics, science and religion and much, much more.'

'How long will I have to study?'

'Fifteen Years.' Then, seeing my dismayed face, 'That includes the three years it takes to become a priest.'

'I'll be an old man by the time I finish,' I gasped, shocked by the thought.

Father Josip laughed and said, 'But you'll be a very wise one.' He went on to say that I'd study at a very special school in the monastery of Bol on the island of Brač which was in Dalmatia. I remembered the goatskin bottle which had come from Bol. All I knew about the place was that goatskin bottles were made there. I was 13 years old and was being asked to make the most important decision of my life.

I had a sudden thought. 'How would I get to Bol?'

'I'd travel with you,' Father answered. 'We'd go by motor coach, train and then ferry.'

'But my mother couldn't afford the fare.'

'Don't worry. The Church will pay for everything.'

I suddenly saw what an opportunity this was. It was my way out of a humdrum life. It was my chance to travel. Most of all it was my chance to become wise, to be able to understand Latin and Greek, to do scientific experiments. This education would set me apart from the other villagers. It would make me equal to the aristocratic boys I had seen in carriages in Pregrada. No longer would they be able to look down on me. How proud Mama would be.

'Have you spoken to my mother?' I asked.

'Not yet. We wanted to ask you first. You can have a day off to go and ask her, if you like.'

But there was someone I wanted to consult even before Mama. That was my *stara mama*/old mother or grandmother – the wise woman of our family. If she thought I should go to Bol, my Mama would think so too and so would I. I explained this to Father Josip.

'That's an excellent idea,' he said.

'Perhaps I could go with you to see your grandmother?' Kazimira said, looking at the priest.

'Of course.'

Outside Ivan's grandmother's house

My mother's mama, Barbara Solman, lived on the border between Croatia and Slovenia. She was in her seventies and delighted at my unexpected visit. She welcomed us with delicious apple strudel, tea for Kazimira and a cool glass of milk for me.

'I've come to ask your advice,' I said, once our greetings were over.

'Why, what's wrong Ivek? Don't you want to stay with Father Josip any more?'

With Kazimira's help, I explained why I was there. Stara mama was silent for a moment, searching my face with her keen blue eyes and then she delivered her answer with that great big hug. 'Grandson, do it! We'll all be so proud of you. Does your mama know about this yet?'

'No, I wanted to know what you thought first. Now I know that, I'll speak to Mama as soon as I can.'

'How long will all this studying take?'

'Fifteen years.'

A sigh, then, 'Well I shan't live to see it finished but I shall die happy, knowing what a learned and famous man you will be.'

I looked at her, in her in her long black dress and blue patterned headscarf, her crinkly face serious. I couldn't bear the thought that she wouldn't always be there.

I reached across the table and took her hand. 'Don't say that, Stara mama, of course you'll be here.' Before she could answer, two of her sons, my Uncles

Martin and Miha arrived. They were astonished to see us and more explanations and hugs followed.

'You won't want to know us when you're a fine, learned man,' joked Uncle Martin. I laughed but felt uncomfortable at such an idea.

When I broke the news to Mama a day or two later she kissed me and then held me at arm's length to look at me.

'Oh Ivek, it's what I've wished but haven't dared hope for. It's such an honour to be chosen. I'm proud of you.' She stopped for a moment then asked, 'But do you want to do this? Won't you be terribly homesick? You must only go if you want to.'

'I do want to, very much. I want to study and learn whatever there is to know. I will miss you, of course,' I kissed her, 'and I'll miss playing with my brothers but it will be worth it, won't it?'

'It will be worth it because it's the will of God, son. I'll sign the necessary papers gladly.' Lujzek and Stjepan were envious of the fact that I was to 'see the world' but their main concern was that I should share, between them, any clothes I wouldn't be taking.

At Faruh, the nuns were soon busy preparing things for my new life. Clothes for the journey and a suitcase were bought. The next couple of weeks flew by. I only had time for a quick farewell visit home. The bundle of unwanted clothes and shoes I took with me was eagerly pounced on by my brothers. My older brother Martin and sister Marija were there too. Goodbyes were soon over. After hugs and kisses and tears from Mama, I was on my way back to Faruh. Martin called after me, 'I'll be at Pregrada Coach Station to see you off.' It would be a good hour's walk for him.

Journey

The next day we were all up very early. For once I wasn't asked to prepare Pubi and the trap. Franceska did that while Father Josip, Kazimira and I ate breakfast. Sebasjana took our suitcases to the door and then it was time to leave. Franceska kissed me and cried and even Sebastijana shed a tear as she hugged me. 'Now you behave yourself and make us all proud of you,' she said.

Kazimira drove the trap and I waved and waved until the other two sisters were out of sight. My excitement was tinged with sadness as I realised, perhaps for the first time, that my childhood was behind me. A new phase of my life was about to begin.

At Pregrada coach station, I found it hard to say goodbye to Pubi. He'd been such an important and happy part of my life. I rubbed his nose and whispered in his ear, 'I'll be back to see you in the holidays.' I was sure he understood. Kazimira embraced me, wiping her eyes and then she drove away. She didn't look back.

Martin was waiting by our coach stop with messages from Mama and the family. We exchanged the customary kiss on each cheek before Father Josip and I got on the coach and were on our way. I hadn't been on a coach before. Father let me sit by the window and I loved being so high above the road.

We were soon further from home than I'd ever been. Forest, mountains and hills gave way to flat countryside and then to houses and streets. It took about an hour and a half for us to get to Zagreb.

Father Josip had told me we were to spend a night at the *samostan* / priests' training college which was attached to the cathedral. We walked through grey crowded streets. I didn't like Zagreb wery much and I hung on to Father's hand when we had to cross a road. The cars and trucks were so noisy and seemed to be travelling too fast.

At the *samostan* we were welcomed warmly by the duty priest. A boy was waiting for us in the lobby. He was to travel to Bol with us. His name was Branko Kapun and I liked him straight away. The priest took us to the refectory, a large room with shiny wooden tables, for a hot meal and then he showed Branko and me to a small bedroom which contained two comfortable beds. We lay awake for a long time, exchanging information about our families and speculating what lay ahead. Branko and I were to become good friends.

How excited I was, the next day, to get on a train for the first time in my life. Everything about it was magical – the gigantic, roaring engine, the window which slid up and down and was fastened by a strap with holes in it, the rhythm of the train over the tracks and eating a picnic as we jolted along. I wished the journey would last for ever. We travelled through valleys with bare craggy mountains on each side of us and over viaducts. I had not seen scenery like it before. We were on the train for almost eight hours and I was never bored. By the time we reached Split, our destination, my face was black with soot and I'd had two cinders in my eye from leaning out of the window. We arrived in the late afternoon and, as I got out of the train, I sniffed the fishy air.

We walked a short way and then I had my first view of the sea. I couldn't believe my eyes. 'I've never seen so much water,' I cried. 'Just look at the colour.' It was as blue as the sky on the sunniest day with tinges of green and turquoise. We were by the harbour and when I leant over to gaze down at the water it was clear enough for me to see the bottom.

We walked along to a small beach where there were rock pools full of strange creatures. The rocks and small islands off the shore were perfectly reflected in the sea as were the brightly painted boats. Everything shimmered and shone in the late afternoon sun.

'That's where we're going. That's the island of Brač where Bol monastery is,' Father Josip said, pointing to a long island which lay stretched out in front of us beyond a glinting strip of sea.

I wanted to stay and stare at the sea and at Bol but Father said he must show us the Palace of Diocletian. I was disappointed because it wasn't my idea of a palace at all. There were no gorgeous rooms or beautiful princesses. It was dull grey stone and high walls with narrow passageways.

Inside Diocletian's Palace today

All I longed for was to be back on the beach, leaning over to look into the water and trailing my fingers through it. We couldn't dally too long as we had to catch the 8 pm ferry to the island of Brač.

That ferry! I felt almost dizzy as we went aboard. I'd been in small rowing boats on the river, of course, but this was a throbbing giant with decks and saloons and even toilets. Branko and I hung over the side with the wind tearing at our hair and clothes. My face was numb with it and the sea air filled my lungs and made my inside feel fizzy with happiness. I turned to Branko and had to shout to make myself heard. 'When I have to do my national service, I'm going to join the navy. This is the best thing ever!' Father Josip had come up behind to warn us not to lean too far over the deck rails.

'That's many years away, Ivek. You'll probably have changed your mind by then,' he smiled. I didn't argue, of course, but I knew he was wrong. 'You can't see the monastery from here. It's round the other side of the island,' Father told us. It was getting dark but I could just make out forested hills across the middle of Brač. They reminded me of home and I wondered what Mama and the sisters were doing. It seemed so long ago that I'd last seen them.

We sailed round the left side of the island to a port. As we approached the dock, I saw the silhouettes of several men wearing long skirts. My legs felt a bit wobbly as I walked down the gangway but only for a minute or two. The figures I'd seen were monks, young and smiling at us. Father Josip shook hands with them and each of them kissed his hand. He pointed to me and said, 'This one's mine.' Then they started a conversation in Latin. The monks carried our cases for us and walked ahead.

'Look at their heads,' I whispered to Branko. They all had tonsures.

'Our hair will be like that one day,' Branko whispered in reply.

We walked out of the town and along a path close to the sea, following the grown-ups closely because they had lamps. There were the lights of another island across a narrow stretch of sea from us.

'That's the island of Hvar,' Father Josip called to us.

We reached Bol Monastery after about half an hour's walk. I remember the high walls and the huge wooden, iron-studded door. I can still hear the clang as the heavy metal bar came down to lock it once we were inside. I can remember thinking that it was shutting out the world I'd known. I felt as if I were inside a new world. In spite of my anxiety and uncertainty, I felt a surge of excitement. 'Now I'll start to learn all the things Father Josip promised,' I said to myself.

1949 – 1953

By 1949, Marshal Tito had opted for the independent development of communism in Yugoslavia, choosing not to join Stalin's Communist Bloc. In retaliation, Stalin revoked the treaty of friendship between the USSR and Yugoslavia. The relationship between the two states was always uneasy – sometimes there were high profile visits from one to the other, sometimes trade flowed between the two but there was never real trust.

Yugoslavia was elected to the council of the United Nations. Financial aid from the USA, Britain and France followed.

Josef Stalin died in March 1953.

Ivan
1953-1958: aged 13-18 years

Monastery

Bol Monastery on the Island of Brac

I felt light-headed with tiredness as Father Josip said 'Good night' to us and went in one direction and one of the brothers took us in the other. We walked along a passage and I saw that there were rooms on our left. We stopped outside a door which had my name on it. The brother opened the door and I saw the little room which was to be mine. It had a small window which couldn't be opened, a narrow bed with one blanket on it (this was to be all we had, summer or winter). There was a crucifix above the bed, a cabinet, a bowl for washing and a pair of sandals. I put down the few clothes I had brought with me and we followed the monk to Branko's room which was further along the passage. Then we went outside and into another building to the refectory.

I was so tired that I hardly remember the meal and the kindly nuns who looked after us then. We kissed their hands as we said 'goodnight.' One showed us where the showers were – separate cubicles so that we did not suffer the embarrassment of seeing each other naked on that first night. Finally I threw myself on my hard little bed and was asleep in an instant.

We were given our uniforms the next morning. Except for having cream rather than white tabards, they were the same as the brothers wore. On the cord around my waist, I carefully hung the rosary I was given.

We were shown round the monastery. It seemed bleak and cold even on a sunny day. There were three separate buildings, at right angles to each other, forming three sides of a square with a garden in the middle. Our bedrooms, a hall and some offices made up one side of the square, the kitchen, refectory and classrooms another and the monks' cells and chapel the third.

After our tour we participated in communal prayers and were told we could have a few days to settle in and get our bearings. As Branko and I walked back to our rooms, we saw Father Josip who stopped and shook our hands.

'I'm leaving now. I hope you both do well,' he said and, looking at me, 'work hard Ivan, I've told them to expect great things from you.' He turned and I watched the last part of my old life disappear. With a sick feeling in my stomach, I wondered if I'd be able to live up to his hopes for me.

At the beginning of the next week we were called together in the hall. There, *Velečasni*/Father Monk gave us our timetable of lessons and explained to us how our days would be spent. He introduced the teachers and our *odgojitelj*/mentors. The latter were senior monks, each of whom had four students in his care. Mine was a very caring man. Throughout the time I was at Bol he helped me in many ways. He was always willing to discuss any problems as well as making sure I attended to my studies. He also checked my homework. The next day our working lives would begin in earnest and I was very excited by the prospect.

I missed Mama and my family and the nuns at Faruh. I missed Pubi too but, at first, I wasn't as homesick as I'd been when I went to live at the priest's house. I quickly made new friends. Branko and I were inseparable and, above all, I was excited by the lessons where a whole world seemed to open up before me.

There was a strict routine to our lives. We rose at 5.30 am, washed and attended prayers then had breakfast. We were in classes from 8 am until noon. We were allowed an hour for lunch after which we prayed for half an hour. Afternoon classes were from 1.30 until 4. Then we participated in physical activities – exercises, gym, basketball, football or running. After exercise we showered. By now we were using communal showers. We undressed and stood in a line under the shower nozzles. When we were ready the showers released some lukewarm water over us. When the water stopped, we had to quickly soap ourselves all over. Then the showers released a little more water and we rinsed ourselves. We never grumbled because we'd heard of some monks who had to shower in cold water and we didn't want that to happen to us. Next we had tea and then did homework.

On one day of every week we had to remain in our rooms all day to read holy works, meditate and pray. Our meals consisted of bread and water on that day and we could only leave our rooms to visit the toilet. We were forbidden to speak to anyone we happened to meet. It surprises me now to think that, although we didn't like it, we never questioned this solitary confinement.

Our studies comprised Latin, Greek, German, Russian, history, geography, mathematics, science and, of course, religion which was considered the most important subject of all. As well as an in-depth study of Roman Catholic theology and history, we were introduced to other faiths. We learned about Judaism, Greek and Russian Orthodoxy and even a little of Islamic beliefs. When I was much older and started to read history books, I discovered that a lot about the bloody history of the Catholic Church was missed out of our curriculum.

We were free for the last part of the evening before prayers and bedtime was at 10 pm. Once a week we went to a secluded and private beach which belonged to the monastery. We stripped off and ran into the clear blue water, splashing and shrieking. I absolutely loved it – the waves, the salty tang, the feeling of my body gliding through the cool water – whenever I thought about Heaven, I knew you'd be able to swim in the sea there. There would be one difference, though. In Heaven there would be no sea urchins to give vicious stings. How we hated them with their spines which hooked into our flesh so painfully. We soon learned that it was best to leave them for about 10 minutes before pulling them out. By that time their hooks had straightened which made the operation much easier. We had Saturdays and Sundays off except for Mass, prayers, an hour of music tuition and homework.

During our free time we played chess, read (religious books), or played table tennis and sometimes we organised informal games of football or basketball outside.

We took it in turns to help the older brothers in the garden. It was there I learned about the healing qualities of herbs. I remember that woundwort leaves were good for cuts. I was also told that cow pats would soothe burns. I liked to spend time with the donkey, the cows and goats because they reminded me of home. I still missed Pubi every day. As life settled down, I became very homesick. At nights, I cried myself to sleep. I longed for my old, relatively carefree life and even a hug from the stern Sebastijana would have been welcome. However, I wrote cheerful letters to Mama and to *Faruh*. I wanted everybody to think that I was happy in my new life and, indeed, I was happy whenever I was engrossed in my studies.

We were always hungry. There was never enough to eat but the food we did have was good except for one thing, Right from my first day at Bol I'd noticed that the soup was different from any I'd had before. Whatever its flavour, there was a strange smell to it and a tang that stayed in my mouth afterwards. I mentioned it to Branko but he shrugged and said that the food was better than his mother had been able to afford.

One day we were in the laboratory for a chemistry lesson. The teacher was introducing us to a variety of chemicals which were in named jars on the bench. He talked about their different properties and how they reacted with each other and then he invited us to remove each stopper, in turn, and sniff the contents. Half way through this exercise I sat up straight and then I sniffed the top of one of the bottles again. Its smell was exactly the same as the one I'd noticed when soup was served. I didn't say anything but looked at the name on the bottle's label *Bromide*. That evening I went to the library and looked in big chemistry reference book. I found 'bromide' and scanned the relevant information. There I read, '*This suppresses sexual desire*'. Innocent as I was, I knew what that meant. I was too embarrassed to say anything even to Branko but suddenly I understood what had happened a few days ago. I'd 'borrowed' a ladder and climbed up to look over the high monastery wall. A troupe of very beautiful girls in tight fitting clothes had sauntered past. Two of them had seen me looking down on them and had blown kisses to me but I had felt no sexual stirrings at all. Now I knew why. After thinking about it for some time, I decided to continue to eat the soup. I thought it would make for a calmer life. It would allow me to concentrate on what was really important to me – learning.

When we had been at Bol for about six weeks, I had my first experience of what it meant to be a trainee monk in the wider world. We were taken, on the ferry, to Split where we were to look at the cathedral and several churches, study their architecture and hear about their history. As we walked in a crocodile, hands held before us as if in prayer, people looked at us and some bowed their heads. There were very few cars about but, seeing us, a policeman walked into the middle of the road to stop any traffic which might come along. When we were safely across I heard him call to a colleague, 'We must keep the holy men safe. Who knows, one of this lot might be our future *Papa*/Pope.'

They both laughed and I felt uncomfortable but when I asked one of the brothers why the policeman had said that, his answer was, 'Just ignore it Ivan.'

Our first visit was to the Cathedral of St Dominius. I was impressed by its octagonal shape and two sets of columns. At midday we were standing by the ancient black stone sphinx, at the bottom of the bell tower, when the cathedral clock started to strike. We all stood quite still and then sank to our knees and crossed ourselves as we had been instructed. Unsurprisingly, we attracted attention once more.

Next we went to the Baptistry of St John which had been the Temple of Jupiter in Diocletian's time. There is a statue of St John there now. We had a picnic lunch of bread, cheese and fruit and ate it sitting by the sea, looking towards Brač but there was no gazing in rock pools or running our fingers through the clear water that day.

Most of the afternoon was spent in prayer in the Church of St Francis. It was a welcome relief to reach the local nunnery where we were given a good meal before catching the ferry back to Brač. Everyone was very tired so we were allowed to have showers and prayers early and be in bed by 9 o'clock.

Christmas came and went with very little excitement. There was no special food and certainly no presents. Some of the brothers made paper chains and paper flowers to brighten the refectory. We attended midnight mass on Christmas Eve and said special prayers on Christmas day itself. The timetable was suspended for just one day.

Twice a year we had vacations from the normal routine. One was in January. We weren't allowed home then but had what was known as 'study leave' when we followed up on anything which particularly interested us and worked on special projects concerning ancient texts.

'It's only January,' I said to Branko. 'We've only been here four months but it seems as if we've been here for ever.'

He nodded but then looked more cheerful. 'But in June we'll go home for a month and a half. Just think of it – seeing everyone again, staying in bed longer...'

To me, June seemed a long way away.

But somehow, after January, time went by quickly. We became busier, I got used to being so far from home and my nightly tears ceased. Suddenly it was June, we were given our tickets and were on our way home. We were not accompanied and as soon as we stepped aboard the ferry to Split the sense of freedom overcame us. Although we had been told to be shining examples in a sinful world we gave a loud cheer and, when we were out of sight of the quay, dashed round the deck uninhibited by our long robes.

Vacation

At Split, a group of us caught the train to Zagreb. Women offered their seats to us, the 'holy ones'. I'm ashamed to say we accepted them, basking in the awe with which we were regarded. When we arrived in Zagreb, we gathered on the platform and many heads turned in curiosity. We must have been a strange sight – a group of adolescent boys in monks' clothing. The ticket collector bowed to us as we swept through the gate.

Outside, we went our various ways. Branko and I walked to the *samostan* in which we had stayed on our way to Bol. We knocked on the heavy door, a small shutter opened, we gave our names and were admitted. By now it was evening so after a wash, prayers and supper we went to bed.

The next morning I said goodbye to Branko and caught a train to Hromec. From there it would take me about two and a half hours to walk home to my mother's house.

The excitement of going home had been mounting for weeks. I could hardly believe the day had come as I hurried over the hills and through the forest. Soon I was in familiar territory. With my heart beating fast, I saw trees I'd climbed, the river where I'd learned to swim and then the small village that was next to the one in which I lived. The people I knew so well waved and called to each other, 'It's Ivek. He's home.' Others came out to look, women crossed themselves and my friends ran up to shake my hand and admire my robes. Some mothers of my friends kissed my hands and one said, 'Shall I call you Father?'

'No, not yet,' I replied awkwardly.

Men and women working in the fields looked up and shouted, 'God bless you Ivek and give you luck.'

I felt as if I were in a dream as I entered my own village. Here, people were on the look-out for me. They came running from their houses to greet me. A crowd of children ran ahead to tell my mother I'd arrived. And there she was, Mama, rushing towards me, hugging me tight, sobbing and laughing together. I had a big lump in my throat but I didn't cry. I felt sick with excitement. When Mama released me, Martin, Lujzek and Stjepan almost knocked me over with their hugs and thumps on the back. My sisters, of course, were living away. Dragica was married and Maria in service.

The marriage of Dragica and Franz

We went inside and, because the habit had been drilled into us at Bol, I asked if I could wash before the meal. Everyone was surprised and even more so when I said, 'Now I must pray.'

'How many prayers do you know?' Mama asked.

'A lot.'

'Teach us one,' Martin said. 'Teach us one so we can all say it.'

'Let's say one we've all said before,' I said, '*In Nomine Patris et Filius et Spiritus Sanctus. Amen.*' As I said this, I crossed myself, of course. It was a strange moment. Everyone was so serious as we repeated the well known prayer together.

What a feast we had. I'd never appreciated Mama's cooking more. She had roasted one of our own chickens served with vegetables, fresh from the garden. Over the meal, I talked and talked about what I'd seen and done and what I'd learned. Then our neighbours drifted in. Soon our kitchen was crowded with people who wanted to look at me and hear about my life at Bol.

I was very tired and opted for an early night. In fact, we all retired early as the bed in which my brothers and I slept also doubled as the kitchen table. At bedtime, the heavy top was lifted off and a big board and straw mattress were put in its place. I slept brilliantly all night, feeling absolutely comfortable next to Martin with Stjepan and Lujzek sleeping at the other end. I wasn't popular the next morning when I was up at 5.30. My body clock was still set to Bol time.

Mama prepared my favourite breakfast of *žganci*/dumpling, served with hot milk. I wanted to look round our farm, vineyard and my best loved part of the forest. It was a lovely day and my brothers and I spent the morning chasing along well known paths and repairing a den we'd made the year before.

Our hunger drove us home. The familiar smell of Mama's famous strudel met us. Mama had been looking out of the kitchen window and, as we trooped inside, she said, 'We've got visitors. See who's coming down the path, Ivek.'

I looked and saw Kazimira and Franceska approaching. All the joy of the morning drained away. I knew why they were here. 'They've come to take me to Faruh,' I said.

'Not yet!' shouted Martin. 'That's not fair. You've only just come.'

'Be quiet Martin,' Mama said sharply. I looked at her face. She knew I was right.

Slowly I went outside to meet the sisters. Franceska ran forward and took me by surprise by kissing my hand and then she hugged me close.

'We have missed you,' she whispered. Kazimira kissed my hand too and gave me a hug which almost toppled her big glasses from her nose. I felt bad about my earlier disappointment at seeing them. They seemed so pleased to see me.

'Come inside Sisters, do.' My mother was at the door. 'Will you join us for a meal? Will you take tea?'

'Just some tea, please,' answered Kazimira. We were soon sitting at the table. Kazimira went on, 'We cannot stay long. We must get back to *Faruh*. Father Josip is looking forward to seeing Ivan.'

'Must he leave so soon, Sister?' Mama asked. 'Can't he stay just a few more days?'

I knew the answer before it came. 'I'm afraid not. Father Josip is very keen to see him and he has much study to do before he returns to Bol.' And that was the end of the discussion.

My young brother, Lujzek, always with an eye for the main chance, said, 'Will you leave those sandals for me, Ivek? Mine are completely broken.'

It was hard to tear myself away. In spite of being barefoot, my feet and legs felt heavy. How I longed to have more time with my family. The only cheering thought was that I should soon see Pubi.

'Do you like it at Bol, Ivan?' asked Kazimira. 'We know life is hard there. There's so much work to do and such a strict routine.'

'I loved it at first,' I said. 'It was all new and exciting. But then I got very homesick and...'

'We understand,' broke in Franceska and she put her arm round me. 'Father Josip has been receiving regular reports on your progress at Bol. So far he's very pleased.'

I felt relieved. 'How's Sebastijana?' I asked.

'More or less the same, only a bit more grumpy with her rheumatism.'

Once more, people working in the fields stopped to look at me and shout blessings and good wishes. 'You're quite famous,' smiled Kazimira. 'Don't let it go to your head.'

I picked a bouquet of wild flowers for Sebastijana and, within half an hour, we could see the church and Faruh. Sebastijana came out to meet us. She hugged me to her, almost crushing the flowers. 'I'm not crying,' she said as tears ran down her face. She took me by the hand. 'Come in and eat but first we must pray.'

The nuns were impressed that I could now join in with all the Latin prayers. 'They've taught you well,' said Sebastijana as she served our meal.

As we were finishing, I heard the sound of horse's hooves. It was Father Josip on Pubi. I ran out to greet them – well to greet Pubi really but I knew I must be polite and speak to Father first.

'Ah good, you're home my son.' He dismounted.

'Yes, Father.'

I kissed his hand and he made the sign if the cross in front of me. Then he put his hand on my shoulder. 'You've done well at Bol. I'm pleased with you.' As we stood, Pubi had been tossing his head and whinnying with pleasure at seeing me. Now I was allowed to pat him, kiss his sweating nose and lead him to the barn.

'Please may I ride him later, Father?'

'Have you shorts or trousers with you?'

Oh no! I thought. We had been told only to bring underclothes, robes and sandals home with us. 'No, Father. We had to leave them behind.'

'You'll have to wait for your ride then. I'll take you tomorrow to order some trousers. Meanwhile you'll have to make do with grooming Pubi.'

Father Josip was as good as his word. The following day we visited the tailor and cobbler. Within four days shirts, shorts, long trousers, a jacket and new sandals were delivered to *Faruh*. 'A present from the Church,' said Father.

At last I was able to ride Pubi. We cantered round the field near the house then I rode him, bareback, into the forest. I felt free. I felt happy and at peace.

It was strange being back at Faruh but without the old familiar routine. Apart from feeding and grooming Pubi, I was no longer allowed to care for the animals. There was no mucking out, taking the cows to pasture or helping with the milking. No longer was I called on to run errands and do odd jobs. Life had a different pattern with time spent in study, reading and prayer. I rode Pubi every day and I also had a new hobby. At Bol I had started to learn to play the piano so I begged the vestry key from Sebastijana and went every day to practice in the church. Sometimes she came too and gave me a lesson.

I also asked Kazimira to teach me how to extract honey from the hives. I loved putting on the protective clothing, taking the combs from the hives and gently shaking off the bees. Most of all I loved the crunchy honey-filled comb – delicious! Once I was allowed to help smoke a swarm of bees which had clustered on a tree. When they became sleepy, I netted them and placed them in a hive. I thought that I would like to keep bees one day.

Although I attended Mass every morning, a new boy had been appointed to serve at the altar, a local lad who didn't live in. I now sat with the sisters on their special pew and was able to make the responses and join in the prayers loudly, in perfect Latin. I had one duty at Mass which was to mix the wine and water together in the chalice. This I did carefully, conscious of my robes and new status. On the second Sunday, I was to participate in Mass, my mother walked to St Mirko's Church to see me. She gave a little wave as I sat down but her eyes were full of tears when I stood to perform the ceremony with the chalice. It was to be over a year before I understood why.

After Mass, Mama came to *Faruh* for a cup of tea. As we walked there together, several girls gathered round, staring at me as if I'd dropped from the sky. Among them was the very pretty Ljubica Mežnar, daughter of the sexton. She was a little younger than I but quick and intelligent. She wanted to hear about Bol and later she asked me to help her with some homework. We became firm friends that summer, under the watchful eyes of the sisters of course. Once, escaping for a few minutes, we even held hands and I experienced some interesting sensations. The effect of the bromide had worn off.

That night, in bed, I felt guilty because I had been told that God had chosen me to be celibate. Perhaps for the first time I thought about the life ahead of me. I had always focused on the education, the learning which still excited me. Now I wondered about a life without a wife. What would that be like? I had heard some of the novices at Bol talk about a vocation, about a moment when they'd heard God's call to service as a monk and a priest. I had had no such experience. Life had always been a struggle for my mother and I had often been told 'God will provide.' It had seemed to me that when Father Josip had taken me under his wing, God was providing for me. This seemed even more true when I was accepted at Bol. I fell asleep, reassured by that thought. I was 14 years old.

It was at this time that I first noticed that the sisters were wearing rings. 'Why are you wearing wedding rings?' I asked.

'They aren't wedding rings,' answered Sebastijana, 'They are betrothal rings.'

'We are betrothed to Jesus Christ,' added Kazimira.

'What, all of you?'

'Yes, all sisters are.'

'Well, Jesus Christ must have a lot of fiancées then.' I laughed at my joke but then stopped to look at their faces. I was relieved to see them laughing too.

Half way through the holiday Franceska and I went to see my grandmother. As soon as she saw me in my robe, she began to cry. 'You're so grown up, Ivek. God bless and keep you.'

Soon her little kitchen was crowded with aunts, uncles and cousins, all anxious to hear about Bol and to gaze at me. It was my custom to pray at noon but my family wouldn't let Franceska and me go into another room and pray quietly. 'Pray here,' they said. 'We'll pray with you.' So we stayed and although Franceska used the usual Latin for prayer, I prayed in Croatian so that my grandmother and everyone else could join in.

'God bless you,' said Stara mama again as we got up to leave. 'Always be a good boy.'

'I am good,' I replied as I hugged her.

She laughed and said, 'Now, now, don't boast Ivek. A truly good man has no pride.' But I knew she wasn't serious and that she was proud of me.

Just before the end of the holiday, I was allowed to ride Pubi home to Mama's, to say goodbye. Once more the house was full of relations, friends and neighbours. Mama was pleased with the food parcel, sent by Sebastijana, but she seemed very reluctant to let me go at the end of my visit. Several times during the day, she seemed about to say something but then to change her mind.

'You really are happy, aren't you, son?' she said as we parted.

'Yes, Mama. I love studying. I am learning so much.'

She clung to me for a moment and tears ran down her cheeks. 'May the good Lord look after you,' she said. I kept turning to wave until she and all the other well-wishers were out of sight. Then I spurred Pubi to a canter and lost myself in the happiness of the ride.

Monastery: Second Year

At the end of the vacation Kazimira and Sebastijana took me to Pregrada in the trap. I kissed Pubi's nose and promised to be back next summer. Several people stared at the sight of two nuns hugging a robed novice as he boarded a bus for Zabok. One old lady touched me lightly on the arm. 'God bless you, my son,' she said. On the journey a man, drunk I think, turned round and shouted, 'How're you doing *popovšak*/religious idiot?' Other passengers shushed him and I felt my face burning but I said nothing.

From Zabok I caught a train to Zagreb and, as usual, went to the *samostan* for the night. A novice, older than me, opened the door and welcomed me. 'My name is Rudi Petrak,' he said.

'That's a coincidence,' I said. 'My sister Dragica's married to a man called Franz Petrak. I'm Ivan Vesligaj.'

'Good gracious,' said Rudi. 'We're almost related. Franz is my brother.'

'It's good to meet you,' I was surprised because I hadn't realised that Franz had a trainee priest in his family. 'How long have you been here?'

'I've been studying here for ten years. In two more years I shall take Holy Orders.'

I was disappointed to hear I had missed Branko as he had gone to Bol the previous day. However, I wasn't short of company. Rudi and I talked for the whole evening and the next morning he saw me on to the Split train at 7 am.

At Bol, it was good to see Branko again and to exchange news. We soon settled down to work and I remember one excursion we made that year. We went, on the monastery's boat, to the island of Korčula to visit the nuns' novice house. There I met the young women who had stayed at *Faruh* a couple of years earlier. By now they had all taken the veil. Their heads were covered and I knew their beautiful long hair would have been cut. They were very surprised to see me and we were able to talk for a short while, reminiscing about the walk and picnic. Vilma, who I couldn't help noticing was still very pretty, laughed and said, 'Do you still hate leek soup?' I made a face and she laughed again. Later she and I sat near each other in the refectory.

'Now you have taken the veil, Sister, where will you go?' I asked.

'I don't know yet,' she said. 'Mother Superior is waiting to hear from the Vatican and then she will let us know. It could be Italy, Africa…anywhere.'

'How about Potkostel? I'm sure that Father Josip and the sisters would be pleased if you went there and so would I. What do you think of that idea?'

'I'd love to go there. I really liked the countryside and the people but it's not up to me.' No, I thought. Nothing's up to you once you've taken the veil or taken orders, for that matter, but I kept my thoughts to myself.

I had been becoming increasingly worried about my mother. I still wrote cheerful letters home but her letters were full of the fact that she was finding life very hard and could no longer manage on what she made from selling the farm and vineyard produce. In one letter she told me she'd been to the local government office to apply for a widow's pension.

'They refused because your father was in the German army when he died,' she wrote. *'They told me to go to the German consulate, in Zagreb and ask them for a pension. I shall do this.'*

In her next letter she said she'd been to the consulate and been granted a small pension of 45 deutsch marks a month but her complaints soon began again. The pension didn't stretch very far. She couldn't afford to buy a warm winter coat. I lay awake at night worrying about her. I couldn't understand why she hadn't applied for a pension straight after the war when she had a house full of children and two sons serving the State: Josip, a captain in the army and Milan in the navy. She'd managed to make ends meet in the hardest of times. Why couldn't she manage now?

I had a sudden idea. I wrote to her straight away.

'You must ask Josip to help you. He belongs to the Party and has friends in powerful positions.'

A couple of weeks later I received Mama's reply.

'It was a good idea of yours to ask Josip for help. I wrote to him and forwarded your letter. I should have thought of asking his advice before. He took me to the government office, had a long talk with the local official and I came away with the promise of a monthly pension of 4,500 dinars.'

After that, I heard no more complaints.

My second year at Bol seemed to go much more quickly than the first. I often longed to be with my family or riding Pubi but I was reconciled to being away and I was still enjoying my studies.

At the start of the vacation, Father Josip met me off the coach at Pregrada with Pubi and the trap. Once more Pubi and I greeted each other gladly. Father Josip shook my hand and told me I'd grown. 'Yes, my long trousers are too short now,' I said.

'We'll get you kitted out with new things as we did last year,' he promised.

The sisters had prepared a feast for my return. It was good to see them but I was anxious to see Mama and my brothers. After a couple of days I was allowed to visit and to stay for one night. Again I was welcomed in the village as some sort of holy person and again I enjoyed Mama's cooking and every moment of chatter and laughter. I was aware of something amiss with my mother, however. She kept asking me if I were happy at Bol and, whatever I said, I seemed unable to reassure her.

On the first evening a crowd of my friends, boys and girls, came to the house and I couldn't help noticing how pretty some of the girls had grown. Indeed, they were now fine young women either working locally or in service nearby.

I studied hard with Father Josip and half way through the vacation my mother sent a message to say she wanted to see me. Father gave his permission and I set off, on foot, in the morning on the understanding I'd be back in Faruh before dark. After our usual affectionate greeting, Mama made some tea and we sat together at the kitchen table. There was no-one else at home. 'Ivek, if I give you some advice will you take it?'

'Of course, Mama.' My voice was calm but I felt a jolt of alarm. Even so, nothing had prepared me for what she said next.

'My advice is that you should leave the monastery. In fact, it's not just advice. It's what I wish you to do.'

A Change of Direction

'Leave Bol?' I heard a squeaky voice quite unlike mine. 'You mean leave Bol for ever?'

'Yes, Ivek, for ever.'

'Why?'

'I have my reasons.'

'But Mama, what are they?'

'As a priest you will never be able to marry and have children. You won't live a normal life. You know how the girls are always round you – like bees round a honey pot. Just imagine, you'll never be able to take one of them in your arms. You are forbidden. Apart from that, you have so many years of study left to do and then you'll have National Service. After that, the Church could send you anywhere in the world. I might never see you again.'

'But Mama, you knew all of this when you said I could go to Bol. You seemed so pleased I'd got a place there. Why have you changed your mind?'

'I have my reasons.' And that was all she would say.

I sat still trying to take in what she had said. I felt as if a pit had opened in front of me. I might sometimes have wondered about my vocation but at least my future had been secure. I loved to study and I had known I'd be able to study for the rest of my life. Now, I knew nothing for certain.

'Has all my hard work for the past two years been wasted?' I said.

My mother simply repeated, 'I have my reasons.'

'What will I do?' A picture of my life as a workman or farmhand flashed in front of me. Shabby clothes, thick boots, filthy hands. Or I might end up working at some menial task in an office – surely Mama didn't want any of this for me?

'You'll find something,' she said. 'You've had a good education.'

'What about Branko, my best friend at Bol. What will he think when I don't go back?'

'He'll get over it.'

Suddenly I thought of Father Josip. He would be so angry if I didn't return to Bol. And what about the sisters? I couldn't bear to think of their sad faces when they heard the news. 'Are you sure, Mama?' I managed to say in my normal voice. 'Are you absolutely sure you want me to leave Bol and come home?'

'I'm sure.'

'Then *you* must go and tell Father Josip and the sisters. I can't.'

'I'll do that,' she said, 'and I'll go now.' With that, she got up and walked through the door. She turned back and said, 'You know Ivek, it's better to be a good Catholic than a bad priest.' And she was gone, leaving me in a state of shock.

I don't know how long I sat there, staring in front of me but seeing nothing. I felt angry with my mother for springing this on me. I thought of all the people who had treated me as a special, holy person and what they would say. I thought about Father Josip and the Church's money which had been spent on me. I thought about the three sisters. Kazimira had often said I was a son to them. The son they could never have. Then I remembered Pubi. That's when the tears came. We'd miss each other so much. I'd never be able to ride him again. Finally, something new and unexpected filtered into the tumult of my mind. It was a feeling of freedom. I was free to do what I wanted, to miss prayers, to leave the homework unfinished, to read what I chose, to try to find some sort of career and even to go out with girls. I could be a normal fifteen year old. No more bromide.

In my most homesick moments at Bol, I had played with the idea of finishing my education there and leaving before I took orders. However, I'd never thought about it seriously and now it was out of my hands. The unfortunate thing was that my fine education was not complete. I had to find a way of continuing to study. I remembered that a friend of mine had passed an examination to a polytechnic college. I knew that these colleges provided training for a wide number of professions. My mind was made up in an instant. That was the only way forward for me.

I saw Mama walking along the path towards our house. She had a big parcel under one arm and my suitcase in her other hand. I ran to meet her and relieved her of her burdens. 'What happened? What did they say?'

'All the sisters cried, even Sebastijana. They send their love and say they'll miss you very much.'

'What about Father Josip?'

By now we were indoors and Mama sat down heavily. 'He took me into his office. He asked me whose decision it was. I said it was a family decision. "Do you really think it's the right decision?" he said and I said, "Yes." He went quiet for a moment and then said, "You do realise what you're doing, don't you? You're depriving a very bright boy of a secure and possibly a distinguished future." I said I understood but I thought this was best for you and that you would do what I wanted.'

'What did he say to that?'

'He couldn't say anything could he? He's always preaching that children should honour and obey their parents. He wants those robes you're wearing back but has sent all the new stuff he's bought for you. He says you can keep it.'

I felt a peculiar sadness as I looked at my belongings brought back by Mama but I knew I had to move fast if I were to be awarded a place at a college in the coming September. I didn't say anything but I took the case and bundle to Mama's room. I didn't want to cry but tears ran down my cheeks as I removed my robes for the last time. I felt so mixed up inside. Slowly I put on my new trousers and shirt and returned to the kitchen.

'I want to go to a polytechnic college,' I said and as I spoke I began to feel better. 'I need to go to the Education Office as soon as possible.'

Mama was obviously surprised at my swift decision but said, 'I'll come with you.'

The young woman who dealt with us at the Education Office had a name badge pinned to her blouse. She was 'Georgia Horvat'. I presented my reports and certificates from my primary schools and from Bol.

She looked at me with interest as she said, 'It's too late to apply, really, but you seem to have had an excellent education so far so I think I can make an exception.' I smiled in relief and she looked through a sheaf of papers. 'I've only one polytechnic place left, I'm afraid, so there's no choice of subject for you.'

'What will I study if I take the place?' I knew I would take it whatever the course. I had no alternative.

'It's called the 'The Technology and Chemistry of Leather.''

Leather? I thought. I knew nothing about it and wasn't particularly interested in it but the words 'technology' and 'chemistry' had caught my interest. I looked at Mama who nodded.

'What about the cost?' I asked. I'd worked out that if I lived at home and got a part-time job, Mama and I, between us, could probably just about afford to pay for my studies at a polytechnic.

'It costs 5,000 dinars a month, including board. You'd have to live in because this one place I can offer you is in Karlovac. Seeing my face drop she said, 'Don't worry. As your mother is a widow, there will be a government grant to cover the expense.'

'Thank you, Miss Georgia,' I said, immensely relieved, 'How long is the course?'

'Three years. You'd have to report to Karlovac Polytechnic on September 15th. Will you accept the place?'

I didn't hesitate. 'I accept it. Thank you very much.'

The following weekend I met Father Josip at St Ann's Church. He shook my hand and said, 'I am very, very sorry you have left Bol, Ivek, but I understand it was your mother's decision.'

'Yes, Father.'

'What do you plan to do?'

'I'm going to Karlovac Polytechnic, Father.'

'I wish you every success.' He patted my shoulder and walked away.

A couple of days later I spoke to Mama about something which had been on my mind. 'I want to go to see Stara mama,' I said. 'I went to see her before I went to Bol and now I've left, I should go and explain why.'

My mother looked rather disconcerted but said, 'If you're going, I'll go too.'

My grandmother's face lit up when she saw us. 'How good to see you,' she said as she kissed us.

'I've come with some news,' I said.

'Tell me.'

My mother said nothing so I went on, 'I've left the monastery. Mama wanted me to.'

There was a moment of silence then my grandmother turned on Mama. 'Why in God's Holy Name?'

'I have my reasons.'

'Your reasons? You stupid woman! This decision will destroy his future. Call yourself a mother? You're selfish and idiotic.' There followed the most enormous row.

I remember my mother shouting, 'He's bright enough to do well in another profession. He's my son, not yours.' They seemed to forget I was there and I walked outside. Finally, my mother stormed off towards home.

Stara mama kissed and hugged me, crying loudly. 'I'm so sorry. God bless you in whatever you do.'

My brothers and sisters were almost as shocked as I had been with Mama's decision. Only my communist brother, Josip, was pleased. When he visited, he clapped me on the shoulder and said, 'Glad to hear you're done with that mumbo jumbo.' The others grumbled at Mama but agreed, between themselves, that it was typical of her to suddenly change her mind about something, make an instant decision whatever the consequences. Neighbours and friends, while feeling sorry for me, cast their eyes to Heaven and said,

'How like Hanika to do such a thing.'

On 14th September Mama and I travelled by train to Zagreb where we stayed a night with her cousin, who lived opposite the railway station. The next day we caught an early train to Karlovac and found our way through the town, with its narrow streets of shops and tall factories, to the massive building which housed the polytechnic college. At the office, we presented my certificates and also the papers relating to the grant I was to receive.

'Oh,' commented the director when he saw the cross and the word 'Bol' at the top of my certificates from the monastery. He looked at me closely.

His secretary, glancing over his shoulder, said to me, 'You're qualified enough to work in any of the offices in this building, you know.'

I was surprised and answered, 'But I want to study.'

The director laughed and said, 'Well, you've come to the right place.' He wrote a short note and put it in an envelope. 'Take this to the accommodation block. It's to confirm your grant.'

He gave us directions. We crossed the River Kupa, walked past more shops and, in ten minutes, we were in the office of the manager of the students' accommodation block.

The manager had dark curly hair and a fine black moustache which he stroked as he read the note and nodded. 'That's all in order. Good.' He rang a bell and a young man entered. He was a couple of years older than me, tall with a kind, round face. He had obviously been waiting close at hand. 'This is Zdenko, Ivan. He will be your guide. He will also be your mentor for your first two years at college.' Zdenko and I shook hands.

'There's no need to worry about Ivan,' he said to Mama, 'I'll look after him.'

Mama smiled a thank you.

We went out of the room and through another door into a large courtyard. I could smell cooking and realised I was hungry. 'It's lunch time,' said Zdenko. 'I'll give you a few minutes to say your goodbyes and then you and I, Ivan, had better go and eat before all the food disappears.' Mama gave me a hug. She didn't kiss me but walked quickly away, not looking back. I think she was crying and I felt like doing the same.

Polytechnic: Year 1

Zdenko and I had a good meal of roast lamb and vegetables and then he led me out of the restaurant and into the courtyard to start our tour of the accommodation block. A raucous babble of different languages hit me. I just managed to stop myself putting my hands over my ears. The noise, echoing off the walls, was almost unbearable. A crowd of young people filled the yard. As well as Croats there were Bosnians, Serbs, Bosnian-Croats and Muslims from I knew not where. On top of all this, I could hear heavy traffic outside, the hoots of horns and the siren from a passing ambulance. I stood still. What am I doing here? I thought. Why didn't I stand up to Mama and insist on going back to Bol? I can't survive in this. How will I ever be able to work among such a mixture of people and in such noise? I suddenly realised how protected I'd been at Bol, how everything there had been done quietly and in order. I thought longingly of the quiet rooms, the beautiful peaceful walks and, above all, of the orderly calm.

Zdenko was looking at me and tugging my sleeve. 'Come on Ivan. I'll show you round.' I pulled myself together and looked about me. Zdenko had to speak loudly, above the excited chatter. He pointed out the accommodation blocks and the meeting room and then we collected my case and he took me to my bedroom. I was dismayed to find it had two bunk beds which meant that I was sharing with three other boys. I was a little comforted by the fact that, from the start, I hit it off with Ostoja, a boy who was already in the room when Zdenko and I arrived. In due course, I discovered that Bosko and Marko the two others I was to share with were pleasant enough but it was Ostoja who became my close friend. Later I learned that his father, too, had been killed in the war and his mother had died when he was 10. Since then he had been brought up in a children's home.

As soon as we'd finished unpacking, we were called into the courtyard to meet our professors. The one I liked most was the professor of literature, Ana Luznik. She was Croatian, small and plump with glasses. She had a kind face and attractive voice. I was to enjoy her lessons about great writers of the world and their works.

At the end of the introductions the professor of music made an announcement. 'To the right of this building is a music studio. One of our local musicians, Oto Rebič, wishes to start a young people's orchestra. Anyone interested in joining it should go to the studio at 7.30 tomorrow evening when auditions will be held.' I decided straight away that I would try for the orchestra. I'd loved playing the organ at St Mirko and had made reasonable progress.

I didn't sleep very well that first night. I was unused to traffic noise and had grown to like having my own room at Bol. True, I always shared with my brothers at home but that was different. I lay awake mulling over how suddenly and completely my life had changed. I thought longingly of my rides on Pubi. I can honestly say that not a day went past, that first year, when I didn't think of 'my' beloved horse.

Ostoja and I walked together to the college the next morning. Lessons started at 8 am. 'Let's stick together so we don't get lost,' he said and I felt pleased that I'd made a friend already.

The polytechnic building was huge. It housed several colleges apart from ours. Trainee teachers, doctors, lawyers and foresters inhabited other parts of the building but the leather technicians were on the ground floor. A notice directed us to take the first corridor to the right off the entrance hall. Our room was the first on the right. There were about twenty students in our year group.

I found, as time went on, that the curriculum was wide and that religious studies was missing. Karlovac Polytechnic College was of course a secular college in a communist state. Most of the work seemed very easy. At Bol, we had covered much more in mathematics, geography and biology. The literature was different because it wasn't religious but I thought that the history was extremely basic. It dealt only with the First and Second World Wars, the Balkan War and a little German and Russian history. At the monastery we had looked in depth at the history of the Byzantine, the Greek and Roman Empires as well as at Venetia, ancient Croatia and much more. The subjects I liked best were industrial chemistry, technology and physics.

Ostoja came with me for the audition for the orchestra. We were both nervous. Oto Rebič was a young man with a kind, pale face and outsize glasses. He smiled encouragingly at us as we tried to show him that he needed us in his orchestra. We passed the sight reading test, using tonic solfa and were accepted. We were selected to play little stringed instruments called biserkas. I was to look forward to the orchestra rehearsals and performances through the whole of my college life. It was time away from the crowd. The atmosphere, as we worked together on a new piece, sometimes reminded me of the atmosphere at Bol. I'm not sure why.

As ever, I enjoyed my studies even though I didn't relish this very different sort of communal life. I couldn't help noticing the bad table manners and crude behaviour of some of the students. I didn't say anything, of course, because I would have been called a snob. Similarly, I didn't pray openly. I tried to pray inside my head but it wasn't the same as the regular prayer times we'd had at Bol and *Faruh*. I was surprised how much I missed the structured prayers and times of meditation. Here, life was all bustle. Even in my bedroom I was rarely alone.

I buried myself in the work, trying particularly hard in science and technology. We were taught about the structure of skin and learned about all the chemicals used in treating and curing pelts. We mixed them and tried them out on small pieces of leather. We learned about different types of skins and how to recognise each. We had homework every weekday evening. Zdenko supervised the four of us who shared my dormitory. He made sure we finished our work and helped us if we were stuck.

I looked forward to the weekends. On Saturdays we went to a small local leather factory to practice the theory learned at college. The students' workshop was on the first floor and the qualified craftsmen, the *majster*s/masters carried out their work on the ground floor. Each came up to instruct us in his particular specialty.

Downstairs, in the factory, we could watch the machines at work. I had never had much to do with machines and certainly had no idea of the mechanics which lay behind them. For the first time I had the chance to observe, close up, how the rollers, cutters and conveyor belts worked.

I was fascinated by the chemistry involved in the production of leather. We were taken to a warehouse and shown how to select the pelts and then, in the factory, we saw the whole process through to the finished leather which was ready for making into goods. We were able to observe all our laboratory experiments on a large scale.

The raw pelts were first soaked in a huge tank of brine then spread out and buried in sawdust for a week. Finally they were immersed in a tank of chemicals (such as we had mixed in the lab) to remove the hair or fur. We wore protective clothes and goggles but it was heavy work. For two years I had done very little physical labour so, for the first few weeks, I felt stiff and sore at the end of the day. I loved the work, however, because I learned something new every Saturday.

On Sundays we were free. I'm sorry to say I didn't go to church. The ethos of the college was fiercely secular, dominated by members of the *Omladina*/Communist Youth League. I would have been badly teased and probably bullied had I braved the local church. I did try to have a few minutes by myself each Sunday, though, so that I could be quiet and think about God. For a long while I missed the times of worship, the sacred music and the prayers I had grown so used to at Bol.

Most Sundays, when it was warm enough, Ostoja and I swam in the River Kupa or in the Korana, a river at the other side of the city. We also played football and joined the Leather College team. We played matches against other colleges in the poly'. Ostoja was a brilliant footballer in spite of the fact that he had no toes. He told me he'd lost them as a result of surgery which had gone wrong. He and I often went for long walks when there was no football.

Zdenko told us that there was a pile of old skis in the loft of our accommodation block. 'I don't know who left them there,' he said, 'but anyone can borrow them as long as they return them afterwards.'

I'd learnt to ski in my village, using a pair of ancient skis which belonged to my uncle so, in midwinter, when the snow was thick on the hill where Karlovac Castle stood, I showed Ostoja the rudiments of skiing. As a natural sportsman, he learned quickly and soon we were spending many happy hours, on Sundays, climbing to the castle and skiing from there.

One of the things I enjoyed most about living in a town was going to the cinema. To me it still seemed to be a magical experience and it really didn't matter what the film was about. Ostoja and I went as often as we could afford. We made friends with the elderly woman in the ticket office. We called her 'Plum' because of her shape and her pink face. She often let us see a film without tickets, putting her finger to her lips and hurrying us in before anyone else noticed.

I was extremely shy with the precocious college girls. Early on I had an embarrassing experience. Each morning, students gathered on the steps outside the building, waiting for the bell. One day I was walking towards the steps with Ostoja when one of the girls jumped up shouting, 'Oh look, here's a lovely new student.' She rushed over, grabbed me and kissed me squarely on the mouth. A cheer went up from the watching crowd and I, with a hot red face, could only push past the girl and rush through the college gate. For weeks I approached college slowly and carefully, looking for the offending girl. If she was in sight, I hung back until she had gone in and sometimes I had to rush into class at the last moment in order to avoid her. Ostoja teased me unmercifully.

I gradually became acclimatised to the clamour and rush of college life. I still longed for silence sometimes. I had come to realise that what I missed most was the inner peace I had acquired at the monastery. Ordinary people seemed to thrive on noise.

I was worried, however, when the local director of Social Services sent for me. In spite of all my reservations, I did not want to be forced to leave. Perhaps my grant was going to be withdrawn for some reason, I thought. The director smiled at me as I went into his office which I saw as a good sign. He invited me to sit down. I sat nervously on the edge of the chair.

'Ivan, we haven't received payment of your grant from your local education office. We've had no cheques for two months,' he said.

I couldn't understand how this had happened. 'But I asked them to send cheques straight to you every month, sir.'

'I know you did and they came for the first two months.'

'Have you been in touch with them, sir?'

'I think it's best if you go and sort it out yourself. I'll give you three days' leave of absence to do so. I have your train tickets here. '

A day later I was waiting outside the office of Georgia Horvat. There was another boy there and he told me that the same thing had happened to him. He'd been given time off from his polytechnic college, to come to the Education Office too. Georgia called me in first.

'Hello Ivan,' she said, 'what are you doing here? Shouldn't you be at college?' I explained the situation and she exclaimed with annoyance. 'I don't know how that can be. The money certainly went out from this office.' She checked in a ledger. 'Oh, I'm sorry, my clerk sent the cheques to your mother instead of to college. That won't happen again, I promise you. Do you think your mother has cashed them?' I had a vision of my mother, always hard up, cashing the cheques but saying nothing. I immediately felt guilty for thinking such a thing.

'Oh no, I'm sure she wouldn't do that. She'd know the money was for college.'

'Sit down for a moment, Ivan.' She spoke to the other boy and then said, 'It's almost lunch time. Are you two young men hungry?' We confessed that we were and she laughed, saying, 'We'll sort the money out afterwards. Now I'm going to treat you both to lunch.'

She took us to a restaurant and bought us a most delicious meal of *srpski pasulj* /smoked sausage and bean casserole. She really seemed interested in us, asking about our families and our college courses.

Back at the office, she went to a large safe set into the corner. 'It must have been a problem with the post,' she said. She counted out ten thousand dinars for each of us. 'Put it in an inside pocket,' she instructed. I had never seen so much money before. 'Now here is money for any travel expenses not covered by your colleges and a little something for you to spend.' To my surprise and delight she handed each of us another 200 dinars. I stammered my thanks but she brushed them aside with, 'That's settled, then.' She made a note in her ledger. 'In future there will be no mistake. The money will be sent straight to your colleges.' Then she surprised me again by giving each of us a hug. 'Off you go. Good luck to both of you and let me know if at any time there is anything you really need.'

I felt happy as I made my way home. Not only did I have my college fees but I had some extra money too. I thought I'd share it with Mama. In the village which lay next to ours, I met Stanko, one of my cousins. 'Why are you home?' he asked.

'I had to go to the Education Office in Pregrada,' I said. 'I'm going back to college tomorrow.'

'Now let me guess why you had to go to the Education Office,' Stanko said mysteriously. 'Could it be because you haven't received your grant?'

'How do you know?' I was astonished.

'It so happens that I was in the bank when I saw Auntie Hanika cashing your cheques. I was right behind her and heard her tell the bank clerk that they had come to her house by mistake.' I couldn't say anything for a moment. I was shocked and hurt and, making the excuse that I had something I needed to do immediately, I hurried home.

Mama was surprised to see me but greeted me affectionately. 'What brings you home in term time?' she asked.

I couldn't bring myself to say anything about what Stanko had told me. I simply recounted the facts of the interview with the director and my successful visit to the Education Office. I didn't mention the extra 200 dinars from Georgia Horvat. I was waiting for her to tell me she had cashed my cheques, to offer me the money and say I should return what I'd been given today although I think I knew, in my heart of hearts, that she wouldn't. I noticed she was wearing a dress I hadn't seen before and that there were one or two new items in the kitchen. Still, I couldn't challenge her. From that day, however, I never again felt I could absolutely trust my mother. I have often thought that the fact that the cheques had been cashed must eventually have shown up in Georgia Horvat's accounts. Why didn't she follow it up and why didn't she demand repayment of the money she gave me? Years later, I asked my mother about the incident. 'I knew they'd give you more,' she said. 'They wouldn't let you starve. Son, I needed the money at the time.'

Vacation

The year seemed to pass quickly and it was time to go home for the summer vacation. On the way, I planned to visit my sister Dragica who was living in Zagreb. I wanted to impress her with my new found sophistication and smartness. On the last morning at college, I ironed a new cream cotton shirt and laid it on my bed next to my trousers and underclothes. I went for a shower and when I returned the shirt had disappeared. At first I thought Ostoja had hidden it as a joke but when he came back from the bathroom and I accused him, he swore that he hadn't seen it. The others from our room had already left for home. I was very angry as I hadn't another respectable clean shirt. I went straight to Zdenko.

'Most of the other boys have gone, Ivan. I don't think I'll be able to track it down for you but I'll try.' He went off to investigate but soon returned. 'I'm sorry I'm afraid it's likely that whoever took it is on his way home by now. He's unlikely to bring it back here next term because you'd recognise it, wouldn't you? Have you another one you can wear?'

'No, I haven't, not a clean one. I've just got this sleeveless vest I was going to wear under my shirt.'

'You'll have to make do with that. Sorry. Have a good break.' I wasn't in a very good mood when I said goodbye to Ostoja but by the time I'd walked to the station, the sunshine and the prospect of the holiday had cheered me.

The guard on the train I was to catch to Zagreb stopped me as I was getting on. 'Why are you half dressed? Put something else on. Make yourself respectable.' I explained about the theft and he laughed. 'I haven't heard that one before. All right, I'll let you off this time.' I felt self-conscious and was sure everyone was looking at me. It was a relief to reach Zargeb and Dragica's apartment.

'Why aren't you wearing a shirt?' was her first question after we'd greeted each other. Once more I explained. 'That's terrible, Ivan. What a mean thing to do. You can't trust anyone nowadays.' After we had drunk coffee together she said, 'I'm sorry we haven't more space. You'll have to sleep on the floor in our room, I'm afraid. I'll put down a mattress for you.' I didn't mind at all. It was a tiny apartment – only one room and the kitchen. My little niece, Nevenka climbed on my knee as I told my sister my college news.

Dragica, Ivan and his niece Nevenka

68

'You can't go home in a vest,' she said. 'Let's go down to the market. There's a very good fabric stall there. You could do with some thinner trousers for summer as well as a shirt. We'll see what we can find and my friend over the road will make some trousers and a shirt for you.'

By the next morning, I was the proud possessor of a smart pair of grey linen trousers and a white cotton shirt. My sister's friend, the seamstress, had worked all night so that I could look smart when I presented myself to Mama. I thanked her warmly and gave Dragica a special hug. She laughed and said, 'Well, you *are* my little brother.'

It was good to be home and I'd looked forward to seeing Mama and my brothers and to home cooking. I quickly realised that this was to be very much a working holiday. It was time to weed the corn and for some days my three brothers, Mama and I were up at 3 am. We hoed between the straight rows of corn and soon my hands, unaccustomed to such work, were blistered and sore. 'You'll get used to it,' was all the sympathy I got from the family and eventually I did, developing callouses by the time I returned to college. When we'd finished a stretch of the field, my mother brought along a basket full of young chicks to finish the work for us. She went home during the morning to make a hot meal which she carried to us along with a bottle of wine. We drank from a nearby spring too and rested for a while in the heat of the day. When we got back to the house the first evening, I was so tired that I could hardly eat the delicious salad of young dandelion leaves and kidney beans. Everyone else went outside to enjoy the cool evening but I climbed into bed and fell instantly asleep.

When the weeding was done, I was given some respite. I walked in the familiar forest and mountains, sometimes alone and sometimes with my brothers or my friends. How I longed for Pubi. How I would have loved to canter over the hills, feeling the rush of wind on my face but I knew this would never happen again.

It was soon time to return to the cornfields. We gently worked the earth around the base of each plant and mounded it in a cup shape, making sure the roots and base of the stem were covered. Although it was back-breaking work it was easy to follow the straight rows of plants which had been sown in the spring by my mother and brothers. My mother made her own string from *konoba*/cannabis and the field had been divided by lengths of this into squares to guide the planters. There was no wastage.

I let my mind wander as I worked. I thought of the different parts of my life, of Faruh, the sisters, and Pubi, of course. I remembered Bol, my studies in the quiet of the monastery and I wondered how Branko was. I thought of my new hectic, noisy life at college and hoped that Ostoja was enjoying his vacation. I concluded that, on the whole, I was content. I was well fed and had a little money for clothes. I still enjoyed studying, I had the prospect of work when I left college and I had a good friend in Ostoja. Life could be a lot worse.

Once we'd finished with the corn, we moved on to work in the vineyard. First we weeded between the vines then we carefully pruned them, grafting the new 'wild' shoots on to the main stems. Next we must spray the plants against pests. I enjoyed making the spray because it reminded me of chemistry lessons.

The final liquid was midnight blue and we used spray guns to apply it. We tied handkerchiefs round our faces to act as masks. When the job was done, the top halves of our faces was deep blue, beside which, the part which had been masked looked startlingly white. Our hands, arms, legs and feet were blue too and it took a great quantity of warm water and carbolic soap to wash ourselves clean. The next day I climbed the hill which overlooked our land. In the bright sunshine, the whole vineyard shimmered, blue. Through half closed eyes I could almost imagine it was the Adriatic Sea.

Mama said that Lujzek and I could have a few days' holiday from farm work. I'd heard that a fruit and vegetable retailer, about an hour's walk away, wanted fresh blueberries and would pay a good price. I knew splendid blueberries grew just over the Slovenian border and persuaded Lujzek to come with me. We set off at 3 am, carrying Mama's largest saucepans with handles made of string. By 7 we'd arrived at the spot, having waded across the River Sutla and crossed a mountain into a fertile valley. On the slopes around, blueberries grew in abundance, large and succulent. No-one else was in sight so we had them to ourselves. I'd invented a special picking instrument, constructed from wood and Mama's sewing needles. It meant I could gather the berries without removing the bloom. We ate a picnic breakfast of bread, pork fat and crackling and drank from a stream before setting to work. It took some time to fill the big pots and we had to be careful of the snakes which came out to bask in the sunshine.

Refreshed by another drink, we retraced our steps until we'd crossed the river then we diverted to the village where we hoped to sell our berries. 'Oh no!' Lujzek groaned when he saw a queue of people lined up outside the store. Each was holding a container of either blueberries or mushrooms.

'Don't worry, they need plenty,' I said but I wasn't too happy at the prospect of a long wait. We joined the queue and, as I looked round idly, I noticed a girl watching us from the high window of an apartment which was behind the store. A man appeared beside her and I recognised him as the manager of our local coal depot. They both disappeared from sight and then I saw the girl walking slowly along the line of people, looking at everyone's blueberries. When she came to me she stopped.

'They look nice,' she said. It must have been the bloom.

'Taste one,' I invited.

'It's delicious,' she said. 'How much is the store paying?'

'A hundred dinars a kilo.'

'How many have you got?'

'About 3 kilos, I think.'

'We'll give you 400 dinars for your 3 kilos.' I accepted her offer straight away and she handed over the money. Lujzek had to wait his turn in the queue and was paid 300 dinars by the store manager for his 3 kilos.

'You've done well,' the store owner said. 'These are of good quality.' We left the store highly delighted with our day's work.

On the way home we bought some sugar, oil, bread, flour, salt and other provisions. We spent 400 dinars and stuffed our rucksacks full. As we were leaving the shop, the owner called us. 'Is there any chance of you getting hold of some mushrooms for me? There should be plenty about. I'll pay a reasonable price. I'll pay an even better one if you dry them before you bring them in.'

I answered straight away. 'Yes, we'll get some for you and my mother will dry them. What we need is a good thunder storm. That'll make then grow.'

Mama was pleased with us when we got home. As well as the food, we gave her 100 dinars and kept 50 dinars each for ourselves. We'd walked over 20 miles that day.

In the night, there was a violent thunderstorm. We were up at 3 am again and this time took *kos*/long baskets which we carried like rucksacks. We climbed the mountain close to our home. We knew where to look and found masses of *vrganjis*, a large brown plate-like fungi. It didn't take long to fill our baskets and we decided to treat ourselves to some lemonade at an inn on our way home. As we were removing our loaded baskets from our backs, a young man came out of the door.

'You've got some fine mushrooms there. Can I buy some of them?' He bought 100 dinars worth. and I realised he was looking at us closely. 'Haven't I met you before? I know your mother and, once a long time ago, I met you with your big brother – what's his name – Adalbert Vesligaj?'

'Yes, he's our brother,' I said although I didn't remember the man.

'You've got a vineyard, haven't you?' We nodded. 'My name's Bešenski and I've just taken over this place. I could do with a bit of help today. Do you want to earn a few dinars?'

'Yes.' This time we nodded enthusiastically.

'Do you know how to clean a big wine barrel thoroughly – a 1,000 litre one? Really clean it, I mean, so that I can re-use it?'

'Yes, we do. We've done it lots of times for our mother.' He led us to the back of the inn. The barrel was as tall as I was. We helped him push it over on to its side.

'We'll need lots of water please, warm to start with,' I said, 'also two scrubbing brushes, some clean cloths…and have you any mustard plants?' These grew as wayside flowers and weeds. They could be found almost everywhere,

'Yes we have. I'll get the things you need.'

We put our mushrooms in a shady place and covered them with a blanket, the man lent us, then we took off our shirts and climbed inside the barrel. He returned with the warm water and brushes and left us to get on. It took a long time to scrub the enormous barrel properly. We called Mr Bešenski several timed to roll it a little so that we could properly reach every nook and cranny to remove the thick red sediment. Then we used bunches of mustard plants he picked for us. We rubbed the whole of the inside of the barrel with them until it shone green. This was to remove bacteria. Finally we rinsed the entire thing with cold water and the job was done. We emerged wet, grubby but satisfied. We washed ourselves down and sat for a rest.

As the sun began to dry us, Mrs Bešenski came out, carrying a roasted pig's head and bread for us. We thought it was as good as anything Mama could produce and I remember it as one of the most delicious meals I ever had. We were also paid 100 dinars each for our labours.

As we left the inn, tired and very full, Lujzek gave a sigh of contentment. 'Another good day's work,' he said. I agreed and we walked on in happy silence.

Polytechnic: Year 2

In spite of the hard work, I'd enjoyed my vacation and felt a bit glum as I boarded the train for Zagreb in September. I hung out of the window as the familiar countryside slid away, quite forgetting to close it as we approached a tunnel. I was not popular with the other occupants when the carriage filled with smoke. I sat down, embarrassed.

Once more I stayed one night with my sister and early the next morning I was on my way to Karlovac. When I arrived, Ostoja was looking out for me. 'Come on, dump your bag in our room and then let's go for a cup of coffee. There's something I want to tell you. Ten minutes later, we were facing each other over our coffees at a student café.

'What's this exciting news?' I asked.

There was a moment's silence then, in a rush, Ostoja said, 'I've met my father.'

I stared at him. 'You said he was dead.'

'I thought he was.'

'Where's he been all this time?'

'He's living in Serbia, on the Hungarian border. It's a long story. He, my mother and I were living in Bosnia in 1941 when the Germans came. Of course I was just a baby. Many people were killed but my parents managed to escape. We had to live in the open and it was bitterly cold. My toes were frost bitten and that's how I lost them – not by bad surgery. That's the story I've always told people because it seemed simpler than going into all the stuff about running away and the snow. Anyway, somehow my mother and I got separated from Father. When I was old enough to ask about him, my mother said she'd been told by the authorities that he was dead. What actually happened was that he hid in the hills and managed to avoid capture. When, eventually, he went back to our village to look for us he was told that we'd both died. We'd moved by then, you see. Father had to find work and start a new life.

It took a moment for me to take it all in. Then I said, 'How on earth did you find each other?'

'I had to go to the local Social Service Office about my grant for this year. I was told that, while they were updating my records, they realised that there had never been any confirmation of my father's death. There was no paperwork to back it up. They didn't really expect to find him but they asked the Red Cross to try. It was they who discovered him – married with two daughters. He was astounded to learn I was alive and immediately came to the children's home to meet me.'

'So you've got half sisters! Did you get on with your father?'

'Straight away. He was a good footballer too. We had so much to talk about. I can't tell you how amazing it was to see him. I've got a photo.' He dug a small picture out of his pocket. His father was smiling but looked old and careworn. It was clear he had endured great suffering.

'Will you see him and your stepmother and sisters next vacation?'

'Yes, next summer. It seems a long time to wait but we're going to write to each other. At last I have someone to write my news to.' I felt so happy for Ostoja. Until then I'd never really thought how lonely he must have been. However many friends you have, I concluded, there's nothing like family.

One night, soon after our return to college, I was woken by a loud babble of voices from the courtyard outside the bedroom. I could hear children crying and women shouting in a foreign language. Before we could investigate, there was a knock on the door and Zdenko came in.

'Get up quickly, everyone. Get dressed and pack a change of clothes in your small bags. Bring your college work too and assemble in the study room. Be as quick as you can. I'll explain everything to you there.'

He was gone before we could ask any questions and, as we obeyed his orders, we were trying to guess what had happened.

'Perhaps it's a fire.'

'No, you just run out then. You don't take stuff with you.'

'Maybe we've been invaded by a foreign army.'

'Invaders don't bring children with them. Listen to those babies crying.'

'Perhaps there's a flood.'

'Could be, I suppose. We'll know in a minute.'

By this time we were on our way downstairs. As I looked out into the courtyard, I saw that it was heaving with people. I could see, by the lights which streamed through the downstairs windows, that most of them were women and children.

'There is an emergency in Hungary,' Zdenko told us. 'The people in the courtyard are refugees. They have been brought here in trucks for safety. They will need to stay for a bit, therefore they will use our beds and eat in our restaurant. Alternative arrangements have been made for us. The trucks which brought them are waiting to take us to an army camp on the other side of the city. Come along quietly please and I'll show you where to go.'

'Will we still go to college?' I asked.

'Yes. College will be as usual.'

'How long will it be for?' someone enquired.

'We don't know yet. No more questions now. Hurry along.' As we passed the restaurant and kitchen, we saw there were army cooks in charge, preparing a meal for the newcomers.

What an adventure it was for us. We climbed aboard the trucks, helped by soldiers who, although they were armed, cracked jokes with us.

'Want to join the army? You'll have to brush your hair first.'

'Do you know how to salute? Not bad but you need more practice.'

As we bumped along the road, I wished my friends in the village could see me. They'd be very jealous.

It didn't take long to reach the camp. We were waved past two sets of armed guards. There was a high wall around the complex. At each corner of the rectangle was a tower. On the top of each I could see the silhouettes of more soldiers. The camp was lit up for our arrival. Army cooks were bending over a camp stove and I wondered what they were cooking at this time of night. A sergeant greeted us as we got out of the truck.

'Welcome,' he said. 'My corporal and I will take your names and home addresses and then these soldiers will show you where you are to sleep. You will be woken by reveille in the morning. Get up when you hear it, wash and dress and report to the canteen for breakfast. It's over there.'

Our particulars were soon taken and we were counted off, twelve at a time, and shown into dormitories. By now it was 2 am and we were very sleepy. I climbed into the bunk above Ostoja's and pulled a sheet and blanket over myself. The bed was hard and I lay awake for a few minutes, listening to the unfamiliar sounds. I thought I'd never get to sleep but I did and was woken by the sound of a bugle.

We slept at the camp for three nights and were taken, by trucks, to college each morning after a breakfast of porridge. The evening meals were excellent. I particularly remember the goulash and the fresh warm bread. On the second day after lectures, Ostoja and I walked to our accommodation block to find out what was happening. Most of the Hungarian refugees were inside, where we had been forbidden to go. However, there were a few people by a Red Cross bus which was parked outside. Clothes were being handed out to them. I wandered over to look. 'Do you want something?' asked the man in charge.

'I could do with some new trousers,' I said cheekily.

'Well, why not? We've got plenty of stuff here. Come inside and see if there's anything to fit you.' I emerged with a pair of trousers and a shirt and I was delighted. Ostoja laughed at me but I think he was envious. To this day I'm not sure if the man thought I was a refugee.

When we were able to return to our accommodation, we found everything spotlessly clean and tidy. Tidier than we had left it, certainly. The director called us to the courtyard.

'The refugees were very grateful for the use of your rooms and the facilities here,' he said. 'Hungary is not a safe place to be at the moment. Some rebels have made a lot of trouble so, for the moment, the people who were here have been sent to places of safety in either France, Germany or Britain.'

A few weeks later there was almost another international incident when a bus-load of Italians happened to stop outside college. Yugoslavia had just beaten Italy in a football match and we danced round the coach, gesticulating and chanting, 'Six-one, six-one.' Fortunately the traffic lights changed to green and the bus moved off before any of the Italians could leap out and take revenge.

At about this time, all the students in our year moved to new accommodation not far from the main campus. The old block was to be refurbished. I wasn't pleased to learn that ten of us were to share a dormitory. Fortunately Ostoja and I were still together. As we were unpacking our belongings, I sat on a lower bunk.

'Rock hard,' I said. 'Where on earth did they get these bunks from?'

'From the army, I heard,' laughed Ostoja.

'Good job I'm joining the navy then.'

We had more independence now we had moved out of the main accommodation block. We had tokens so that we could eat at any of the student restaurants in the town. We supplemented our diet with fresh fruit when we could. There was a fruit shop opposite our digs and the young woman who worked there took pity on us, two poor students, and often slipped us free apples.

I still enjoyed Saturdays at the factory. One episode stands out in my memory. It shows that although I was, on the whole, a serious minded and conscientious student, I wasn't above playing the odd practical joke. We were in the students' workshop and the *majster*/master was demonstrating a process which could be used on leather. Suddenly he realised he had forgotten to bring the ammonia he needed.

'Ivan, go downstairs and fetch some, will you,' he said. 'It's in the big bottle on the left of my bench. You can't mistake it. It's red and it's labelled. Pour some carefully into this flask and bring it up as quickly as you can.'

As we'd been handling chemicals, I was already wearing protective clothing, a mask and goggles. I found the ammonia bottle, lifted out the clay stopper and, with utmost care, poured some into the flask. I re-stoppered it and replaced the bottle, left the workshop and started up the stairs. The janitor, a bossy little man, was coming down and for some reason carrying an axe. He didn't like students very much and made our lives as difficult as possible, reporting us to the *majsters* for the smallest thing.

'What have you got there?' he asked importantly.

Knowing his liking for alcoholic liquor, I couldn't resist saying, 'Cognac.' (The ammonia I was holding was the same colour as certain brands of cognac.)

'Cognac? Lovely! Let me sniff it.' I held out the flask, he bent his head over it and inhaled deeply.

His reaction was violent. He reeled backwards, spluttering. He tottered, lost his balance and fell sideways on to the stairs. His eyes were watering and he coughed and swore violently when he could get his breath. I stayed long enough to check he wasn't seriously hurt and then I ran upstairs, holding the flask at arm's length. He gave chase, brandishing the axe but he was still gasping and I was too quick for him. I knew he wouldn't complain about me because doing so would make him look stupid. I also knew that, in future, I'd have to be very careful to obey all the factory rules to the letter. If by any chance he'd recognized me, he'd certainly not miss an opportunity to catch me out.

Ostoja had something to do after college that day so I walked home alone. I was laughing to myself, remembering the janitor's reaction and hurrying because I wanted to finish some work. I reached the bridge over the River Kupa and dashed across the main road without looking properly. There was a scream of breaks and a truck pulled up less than half a meter from me. I stood stone-still for a moment then I heard a door slam and the truck driver was in front of me. For the second time that day, swear words were hurled in my direction. The driver made as if to punch me. He clearly intended to teach me a hard lesson. I dodged out of his reach, doubled back and raced as fast as I could along the pathway. I glanced behind. Regardless of the fact that the truck was blocking the road, its driver was still in pursuit. Fortunately he was no match for me. Not only was I considerably younger than he, and fitter, but I knew the alleyways and short cuts and soon left him behind.

A week or two later, adverts appeared around the city for a day of festivities. 'Army Day' would celebrate Yugoslavia's glorious defenders. Ostoja and I decided to attend as a welcome break from routine. Soldiers marched through the streets to the music of brass bands and the market square was transformed into a showground for military equipment. We were still child-like enough to be thrilled by sitting in a Russian T34 tank, wearing helmets, handling the machine gun and peering through the powerful binoculars.

We wandered from stall to stall, talking to the soldiers and listening to a variety of reasons why, when it came to the time for our military service, we should choose to join the army. Ostoja was impressed but I didn't waver from my determination that my choice would be the navy.

The highlight of the day was the flight of a military plane over the city. A ladder was lowered from it and a man, climbing down, performed a series of acrobatics. For the finale he descended to the bottom and hung from it. It seemed miraculous because his arms and legs were outstretched. Then the loud speaker crackled into life and the announcement was made, 'Now he is holding the ladder only by his teeth.' Ostoja looked at me and laughed. 'I bet no-one in the navy could do that,' he said.

There was an attic above our dormitory where our suitcases were kept. There were also lockers where we stored any of our belonging which we weren't using at the time. Some evenings I'd go up to the attic on my own. I'd crouch in front of my locker and think about my brothers, sitting with Mama and our neighbours outside our house, chatting or singing together. In spite of Ostoja and all that I enjoyed about college, I still suffered from severe bouts of homesickness.

Playing in the orchestra was one way of forgetting all my negative feelings and worries. I was excited when Oto Rebić made an announcement one evening.

'I have entered you for a competition next month. You will compete against the orchestras of the other colleges which come under the auspices of this polytechnic. We will play some pieces you know already and we will learn two new pieces. This will mean some extra practices. Is everyone willing to take part?' We were all enthusiastic but I was very concerned when the conductor went on to explain what we would wear for the competition. 'It is important that you look smart and I have selected a uniform for you. From now on we'll be giving occasional concerts and entering other competitions so the uniform will do for those too. I want everyone to wear dark blue trousers, white long sleeved shirts and black well-polished shoes.'

He went on to say where we could buy the trousers and the price – 2,500 dinars. I stopped listening. I never had that sort of money to spend. I had enough for my day to day needs but very little over. I knew there was no point in asking anyone in my family but suddenly I remembered something which had been said to me over a year ago. 'Let me know if there is anything you really need.' In my mind's eye I saw the kindly face of Georgia Horvat.

That evening I wrote to her, explaining my situation and asking her if there were any way her department could pay at least part of the cost. Within four days I received a letter from Georgia and a cheque for the whole amount.

'Dear Ivan,' she wrote.

'I am pleased you contacted me about your need for a uniform for the orchestra. I enclose a cheque which will cover the cost of the blue trousers. You will look very smart.

Congratulations on gaining a place in the orchestra and on working hard enough to merit performing in the competition. I'm sure you will do well.

I know that at the end of next year, when you are about to finish your college course, there is an expedition planned for the senior students. When the time comes, please do not hesitate to let me know how much money you need in order to participate. Please tell me exactly. Try not overestimate. I will do my best to obtain the money for you.

Good luck in the competition,
Yours sincerely,
Georgia Horvat.'

The great day of the competition arrived. It was to be held in a huge amphitheatre and we were all very nervous as we waited to go on the raised stage. Ostoja was shaking and my throat felt dry and prickly. When it was our turn, we walked on as we had practised and a cheer went up from the members of our college who were in the audience. I felt better and a smiling Oto Rebić, standing in front of us, calmed me. Once he lifted the baton, I forgot the audience and judges, concentrating on all he had taught us. When we'd finished there was loud applause. Even a couple of the judges clapped. We had done our very best and, as I walked off the stage, I felt almost as happy as I had when cantering on Pubi. Of course we had to wait until every group had performed to know how we had done. I thought the medical students, with their violins and cellos were particularly good. Were they better than us?

At last the performances were over and the tension heightened as the judges bent over the mark sheets and talked in low voices. Finally, the chief judge mounted the stage. He said all the usual things about the high standard, the difficulty in choosing. Then he said, 'I will announce the winners in reverse order. Third, the Teachers' College (applause). Second place, the Medical College (louder applause). But I am delighted to announce that, in first place, winning this year's Musicians' Plaque is...the Leather Technicians' College Orchestra, conducted by Oto Rebić.' There was tumultuous applause. Our fellow students in the audience jumped up and shouted their congratulations and we clapped each other on the back and laughed. I was excited, exalted. Ostoja and I even hugged each other and I grinned until my face ached. The sweetness of that success stayed with me until the end of term when I travelled home and Ostoja set off to see his father again and meet his new family.

Vacation: Marica

The summer holiday started by following much the same pattern as the previous one. I worked in the fields and vineyards and between tasks I had some time to myself. It was during one of these lulls that our neighbour, Mirko Petrak, came to our house to see me. I liked Mirko. He was in his mid-twenties, had been married to Marica for six months and worked very hard on his small farm. 'Ivan,' he said, 'I wonder if you would do me a favour?'

'Of course.'

'Are you free tomorrow?'

'Yes.'

'Yesterday I cut the grass in my top meadow. This afternoon Marica and I started spreading it but we didn't finish. I have to go to the vineyard tomorrow. Could you possibly go with Marica, in the morning, to finish it off?'

'Yes, certainly,' I replied. I could not know, at the time, what an impact that simple agreement was to have.

Marica was ready to leave at 10 am the next day. She carried a picnic basket and I couldn't help noticing how beautiful she was. I'd never really thought about it before but that morning she seemed to shine with health and energy. Her large eyes were brown, her lips full and she had tied back her long dark hair. As she walked along the narrow footpath in front of me I was mesmerised by the swing of her hips. I tried to look away but always my eyes strayed back. I was pleased to arrive at the meadow and start work, spreading the cut grass with a long wooden rake. Still I couldn't stop my eyes being drawn again and again to Marica, at her cleavage as she bent forward, at the way her breasts moved inside her white cotton blouse.

We rested at noon and shared a simple picnic. I could smell her as she handed me the bread and cheese. She was sweet with the soap she used and the scent of the hay and there was an underlying womanly smell of heat and sweat. I felt light-headed, unable to think of anything to say.

'I have to go home now, Ivan,' she said. 'I must milk the cows and prepare the evening meal. Could you meet me back here at about four?'

'Yes,' was all I could manage.

'We'll make the haystacks then so the grass will be ready for spreading again tomorrow. Is that all right?'

'Yes.'

She gathered up the picnic things and walked away. I sat until she was out of sight, trying to sort out my feelings. I'd never felt like this before and I'd certainly be back promptly at 4 o'clock.

When I arrived, she had already started raking the grass into piles and shaping it into little mounds as was customary in our area. I started work from the opposite side of the field and, as the shadows began to lengthen, we met in the middle. Marica stood up, stretched her arms above her head and sighed. 'We've earned a rest and a glass of wine,' she said. 'Come on, let's go into the shade.' I followed her to a sheltered corner of the field. There was forest on two sides of us and haystacks on the others. She retrieved a bottle and two glasses from the edge of the field and poured us each a glass of red wine. She drank from hers and I took a gulp of mine. I wasn't used to drinking, I didn't like wine very much and that mouthful seemed to sear my throat. I felt heat rise to my face. I became even hotter when Marica put her hand gently on my knee.

'Can I ask you something?' she said softly. 'Can I ask you without giving offence?'

'Yes,' my voice seemed too loud and shaky. I was the victim of all sorts of sensations, new to me. I should have guessed what was coming but I didn't.

'You spent all that time in a monastery, I know. You're at college now so you have much more freedom. Are you still a virgin?'

By now I was burning all over. I was overcome with embarrassment and desire. Another 'Yes' was all I could get out.

She turned to face me. 'Do you know how to make love to a girl?'

'No.'

'All that's going to change, Ivan, because I am going to teach you everything. Would you like me to do that?'

I couldn't answer. I took two more mouthfuls of wine. My head was swimming, I felt desperate with desire. Before I was able to say anything she leant towards me. Again I caught her scent, as intoxicating as the wine. She took both of my hands in hers and kissed me on my mouth. It was a long kiss and I found myself responding but, when I felt her tongue probing inside my mouth, I drew away, in spite of myself.

'Marica, we can't. You're married.'

'So what? He'll never find out if we're careful. You won't tell. I won't tell. It'll be our own little secret.'

What could I say? I've often thought I should have got up and walked away. But I didn't. I stayed and she showed me what to do, how to please a woman and how to satisfy myself. Of course, I didn't learn everything that first time. On reflection I know I lay there, that warm summer evening, rather like a tailor's dummy. I allowed her to have her way with me from the moment she delicately removed my shorts until the end when she stood up, shook her skirt straight and briskly said,

'We'd better get back now.'

I let her go ahead and trailed behind. Emotions boiled inside me. My sexual desires had been blunted by bromide for the two years I was at Bol and my only experiences up to this time had been holding hands with Ljubica Mežnar, the unwelcome kiss from the precocious college girl and a few rather inept dances at discos. Nothing had prepared me for what had happened that afternoon. I thought that at last I knew what life was all about. The experience amazed me, seemed to stretch my senses until I thought something must break but now I felt flat and exhausted. I wanted more of the same. I wanted to live at that pitch for ever.

I said nothing to anyone of course. I had a headache and my mother was surprised that I seemed to have lost my appetite. There was a loud knock on our door at about 8 pm. I jumped up guiltily, the victim of my conscience. I looked out of the window and saw Mirko standing outside. I was seized by panic and couldn't move. Marica must have told him. He'd come to kill me. He had something in his hand – an axe?

Meanwhile, Mama had opened the door and Mirko stepped in, all smiles. He handed a bottle of wine to Mama. 'This is for Ivan but I expect he'll share it with you,' he said. He turned to me. 'Thank you very much for what you've done in our field. Marica says you worked very hard. I'll quite understand if you aren't available but could you possibly give her a hand for one more day? I'll repay by helping you out when you need me in your fields or vineyard.'

'I don't need Ivan tomorrow,' Mama said helpfully. 'We're spraying our vines the day after.'

'I want to spray tomorrow,' Mirko said. 'Do you mind helping Marica once more, Ivan?'

Did I mind? I couldn't wait to see her again…to smell her… to feel her…'I don't mind at all. What time?'

'Is about eight o'clock all right? She'll need to bring my lunch up to the vineyard at midday. You should be able to re-spread the grass quite quickly. After tomorrow I'll be free to finish everything off in the meadow.'

'Eight o'clock will be fine,' I said.

I found it hard to sleep that night. I was too excited by what had happened and by what I felt sure would happen on the morrow.

At 8 sharp I was knocking at Marica's door. There was no reply. I knocked more loudly. Silence. I couldn't understand it so I called out, 'Marica! Are you ready?'

'I'm ready!' her voice contained a hidden smile and I followed it into the cowshed. She'd just finished milking and was putting the covered pail into a corner. I stood uncertainly in the doorway. 'Come to me Ivan,' she called. 'Come on. You know there's nothing to be afraid of.' And she took me again, in the fresh sweet hay, with the munching cows moving in their stalls as a backdrop.

I did feel some pangs of guilt. Clearly Mirko trusted me absolutely. It didn't even enter his head that I would take advantage of being alone with his wife – or rather that she would take advantage of being with me. From that day to the end of the holidays Marica and I made love every day. I don't know how we avoided detection. Once or twice, when I had a day off, I walked by myself into the forest I loved. Each time I heard a soft footstep behind me and, turning, found Marica smiling at me and carrying a basket on the pretext of looking for *vranji*/fungi or for eggs laid by her wayward hens. Then we made our way off the main path into the bushes and, lying on the tender moss, I'd look at her and at the outline of the brilliant leaves against the clear sky and count myself the luckiest person in the world.

Polytechnic: Year 3

It was even more of a wrench than usual to leave for college. Marica cried at our last meeting and I felt as if life would lose its flavour. However, part of me was practical and realistic. I knew that nothing could come of our relationship. She was married and I had all sorts of plans for my future which did not include settling down any time soon.

Back at college, Ostoja and I had a great deal to talk about. 'Have you had a good holiday?' he asked. It was a relief to tell him about Marica but he didn't seem as surprised as I expected.

'Much the same happened to me,' he said, 'except that my girl wasn't married. She's a Muslim so everything had to be absolutely secret or it would have created terrible trouble with her family.' We grinned at each other, feeling we were true men of the world.

'What about your father?' I asked. 'How did staying with him and his family go?' He handed me a photo of himself with his father and two teenage girls, one dark haired and the other a stunning blonde.

'I had a great time. We went sight-seeing and swimming. She's gorgeous, isn't she?' He pointed at the blond girl and I could only agree. 'They are very nice girls and wanted to get to know me. Once, I managed to have long talk with my father when we were alone.'

'Did he answer your questions?'

'Yes. I'm now convinced that Father did all he could to find us once he'd evaded capture by the Nazis. As I suspected, he was one of the Partizans who were working in the Kozara Mountains to undermine the German offensive. They weren't successful, of course, and by the time he was able to make his way back to our home, we had left. All the villages were deserted and then, later, he was told we'd been killed during the offensive.'

I was pleased that Ostoja's mind had been put at rest. I looked again at the photo of his father who was small, with just a little grey hair on his head and droopy moustache. Then I looked through narrowed eyes at Ostoja. 'Do you know, one day you'll look just like your dad,' I said.

During the course of that year, Ostoja's father and sisters came to visit him and I was invited to go out with them for the day. It was sunny so we took a picnic and climbed to the castle. Ostoja and his father were easy together and the two girls, a few years younger than us, were very good company. After lunch we went down to the river and cooled ourselves by swimming. I liked Ostoja's father. He had the same ready laugh and sense of humour as his son. He insisted on including me in his plan to have dinner at a restaurant.

'Well, what do think of him – my Dad?' asked Ostoja as we went into our accommodation block.

'Terrific – just like his son,' I said, giving him a friendly punch. 'And as for your sisters…what a pity they don't live nearer.'

'I'd keep them out of your way if they did,' he laughed. I felt happy for him that things had turned out so well.

Ostoja started to receive parcels from home regularly: cakes, biscuits and all sorts of goodies. Characteristically, he shared everything with me.

As term got underway, we found ourselves engaged in more practical work. Our curriculum demanded that we learned, from experience and in detail, how any type of 'finished' leather was produced from the time it was raw to the time it was ready for sale. This could be in any form, from the sole of a shoe to a jacket. We knew that most of us would never have to carry out such heavy and dirty labour again as our futures lay in laboratories as technicians or scientists but we needed to understand the process.

One Saturday, Ostoja, two other students and I were told to transport ten complete cow hides from the workshops, in the small factory where we worked, to the main factory on the other side of the river. We had already removed the hair from the hides and washed them in the huge revolving drums that made them swell to more than twice their original thickness. They were slimy, heavy and difficult to carry. We staggered outside with each and loaded it on a hand-wagon. As the pile became higher, one boy had to stay outside to steady it. The supervising *majster* helped us with the last couple. We tied the skins on to the cart with ropes and set off, two of us pulling the wagon handles and two pushing from behind. The wheels of the wagon, about half a metre in diameter, seemed to have a life of their own. Steering was very difficult and, as we approached the bridge, I noticed the skins had a tendency to shake and judder a little. Once on the bridge, the footpath became less even, a front wheel caught in a crack and the skins, jelly-like and in slow motion, slid gently off the wagon into the road. Wobbling, they spilt in all directions. Brakes screeched, drivers shouted and traffic halted. At first we just gaped but then we began to laugh. Even our *majster* joined in. The motorists didn't appreciate the performance but we and many passers-by did. A policeman soon arrived to direct the traffic round the spillage. It took us an exhausting half hour to re-load. This time we made sure the ropes were properly secured.

Because of the dirt picked up from the road, the skins had to be re-washed and we were glad of the short rest. Then we watched as one of the factory workers used a machine to expertly slice a skin horizontally, separating the derma from the hyper-derma. Next it was time for us to try. We managed but it wasn't as easy as the specialist cutter had made it look.

Our final year slipped by quickly. There were more musical performances, football matches, projects to present and suddenly it was time for the final exams. They lasted nearly two weeks with vivas as well as written papers. We had to wait another two weeks for our results. Rather than waste this time, we went hop-picking to earn some spending money for our upcoming trip. Once more I wrote to Georgia Horvat. Her letter the previous year had said, '*please don't hesitate to ask...*' So I didn't. The required 5,000 dinars arrived within a couple of days with a little extra for pocket money.

The day for our exam results came. I think we all felt a bit sick as we went into college to receive them. The grades were 1-5, 1 being 'fail' and 5 being 'distinction'. I was delighted to receive a 4 for the Technology of Leather and 5 for all academic subjects. Ostoja received 3 for technology and a sprinkling of 3's and 4's for everything else. He was satisfied and said, with a grin, 'Maybe I shouldn't have played so much football – but it was worth it!'

Expedition

We had a few weeks before the trip so the orchestra put on a concert and Ostoja organised a football match. Attendees at both events were invited to make contributions towards the expenses of our trip. We visited many stores in the city, asking for donations of tinned food, toiletries, batteries and other useful items. The professor in charge, Professor Pepi, shared everything between the participating students. Professor Ana Luznik was also accompanying us on the trip.

On the morning of our departure, thirty of us and the two professors assembled in the courtyard. We were all carrying rucksacks stuffed to the brim. Amid excited chatter we walked to the railway station. I realised, from snippets of conversation I overheard, that some of the students had never seen the sea and neither had Prof. Anna Luznik. Our train would carry us to Rijeka, on the Adriatic, where we were to board a ship for Zadar which was further south but still on the coast.

Prof. Pepi had booked two entire coaches for our party on the train and, once we were settled, he produced bottles of *Karlovaco Pivo*/beer made in Karlovac for us to share. 'You're all 18 now, all men and women, you've worked hard so you're entitled to a drink. Let's have a party.' So we did. The Professor had a small radio and some of us danced and sang along with the music. That set the tone of the whole trip – light hearted and full of laughter. No-one drank too much but everyone was happy.

The excitement peaked when we arrived at the quay-side in Rijeka and had our first glimpse of the sea. There were gasps of 'I didn't think it would be this big,' and 'How can those heavy iron ships float?' as we were ushered aboard a ship called *Jadrolinija*. We hung over the rails as we left the dock and then sat on benches while the professors retired to their cabins. We ate the picnics we had prepared for ourselves. Ostoja and I had sausage and bread. We wandered about the ship until, exhausted, we each curled up on the deck or on a bench and slept. I woke up next to Ostoja in the middle of the night. Although the day had been warm, the night was cool. I walked for a bit, looking out at the blackness of the sea and gazing into the midnight blue sky, so full of stars. I fished a sweater out of my rucksack, put it on and leant over the rail, imagining I was a sailor and off on an exciting voyage. Then I settled down again to sleep until morning.

We woke early and had breakfast on the ship after which we docked at Zadar. There we visited a liqueur and bon-bon factory and came away with free samples of both. Later we swam in the clear, warm sea – a particularly memorable experience for the several who had never even seen the sea before. We stayed at a youth hostel with extremely basic accommodation. Mattresses had been placed next to each other all round a large hall. We were allotted one each with girls and boys on alternate mattresses, feet facing the middle of the hall. I was next to Prof. Ana and, during the night, I somehow managed to turn 180 degrees so that my first sight in the morning was of her feet. I was teased a great deal about this – even more so when Prof. Pepi called over, 'Leave the poor boy alone. We know he's good and moral. After all he used to live in a monastery.'

We spent two days sightseeing. In spite of the considerable damage to the city in the Second World War, a few relics of Roman occupation were still to be seen. I was interested to visit the Church of St Donat because I had seen pictures of it when we'd studied Byzantine history at Bol.

We sailed, overnight, to Split and once more Bol came to my mind. I pointed out the island of Brač to Ostoja.

'It all seems so long ago now,' I said. 'My life there was nothing like our life at college.' I gazed at the island for a while, memories flooding me. How innocent I'd been. I really had thought that God had arranged my life but how differently things had turned out. I wondered what fresh turns my life might take.

In Split I became the guide. I knew it well and showed the group the palace of the Roman Emperor Diocletian, explaining its history and architecture.

Split Harbour. Brac Island just in view.

Our next stop was the walled city of Dubrovnik and I thought I had never seen such a beautiful place. The houses were white with orange tiled roofs. We had a splendid view as we walked round the city walls. The solid, bulky Fort of St John, built into the wall, stood facing the Adriatic. As we looked out to sea, we could see small islands, covered in maritime pines.

Perhaps the visit I most enjoyed, in Dbrovnik, was to the Maritime Museum. There the seafaring history of the city was told through a collection of model ships, pictures and diaries. Ostoja nudged me out of my dream of being at sea in one of the fine sailing ships. 'You won't sail in anything like that if you join the navy,' he teased.

'That doesn't matter,' I said, 'I don't care what the ship's like. I just want to go to sea.'

Our party stayed in Dubrovnik for almost a week, in bed and breakfast accommodation throughout the city, which gave us some measure of independence. Ostoja and I boarded together, of course. On our last afternoon Ana Luznik surprised us. She called us to one side and said, 'Have you two ever been to a nightclub.'

'No.'

'Well, now's your chance. I'll take you to one this evening. Make yourselves smart and I'll collect you at nine o'clock.'

'Why has she chosen us?' I asked Ostoja.

'Because we're not only the most handsome students, we're also the most intelligent, of course,' he grinned.

Prof. Ana looked very attractive when she arrived at our digs. Her long blond hair, usually pinned back, was loose and she was wearing a thin dress I hadn't seen before. She was in her 30s I should think, nicely rounded in the right places and with big blue eyes. We felt rather self-conscious as we walked with her to the club but, when we got inside, we understood why she had asked us to accompany her.

Waiting in the foyer was a young man, a visitor to Dubrovnik, we gathered. He embraced Ana and she introduced him as Zdravco. We went into the dance hall.

'Sit here, boys,' he said, pointing at a small table. 'We'll be just over there. What would you like to drink?'

'Beer, please.'

A waiter brought our beers and Zdravko said, 'Put whatever these young men want on my bill.' Soon Zdravco and Ana were deep in conversation, heads close together.

'Isn't she married?' Ostoja said softly.

'Yes, to an officer in the army, I heard.'

'Bringing us here was her excuse to come, wasn't it?'

'Yes,' I agreed. 'It's not because we're so handsome and intelligent.' We looked at each other and began to laugh and we found it hard to stop. Fortunately Ana and her friend were dancing by this time so they didn't notice. We ordered more beers and soon we started to find everything amusing.

At about midnight, I pulled myself together, realising we'd had enough to drink and needed to be up at a reasonable time in the morning. Ostoja agreed that it was time to go and we went over to Ana to say we would like return to our digs. She said that was fine. We were a little tipsy as we wound our way back. We felt older and wiser and very surprised to see a completely different side of our favourite professor.

The next morning was our last in Dubrovnik and we woke at 7.30. At 8 o'clock we called at Prof. Ana's digs. They were close to ours and, during the week, we had usually walked with her to the group's meeting point. The landlady came to the door. 'She's not in, I'm afraid,' she said. 'She must have gone for a walk first thing and hasn't returned.' Ostoja and I glanced at each other knowingly,

'Could we wait here for her to come back, please?' I asked. 'We need to speak to her. The landlady said we could wait in the hall and she went into the kitchen.

'She didn't come home last night, did she?' whispered Ostoja.

'I don't think she did. She'll have to come back to collect her things before we leave Dubrovnik.' I felt a bit uneasy. Suppose something had happened to her…

After about half an hour the front door opened and Ana walked in. She was surprised to see us and flushed. 'How nice to see you both. I see you've got your bags. I'll just fetch mine.' In five minutes the three of us were outside. 'It was too late to come back here last night so I stayed in a hotel,' she said.

'Did Zdravco turn out to be a nice man?' Ostoja asked boldly.

'Very nice thank you,' she smiled, blushing again. 'I have to ask you something. If you meet my husband, in Sarajevo, please don't say anything about our going to the night club. Will you promise?' We made the promise solemnly and felt very important to be in on a secret which involved one of our professors.

Our party travelled by train to the beautiful and ancient town of Mostar, in Hercegovina. Mostar means Bridge-keeper. Its magnificent bridge (*Stari Most)* over the Neretva River is of creamy stone which reflected the gold of a particularly glorious sunset we were lucky enough to see. I remember Mostar as a city of graceful minarets, reaching up into a clear deep blue sky.

Two days later we caught a train to Sarajevo.

'Look,' Ostoja said as we walked up the platform. 'Guess who that is.' An army officer stood by the exit. We saw Prof. Ana hurry forward. The officer took her bag and embraced her, She looked round as we drew level.

'Miloje,' she said, 'Let me introduce you to two young men who have looked after me – been my chaperones – Ivan and Ostoja.' Ana's husband shook our hands, smiling.

'If that's the case, you must come for a meal with us. As a thank you.'

An hour later we were sitting in one of the best restaurants in the city, tucking into succulent steaks.

In bed that night, I reflected on the strange turn events had taken. I had conspired in an illicit love affair and been rewarded for it. I, myself had been involved with a married woman last summer. What had happened to Ivan of the priest's house and Bol? Is this what 'growing up' means? It was my last thought before I fell asleep.

We spent several days in Sarajevo. I particularly remember standing on the spot of the assassination, in 1914, of Crown Prince Franz Ferdinand. The guide told us the story of the radical student, Gavrilo Princip, who shot the prince as he travelled with his wife in their motorcade. 'This was one of the acts that triggered the First World War,' he said.

'Was the assassin executed?' someone asked.

'No, he died in prison – of TB.'

We were allowed to wander round the old Turkish quarter on our own. Its narrow lanes were paved with marble which reflected the afternoon sun. Old men sat outside small cafés, smoking and drinking coffee. The scene could have been from a history book.

We left Sarajevo very early the next morning. We didn't have time for breakfast and there was much muttering about this on the train but Prof. Pepi laughed and said that we had to be patient. After half an hour we alighted at Visoko where the professor had arranged for us to visit the most famous leather factory in Bosnia. Outside the station were two Mercedes coaches waiting to carry us there.

We were welcomed by the young director who made himself immediately popular by leading us to a gleaming restaurant and offering us a breakfast of fresh warm rolls, butter, cheese, cold meats, coffee and fruit. Next, we divided into smaller groups to look round the large modern factory. The director joined our group. 'Students from your college are particularly welcome,' he said. 'As you know, the college leads in up-to-date leather technology and in its training programme. Young people with your qualifications are very scarce.' He explained that his firm had the contract for supplying much of the clothing for the army. They made its long leather trench coats, belts, map-bags and boots as well as a variety of goods for sale to civilians. As we walked along a corridor, several men came out of a room to our right.

'What's in there?' I asked.

'It's a store room for our finished goods. Come and have a look.' I love the smell of leather but in the store it was almost overpowering. There were racks and racks of coats and jackets, boxes of belts and bags and shelves of boots and shoes. I reached out and felt one of the short black jackets. It was soft and pliable. The stitching was perfect.

'This is beautiful,' I said. 'How much would it cost?'

'30,000 dinars.'

'I'll have one like it one day.' I was about to move on when the director said, 'Would you like it?'

'Like it? Yes I would of course, but I can't...'

'Try it on.' It fitted perfectly.

'Take it,' he said. 'Carry it over your arm so that your friends won't realise it's new.' He waved my thanks aside and asked my name.

He took out a notebook and I watched him write in it – '*Ivan Vesligaj.*' He jotted down a serial number and then it large letters wrote '*GIFT*'. The jacket was mine.

I caught up with Ostoja and he noticed my acquisition immediately. 'Where did you get that?' he demanded. 'You didn't help yourself to it, did you?'

I was offended. 'Of course not.' I explained what had happened.

'Good for you,' he said generously but when the director came to walk beside us, Ostoja said to him, 'I hope you don't mind my asking, but would you be able to spare one more jacket – for me – please?'

The man laughed and looked round as if worried that he would be besieged by students with similar requests. 'Not now,' he said softly. 'You can have one before you go but don't talk about it. I can't give more than two away.'

Ostoja grinned happily. 'We'll be the best dressed men in town.'

We were shown leather at all stages of preparation and also watched as some pieces were made into handbags which would soon be in the shops. We were familiar with much of what we saw but everything was on a huge scale. I had always been most interested in the chemical processes involved so I asked the director about the work that went on in the laboratory.

'You may find it hard to believe,' he replied, 'but we haven't really got a laboratory. It's more a small testing station. We've one elderly man in charge. He's been pretty successful but there have been some expensive mistakes. Would you like to meet him?' We said we would and were soon in a small room which resembled our laboratory at college. 'This is Željko,' the director said and we shook hands. Ostoja and I asked Željko about the proportions of fats and chemicals he used at various stages in the preparation of the leather. He produced a little notebook in which he had written them down. We stared at it in amazement.

Noticing our expressions, the director asked, 'What's wrong?' I felt awkward. How could we say that these proportions were wrong? We'd spent so long experimenting, finding the best mixtures for ourselves and then learning by heart what they were. No wonder the director had said they'd 'had a few problems'.

'It's just that they're different from what we use,' Ostoja said diplomatically.

'You could check with our professor,' I added. 'He's head of leather technology at college.'

Željko had, of course been listening. 'Please write down in my notebook the proportions you have learned,' he said.

'I was about to ask you that, myself.' This, from the director. I wrote, saying each set of figures aloud as I did so and glancing at Ostoja for confirmation.

When I handed the notebook back, Željko thanked us. 'My family were farmers,' he explained. 'We kept cows and used their hides to make leather. We had our own recipe for preparing the skins, using *vapno*/lime. It was all trial and error. It's been very much the same for me here.'

The director had been quiet for a few minutes. Suddenly he said, 'Would you two lads like to work for me? We need trained technicians and I'll pay you well.' Ostoja started to agree but I said quickly,

'Thank you for offering. We feel very honoured but we haven't even been given our diplomas yet. May we contact you after that, please?' I wanted to keep my options open. I knew there were similar posts available in Zagreb which was relatively close to my home and, of course, where my sister lived. I planned to try there first.

'Of course,' the director replied. 'Just bear my offer in mind.' Ostoja and I grinned at each other. This was turning into a very good day.

We were served a sumptuous lunch. There was a choice of roast meats, with vegetables and all appropriate trimmings. A line of carafes full of wine stretched down the centre of the long table. Neither Ostoja nor I drank wine so we asked for water and were presented with cold spring water from a source very close to my family's vineyard. We noticed how swiftly the wine was disappearing. 'We'll be the only ones who are sober,' muttered Ostoja. How right he was.

After lunch, the director announced that a special show had been organised for our entertainment. There was a local band and also dancers in national costume. Everyone in our party was very merry by the time we had to leave. Prof. Pepi managed to thank the director in a rather slurred voice and Prof. Ana hung on to my arm as we walked out to the coaches. 'What a brilliant time they gave us,' said Ostoja, clutching his leather jacket, slipped to him by the director.

'Yes,' I said thoughtfully. 'You know why, don't you?'

'Why?'

'Because they're desperate to recruit some properly trained technicians.'

Ostoja laughed and said, 'I wouldn't mind working there. The food's brilliant.'

The coaches dropped us at the railway station and as we went in, Prof. Pepi caught up with me. He was weaving from side to side and put his hand on my shoulder for support. 'Stop a moment, Ivan,' he said in a loud voice and I stood still. 'Here Ivek, take this. It contains all the tickets, meal vouchers and money. Take good care of it. It's very important.' While speaking, he pushed his briefcase into my hand.

'I can't take…,' I started.

'Take it Ivan. Take it and look after it for me. I am drunk and you are sober.' And with this, he staggered away into the midst of the students, many of whom were in an even worse state than he was. I shrugged at Ostoja, extended the strap on the briefcase and put it across my shoulders. Leaving everyone else to follow, we went on to the platform. The train was just arriving.

'Let's stay away from that lot,' Ostoja said. 'It's no fun being sober among a crowd of people who are merry. We found a quiet compartment and started to talk about our day at the factory. The train soon drew out of the station and the ticket collector arrived.

'This ticket is for us, twenty eight other students and two professors who are in another part of the train,' I said, handing the man the group ticket.

'This ticket is for Zagreb,' he said.

'Yes, that's right.'

'This isn't the Zagreb train. This one goes to Sarajevo.'

Ostoja and I stared at the man and then at each other. 'To Sarajevo?' I repeated stupidly.

'Are you sure?' said Ostoja.

'Of course I'm sure.' The collector looked annoyed. 'You'll all have to get off at the next station and catch a train going in the opposite direction.'

When the man had gone, Ostoja and I walked the length of the train, looking for the others. There was no sign of them and we had to admit what had happened.

'They must have got on the right train,' I said.

'Yes and I wonder where they are now. They won't get far without tickets.'

I began to laugh. 'And we were supposed to be the sober ones!' We laughed together then and suddenly the train stopped. It was dark by this time and we could see lights outside.

'It's the signals. They're red,' called Ostoja, leaning out of the window.

'Let's get out,' I said. Afterwards I realised what a stupid idea this was. We could have been anywhere. I didn't even think about not being able to catch a train from a signal halt. It just seemed important to get off a train that was going in the wrong direction, so we did, clutching our rucksacks and the precious briefcase. We scrambled up the steep bank for safety, the train moved off and we watched its tail lights disappear.

'Now what?' Ostoja looked at me. 'We're miles from civilisation.' It was pitch black except for a sliver of moon and millions of brilliant stars.

Then I saw something in the distance. From the direction we had come there was a faint yellow light. 'That's where we're going,' I replied. 'There, can you see it?'

'Just about.' In silence, at first, we walked beside the track towards the hopeful glimmer. As we drew closer, we saw more lights. It was a small station. The train had rushed through it without our noticing. Now it was our salvation. We decided what we'd do when we reached our goal and quickened our pace.

There was no-one on the platforms but there was a light in the stationmaster's office. Ostoja knocked the door.

A tall man, in uniform, opened it. 'Yes, what do you want?' I suppose we were rather dishevelled by this time – not a prepossessing pair. Between us we explained our dilemma and showed him the tickets.

He grinned at us, 'Well you have got yourselves into a tricky situation, haven't you? And what about the other poor blighters in your party? Where are they?'

'We wondered if you could phone Visoko station and the stations beyond to find that out, please? If they got on the correct train, thinking we were already on it, they would have been made to get off once the ticket collector found they had no tickets, wouldn't they?'

'They certainly would. You're lucky I'm not busy. Wait here and I'll see what I can do.' He came back a few minutes later. 'They're at Zavidovići. That's beyond Visoko. Your mates did indeed have to get off once it was discovered that they hadn't got one ticket between them. I don't think you're very popular.'

We laughed uneasily. 'What time's the next train to Zavidovići?' I asked.

'10.30.'

I looked at the station clock. I could hardly believe it was only 8.15. So much had happened since we'd left the factory in Visoko.

'It's the Zagreb train so you won't have to change. Just make sure that when it stops at Zavidovići you attract the attention of your party. It's a slow train, I'm afraid. It'll stop at every station. You won't get there until 3 a.m.'

We thanked the stationmaster and settled down to wait. I felt we'd done our best to rectify our stupid mistake but I didn't look forward to meeting Prof. Pepi.

When I said this to Ostoja, he smiled and said, 'It'll teach him not to get tipsy on college trips!'

The train was on time and we dropped off to sleep to its steady rhythm but fortunately woke at 2.30 am. As the train slowed to a halt at Zavidoviči, we saw our college colleagues standing in a long line, facing the train. We opened the door, waved and shouted and everyone scrambled aboard. Prof. Pepi got into our compartment with a few of the students. He stood and looked at us and then swore but he was smiling.

'You two! I thought you were the sober and responsible members of our party. What the hell did you think you were doing – going off in the wrong direction? Always have to be different, don't you? Hadn't you had enough of Sarajavo?'

Before we could answer, one of the girls flung her arms round my neck and kissed my cheek. 'That's for making our holiday a day longer than it would have been,' she said and everybody laughed. It was a relief to hand the briefcase back to Pepi.

Later Ostoja whispered, 'I think we got off very lightly.' We made the most of the time we had on the train. There was no beer, which was probably just as well, but we sang and told jokes and reminisced.

It was 8 am when we reached Zagreb which was the last stop on our itinerary. Prof Pepi turned to me.

'This is your city, Ivan. It's time for breakfast. Where's the best student restaurant? And don't take us in the wrong direction!' I knew I wouldn't be allowed to forget the mistake in a hurry.

I led the party to the restaurant and after breakfast showed them the old city. We walked its narrow streets and admired the church of St Mark with its dramatic roof, the coloured tiles of which are patterned to form the coats of arms of Croatia, Dalmatia, Slavonia and Zagreb.

Church of St Mark, Zagreb

The rest of the day was ours to do with as we wished. I took Ostoja to see Dragica and she made us a fine meal of goulash. Then it was time to go to the station for the final train journey together. Our trip had been a wonderful experience. I had seen so many places which, until now, had been names on the map of Yugoslavia. I had enjoyed companionship, the odd adventure and lots of laughter but now it was over. It was almost time to face the future as a grown-up.

We had two days of term left during which we collected our diplomas, packed our belongings and said goodbye. Ostoja and I went to thank Prof. Pepi. He had organised every aspect of the trip – all the finances, the travel, accommodation and food vouchers. He had been such good company too. Next we saw Prof. Ana. We had kept her secret and she gave each of us a hug, saying, 'I'll miss my chaperones.'

There were two other people we wanted to thank. The first was the young woman in the fruit shop who had kept us supplied with free apples. Secondly, we went to the cinema to say goodbye to 'Plum' the elderly woman in the ticket office who had allowed us to see so many films without tickets. She kissed us and wished us luck.

Then it was time to go. Ostoja and I walked to the station together. We didn't speak much. It was the end of an era. It was hard to believe that my formal education was over at last as was the almost constant companionship of Ostoja. We shook hands and promised to stay in touch. My throat was tight as I waved him off on his train. He was going to stay with his father for a short holiday and had decided to take the director of the factory in Visoko up on his offer of a job.

As I turned away I noticed a face that was familiar to me. It was Josip Puškar, a boy who had been in my year at college but who I didn't know very well. He came over.

'Are you waiting for the Zagreb train?' he asked.

'Yes.'

'So am I. I plan to apply for a job at Almeria.' This was the well known leather and tanning factory that I also had in mind.

'I'm going to apply there too.'

'Brilliant. You can show me where it is.' When I discovered that Josip had nowhere to stay, I suggested we should go to Dragica's. She hadn't a spare room but she'd know someone who had.

We spent the night in an apartment next to Dragica's house. She was looking after it while the occupants were away and knew they wouldn't mind but they were due home the next day so we'd have to make other arrangements. The next morning we smartened ourselves up as well as we could, in our student suits, and set out for Almeria.

In 1953 relations between Yugoslavia and the Vatican were terminated although the practice of religion was tolerated and it remained possible for young men to train for the priesthood. The school at the Monastery of Bol, where Ivan received two years education, was run by Franciscan monks who are characterised by rigid poverty, simplicity, love of all creatures and for work among the poor.

Away from religious establishments, in communist Yugoslavia, there was suspicion of practising Christians. Thus Ivan received an exclusively secular education at the polytechnic college.

In 1954 there was outrage and public protest in Croatia when the Yugoslavian Council of Culture and Education declared Serbian and Croatian to be the same language. Throughout the 1950s and beyond there were nationalistic tensions which flared into protest and violence periodically. Government propaganda might proclaim that Yugoslavia was united by the fact that each person thought of him or herself, first as Yugoslavian and only secondarily a member of his/her 'birth nation' but this does not seem to have been the case in ordinary everyday life. Indeed, as John was telling me his story, I noticed that he always specified the nationality of any new person he mentioned. It took me some time to realise that this was a sort of shorthand for describing different types of people. For example, in the eyes of the young Ivan, Serbians were pushy, craved power and occupied the top jobs and Montenigrans were not very clever whereas Slovenians were almost as worthy as Croatians, the cream of Yugoslavia. However, in spite of undercurrents and tensions, Marshal Tito managed, on the whole, to maintain a peaceful co-existence between the nations

In foreign affairs, relations between Yugoslavia and the Soviet Union improved with the recommencement of trade and an exchange of visits between Marshal Tito and Khrushchev and Bulganin of the USSR.

In 1956 Ivan witnessed a little of the collateral damage of savage reprisals taken by the USSR against an uprising in Hungary. He saw Hungarian women and children given shelter in his college accommodation although he had no way of knowing what had caused them to flee. In fact a student demonstration in Hungary had sparked a nation-wide revolt against Soviet-imposed government policies in that country. There were summary executions and, in spite of a spirited defence, the Hungarians were finally defeated. About 2,500 Hungarians were killed in the fighting. The Soviets installed a new government and repressed any opposition. In spite of Marshal Tito's reputation for comparative benevolence, he did not condemn the savagery of the Red Army against the whole Hungarian nation, military and civilian alike.

Footnote

There are recurring mentions of the Palace of Diocletian in Ivan's story and I was fortunate to visit this magnificent building recently. Its background is as follows:

The Roman emperor, Diocletian, came to power in 284 AD. He commissioned two architects to build a splendid, fortified palace, overlooking the bay at Split, on the Dalmatian coast. After his death, in 316, the palace was used as administrative offices.

Since Roman times, the various spaces within the palace have had a myriad of uses. For example, what was Diocletian's mausoleum was consecrated as a cathedral in the 7th century. Today, in other parts of the building, market stalls abound with bars, restaurants, shops and art and craft displays.

Ivan Vesligaj
1958-1960: aged 18-20 years

Work

The security officer at the door of Almeria was a self-important little man. 'Yes?' he said. 'What do you want?'

'We'd like to see the personnel officer, please.'

'Why do you want to see him?'

'We want to ask about the possibility of employment here.' The man's manner annoyed me.

'There are no jobs going. I can tell you that.'

'Are you sure?' Josip said. 'We heard that…'

I cut across him. 'I don't think it's for you to say whether there are jobs or not. You don't know who we are or what sort of qualifications we have. Please ask the personnel officer if he is free and, if he isn't, if we can make an appointment to see him.' The man mumbled something into his sparse moustache, picked up the internal phone and dialled a number.

'There are two lads wanting to see you, sir,' he said. 'They're after jobs.' He cast a scornful look in our direction. He listened to the reply and put the phone down. 'He says to send you up.' Then, quickly, seeing my triumphant expression, 'That doesn't mean anything. He only wants to look at you. He's first floor, second door on the right.'

The personnel officer was a huge man with a mass of black hair. He smiled at us. 'Sit down lads. I'm sorry but you've had a wasted journey. We have no vacancies in the factory at the moment. Contact me in a couple of months. I might have something then.'

I was furious. He hadn't even asked us what sort of work we were seeking. He'd looked at us and made the same assumptions as the security officer – that we were labourers. I didn't answer but got up and walked to the door. Astonished, Josip stared at me. 'Come on Josip. It seems as if our three years at college would be wasted at this place. Let's find a leather works where we'll be appreciated for what we've learned.' Josip got up as I opened the door.

The personnel officer leapt up. 'Stop! Don't be so hasty. What qualifications are you talking about?'

We pulled our diplomas from our pockets and I said, 'Just these – from Karlovac Polytechnic. Still, as you're not interested…'

'I didn't realise you were qualified technicians. That makes all the difference. Sit down, please and I'll call the director. I know he'll want to see you.' Josip and I grinned at each other as the man lifted the phone. 'I've two leather technicians here, sir, looking for employment. In view of what you were saying yesterday…Yes sir.' He put the phone down. 'He's coming right away.'

96

The director arrived almost immediately. After introducing himself as Drago, he sat down. 'Fetch us all some coffee, will you, please,' he said to his secretary, who had followed him in. When she'd gone he examined our diplomas and smiled. 'Excellent. You're just what we need. I can certainly offer you both jobs, I'm pleased to say but you'll need to have a medical examination first and I'm afraid it will cost you 10,000 dinars.'

The excitement of success evaporated in an instant. Where could I get hold of such an amount? I felt determined not to fail, having come so far, however. I'd call this man's bluff. I got up again. 'Thank you for your offer,' I said, 'but I can't accept it as I cannot pay 10,000 dinars. I have only a very little cash and I need that to buy food. How about you, Josip?'

'I'm the same,' he said, getting up.

'Hey, not so fast.' Drago was on his feet. 'I'm sure we can find money for the doctor's fees on this occasion.'

'That would be wonderful. Thank you,' I said. And we all sat down again.

The secretary arrived with the coffee and the director asked her to fetch the financial director. She came immediately, a large woman with a forehead that was wrinkled – as if she were always puzzling over difficult calculations.

'These two young men will be working for us, Ana,' he said. 'They have just finished college and are highly qualified leather technicians but, at the moment, they are financially embarrassed. I don't want to lose them so the firm will pay for their medicals.'

Ana's forehead developed new wrinkles as she answered, 'If you say so, Director. I'll fetch the cash now.'

While we drank our coffee, the director told us a little about the factory. 'We simply produce finished leather here,' he said. 'We don't make it up into clothing or shoes. Most of our leather is exported to Germany and we also supply a lot to the army. It's of a very high quality.' Then Ana came back and counted the money on to the desk. She divided it into two, pushed it into envelopes and handed one to Josip and the other to me.

'Let's see, today's Tuesday,' said Drago. 'Providing your medicals are satisfactory, can you start tomorrow?'

'Would it be possible for us to start next Monday?' I asked. 'We need a few days to sort out accommodation.'

'Monday it is, then. You'll do shift work, being on duty alternately, one week working from 6 am until 2 pm, and the next working from 12 noon until 8 pm. All right?' We nodded. 'But on your first day, come together at 8 am for induction. I'll show you round the works and, once we've agreed on your salaries, you can sign your contracts. Now, go straight away for your medical. My secretary has advised the doctor that you're coming. The clinic is just round the corner. Just one thing, as we have just handed over 20,000 dinars to you, I'm sure you'll understand if I hang on to your diplomas until after your medical – as insurance.'

An hour later we had both been passed as A1 fit and were given certificates to prove it. We took them into the factory and Ana returned our diplomas. We felt extremely pleased with ourselves.

Josip found some temporary accommodation and Dragica said I could sleep on a mattress on her floor. I wished it were Ostoja starting work with me. I wondered how he was getting on. I missed him. Josip was nice enough. He had the same sort of village background as I had but I couldn't imagine going out in the evenings with him or he and I falling about with laughter as Ostoja and I had done so often. I combed the local newspaper for possible lodgings and found an apartment block with rooms to let. Josip and I went to look and decided one of them would do for us. The rent was 1,500 dinars a month.

We moved our few belongings in and as I looked at our humble room, I felt a surge of pride. I'm an independent man of the world, I thought. On Monday I'll be a working man, a technician, earning a salary. Then I thought of what great plans I'd had for myself. I'd wanted to study for a further seven years at Bol. I'd wanted to become one of the most learned men in Croatia. I hadn't been sure of my vocation and I might not have completed the last three years priest's training, nevertheless, at the end of nine years' study, I would have had the pick of academic posts in Croatia and beyond. Yet here I was, a leather technician, with no chance to use all the knowledge I'd acquired at the monastery. Just then Josip came into the room and brought my reverie to an end. By the time we'd walked outside and were making our way to a restaurant, to celebrate our good luck at finding work and accommodation, I was feeling cheerful once more.

Monday arrived and we reported to Almeria at 8 am, having sailed past the security guard, waving the passes we'd been given. The director was busy and the personnel officer called us into his room. We filled in some forms and then the officer said,

'Now we'll talk about your salaries. How much do you think you should earn?'

I was surprised by the question. I looked at Josip who gave a small shrug.

'Well, remembering our qualifications, what do you think we're worth?' I asked. Before he could answer, the director walked in. Afterwards I couldn't imagine what possessed me but the words were out before I knew it. 'How much does the director earn?'

Drago answered, laughing. 'You've got a nerve! I don't mind telling you though. I earn 35,000 dinars a month. I'm the boss and carry heavy responsibilities. The ordinary factory workers earn between 12,000 and 15,000 a month, according to their job and their experience.'

I was sitting next to Josip and I looked at him. 'Try 23,000,' he whispered.

'28,000,' I said.

'25,000,' Drago said. '25,000 a month, paid in two instalments, each of 12,500 dinars. There will be the chance of an increase, if and when, you prove yourselves. I honestly can't offer you more than that.'

Josip was nodding at me. 'Done,' we said together and we shook the director's hand. We signed our contracts with a flourish.

After coffee we started the tour of the factory. All we saw was familiar to us from the small college factory or from the larger ones we'd seen in Karlovac and Visico. Working conditions were good and the workforce cheerful and friendly. The men regarded us with interest. Most of them had worked there for years and were sceptical about whether we could teach them anything. 'Welcome lads,' one worker said with a smile. 'Am I getting older or are you only just out of school?'

'Just out of college,' the director corrected him. 'Just out of college with a diploma to prove their expertise.'

'We'll have to make sure we prove ourselves,' I said to Josip quietly. 'One slip and they'll never trust us again.'

'Then we mustn't slip up, must we?' he replied.

When we'd finished looking round the factory floor, I asked the director where the testing station was. 'I was leaving that until last,' he said. 'Through here. It's in an annex built on to the main building.' There was one man of about forty five in the room who was introduced as Miško. He was writing something in a large black book.

'This is the Production Book and I'm just writing down the chemicals which have been used today,' he explained. He handed it to me. I noticed immediately that he'd recorded the amounts of the different chemicals but had noted the number of skins treated instead of their gross weight.

'Look Josip,' I said.

'No weights shown,' he said immediately.

'What's wrong?' Drago had heard us whispering. It was the same difficult situation that I'd found myself in at the factory in Visico but in this case we were actually going to be working with Miško. We didn't want to upset him or get him into trouble. However, he made it easy for us.

'I understand that you are fully trained for this sort of work?' he said. We nodded. 'Then don't be afraid of offending me. There was no such thing as a leather technology course when I was your age. I used to work on the machines here in the factory and am absolutely self-taught. I shall be pleased to learn from you.'

We shook hands with him and the director smiled and exclaimed, 'Well said, Miško. You are senior to these young men so make sure you keep them in order. But as far as technical matters are concerned, I expect you to do as they say.'

'Certainly sir.'

'I'm sure you'll all work well together, as you'll be a supervisor, I'll put up your salary at the end of the month, Miško.'

Drago stayed with us for most of that first morning. As we were supervising the weighing of a batch of skins, he showed us a small, windowed office right in the centre of the main preparation room. 'This is yours,' he said. 'You can see everything from here and will be able to check all is being done as it should be. Here's a new book for recording precisely the processes you use. We'll start afresh.' I couldn't help smiling – a splendid new leather-bound ledger and an office of our own – we really had made it!

We got to work straight away. The skins ready for processing required three washes. During two of them certain chemicals and fats were applied. We realised that Miško had washed the skins at too high a temperature and we made the necessary adjustment. We also calculated that he had been adding too much fat and more chemicals than were necessary so we changed those amounts too. At one point Miško couldn't stop himself saying, 'That'll never work.'

'Wait and see,' we said. It did work. The quality controller came to test the flexibility of the leather.

'Let's see your miracle,' he said. 'I've been here ten years. Let's see what you've done in a day.' He was so impressed that he called the director to look. We explained to him the changes we had made.

'Washing at lower temperatures and using smaller amounts of chemicals will cut our overheads considerably,' he said. 'If you go on like this, you'll force me to give you a pay rise.' We laughed but secretly we were pleased and relieved that our hard work at college was paying off.

Our final task was to mix the black dye and supervise its application. We watched as the skins were pegged out in a huge drying room, where hot air blowers would be in action until midnight. The next day the skins would be pressed and then trimmed and polished. We left Almeria at 10 pm, exhausted but content.

Ostoja

I spent a good deal of time in the British Consulate reading room where the daily papers and western publications, some translated into Croatian, could be found. These were my window into a wider world. I was in the library one day, a couple of months after I'd started at the factory, when I came across an article in a leather trade magazine. It described a new method of drying skins, using a slatted rack system which was manufactured in Germany. Many more skins could be dried in less time and, because of the way skins were pegged on the racks, there was no need for them to be pressed. I made some notes on the article and copied the accompanying illustrations.

The next day I took the information to Drago. He looked at it with interest.

'You're a great one for cutting overheads,' he laughed. 'This certainly appears to be an efficient system.' He pointed at the name of the manufacturer. 'We deal with this firm. Next time the rep comes, you and I will talk to him about it and I'll ask Rogaška to come and translate.' Rogaška, one of the managers, spoke German fluently.

I couldn't believe how easy it was. The rep came, the director ordered the equipment and two weeks later a team of Germans came to erect the racks and show the workers how to use them. Within a month, the system was installed and running. Drying time was cut from six to three hours with three times as many skins dried at a time.

'I'll have to take on more technicians,' the director told us. 'Our production will go up now and we can't afford any mistakes with the technical side. You don't know anyone else from your college who's looking for a job, do you?' We said we didn't but then I had a wonderful idea. I'd contact Ostoja and see if he'd like to come to Zagreb.

I was on the late shift that day and reached home at about 8.15 pm. As I walked through the front door my landlady called from her sitting room. 'Ivan, come in here for a moment. There's someone to see you.' I couldn't think who it could be. I went in and who should be sitting across the table from the landlady but Ostoja! He leapt up and came across to me. We shook hands and clapped each other on the back. It was amazing to see him on the very day I'd decided to get in touch.

'Will it be all right if I sleep on your floor for a couple of nights?' he asked. 'Just until I can find somewhere to stay. This nice lady says she doesn't mind. She'll even supply a mattress and blanket. I've seen Josip and he's fine about it too.'

'You don't have to ask,' I said.

We thanked the landlady and went out into the street. 'Let's find somewhere to eat,' I said. 'Then you can tell me everything.' Ostoja's explanation was simple. He had received my letters praising Almeria and the developments the director was introducing. He was earning 20,000 dinars against my 25,000 and, above all, he missed our easy companionship as much as I did.

'So I gave a week's notice and decided to come and try my luck at Almeria,' he concluded.

'It's such a coincidence. The director said only today that he wants more technicians and I was going to contact you. I'm sure you'll get a job with us. It would be great if we could find accommodation together, wouldn't it?' I said. 'Josip's fine but he's not you. What do you think?'

'You don't have to ask,' he said, laughing.

The next day Drago gladly took Ostoja on. His medical was satisfactory and the contract was signed. He would earn the same as Josip and me and would start work at the beginning of the next week. It was a beautiful day and I decided to spend my short break in the nearby park. I sat on a bench to enjoy the sunshine and a few minutes later an elderly gentleman sat down next to me. We exchanged remarks about the weather and the beauty of the trees and he asked me in which area of the town I lived. I told him and explained that I shared a room with a work colleague but would like to move so that I could share with a friend I'd known for a long time. He was out looking for suitable accommodation at that very moment.

'I may be able to help you,' said the gentleman. He took out his card and handed it to me. His name was Dominik Rebič and he lived in a very pleasant locality. 'I have a spare room to let. It's comfortable and quite big enough for two people.'

I could hardly believe my luck. 'How much is the rent?'

'6,000 dinars a month.'

It was a lot but we'd be able to afford it between us. 'Could we come and see it tomorrow, please?' I asked.

'Certainly. My daughter will show you round and explain everything to you. She acts as landlady for me.'

The room was large, light and airy. The parquet floor shone, there were two easy chairs, polished cupboards and chests and the two beds were covered in cheerful counterpanes to match the rugs. There was a small table with two chairs and the focus of the room was a big ceramic wood-burning stove. Ostoja and I looked at each other and nodded, delighted with what we saw.

'We'll take it, please,' I said to Dominik Rebič's daughter. As Josip was perfectly happy to become sole occupant of our original room and take over the rent, Ostoja and I were able to move without delay.

At the factory, the following Monday, the director called a meeting at which we three technicians were asked to be present. 'I want to reorganise your schedules,' he said to us. 'Now there are three of you, I think each of you could take responsibility for a particular aspect of the process here.' Josip and I had guessed he might think along these lines – it was his logical next move – but we didn't feel quite ready yet. We had agreed what to say.

'Would it be possible to delay the reorganisation for a couple of months?' I asked.

Josip followed up with, 'Now there are three of us, we want to take the opportunity to get everything in order. Between us we can keep the daily chemical work going and at the same time experiment to find the definitive mixtures of chemicals for each process.'

'We'll carry out stringent tests on the leather,' I added. 'We'll be able to ensure we use the minimum amounts of chemicals and fats necessary for top quality results. We're sure we'll be able to cut costs even more.'

'I can see you've thought all this out,' Drago said, laughing. 'Just say which records of processes you need and let me have your report as soon as possible.'

Six weeks later the three of us delivered our report. The director and financial director considered it and were so impressed that our salaries were increased to 28,000 dinars a month. I had been sending my mother money regularly. Now I could send her more and also give some to my sister, Dragica, who had often fed me, allowed me to stay in her home and had had the trousers and shirt made for me so long ago.

Josip, Ostoja and I were now given our own areas of responsibility. Josip had the 'Shoe Leather Department', Ostoja the 'Soft Leather' and, to my delight, I was to be in charge of overall testing. Part of my job was to oversee the early preparation of the leather. I could sit in the central office and make sure the workers did everything correctly. I must say that I felt rather important then. On the other hand, I liked to be out and about on the factory floor, joining in the good natured banter.

Ivan (2ⁿᵈ from left) and friends from Almeria
Ostoja lying in front

Soon after our salary increase, I arrived at the side gate of Almeria just before 6 am, for the early shift. I was surprised to see the big gates open and a large truck backed right up to the despatch bay. I couldn't see anyone and there was a strange silence – none of the shouting and laughter that usually accompanied loading. I had never seen a truck by the bay so early so I didn't go through the gate but ran round the outside of the perimeter fence to the security booth. I explained my suspicion to the security officer. He knew nothing about an early despatch so I used his phone to speak to the director. 'I'll phone the sales manager straight away and come back to you,' he said. He rang back after a couple of minutes to say, 'The police are on their way.' Within five minutes six police cars arrived, sirens blaring. The police caught the thieves as they were about to drive away. Among them was one of Almeria's managers.

I continued to go regularly to the British Consulate reading room. I liked looking at the western magazines, particularly at the men's fashions. In communist Yugoslavia no western imports were allowed. Our fashions lagged far behind those of Europe and the USA but most people had no way of knowing this. However, I knew it and I longed for a pair of jeans and some winkle pickers. I was envious of Franco, one of our van drivers, an Italian. His jeans were tight and his shoes were pointed. One day I asked him if he could get me some similar gear.

'Sure,' he said.

'I'd like a leather belt like yours too, if that's all right.' He wore a leather cowboy belt. It sported a buckle in the shape of a saddle, on which were imprinted two guns.

'I can get all that for you from Italy,' he said. 'It will cost you about 10,000 dinars altogether. It was a lot of money – more than a month's rent, over a third of what I earned a month but it would be worth it.

'That's fine,' I said. 'I'll pay you tomorrow.'

I could hardly wait for my order to arrive. I'd been very pleased with my coloured shirts which weren't available in local shops. Ostoja and I had managed to amass a selection by giving our white shirts to my brother, Josip, who worked at a dye factory. He was able to return them in whichever colour we'd requested. Shirts were one thing but the jeans, winkle pickers and special belt were another – the prospect of those was much more exciting.

Franco brought my longed-for clothes to the factory a month later. After work I rushed home and tried them on with my red shirt. Everything fitted perfectly. Ostoja laughed as I strutted round the room. 'A peacock,' he said.

'You're just jealous,' I replied.

It was at about this time that I met Stela Novak my first girlfriend not counting Marica of course. Stela was an actress. I waited outside the stage door for her one evening after I'd seen her in a show. She accepted my offer to walk her home and later to come for a drink with me. She was a sweet, pretty girl, with rosy cheeks and a beautiful smile. We enjoyed each other's company and had a similar sense of humour. She was working most weekday evenings so we could meet only on my occasional days off, late in the evening after the shows or on Sundays.

One Saturday evening Ostoja and I went to a disco. The first person I saw, as I entered, was Branko Kapun. I hadn't seen him since I'd left Bol. Our eyes met and we dashed towards each other, shook hands, exclaiming in delighted surprise.

'This isn't the place for a Bol student,' I said.

'I'm not there any more. In fact I left soon after you. It just wasn't the same without you and I'd got to the stage where I couldn't stand it any more – the discipline, the work. I felt as if I was wasting my life so I asked my mother to allow me to leave. Honestly, I never did feel I had a vocation. We were so young when we were asked to make the decision, weren't we?'

'Yes we were. Are you living in Zagreb?'

'Yes. I'm working at a big printing firm. I'm in charge of the office. There's one thing you can say in Bol's favour. It gave us an excellent education.'

I had another surprise the next evening. Dragica and her husband Franz had been invited to take me for a meal at the house of Franz's aunt. When I walked into the living room, who should be sitting there but Rudi Petrak, the trainee priest who had kept me company when I'd stayed at the *samostan*. Rudi was, of course, Franz's brother but I hadn't seen him since the time he'd waved me off on my way to Bol. We shook hands warmly. 'Are you still in training?' I asked.

'One more year to go then I'll be a fully fledged priest. I'd heard you'd left Bol. What are you doing now?'

I told him about the factory and my work there as we sat down to eat. After the meal, I thanked the hostess and prepared to leave. I had arranged to meet Stela at a nightclub.

'Why don't you come with me Rudi?' I said. 'Come and see how the other half lives.'

'I'd love to but I haven't any money and no civvies with me. I can't go like this.' He was wearing his priestly robes.

'The evening's on me,' I said 'and Franz will lend you some clothes, won't you?' I looked at Franz. He was about the same size as Rudi.

'Of course,' Franz answered. 'Let's go home now and I'll fix you up. It won't take long.'

When Dragica realised what was happening she was furious. 'No Franz, you can't. Rudi's almost a priest. He shouldn't go to a place like that.' She turned on me. 'And you should know better than to ask him.'

Franz laughed, 'Come on Dragica. The man deserves a bit of fun. It's a perfectly respectable club.' And, ignoring Dragica's angry protests, we walked out.

Franz did Rudi proud with an almost new suit, crisp white shirt, blue tie and black shoes. 'I don't recognise myself,' he laughed as he gazed in the mirror.

At the club, we met Stela. With her was her friend, Ana, a dark sparkling beauty. By the time I had bought us all some drinks, Rudi and Ana were dancing together and they were inseparable for the whole of the evening. They danced until they were tired then they sat and talked until they felt like dancing again. Rudi got through a lot of wine but I kept a clear head. I knew I must get him safely back to Dragica's and I was on the early shift the next day. It was 3 am before we left the club. Rudi was very merry and I heard him telling Ana where, in Zagreb, his aunt lived. 'I visit her the first Saturday of every month,' he said, clasping her hand.

'I'll come and see you there,' she promised. We left the girls at their door and somehow I managed to get Rudi to Dragica's house. He was very much the worse for wear and stumbled through the door, waking the household. Franz came down and helped him to bed while Dragica harangued me.

'You're a disgrace!' she shouted. 'What did you think you were doing? Rudi's a good man, a man of God. You've led him astray this evening. May God forgive you!'

I didn't excuse myself. I knew Rudi had thoroughly enjoyed himself. I thought that, if he was secure in his vocation, a few drinks and dances would do him no harm. If he wasn't secure…then it was better for him to discover that now rather than after he'd taken orders. I turned away and hurried home to grab a couple of hours sleep before work.

Later I learned that Rudi and Ana's friendship lasted until the end of Rudi's training. Often when he visited his aunt, Ana would arrive to drink coffee with them or to take a walk with Rudi. He always brought fruit for her from the monastery orchard. I truly believe the friendship was innocent and that I had no reason to take to heart the accusations Dragica had thrown at me on that unforgettable night.

Folk Group

In spite of the company of Stela and Ostoja, in spite of night clubs and discos, I felt jaded and bored once the 1959 New Year festivities were over. Everything was going well at the factory but I wanted something more from life. I wanted to *do* something. I missed studying and playing in the orchestra. I needed a new challenge. One evening Ostoja and I were sitting by the stove in our room and I was bemoaning the lack of things to do. Ostoja said, 'Perhaps there's a local orchestra we could join.'

'There isn't one close enough. I looked for one when I first came to Zagreb.'

Ostoja said, with a laugh, 'I suppose we could start our own.'

'That's it!' I shouted. 'We can. Not an orchestra but a group – you know – with guitars and drums. That's a brilliant idea.'

'What sort of music?'

'Folk. Some people will play and others sing or dance. We'll have to find teachers…we can even dress in national costume. It would be fantastic!' The whole splendid picture was inside my head. There were Ostoja and I, on the stage, playing shiny guitars. There was the sound of sweet singing and, in front of the stage the colourful dancers performed wondrous movements.

Ostoja brought me back to reality. 'Instruments are very expensive and so are costumes and lessons. Where could we get that sort of money?'

He might just have well poured a bucket of iced water over me. The vision faded and I slumped in my chair for a moment. My dream had been so vivid, I couldn't simply forget it, let it slip away. I was silent, thinking hard, and then I sat upright and said, 'The director. We'll ask the director.'

'Any other business?' asked Drago as our weekly meeting with him drew to a close.

'Yes sir,' I said and I laid before him our plan.

He was silent for a moment and we held our breath. His secretary, Jadraka, a friend of mine, spoke first.

'Could I suggest, sir, that Ivan and Ostoja put their plans on paper and make a list of all they will need, with costings. That way you'll be able to see whether or not the idea is feasible.'

'That's an excellent way forward,' he said. 'I'm in favour of the idea, in principle. Such a group would be good for morale and publicity apart from the enjoyment of those who participate. But I do need to know just what it will all cost.' I gave Jadraka a grateful smile as we left the room.

By the next week we had the information Drago required. 'This looks very satisfactory,' he said after he had read everything and checked our calculations. 'I'm pleased you have found teachers willing to show you the skills required. You may go ahead.' He cut our thanks short with, 'Jadraka will place notices around the workshops and offices so that people can sign up to join your group. You will need to elect a committee and run things properly. Make sure all invoices come to me and keep a record of what you spend.'

We were delighted and set about following the director's instructions. Suddenly we had more than enough to do, challenge after challenge, I was in my element. Josip and I elected to play guitars. Ostoja chose the drums. He and I also went to folk dancing lessons. Later I joined the folk singing group too. It was agreed that we should name our new group after the leader of The Peasants' Revolt. We called ourselves, *Fokrolna- Grupa Matija Gubec/* the Matija Gubec Group. Everyone was enthusiastic and we spent every spare moment practising. I had very little time to see Stela as my new passion took over. The relationship between us cooled gradually but we still met occasionally, as friends.

At the beginning of July we gave a small concert to some of our colleagues at Almeria. The director attended and was so pleased that he asked us to repeat it a couple of weeks later. This time we performed in front of the board of directors of a subsidiary company of Almeria. They had travelled the 100 kilometres for a meeting, were wined and dined and entertained – by us.

'Thank you very much,' said one of the visitors at the end of the concert. Turning to Drago he continued, 'Would you consider allowing these talented young people to come to my factory to entertain my workers?'

'Certainly,' answered Drago. I was elated. Ostoja and I had made this happen. Suddenly I felt that I could do anything.

Three weeks later we travelled, by minibus, to the smaller factory and performed in front of the office and factory-floor employees. Away from home, I was nervous and forgot the words to my song. Ostoja, on the drum, mouthed two words to me and I managed to continue almost without a break. No-one seemed to notice and we were very well received. Afterwards we were taken to the restaurant and given a splendid meal. Next, the restaurant chairs and tables were cleared away for a dance. As a musician began to play an accordion, I saw a beautiful girl at the other side of the room. I went swiftly across and asked her for a dance. Her face lit with a smile as we walked on to the dance floor. She had a round face and dimples. Her complexion was creamy and her glorious brown hair fell to below her narrow waist in two shining plaits.

'I'm Ivan,' I said.

'I'm Štefica.'

That's all we said then but, later, as we danced throughout the evening, I discovered that she taught in an elementary school and her cousin worked in the office at Almeria. Before we parted, we exchanged addresses and promised to write. Ostoja teased me on the way back.

'I thought you said you were going to concentrate on the group for a bit and not bother about girls.' I gave him a friendly punch. I was feeling too happy to argue. Our concert had been very successful and I'd danced the whole evening with a lovely girl. What more could I ask?

Štefica and I wrote to each other. Those were the first love letters I'd written or received. Her cousin told me how much she liked me but she lived too far away for us to meet although I often thought about her.

After about three months I heard, from Štefica, that she was bringing a class of children to Zagreb to see the museum and the zoo. I was very excited. I didn't know if we'd have even two minutes to talk privately but I couldn't wait to see her. I arranged to have a day off work so that I could meet the coach in the city square.

Štefica gave her wonderful smile when she saw me and she looked as gorgeous as ever as she helped the children from the coach. I hadn't anticipated that there would be three other teachers with her. She flushed as she introduced them.

The oldest one smiled in a kindly way and said, 'We've got a little surprise for you. We've decided the three of us are quite capable of looking after the children, Štefica. You two young people can have the day together and meet us back here at six o'clock. How does that suit you?' It suited us very well.

When the school party had disappeared, I put my arm around Štefica's shoulders and said, 'Let's go and get something to eat and you can think about what you'd like to do with our unexpected day.'

'I'd love to go to the mountain, to *Medjevica*, I've heard it's beautiful and has views over Zagreb.'

After lunch we wandered upwards through *Medjevica*, the mountain forest which lies to the north of the city. We admired the views of the river valley and also of the city itself, nestling, as it does, between hills. Then, leaving the path, we sat down on the dry leaves.

Thoughts of another forest and another woman flashed through my mind. How different this was. Štefica was shy, diffident and I was the one taking the lead. We kissed and held each other close but as my hands strayed, to take in the curve of her breasts, she pulled away.

'No further,' Ivan she whispered. 'Just kissing. That's all until we're married.'

Then *I* moved back. Married? Štefica's thoughts were rushing too far and too fast. She was lovely, she was desirable but I had no wish to marry for a long time. I supposed I would want to settle down and have a family one day but certainly not yet. There was too much I wanted to do first. I didn't say anything. I didn't want to spoil Štefica's day. We continued our walk, talked about our families and our work. We had coffee and torte when we got back to the city and then it was time for her to go.

'Did you have a good day?' the teacher in charge asked as we stood by the coach.

'Marvellous,' we both replied. Štefica was not too shy to kiss me in front of the children and teachers. I was the one who was embarrassed.

She and I saw each other only once more, just for half an hour when she came with her parents to visit family in Zagreb. We continued to exchange letters for several years, however.

On the following Tuesday, the tram in which I was travelling home from work, suddenly halted. I realised that a row of trams was stationary in front of us.

'Everyone off!' shouted the driver.

'Why?' I heard somebody ask him. 'What's happened?'

'There's some sort of demonstration I think. Bloody students.'

It was a beautiful day, I had nothing to hurry home for and I had some student friends so I decided to go and investigate the protest. I followed the noise into *Savska Cesta*/River Road. Hundreds of students were parading towards the student accommodation blocks. Some carried banners with the slogans, *Long live Communism, Give us bread, We are hungry* and *Down with corruption.* They were chanting the same messages. As it wasn't long since I'd been at college, still had friends there and I sympathised with the students' cause I joined them, shouting along with the rest. When we arrived at Marshal Tito Square, we were greeted by ranks of police in riot gear. The procession halted and students crowded into the square, facing the police. Somehow I had worked myself toward the front. There was the sound of marching and a shout from the other side of the square and I turned to see that a number of soldiers had halted there. They were carrying fixed bayonets. An army officer pushed his way through the crowd and stopped by the police chief, close to where I was standing.

'What do you want us to do?' I heard him ask.

'Disperse these hooligans. Use your weapons.'

The officer drew himself up. 'We are the People's Army,' he said sharply. 'Our sons and daughters may be in this crowd of young people. We will not attack them.'

Before the police chief could answer, the officer had turned and was making his way back to his men. 'About turn,' he bellowed. The soldiers turned and marched away.

The police chief gave the order to attack the students who retaliated by throwing stones and bricks. I decided it was time to run. I slipped quickly to my left and made for the park railings. I could hear footsteps behind me. I glanced over my shoulder and saw a police officer. I sprinted and took a flying leap at the railings, gripping the top and starting to heave myself over. I was almost there, at the tipping point, when I felt a heavy blow on my rear. I scrambled over, out of danger and looked back. The policeman was brandishing his truncheon. My bottom was bruised but I knew I'd got off lightly.

When Ostoja got home from work, on the day of the protest, I showed him my injury. He was sympathetic but couldn't help laughing when I tried to sit down sideways. It was over a week before I could sit comfortably.

Later I heard that a couple of student leaders had been arrested. It appeared, however, that the government intended to play down the whole incident. The leaders were soon released and a fine new student restaurant was opened. There, excellent food could be obtained in exchange for special student tokens. A couple of my friends gave me tokens and took me there to eat as a mark of appreciation for my support.

An idea had begun to crystallise in my mind. It was an idea that I'd mulled over for some time. Now it was almost time to talk it over with my closest friend.

Although I was enjoying a good social life, was successful at work and very involved with *Matija Gubec*, I was become increasingly unhappy about the petty restrictions imposed on our lives by the ruling communist party. They had no mandate to be our rulers. It is true that elections were held but only members of the communist party were entitled to vote. In our factory, as in every other work place, there was a communist cell called a 'Workers' Council'. Ours comprised about thirty Party members, most of whom were in positions of authority although I knew some of them to be illiterate. They had eyes and ears everywhere, always waiting to denounce a worker who said a word against the government or the prevailing dogma. A few weeks previously I'd made my feelings plain to the communist cell in Almeria. I often saw the cell secretary in the restaurant and one day I stopped her as she was leaving. 'I'd like to join the Party,' I said. 'Please will you put it to your next meeting?'

She looked surprised but pleased. I don't think she'd viewed me as a potential candidate. 'Certainly I can propose you,' she replied. 'Come to the committee room at 6 pm. next Tuesday.'

'Be careful,' Ostoja warned when I told him what I had in mind. They're probably watching you already.'

'I shan't actually be doing anything wrong,' I said. 'I'm sick of the lot of them, sneaking round just looking for things to report. They fabricate them if they can't find anything, simply to make themselves look good. What I read at the British Consulate makes me realise what a difference there is between life here and life in the west. There, even when they live in the countryside, they don't have to wait for a farmer to sell them goods which are carried by horse and cart. They have proper food shops with milk, butter and eggs and much much more in them. They have amazing clothes shops too with lots of styles to choose from. We have nothing.' Ostoja started to speak but I hadn't finished. 'We can't even buy pop records unless they are made in a communist state and as for UDBa /secret police…when you're not being watched by the cell at work, you're being watched by UDBa outside.'

Ostoja laughed at my tirade. 'I should stop going to that reading room if it makes you so cross, Ivan. Anyway, just take care. Don't upset the Party.'

I walked into the committee room promptly at 6 o'clock. Everyone turned to stare. 'What are you doing here?' the chairman asked.

'I've come to join the communist party.' There was silence as they took in my jeans, winkle pickers, red shirt and red socks.

'Just turn right round and walk out again,' barked the chairman. I looked at him with the most disappointed expression I could muster and very slowly obeyed.

Now, after the student protest and the unwarranted vicious reactions of the police, I was ready to confide in Ostoja. I took a deep breathe. 'I want to get out,' I said. 'I want to escape to the west. Will you come with me?'

Plan to Escape

Ostoja stared at me. 'Get out? You mean leave Yugoslavia, leave work, *Matija Gubec*…everything?'

'Yes, that's exactly what I mean. I'll go alone if I have to but I'd really like you to come too. We could do it. We'd plan everything very carefully. It would be a fantastic adventure…and imagine being free to do what you like, to go where you like and to wear what you like.'

There was a moment's silence then Ostoja said, 'It's a huge decision. We might get caught and then what?'

'We won't get caught. We'll make sure of that. Think about it. You and me, against the world – against the communist world, anyway. We've made other things happen. We've changed things at Almeria and look at *Matija Gubec*. We could make this happen too.'

Another silence then, 'Yes, all right. I'll do it.'

We spoke of little else when we were on our own. We bought maps and a compass and talked loudly, in shops, about hiking across Yugoslavia. We listened to tales of successful escapes through Austria and then we heard about people being shot as they tried to cross. Perhaps we should try a different crossing point. Both Ostoja and I had arranged to visit our respective families and we knew we must go through with this. We must act normally or people might begin to ask questions. We'd fulfil our commitments and work as hard as usual at Almeria but, now we'd made the decision to leave, everything else seemed a distraction.

On my way home, there were only two people sitting near me on the train from Zagreb. The first alighted at the next station and the other, a man of about 25, asked me if I minded if he opened the window. He introduced himself as Boško and we were soon chatting.

We discovered we liked the same sort of music, were both going to visit our families and we talked about the work entailed in keeping vineyards. The journey passed swiftly.

Boško prepared to leave the train at the stop before mine. 'It's been great to have company,' he said. 'It would be good to travel back to Zagreb together. Which train are you catching on Sunday?'

'The one that gets back at 9 pm.'

'Me too. Look out for me, will you?'

'Of course.'

The train was slowing and as he reached up get his case from the luggage rack, I noticed, with a jolt, that he had a pistol in a holster fixed to his belt. He turned round and saw I'd noticed the gun. He laughed.

'Don't worry, I'm quite safe. I'm a detective. See you Sunday.' The train stopped, he jumped out and waved as I stared after him.

I didn't say anything about Boško to my mother or brothers. I knew I'd have to be careful in my dealings with him. I thought that, as he was carrying a gun, he was probably a member of UDBa. If I was clever I might be able to get some useful information from him. Of course I didn't tell my family about my plan to escape either. My mother would certainly try to stop me. I simply slotted back into life at home for a couple of days, helping with the weeding of the vines and enjoying Mama's cooking. As I lay in bed on the Saturday night, I was swept by a huge wave of sadness. I don't know when I'll lie here again – if ever, I thought. The new life Ostoja and I hoped for was uncertain and thrilling but I'd be leaving almost everything I'd ever known behind. I gave Mama an extra hug as I left for the station on Sunday evening. She was waving as I turned the bend in the road and I willed myself not to change my mind about leaving Yugoslavia.

Once on the train, I found a quiet compartment. I leaned out of the window at the next station and saw Boško kissing a young woman. He looked round, saw me, waved and climbed aboard. 'My girlfriend,' he explained as we shook hands. We exchanged pleasantries about the weekend and then he said, 'I've been wondering if you and I might spend an evening together – go to club, say. What do you think?'

I thought it would be an excellent chance for me to get some information, discreetly, so I didn't hesitate. 'That's a great idea.'

We arranged that he would come to my lodgings the next Saturday evening.

Boško arrived promptly, smartly dressed. I noticed he had the pistol under his jacket but didn't say anything. We made our way to the nightclub I often frequented and found Stela already there. She came over to speak to me. I introduced her to Boško and she noticed the bulge of his gun. Her eyes widened. 'What's that?' she whispered, 'It's not a …'

'It's a pistol,' I said quietly, 'but don't worry. He's a detective so he needs to carry one. You're quite safe. He's a friend of mine.'

She didn't look altogether reassured but we sat down and I went to buy some drinks. When I came back Stela was being led on to the dance floor by a friend of mine. It was my chance to find out a bit more about Bosko.

'You said you're a detective,' I said softly. 'What sort of detective?' I laughed. 'Do you solve murder mysteries? Are you a policeman?'

'Sort of.'

'Can I ask you a straight question?'

Boško looked round to make sure no-one was listening. 'Yes.'

'Are you a member of UDBa?'

'Yes but don't let that put you off.'

'I won't say anything to anyone. You can trust me,' I said. Then I feigned interest in his work. 'What a fascinating job. You must find yourself in some tricky situations sometimes.'

He looked pleased. 'I do, believe me. A lot of what I do is concerned with people who are discontented and break the law to try to better themselves, either by fraud or by trying to get out of the country. People just don't know when they're well off. They're never satisfied – always thinking things are better on the other side.' The conversation was going just the way I'd planned.

'Why on earth would they want to do that? It's very risky isn't it? How long are the prison sentences for people who are caught?'

'It depends on which court they end up in. We just catch them and hand them over. I think the first time offenders usually get one to three months. For a second offence about six months to a year and so on. A lot of our work comes after we've caught the offenders because we have to investigate all their contacts and discover how they got the information about where to cross and also who may have helped them.'

Stela was now dancing with another admirer so I topped up Boško's drink and pushed him a little further. 'I heard about someone who was caught trying to cross into Austria.'

'We catch lots of people there. It used to be a relatively easy place to cross but we've tightened up security on that border.'

I felt I had learned all I could without making Boško's suspicious so I changed the subject. Stela came back to the table and I asked her for a dance. Boško found a girl to dance with and the evening passed pleasantly.

Stela was ready to leave by 3 am so the three of us went out into the cool night air. There were three teenage boys lounging outside the club, the worse for drink. Beautiful Stela often turned heads. Now she glowed with the exertion of dancing and one of the lads walked over.

He leered at Stela. 'Dump him,' he said, nodding in my direction. 'I'm a better bet.' I recognised him as the son of a high ranking judge. His photograph had recently appeared in the newspaper in relation to a drunk and disorderly charge.

I put my arm round Stela's shoulders and as we walked away from the group I heard Boško shout sarcastically, 'Why don't you little boys go home to your mummies?' The judge's son turned on him as if he was going to land a punch. Boško dodged and, leaving Stela well away from the trouble, I ran to his side.

'Calm down everyone,' I pleaded. Out of the corner of my eye I saw Boško take the pistol from its holster. 'Boško,' I whispered, 'Don't be stupid. Either put that away or take the bullets out.' With relief, I heard a click and he slipped the bullets into his pocket. When I looked round, the three boys were moving towards Stela.

'Come on darling, give us a kiss,' one of them called and I ran over to Stela. The boy turned and raised his fist but I was faster. I punched him on the nose and he went down, bleeding. The judge's son kicked the pistol out of Boško's hand. It fell to the ground and the third boy picked it up. The next moment Boško was flat on his back, punched by the judge's son. His mouth was bleeding.

Suddenly the police were there. They took in the situation and bundled the three boys into the police van. Boško produced his UDBa card so they turned away from him and looked at me. 'You too,' said one of the officers, grabbing my arm.

'Leave him,' ordered Boško. 'He had nothing to do with it.'

The officer let go and grinned at me. 'You'd better take the young lady home,' he said.

I was just dropping off to sleep when there was a knock at my door. Boško was standing outside.

'Can you let me have a bed for the night?' He asked. I didn't enquire why he couldn't go to his own lodgings. I simply handed him clean sheets and said he was welcome to sleep in Ostoja's bed.

I had the next day off so Boško and I breakfasted together. Out of interest, because I couldn't imagine why anyone would choose to join such a hated organisation as UDBa, I asked, 'Are you happy? Do you like your work?'

'The money's good but it all gets me down sometimes. Some of my friends have escaped. I think about it sometimes.'

I didn't pursue the matter and he left after breakfast. I never came across him again.

Escape

Ostoja arrived back from Bosnia but before we could put our plan into action, I received my call-up papers for National Service. In order not to raise suspicion it was important that I should turn up for the medical. I passed A1 and was selected for the navy. It was what I'd always wanted. It was ironic that I now hoped to be long gone before the start of my training.

'It's now or never,' I said to Ostoja. 'Your papers will arrive soon and I'll be off to the navy and we'll never actually get away. Shall we do it now?'

'Yes.'

We pored over the map and decided to try to get to Italy. Although others at work, who toyed with the idea of escape, always spoke about going to Austria, I had my conversation with Boško in mind. We planned to cross the Italian border, at night, near a town called Sežana which is in Slovenia.

'We can go by train to Rijeka and then on to Sežana by another,' said Ostoja, tracing the train line on the map.

'Sežana is right on the border. It has a crossing point,' I said. 'I don't think we should risk going the whole way there by train. Questions may be asked when we buy the ticket. Let's go as far as Senožeč by train and walk to the Sežana border. It's about 30 kilometers.'

'I think you're right. There's forest almost all the way so there'll be plenty of cover.' Ostoja agreed. 'We'll have to swim across this river to get to the actual border.'

We didn't mark our route on the map in case we were stopped and searched by police but we soon knew it by heart. Seeing the place names on the map made our journey seem real. For the first time I felt sure we'd do it.

Ivan's brothers. Lujzek and Stjepan

My brother, Lujzek, was working in Zagreb and we often met for a meal. I knew he was likely to call at our flat at any time and would wonder where I was. I wrote a short note to him telling him of our plan to escape but giving no details. I put it inside a book which I placed on top of the wardrobe in our room. 'If my brother comes at any time when I'm out,' I said to the landlady, 'please would you give him the book which is on top of the wardrobe?' I hoped Lujzek would open the book and flick through the pages. This was the best I could do to inform my family about my plan – when we were safely underway

A few days before our departure, we bought small binoculars, a sharp little knife and torches and talked again in public about the hiking holiday we were planning. The day before leaving, we went to work as usual and drew our half month's salaries. On the way home I bought bread, a good deal of salami and, as an afterthought, some cayenne pepper. I'd heard it would put dogs off a scent – and I knew that we might have to contend with guard dogs.

After packing our purchases and as many clothes as possible into our rucksacks, we went to bed but neither of us could sleep. I could hear Ostoja restless in his bed. I must have dropped off eventually for suddenly Ostoja was shaking me. 'Time to get up,'

I could tell he was very nervous. 'It's not too late to back out,' I told him. I was excited by the prospect of the adventure but didn't want to put pressure on him.

'I don't want to back out but let's go and get it over with.'

It felt as if everyone was looking at us on our walk to the station. We had decided to masquerade as tourists off for a seaside holiday. I was sure a large, dark-haired man was following us until I turned round and saw him turn into a side street. We caught a train to the resort of Rijeka, on the Adriatic coast. Having spent a few hours there at the beginning of our college trip, we had a vague idea of its layout. Ostoja began to relax as we had a picnic on the train, cutting thick slices of fresh bread to eat with salami. We arrived at 2 pm and strolled, with other tourists, to the beautiful beach.

After a swim, we joined sightseers, visiting the Cathedral of St Vitus and the Maritime Museum. As evening approached, we bought more bread and had a meal in a restaurant. Then, walking casually out of the town, we looked for somewhere to sleep. It would be risky to stay at a hotel or guest house because police often visited these establishments to check identity papers.

Within about twenty minutes, we came to an isolated and deserted building site. In the corner were some huge concrete pipes. 'Let's use one of these as shelter,' I said. Crawling inside, we spread our clean clothes out as a mattress, lay down and in a surprisingly short time were fast asleep.

It was I who woke Ostoja early the next morning. After more bread and salami we went to the station and found there was a local train for Senožeč due to leave at 7 am. We had time to make ourselves presentable in the washroom before boarding a very slow train. How impatient we were.

'We could walk faster than this,' I whispered.

'Sh!' hissed Ostoja, looking to see if anyone had overheard. The crawling train was making us both jumpy but at last we came to Senožeč.

We checked, with the compass, which direction to take but had already decided to walk away from the border at first. Once we were out of the town we would double back through the forest. As we went we saw men and women working in olive groves and vineyards, backs bent to their tasks. One woman gave a friendly wave. Somehow, ordinary life seemed unreal against our risky adventure. We didn't talk much. Ostoja found some wild figs which we relished. They were the first of many that we gathered to supplement our dwindling bread and salami supplies.

Once we were sure there was no-one about to see us we entered the forest and turned in the direction of the border. It wasn't long before we reached the edge of the trees and could see the river just below. I looked through the binoculars and scanned our side and then the other. No-one. I handed the binoculars to Ostoja.

'Can't see anybody,' he said, 'unless they're lurking in the trees.'

'Let's go then.'

We stripped and pushed our clothes into the rucksack. We wrapped the bread, binoculars, torches and compass in dry clothes, hoping that would afford protection from the water. The river looked green from reflections of the overhanging trees. I slipped in first and gasped as the cold hit me. We were both strong swimmers and managed to keep the rucksacks more or less above the water. We were soon over the river and hid in a bush to dry and dress. We ate a small piece of bread each to celebrate its escape from a soaking and, using the compass, set out on a three day walk to our chosen crossing place, just north of Sežana.

All the time we listened out for voices and footsteps in the forest and when we were forced to emerge into open country, we used the binoculars to check for any sign of life. If we saw or heard anyone, we hid among the trees or in bushes and once in a deserted building. We spent the nights in the forest off the path.

Late on the third afternoon we were in sight of the official Sežana crossing point and saw Italy beyond. '*S-F-R-Y*' I spelt out as I gazed through the binoculars at a notice by the bridge, on which were guard rooms and a checking station. The letters stood for *Socijalistick Federal Republiks Yugoslavia/* Socialist Federal Republic of Yugoslavia. 'Nearly there,' I whispered. 'Soon we'll leave *S-F-R-Y* and all its stupid rules behind. We'll be in Italy – the West – Freedom!'

Ostoja brought me down to earth. 'Don't speak too soon. We're not there yet.'

'We'll get there. See how they've cut down the forest each side of the road to the bridge. We always knew we'd have to go a bit to the north for cover and because there are bound to be too many guards just here. Come on.'

We threaded our way through the edge of the forest for about two kilometres and saw, in the distance, to our right, a watch tower. 'This is the best place to cross,' I said, 'about half way between the bridge and the tower. We'll have to dodge the border guards though.'

'Let's watch them parading up and down – see if we can find out how they organise themselves,' Ostoja said.

We lay on the ground close to some bushes and watched through the binoculars. The guards were armed with submachine guns. Each had an Alsatian dog at his heels. The men worked in pairs, starting about half a kilometre apart, and walking towards each other. When they met they lit cigarettes and chatted. Then they walked past each other and continued on along the border until they came to what was obviously the end of the area for which they were responsible. They then turned round and walked towards each other, stopped, lit cigarettes, chatted again, crossed over … and so on.

'Let's count the seconds it takes for the guards to reach their furthest points,' I suggested. 'We'll make our dash when we reckon that they are about half way there. That will give us the best chance.'

'We won't go until it's dark, though, will we?' Ostoja asked anxiously.

'No, let's just time them now and then we can rest for bit.'

Night fell. We could see glows from the cigarettes of the two guards who were closest as they stood together almost directly in front of us.

'It's dark enough,' I whispered the words although the guards were too far away to hear.

'This really is it,' Ostoja's voice was shaky. We crawled behind a bush, Ostoja pulled the cayenne pepper out and then we packed everything else away and shouldered our rucksacks. We watched the two glowing cigarettes move apart.

'Now!' I hissed and we ran.

Italy

Bending low, we ran as fast as we could through the undergrowth. Reaching the broad band of cleared land which ran round the boundary, we straightened and sprinted across it. My heart was thundering. In my mind's eye all I could see were submachine guns and snarling dogs. I glanced behind me. Ostoja was at my heels, the tin of pepper in his hand. He was leaving the trail to confuse the dogs. The distance, which had seemed short from the shelter of our bush, now seemed endless.

There was a shout. We'd been spotted but the terrain had altered. It was untrodden and scrubby. There was no wall or fence to tell us but I knew where we were. 'No man's land,' I gasped. A bush loomed to my right and I pulled Ostoja behind it as I paused to catch my breath, I could hear the panting of the dogs and just make out their shapes. They stopped suddenly and started to sneeze and cough. We heard them thrashing about, no longer in pursuit. The pepper had done its job. We turned and ran on, trying to stay in the shelter of small trees. And then we reached it – a huge glorious sign on which was written the word *ITALIA*. We clutched it, Ostoja kissed it. We each took a flying leap past it.

'We're here! We've done it! We're in Italy!' Ostoja shouted and, pulling off our rucksacks, we flung ourselves on the ground, exultant, gasping, laughing and crying too – with the relief of it all.

I'm not sure how long we lay there on the rough grass. Terror had masked our exhaustion but now we were safe we couldn't raise the energy to get to our feet. At last Ostoja rolled over and sat up. 'Look,' he said, pointing to lights on our left. 'That must be Trieste.'

I sat up. 'Civilisation at last,' I reached into my rucksack for the last of the salami. The bread had long gone. We ate and wearily got to our feet.

'Police station?' asked Ostoja. I nodded.

We started to walk in the direction of the nearest light and, within a few minutes, came to a narrow road which we followed. I couldn't believe it was only 9 pm. It felt as if days had passed since we'd first arrived at our crossing point. A woman was standing outside the first house we came to.

Ostoja addressed her in Slovenian, 'Excuse me madam, do you speak Slovenian or Croatian?'

She answered in Slovenian. 'Can I help you?'

'Could you direct us to the police station, please?'

'Have you just come across the border?'

'Yes, we want to report to the local police.'

'You're not the first people to say that to me. The police station is about 500 metres along this road. You can't miss it. Good luck.'

We thanked her and in a short time we arrived at a building with *Polizia* written over the door.

Clearly the officers were used to receiving people from across the border. They all spoke fluent Slovenian and Croatian and could not have been more welcoming.

'Can I get you anything to eat or drink?' asked the policeman in charge of us. Suddenly I realised I was almost unbearably thirsty but before I could reply, Ostoja said, 'Just a big drink of water for me, please.'

'For me too,' I said.

'*Aqua* it is.' The officer returned with a jug of iced water and two glasses. Never was a drink more delicious. He noted our details in a large black book and then explained that he would take us to a refugee reception centre nearby – to a camp called 'Aurisina'.

As we climbed into a police car, it occurred to me that I had not thought of us as refugees. I said to Ostoja, 'Do you remember when we had to get out of our rooms at college for the Hungarian refugees?'

'Yes. Never thought *we'd* be refugees did we?'

'No.' In those innocent days I could never have imagined the situation in which we now found ourselves.

Aurisina was composed of a number of huts. The car drew up outside one of them and our police officer took us inside and gave our names to the man in charge. 'You'll be all right now,' smiled the officer. 'Sleep well and good luck.'

'I'm the duty officer,' the man behind the desk said in Slovenian. 'We have people of many nationalities here – Bulgarians, Albanians, Hungarians, Macedonians and so on. All have managed to escape from the grip of communism. All want to be free citizens.' We smiled, not sure what to say. 'Still, you don't want to hear anything more from me do you? You must be very tired.' He gave us forms to complete on which we had to give our names, ages, home addresses and nationalities. As we handed them back he said, 'If you go next door to the canteen, they'll feed you. Then come back and I'll tell you where you can sleep. Tomorrow, after breakfast, you'll hear about your allocations.'

The spaghetti bolognese was superb and the beds were clean, though fairly hard and in a noisy bunkhouse. This didn't trouble us. In fact nothing troubled us. We were in a free land and we had received nothing but kindness since our arrival. Looking back, the word 'allocations' should have rung alarm bells but it didn't. Blissfully unaware of the trouble to come, we were asleep within a couple of minutes and I slept deeply and dreamlessly throughout our first night on the other side of the border.

'Ivan Vesligaj,' shouted the man sitting behind a table labelled 'AUSTRALIA'. I walked over. 'Sit down,' he said. 'You have been allocated to Australia. I'll just run over your details and you can sign the agreement. The ship sails from Naples in four days. Meanwhile you can stay at this camp.' Numbly I confirmed my name and date and place of birth. 'Profession?' the man asked.

'Leather technician.'

'Excellent, excellent. You won't have any difficulty getting a job in Australia. You'll be sought after.'

I had a sick, sinking feeling in my stomach. This couldn't be right. I wanted to go to Britain or Germany. I certainly didn't want to be forced to go to the other side of the world. This hadn't been part of the plan.

We'd been told to assemble in a large hut at 10 am. Ostoja and I had arrived early to find six tables set up, each bearing a notice on which was the name of a country. 'Australia' was near the door. Next came 'Germany', then 'France', 'Spain', 'Great Britain' and 'Sweden'. We'd often discussed where we'd like to live. We wanted to stay together and had agreed, Britain, first choice, Germany second. We didn't really mind which.

'It looks as if we can choose from these,' I'd said. 'Let's see who sells his country better, the Brit or the German.' We'd laughed and sat down, watching the other refugees drift in. By 10 there were thirty five of us altogether.

'They look a rough lot on the whole,' whispered Ostoja. 'But I suppose they've all had a tough time getting here.'

'Still, they could wash and smooth their hair.' We'd laughed again. By then the various representatives had arrived. We were sitting near the French desk. I noticed that several of the people who were called there couldn't sign their names but simply put crosses instead. It was then I'd heard my name called.

I pulled myself together. 'I think there's been a mistake, sir. I've never said I wanted to go to Australia.'

'You've no choice. You've been allocated to Australia.'

'Is there any chance the allocation could be changed?'

His face went red. 'None at all.'

I sat still, trying to take it in. I was struck by a dreadful thought. Suppose Ostoja had been allocated somewhere different. I decided to change tack. I smiled. 'You say that leather technicians are in demand in Australia, sir?'

'Yes.'

'My friend Ostoja Dragojevic is a leather technician too. Please could you tell me if he's on your list.'

Impatiently, he glanced at the paper in front of him. 'Yes, he's on it. Now will you sign this agreement and I'll give you 500 lire for your expenses until the ship sails. Meanwhile, you can sleep here and will be told about transport to Naples in due course. There are no restrictions on you. Go out and do some sight-seeing. You can come and go as you like.'

I thought fast. At least Ostoja and I were in the same predicament. If the worst came to the worst, we'd end up in Australia together. In the interim we may be able to find a way out. 'Yes sir, thank you,' I said. I signed the agreement, took the money, shook his hand and hurried back to Ostoja. I just had time to tell him the news. He started to speak but I broke in. 'Don't say anything. You're next on the list. Just sign and take the money. We'll think of something.' At that moment his name was called.

'Let's get out of here so we can talk,' Ostoja said as we left the hut. We walked out of the camp in silence and boarded a bus bound for Trieste. We didn't speak at first, both sunk in gloom. I had imagined that we'd thought of every possibility – getting caught, beaten, imprisoned even dying in our attempt to escape but never, in our wildest dreams, had we thought of being deported to Australia. Ostoja broke the silence. 'What on earth have we got ourselves into?'

'We thought we were so clever,' I answered bitterly. 'How can we have been stupid enough to think we could just walk into any country we fancied.' I was angry with myself and with the system. Suddenly I knew that I wouldn't let myself be forced into something I didn't want to do. 'Let's discuss it all when we can't be overheard,' I said, forgetting, for a moment, that no member of UDBa would be lurking on the bus.

We got off the bus in central Trieste, bought some sandwiches and walked to a pleasant park. I was dismayed to see many people begging on the streets. 'So much for capitalism,' commented Ostoja.

We sat under a tree to eat the sandwiches and I said, 'We don't have to go, you know.'

'Let's not be hasty,' he replied. 'We're free now. We're in a free country. I can feel the difference.'

'But we're not allowed to stay here, are we? We've no idea what Australia is like. If we don't like it, it will be very difficult to leave. We'll be so far from everywhere else and, anyway, no other country is likely to take us in if we turn this offer down. Alternatively, we know we'll be in terrible trouble if we go back to Yugoslavia openly. I think we should sneak back over, use the same technique as we did to get here. It's up to you to do what you want to, of course. Don't be influenced by me…but if you decide on Australia, please keep in touch.' I couldn't go on. I fervently hoped Ostoja would come back with me but I had to let him decide for himself.

There was a long silence and then, unexpectedly, he began to laugh, 'How ridiculous! All that danger and effort and our triumphant entry into Italy has come to this. To us slinking back, tails between our legs.'

'You're right it does seem silly but at least we gave it a go. If we hadn't, we'd always feel we'd missed an opportunity. Anyway, you don't have to come back…'

He interrupted me with, 'I'll come, of course I'll come back with you. We're mates.' And laughing again, 'How could you possibly manage without me? We'll slip back and no-one need know a thing about our adventure. When shall we go?' I was so relieved, that the journey ahead suddenly seemed a simple affair.

'Tomorrow I think. We'll try to get a good night's sleep and set out in the morning. We can say we're going to the laundry to wash our clothes if anyone asks why we're carrying full rucksacks. We've still got everything we need to get across the border and we've got some dinars left.'

'We can wait until dark to cross,' Ostoja said.

'Yes. We'll spend the day in Trieste and have a good meal.' I pulled the map out and we bent over it. 'I don't think we should risk crossing at the same point as last time,' I said. 'They'll be on full alert because of spotting us when we came over.'

'Here.' Ostoja was pointing north of Trieste to a place called Drovlje. 'This looks possible. It's not too far.'

'And it's only about 20 kilometres from Sežana, a day's walk.' I traced the line with my finger. 'We'll go south from Drovje to Sežana and catch a train to Zagreb. We've got enough money for the fare.'

'Yes, that sounds fine. Let's go for it,' Ostoja said.

We caught a bus to Trieste the next morning. We bought some bread and sausage, had a large meal and hung around, in the city, until about 6 pm. Then we started the 7 kilometre walk to the border. There was no need to lurk in trees and undergrowth. We followed a dirt road and even saw a sign post pointing us on our way. *'To the Border'* it proclaimed, in Italian and Slovinian.

By 8 pm we were in position. There were no guards on the Italian side of the border but we saw, through the binoculars, the ones on the Yugoslavian side. They were working to the same pattern of patrol as we'd seen at Sežana. We waited until 9 pm and complete darkness, then started the now familiar procedure of 'getting across'. Once past the *Italia* post, we had to be very careful making our way through No Man's Land and I actually bumped into the post displaying the letters *SRFY* and stumbled against Ostoja. There was no sign of the guards so we scuttled straight ahead out of their path and into a vineyard.

'We're home! I can't believe how easy it was,' I gasped. After a short rest we picked some ripe grapes and made our way on to a wooded hillside. We decided to rest and slept fitfully under cover of a bush. I woke at 3 am and roused Ostoja.

'Let's get going. It would be best to get away from the border before there are too many people about.'

Using our map and our compass, to determine the direction of Sežana, we found a narrow road. 'Let's make it easy for ourselves, there's no need to lurk among the trees, we're in Yugoslavia now. We're walking away from the border and have every right to be here,' I said confidently.

There were very few people at first. We stopped at midday, ate some bread and the fruit we'd picked along the way and then rested for a couple of hours. We made good headway in the afternoon, and when I thought we must be almost there a woman passed us, carrying a pitchfork over her shoulder. 'How far is it to Sežana, please?' I asked her.

'About 3 kilometres.'

'Nearly there!' Ostoja remarked. At that moment a motor cyclist rode towards us. He went past and then stopped. We looked back and saw him dismount and fiddle with something on his front wheel. As we started to walk away, there was a shout.

'Stop! Turn round and put your hands up or I'll shoot.'

We spun round, hands in the air. The man was pointing a Luger straight at us.

Prison

Still pointing the gun at us, the man approached. My mind was racing. I knew that somehow our little trip into Italy had been discovered. I cursed myself for my smugness at the ease of crossing and for my carelessness over our walk to Sežana. I knew now that we should have made our way across country and not strolled casually along the road.

'Where have you come from and where are you going?' The man barked.

Ostoja seemed tongue-tied so, ignoring the first question, I said, 'We're going to Zagreb. We work there. We're on our way to the railway station.'

'Stay where you are. Don't move. Keep your hands up.' He walked backwards to the motor bike but turned to get his radio. As he bent over the bike I hissed to Ostoja, 'Knife, compass, ditch!' I fished in my pocket for the map. By the time the man stood upright, radio in hand and looked at us once more, the knife, compass and map were hidden by long grass, in a nearby ditch.

We stood with our hands up for almost half an hour. My anger with myself had been replaced by fear. Visions of firing squads came, unbidden, into my mind. I looked sideways at Ostoja. He was pale and his hands were shaking. Eventually, scared that he might faint, I timidly asked the man if we could put our hands down.

'We're not armed,' I said. He gave a scornful laugh and nodded his head but I saw him tighten his grip on the Luger.

At last he greeted someone who was approaching from behind us. I daren't look round but heard footsteps. Two uniformed policemen appeared beside us, looked at us and one of them said something in an undertone to the man with the Luger. They all laughed and looked at us again. I felt ridiculous standing there. I *was* ridiculous. I'd been an idiot to run the risk of discovery by sauntering along a main thoroughfare and now we would pay the price. I realised that we were in real trouble. The man on the motorbike was clearly a plain clothes border guard. After all our care on the two borders, we'd been caught just as we were almost safe. If we'd managed to get on the train to Zagreb we would never have been traced.

'Over to you!' said the guard to the policemen and he roared away on his bike.

'Come on you two,' one of the policemen placed an arm on my shoulder. 'This way.'

'Where are you taking us?' Ostoja asked and I detected a wobble in his voice.

'Police station, It's not far. No need for handcuffs is there? You don't look dangerous.' He laughed again and I felt like a little boy. I was deflated, my pride in tatters.

At the police station, our names were taken. 'Where have you just come from?' asked the officer behind the desk.

I knew there was no point in lying. They clearly knew the answer and were checking whether or not we would tell the truth. 'Italy,' I said.

'Sign here,' He pushed a paper in front of each of us. It was an admission that we had crossed the border illegally. We signed. We were taken to a cell which had sloping wooden benches around the walls. There were six other people already there. The slop bucket was behind a screen in the corner. Almost immediately some black bread and black coffee was brought to us. In spite of our anxiety, we gulped both down. We hadn't eaten or drunk anything for hours.

'We need to get our story straight,' I whispered to Ostoja. 'We'll probably be questioned separately so we need to give the same answers.'

'Let's stick as close to the truth as we can,' he said softly. 'It makes it easier to remember.' We agreed on what we would say. I couldn't sleep. The benches were uncomfortable and the other cell occupants noisy. I kept running different scenarios in my mind – imprisonment, torture, perhaps pardon and release as we were young and first time offenders…or, ever recurring…the firing squad.

It was a relief when, at 6 am, more bread and coffee arrived. Soon afterwards everyone from the cell was lined up in the courtyard, Ostoja and I at the far end. A police officer came in carrying a covered basket. It looked as if he was going to provide a picnic but from under the cover he pulled out handcuffs. He walked along the line handcuffing the prisoners but when he got to us he stopped and said, 'Not you. You're no threat.'

Again my pride was wounded. I knew I should be pleased to have my hands free but I felt insulted and I knew the other prisoners were smirking at our expense. We were escorted to a police truck. Inside, benches ran along the sides. A table was fixed down the middle. Two armed officers climbed in with us. One of them sat next to me. A third sat next to the driver.

It was a nightmare drive, dark, crowded, hot and stuffy. There were small plastic windows, too high to be of use and I was soon very thirsty. I was glad, then, to be free from handcuffs. At times I rested my head on my arms and dozed. Ostoja did the same. At first the other occupants muttered among themselves but gradually an exhausted silence descended. The officer near me broke it once by asking if I smoked. He held a cigarette out to me.

'No thank you. Can you tell me where we're going, please?'

He laughed. 'You'll know when you get there.' Then, dropping his voice, he whispered, 'Sevnica, near Krško. You'll wait there to be sentenced.'

'Be sentenced, be sentenced,' the words throbbed inside me. What would we be sentenced to? The terrifying images which had haunted me since our capture hit me anew. I clenched my fists under the table. I would not allow myself to panic. Ostoja and I would deal with whatever came to us as we had done so far. I took a deep breath and answered the officer in as normal a voice as I could.

'Thank you. How long is the journey?'

'Between six and seven hours.'

After about four hours the truck stopped. 'Out,' shouted one of the officers and we climbed down stiffly. We were escorted to the toilet and allowed to splash our sweaty faces with cold water. Ostoja and I filled our cupped our hands and gratefully drank some. Then we were taken back to the truck.

As soon as we were settled, the back was flung open and a man appeared, carrying a tray of sandwiches. Each was like a small rough white loaf, sliced through and filled with ham, salami or cheese. They were delicious and the weak beer served with them, a wonderful surprise. I began to feel more cheerful. I'd already passed the information about our destination on to Ostoja. Now I whispered, 'Do you know, I've got a feeling that we may get off fairly lightly. Stop looking so worried.'

It was almost 5 pm when we finally stopped outside a grey forbidding castle with heavy fortifications. We got a glimpse of it as the truck turned and backed under a huge archway. We staggered down and found ourselves in a long courtyard. The tall stone walls rose on all sides. Other prisoners were gathered near the gate, clearly new arrivals too. We were sharply ordered to stand in line. There were about thirty of us. Ostoja and I were at the far end of the line, next to a long stone trough, which ran almost the width of the yard. There were taps above it and several men stood there washing and shaving. The one nearest me spoke to the next man, 'The new bunch has just arrived.' I recognised the voice immediately. It belonged to my brother, Adalbert.

The prison officer was speaking to us, 'Get into twos and follow me into the canteen.'

There was a shuffling as the men obeyed and I said softly to my brother, 'Hello Adalbert.'

With a clatter, he dropped everything into the sink. He spun round and stared at me, mouth open.

'Ivek! Where have you come from?'

I just had time to say 'Italy' before we were marched into the canteen.

'Who's that?' Ostoja asked when we were seated at a long wooden table.

'One of my brothers.'

'What a coincidence,' he laughed. 'Are you a family of convicts?'

'As far as I know I have six other brothers and two sisters who are not in prison,' I answered primly.

'What has Adalbert done?'

'I'll soon find out.'

The *šuta*/pasta and minced meat we were given was good. We had black coffee afterwards and, as I started to drink mine, Adalbert came into the canteen and up to me. He put two spoonfuls of sugar into my coffee from a packet he was holding and stirred it.

'This is my friend, Ostoja,' I said. Adalbert handed him the sugar and the spoon. 'Why are you here?' I asked.

'I got caught trying to cross to Austria,' he replied. 'I was sentenced today. Three months in Ljubljana. I'm not sure when I'm going.' An officer was walking purposefully in our direction. 'I'd better go now. We'll talk properly tomorrow.'

After supper we were taken to our sleeping quarters on the ground floor – a room with ten bunks. We had a quick wash and then Ostoja climbed up to the top one and I got into the lower and, in spite of the hard lumpy mattresses, we slept well.

Once more Adalbert supplied us with sugar at breakfast, after which our group was told to assemble in the courtyard. When we were in line, a woman prison officer appeared. 'I need two volunteers to chop wood in the forest,' she said.

Almost before she'd finished speaking, I had my hand in the air, at the same time nudging Ostoja. His hand shot up too. 'Right lads,' she said. 'Follow me.' She turned to face us. 'Now listen. No silly business. No escape attempts. There's really nowhere to go and we'll catch you easily if you try.' We nodded. The best thing to do was to keep our heads down, be model prisoners and hope for very short sentences.

We loaded a covered basket and two axes into the back of a jeep. There was no mention of handcuffs as we climbed in beside the driver. Winding through a forest, we came, at last, to a large clearing. The car halted and we got out. I closed my eyes for a moment. It was a hot, clear day but here there was shade and the air was fresh. Birds sang and I could almost imagine myself in my forest – the forest of my childhood.

'Well, just look at that!' The voice of the officer jolted me into the present. She was pointing to several large piles of neatly stacked wood 'There's been some sort of mix-up,' she said. 'Someone's already done what we came to do. There isn't any wood left to chop.'

'That's a pity,' Ostoja said, disappointed. 'Does that mean we have to go straight back, ma'am?'

'Could we saw some of the small trees down?' I asked helpfully. 'See, some are marked ready. If we saw off their branches, we could chop the main trunk down and then chop the timber into logs like the pile over there.'

'No saws,' replied the officer, 'but full marks for trying. No, we'll just make the most of this lovely day. We're not expected back until this afternoon so if we go back now, they won't know what to do with me and you two will be hanging around. I've brought a picnic in that basket. Let's walk a bit and you can tell me why two nice young lads like you have ended up in prison.' So, quite unexpectedly, we spent a pleasant and relaxing few hours in the forest. The officer had made sure the picnic was a tasty satisfying one, with more huge sandwiches. This time, they were served with salad and fruit. We finished with beer.

As we walked back along the prison courtyard, at about 4 pm, I met Adalbert.

'Where have you been?' he asked. 'I've been looking for you.'

When I told him, he laughed 'You lucky devil. You always were the lucky one in our family. I can't stop now. Let's meet here later, during recreation.'

After supper I found him leaning against the courtyard wall, smoking. 'Whereabouts were you caught?' I asked him.

'Near Kranjska Gora, I wanted to go through Austria to Germany and settle there. The army got me. They roughed me up before they handed me over to the police.'

'Why didn't you get a passport and do the whole thing legally?'

'I tried but they refused. Why didn't you?'

'I don't really know. I just had this idea about escaping and went for it.'

'Typical,' Adalbert laughed. 'Headstrong and stubborn, that's you. You'd best tell the judge you tried for a passport and failed. That'll count for something.'

'Right. Ostoja and I have decided not to tell which crossing places we used. They were relatively easy and if they realise that, they'll tighten up security and make it harder for anyone else who tries the same routes.'

Adalbert was staring at me. 'What do you mean, crossing *places*? Do you mean to say that you crossed to Italy and then crossed back?' I'd given myself away and was forced to tell him the whole story. He roared with laughter and clapped me on the back. 'Well, now I've heard everything!' He laughed again and then became serious. 'I think I'll be moved to Ljubljana early tomorrow, I may not see you before I go.' We shook hands and agreed we'd meet once we were both free. He put his hand on my arm. 'Take care little brother. No more crisscrossing borders.' And he turned and went indoors.

I didn't see Adalbert the next morning and, after breakfast, Ostoja and I were called to one of the prison offices which was serving as a courtroom for the day. We had rehearsed what we'd say at the interrogation. We were both anxious, I felt a bit shaky but was determined not to show it. My name was called first. An UDBa officer sat behind a desk. He was clearly the judge. A secretary sat at a table and a prison official guarded the door. I stood uncertainly, looking at the officer, feeling extremely vulnerable.

'Sit down,' he said sharply. I sat on a low wooden chair so that I had to look up at him. He was leafing through a sheaf of papers. 'What is your name?'

'Ivan Vesligaj, sir.'

'Ah yes. I know everything about you Ivan Vesligaj. I have your address here, I know where you have worked. I know where your mother lives. There is no point in your telling any lies. I have all your details. Understand?'

'Yes, sir.' I didn't know if the man really had all the information he claimed but I'd have to be careful. Now the moment of interrogation had come, I felt calm and strong. I would soon know the worst.

'Why did you run away over the border without the appropriate documents? Why didn't you apply for them in the proper manner?'

I took a gamble. 'I did apply for them but I was refused.'

'Where did you get the idea of crossing unofficially?'

'I attend a variety of youth groups in Zagreb. There was often talk of crossing the border. No one particular person influenced me.'

'Who travelled with you?'

'Ostoja Dragojevic'

'You were picked up in Slovenia. I find that extraordinary. You'd successfully crossed into Italy and then decided to come back. Why?'

I flushed. I knew that what I was about to admit sounded crazy. 'Yes sir, we did get to Italy and stayed a couple of days. Then we discovered that we were to be sent to Australia. We had no choice in the matter. We didn't want to go to the other side of the world so we came back.'

The secretary laughed aloud and even the judge covered his mouth with his hand and turned away. Once more I was humiliated. When my interrogator looked at me again his face was stern. 'You have been very foolish and you have broken the law so you must be punished. I am taking into consideration your truthfulness and the fact that you came back to Yugoslavia of your own volition. I sentence you to fifteen days in prison. You will go first to Petrinska detention centre, in Zagreb, and will be sent to another prison from there. You may go now. I hope this will be a lesson to you.'

In spite of my humiliation I wanted to jump and shout for joy. Only fifteen days – and we'd already served some of them. I winked at Ostoja and gave him an encouraging smile as I passed. I had been worried that I'd be sent to Nova Gradiška prison. My sister, Marija's husband was governor there and I certainly didn't want my family to find out about my stay in prison until I felt ready to tell them. I realised that my final prison destination might be Nova Gradiška but I thought it unlikely as it mainly held long term prisoners.

I was relieved to hear that Ostoja's sentence was the same as mine and that he was also bound for Petrinzka. The next morning he, I and six other prisoners were taken to Krško railway station by truck, driven by the woman officer who had taken us to the forest. Before she drove away from the station, she dropped a piece of paper into my pocket and said softly, 'Don't look now but it's the address of my family home in Zagreb. If ever you need anything, you'll get help there.' I was astonished and moved by her action but could only smile my thanks. Although I never had occasion to take her up on her offer I have always been grateful to her for reaching out to me at a time of anxiety and uncertainty.

We boarded the Zagreb train and I was relieved that we were not handcuffed whereas the two older men were. We were even permitted to sit on the other side of the compartment. We pretended that we had nothing whatsoever to do with the officers and handcuffed prisoners. I don't know if we deceived anybody at all but it made the situation easier to bear. A black Marija was waiting for us at the station and we were soon at Petrinska. How often I'd passed the building without looking at it or thinking about the prisoners inside. We got down from the van just inside a large courtyard and were marched into a hall where we were told to sit down. A well-dressed man sat one side of me. He had come with us from Sevnica but I hadn't spoken to him before.

'Are you here for crossing the border?' I asked.

'Yes but I was on a walking holiday and wandered over the border without realising it. It was a mistake.' I didn't bother to reply. Having seen the guards on the border, I knew he was lying.

We were called in for questioning separately, Ostoja before me. 'All the same questions as before,' he said when he came out. 'Just remember, don't smile.' I didn't know what he meant until it was my turn and I saw the camera in the interviewing room. I really am a convict, I thought as my first mug shot was taken. I have a criminal record and my details are on police and prison files. I think it was only then that this struck home to me. However, determined not to show what I was feeling, I annoyed the prison officer by giving a big smile as the camera clicked for the second photo.

The prisoner who claimed innocence (we dubbed him 'Mr Innocent'), Ostoja and I were taken to a small cell with sloping wooden benches like those we had tried to sleep on at the police station. We were each given a straw mattress and a blanket and later served with excellent belly of pork casserole, passed through a hatch in the door. There was nothing to do but chat with our six cell mates. Mr Innocent still insisted he had been subject to a miscarriage of justice. 'It's all made me ill,' he said. 'I feel dizzy and sick. I'll be seeing a doctor tomorrow morning.' I didn't like him at all. I thought he had a shifty look and a whining voice.

We slept surprisingly well and were woken by a loud shout from the corridor outside, 'Everybody up! Everybody up!' There was a shrill blast on a whistle. Mr Innocent remained in bed, claiming he felt too ill to move. After a breakfast of black coffee and bread the cell door was thrown open.

'Exercise time,' said the officer. 'March into the yard.' For half an hour we walked, marched and ran around the courtyard in a large circle to the taunts of the officer in charge, 'When I say run I mean run. Lift your feet up. You're running like women. March now, one two, one two…keep up, keep up.'

We returned to the cell out of breathe and had just drunk some water when the door opened. 'You two,' said the officer, pointing to Ostoja and me, 'bring your bags with you and follow me.' As we walked towards the office he said, 'Now you'll find out where you'll be serving the rest of your sentence.'

'Please don't let it be Nova Gradiška,' I whispered to Ostoja. He smiled sympathetically.

'You are fortunate young men,' the governor said to us as we stood in front of him. 'You are being sent to Žitnjak…' I didn't hear the rest of his sentence. Žitnjak was just outside Zagreb fairly close to where Dragica lived. I hadn't realised there was a prison in that area. It was too close to Dragica for comfort although reason told me we were extremely unlikely to meet. I pulled myself together. At least it wasn't Nova Gradiška. For that I was grateful.

We travelled in a prison van but one with windows. I kept my head down as we passed near Dragica's apartment and soon we arrived at what looked like a small farm. The gate was wide open, and as we wound up the long drive, we passed men working in fields and in a vineyard. I was amazed. 'This doesn't look like a prison.' I said to Ostoja.

'You're lucky,' said the officer travelling with us. 'This is an open prison and you'll spend every day in the open air.'

The governor of Žitnjak met us and took us to his office. After we'd confirmed our details he said 'We are harvesting grapes and some of the vegetables at the moment. Tomorrow you will be shown what your tasks are. I'll take you to your billet. Any questions before I do?'

'Do people ever escape?' Ostoja asked. 'It seems risky to leave a prison gate wide open.'

The governor laughed. 'You wouldn't get far. It may look free and easy here but we know where everyone is all the time. You can walk through the gate if you like and try to hide from us but we'd soon find you. Then you'd have your prison term trebled and you'd serve it in a much tougher place than this.'

The wooden billet, which we were to share with eight other prisoners, was light and clean. We sorted out our belongings and it was then I realised that my leather wallet was missing. Stuck in the pocket of the rucksack, in its place, was a cheap plastic one. Oddly the little money I possessed was still in it. Not a dinar was missing. Nevertheless, I was furious. I held the vastly inferior wallet at arm's length.

'We know who did this, don't we? Mr Innocent, while we were out of the cell exercising. I knew he was a liar and now I know he was a thief too.'

'At least he didn't take your money,' said Ostoja comfortingly.

'I only had a few dinars. My wallet was worth a lot more than that. Oh look what he's left for me as well. The dirty old man!' I had pulled something through a slit in the cover of the wallet. It was a collection of pictures of naked women in provocative poses.

'Wow! And he looked so respectable,' exclaimed Ostoja. 'Get rid of them quickly. You'll be in trouble if any of the prison staff sees them.' Angrily I tore the pictures into tiny pieces and buried them in a patch of earth outside the hut.

The last eight days of our prison sentence passed quickly. We helped with the grape and vegetable harvests. We ate plenty of fresh fruit and vegetables and slept well on straw mattresses laid on wooden bunks. Our fellow inmates were pleasant and many had committed the same offence as we had. There was one poor lad who was there because a young woman had claimed he was the father of her child. He had denied this and refused to pay her money towards the child's upkeep. 'I wasn't the father. I hadn't slept with her,' he told us, 'but she'd been my girlfriend and everyone believed her rather than me.'

A couple of evenings before our release Ostoja and I were sitting outside the hut. Birds sang in the bushes as the sun set. The breeze was cool and full of the scent of flowers. It was idyllic, certainly there was nothing prison-like about it, but something was weighing me down. There was something that we must, at last, discuss.

'Ostoja, what's going to happen to us when we get out?'

'I've been putting off thinking about it,' he said.

'So have I. It's just been a matter of getting through, taking a day at a time but now we need to make some plans.'

'We're bound to have lost our jobs,' Ostoja said gloomily.

'Yes we are but they owe us money. As they always paid us half a month in arrears they'll have to give us what we've already earned. When we get out, we'll go to Almeria first for our money and then we'll go to see Dragica. She'll give us a meal.'

'So far so good,' said Ostoja, 'then we'd better go and pay the rent we owe. Remember, we always said we'd send it from Italy.'

'Yes,' I agreed. 'But after that what? I suppose I should go and see my mother and give her a bit of help on the farm. I'll be hearing from the navy at any time.' It was strange to think of ordinary life again. The day of my military medical and acceptance for navy seemed a lifetime ago.

'I'll be getting my military papers soon too. They may be waiting for me already,' said Ostoja. 'If you're going to your mother's, I'll go and visit my father and family. After that, I might be able to get my job back at Visoko if I haven't been called up.'

We were silent for a few minutes. I think it struck both of us that once we each went our separate ways, it would certainly be the end of our constant companionship. 'We will stay in touch, won't we?' Ostoja said quietly.

'Always,' I answered with assurance.

Release: Parting

The last day of our prison sentence dragged as we counted the hours to freedom. Next morning we reported to the governor's office. He returned our identity cards and gave each of us 100 dinars to help us on our way. He walked outside with us and pointed in the direction of the gate. 'There's the gate. Walk through it as free men and don't ever let me see you in here again.' We assured him that he wouldn't and shook hands. Without looking back we walked away.

Outside the gate, we stopped for a moment and took deep breaths of the warm air. Ostoja laughed. 'I'm sure free air smells different,' he said.

I spotted a tram. 'Come on, first stop Almeria,' I shouted as I sprinted to the stop.

We hadn't planned what to say when we got to the factory. It would depend on who we saw. Drago might be inclined to give us another chance, we thought, as we had been partly responsible for many improvements in the production process. Our luck was out, however. Drago was away and there was even a new personnel officer. The huge man with so much black hair was nowhere to be seen and in his place was an unpleasant looking individual. He scowled at us as we entered the room.

'Who are you?'

'I'm Ivan Vesligaj,' I answered.

'And I'm Ostoja Dragojevic.' I saw Ostoja give him one of his winning smiles but it was wasted. The man's frown grew deeper and his mouth turned further down at the corners as he slowly nodded his head. 'Oh yes, I've heard a great deal about you two. Where have you been?'

Ostoja spoke pleasantly. 'To Italy for a holiday.'

'I happen to know, from our records, that you haven't got passports,' The man was sneering at us. 'How could you go on holiday abroad without a passport?'

I'd had enough of his attitude. 'We escaped,' I said. 'We successfully got across the border, had a holiday and came back. Any more questions?'

'What do you want from me?'

'Are our jobs still here for us?'

'No they're not. You're sacked.'

We'd expected this. I pulled myself up to my full height and said very firmly, 'You owe each of us half a month's salary. Please arrange for us to have it now.'

He knew it was our entitlement but it was clear he resented writing the cash slip.

'Take this to the finance department, get your money and then leave the premises immediately.'

I took the slip and we walked out in silence.

'What a charmer,' grinned Ostoja.

When we entered the financial director's office we had another surprise. Ana, of the wrinkled forehead had gone. There was a very stout lady more than filling Ana's chair. I handed her the cash slip and she looked in a ledger. 'It appears we owe you 60,000 dinars each she said coldly.' She heaved herself up, waddled to the safe and took out a wad of cash. She counted out the correct amount and closed the safe door. 'Sign here'. She handed us the money and, opening a drawer in the filing cabinet, she withdrew two small booklets saying, 'Here are your *radnicka knjizica*/work records. They are signed up to date. Now please leave the premises.' We walked slowly down the stairs, along the path and past the security office, into the street.

'It seems odd that we'll never come here again,' Ostoja said.

I didn't reply. I had been at Almeria for the whole of my working life. I'd been happy there, had learned a great deal. This was the end of a chapter.

There was no time to brood. It was 10 am and there were two things left to do in Zagreb. 'Come on,' I urged. Let's get to Dragica's. She'll feed us and then we must go and pay our rent.'

'Who is it?' Dragica shouted when I rang her doorbell.

'Your little brother Ivek,' I called.

There was a scream of delight, the door was flung open and I was enveloped in the arms of my sister. 'We thought you were dead or in prison,' she said, holding me at arm's length to scrutinise my face. 'Lujzek showed us the letter you left and we've been worried sick!'

'I'm sorry you've been worried. I wrote the letter to put your minds at rest – so that you wouldn't think something bad had happened to me when I didn't come to see you. I didn't mean to make you anxious.'

By now we were sitting in the kitchen and Dragica was heating a big saucepan of soup. 'What are you doing here? She asked. 'Didn't you like it over the border?'

'It was wonderful in Italy but we were going to be sent to Australia so we decided to come back.'

'Australia! Good heavens.'

Then we told her about our adventures since we'd left Zagreb. We confessed that we'd been to prison. She wasn't too shocked and even laughed at the coincidence of my meeting Adalbert. She served chicken soup, apple strudel and beer. 'You're welcome any time,' she called as she waved us off. 'Give Mama my love, Ivek. Good luck to you both.'

'I thought I'd seen the last of you,' our landlady exclaimed when we knocked on her door. 'I've cleaned your room and was about to re-let it. But you can stay on if you want to.' We thanked her and explained that we had been on an unexpected holiday and were now leaving Zagreb.

'We've come to pay what we owe you,' Ostoja said.

'That's a wonderful surprise,' smiled the landlady. 'You know, I thought it was uncharacteristic of you to leave, saying nothing and owing money. Thank you for being honest.'

When we had paid her I said, 'Please may I say goodbye to your father? He was kind and offered me this accommodation at a time when I really needed it.'

She turned away from us but I saw she had tears in her eyes. 'I'm sorry, you're too late,' she said quietly. 'My father died a week ago. His funeral was yesterday.'

As we walked away from the house, carrying our few belongings, I said 'I can't believe how much has changed while we've been away. It's less than a month since we went.' We were quiet then, knowing that something else was about to change. We were about to go our separate ways and we didn't know when we'd see each other again. I felt a choking in my throat and Ostoja kept blowing his nose. We reached the station in silence, bought our tickets and studied the timetables.

'Platform 3 for me,' I said. 'Train leaves in ten minutes.'

'Mine's in half an hour from platform 1. Shall I come and wave you off?'

I was afraid I was going to cry so I said, 'No, let's say goodbye here. Get it over with.'

Solemnly we shook hands and then Ostoja grasped me in a bear hug. His voice was thick as he said, 'I'll never forget all we've been through. Stay in touch.'

'Of course!' I've got your address and you've got my mother's and my sister's.' We released each other and I turned quickly for platform 3.

'Thank you Ivan, thank you for everything.' I looked back. Ostoja had a tight little smile on his face. I knew he was struggling with tears.

'Thank you too,' I managed to say and then I ran down the steps to my platform.

I was glad of the hour I spent on the train to Lupinjak. It gave me time to compose myself, to look back over my friendship with Ostoja and to start looking forward. It was a lovely afternoon when I alighted from the train and started out across the fields towards my home. As I reached the top of the last hill I looked down at my family's land and the forest I loved. I sat down for a moment and marvelled at the mellow sunlight on the vineyard and cornfields, at the rich greens of the trees. I had never seen my home look more beautiful. Suddenly I found that I had tears in my eyes. If I'd gone to Australia, I might never have seen all this again – but I knew I was also mourning the end of an important part of my life as well as being deeply moved by my homecoming.

Call up

My mother was in the vegetable garden when I arrived home. When she looked up and saw me, she gave a cry. 'Ivek! Lujzek told me you'd gone over the border. I thought I'd lost you for ever. What are you doing here?' She hugged me hard and long and then pulled me inside and sat me down at the kitchen table. 'I'll make coffee. Tell me all about everything.'

I gave her a shortened version of the 'escape' and she laughed when I described my meeting with Adalbert. 'You two!' she exclaimed. 'Both of you have always been awkward.'

'Now tell me about yourself, Mama. How are you?'

'Not as young as I was and now I've only got Stjepan at home, I'm finding the farm and vineyard a bit much.'

'Perhaps you should employ someone to come in and help. Once I get a job, I'll be able to send you some money towards it.' Before she could reply, Stjepan came in so I had to tell my story all over again while we ate mama's special salad for lunch. I promised to stay and help for a few weeks, starting with spraying the vines the next day.

Later I walked to the next village to pick up the materials for spraying. On the way back I met many of my old friends. Several of them were already married and a couple even had small children. How different their lives were from mine. I couldn't imagine being 'settled for life' as they seemed to be.

That first evening, as I was standing outside enjoying the cool air, I heard my name. It was Marica calling to me from her garden. My heart lurched as, in a rush, I remembered our magical summer. I took a steadying breath as she walked over to me.

'How are you, Marica?' I asked.

She pulled a face. 'All right, I suppose. Rather bored though.' She smiled at me. 'Mirko's not up to much…you know what I mean. By the time he gets home in the evening and has had a meal he's so tired he goes straight to bed – to sleep.'

In that instant I realised that I didn't want to get involved with Marica again. It had been amazing, she'd taught me so much but that was all in the past when I had been no more than a boy. I laughed awkwardly, 'It will be better in the winter when Mirko gets home earlier,' I said and was grateful that Mama called me in at that moment.

I sprayed the vines the next day and, in the days that followed, helped in the corn fields and with harvesting the vegetables. I often wondered about Ostoja and, a week into my stay, I received two letters. I recognised Ostoja's handwriting on the envelope of one of them and opened it first.

I've been staying with my family, he wrote. *It was good to see them all again especially my father.*

I received my call-up papers just after I arrived home. I went for the medical but did not pass. They took no notice of how fit I am but were only concerned about my lack of toes! I can't say I mind very much because I have managed to get a job at 'Visoko' again. The director was impressed by all I learned at Almeria and has offered me the same salary as I was receiving there.

I've got a beautiful new girlfriend. Her name is Vanja. I often think about our mad escapade over the border and back again. It seems like a story – as if it happened to two other people! I hope you are well and will get another job but, of course, you'll be off to the navy soon. Let me know how you get on…

The second letter was notice of the start of my military service in two weeks time. There was a list of toiletries I would need and instructions to buy a kitbag too, in which to carry my belongings. The kitbag had to be clearly labelled with my name and address. I felt a surge of excitement. At last my ambition was to be realised…the ambition I had held since my first trip on the sea, on the ferry to Brac Island, when I was 13 years old.

I replied to Ostoja's letter, telling of my impending military service and I worked hard in the fields for the next fortnight but took one day off to visit my grandmother. She had never seen the sea but had heard of pirates and shipwrecks. 'God bless and keep you and bring you safely home again,' she said as she kissed me and slipped some cash into my hand. 'I'll pray for you every day.'

On the last Tuesday in August 1960 I kissed Mama and shook hands with Stjepan. Mama clung to me and cried as she usually did when I left home. I promised to write, disentangled myself and, slinging the kitbag on my shoulder, set off for Pregrada. As I walked through my village and the next, people, recognising the kitbag as a sign that I was off to sea, called out to me,

'God Bless, Ivan.'

'Come back safely.'

'Good luck.'

I felt as if I were entering upon an adventure. I wished Ostoja could start it with me but I dismissed the thought. Nothing was going to spoil the start of this new phase of my life.

When John was telling me about his life during this period, he suddenly stopped and said, 'You've no idea what it was like to be looking over your shoulder all the time. There were always people prepared to denounce you as a trouble-maker – not just the secret police but ordinary people who you met socially or at work and who would to anything to get a bit of credit for themselves.' Among the most dangerous of these people, it appears, were members of 'Workers' Councils'. These groups had been set up in work places in 1949 and, as Ivan was aware when he worked at Almeria, they were ideally placed to seek out and denounce dissidents.

My research for this book revealed that there was a demonstration of national solidarity by Zagreb students, in May 1959. This could have been the demonstration in which Ivan became involved – when the army refused to attack the students and Ivan was chased by a policeman.

Vesligaj
1960-1963: aged 20-23 years

The Navy at Last

At the large military reception hall in Pregrada, I signed in and was directed to wait in the yard for military transport to Zagreb. 'From there you'll go to Pula by train,' said the officer at the desk. The yard was full of young men many with girlfriends or wives, some of whom carried babies or held the hands of young children. I recognised two lads with whom I'd been to school when I lived at Father Josip's house. It was good to see some familiar faces and even better when I discovered they were naval recruits too. One of them, Željko, had his arm round his wife who was sobbing.

A grey coach arrived and an officer stood on its steps and called for silence. 'This coach is for border guard and naval recruits,' he shouted and he read a list of names, including ours.

'Ivan, look after Željko for me,' sobbed his wife as we climbed aboard.

'I'll do my best,' I said and Željiko looked embarrassed when I grinned at him.

We arrived at Zagreb at 5 pm. The border guard contingent was taken to catch a train to Serbia where they would embark on their training. It would include guarding the border in the way Ostoja and I had observed during our 'escape'. I was extremely pleased that I had not been chosen to carry out that monotonous task.

'Our train doesn't leave for Pula until 10 pm,' said our officer to the three of us who were left. 'We'll go to the military waiting room and get something to eat.'

Some naval recruits had already arrived in the waiting room and more joined us during the evening. When we finally boarded the train our group filled two coaches. Some of the men were the worse for drink and there was so much noise that it was impossible to sleep properly. Željko and I sat together and dozed.

'Right you lot. Wake up and get out.' We were jerked to consciousness by a petty officer throwing the door open and shouting. We grabbed our kitbags and bundled out to be faced by a line of petty officers every one of whom, to my bleary eyes, looked grim. Each held a file. The first in the line called out a list of names including mine and the names of my two friends.

'You're my lot. Get into twos and follow me.' We were taken to the naval barracks where straw mattresses were placed around the walls. 'More recruits will be joining you tomorrow,' the officer said. 'Leave your kitbags and come to the canteen for breakfast. You can rest for the remainder of the day as you were travelling all night. Tomorrow the real business will start. I'll collect you from here at 10.00 hours for another medical. Make sure you're ready.'

Over the next few days I turned gradually from a civilian into a member of the navy and I was delighted with the process. I passed the medical and was given my kit (one working, one white and one winter uniform, underclothes, socks, boots, shoes and a blue naval kitbag.) I felt very smart when we changed into whites. Now I'm really in the navy, I thought. We shed the remnants of our old selves when we packed our civvies into the kitbags we had brought and watched as they were loaded into a truck, to be delivered to our homes. I had no regrets about this. I was ready to start my new life.

After the third day of drill practice a warrant officer told us, 'You will now go for your final medical tests. The results of these together with the level of education you have reached will determine which trade you are assigned to.'

The medical consisted of hearing, sight and lung capacity tests. I wasn't anxious about my results. I really didn't mind which trade I was chosen for. I simply wanted to sail away on a ship and see the world. When the lists were posted up my name was on the 'Communications and Signals' list and Zeljko's was on the one for the Catering Corps. I was excited to learn that I would be trained in radio transmitting, Morse code and semaphore communications as well as in the use of radar. I'd always loved studying and had missed it since leaving the polytechnic. Here's my chance to learn more, I thought, and vowed to do my best to excel.

The next day I, along with the fifteen other communications recruits, was told to pack my kit and go to the quay side. About sixteen more men joined us there. We were to sail round the Istrian peninsular to Lovran for our specialist training.

As I shook hands with Željko, I wished him luck. 'I'm sorry I won't be able to look after you for your wife,' I laughed, 'but I'm sure you'll manage without me. Maybe we'll meet on board sometime and you can cook me a tasty meal.' As it happened our paths never crossed again.

Aboard the naval ferry, I leant over the side and felt the sea breeze on my face. I saw the silvery wake as the ship cut through the water. I let my mind wander over all that had happened in last couple of months. I planned what I would tell Ostoja in my next letter. 'I've done it,' I said to myself. I was exhilarated by thoughts of what was to come. I hadn't felt so happy for a long time.

Training 1: Lovran

It was evening when we arrived at Lovran. We disembarked and were greeted by the orders,

'Line up! Get into twos! Left turn!' A number of NCOs hustled us into position. The one at the front shouted, 'Quick march!' and in a surprisingly short time we were marching in an orderly way towards the naval training college. Just before we 'right turned' away from the coast, I saw a number of long rowing boats tied up in the quay. Each would seat about twelve men.

'I wonder what they're for,' I muttered to the man marching next to me.

A sharp-eared leading seaman nearby laughed. 'You'll find out,' he said. 'While you're here, you'll learn what real exercise is.'

We marched past a big, gated entrance with armed guards on either side. The next gate was opened for us. We passed through and, as the gate clanged behind us, I remembered the noise of other closing gates – at Bol, at the prison – but this time I felt no fear. I felt glad anticipation at this next step in achieving my ambition.

We halted in the parade ground. Tall masts flanked two sides of it, each with a light at the top but before I could speculate on their use, we were ordered to leave our kitbags and follow the leading seaman to the canteen. I noticed there was a high wall round the perimeter of the complex with watchtowers on each of the four corners. A number of buildings stood within the walls.

After a meal, we picked up our bags and marched to the dormitory block. My room was on the second of three floors. As I walked along the corridor towards it, I saw that each room had a rack outside and some of these contained rifles. The rack by my room was empty. The room had three bunks and there was already a lad there when I opened the door. He was tall and dark and turned to me with a wide smile. 'I'm Milan,' he said. I liked the look of him. He wasn't Ostoja but I felt instinctively that we would be friends. Later, I discovered that he came from a farming family outside Belgrade. Essentially, our backgrounds were similar but he hadn't had the opportunities of education and travel that I'd had.

The leading seaman had told us to leave our bags in the rooms and report back to the parade ground. Our first duty, on that first day of our training, was to clear every speck of rubbish from the grounds of the establishment.

'Every matchstick and cigarette butt must be cleared. Understand?' he shouted. When we'd finished, he dismissed us. 'You've got some free time now to acquaint yourselves with where you'll be living for the next six months. Lights out at 22.00 hours. You'll hear the bugle.'

Milan and I walked round our new home. We found two lecture theatres, a library and several locked rooms.

'Signalling equipment is kept in there,' said a passing seaman. 'You'll get to use it soon.'

We were both quite tired and got into our bunks early but at about midnight I woke with a sickening start to the sound of a siren. I guessed there must be some sort of emergency and I sat bolt upright.

'What's that?' Milan mumbled, half awake.

'Come on, grab some clothes. We must get outside now,' I said.

Dragging our work uniforms on, we stumbled downstairs and on to the parade ground. Three military trucks were parked to the side and one of the officers hurried us into three groups.

A loudspeaker crackled and a voice addressed us, 'Go to the truck closest to your group. You will be given a shovel. Tonight you will become fire fighters.'

In our lorry, the petty officer told us we were going to the *Mošćenića Draga* Forest. 'The fire brigade at Rijeka has called for our services,' he said. Police waited for us on the main road. They drove ahead, blue lights flashing, sirens screaming.

As we approached the forest, we were enveloped in smoke. The truck stopped, we jumped out and were immediately shown where to dig a trench.

'It will act as a fire stop,' said a fire officer. 'Throw the earth you move on to the other side of the trench to damp down any sparks.'

We spread out and started digging. In front of us, fire officers were spraying flames with sea water. We dug steadily for two hours. Everything had a strange, other- worldly quality – the billowing smoke, the hiss of steam, the orange licks of crackling flames, the heat and dirt and above all the thick, choking atmosphere. I thought that hell must be like this and hoped I wouldn't end up there.

At last, after about two hours, the flames had subsided and we were told we could stop digging. Wearily we walked back to the trucks.

'Thank you lads,' the chief fire officer shouted. 'We couldn't have managed without you.'

We laughed at each other's black hands and faces as we climbed aboard. 'Your own mothers wouldn't recognise you,' said the petty officer. 'When you get back, put your uniforms for wash, shower yourselves and then grab a few hours sleep. Reveille's at 06.00 hours remember.'

Reveille came too soon. We had been told to report to the parade ground, stripped to the waist. 'You'll soon be fit,' the officer said. 'Exercise is what you all need.'

'Exercise' took about an hour and a half. We ran along the road to a path which led us up a mountain to a plateau. There we stretched and bent every part of the body – or so it seemed to me. Then, sweaty and tired, we ran back to camp for a shower and breakfast. Exercise took the same form every morning of the first months of our stay at the training camp. On cold days, steam was rising from our bodies by the time we arrived on the mountain. I found the sessions became easier as time went on but I'll always remember the feeling of exhaustion that first time. I quickly noticed that Milan excelled at all exercise. I was fit but he was fitter and actually seemed to enjoy our morning physical routine. Later in our training, we exchanged exercise on land for rowing the long boats I'd noticed on my first march to the camp. Twelve of us to a boat, we soon became very competitive and our fitness improved even further.

I forgot my tiredness, that first day, with the excitement of being given a firearm. It was a Thompson submachine gun. Milan was given an MP automatic rifle and most of the others in our group had ordinary rifles.

'Each of your guns has a serial number,' said the leading seaman. 'Learn it by heart. You are entirely responsible for the care of your weapon and for the safety of the people around you when you are carrying or firing it. Now go and place it in the rack outside your room. Those of you with submachine guns must use the attached lock and chain to fix them to the rack for extra security. Tomorrow you will learn how to dismantle and clean your guns and have a lesson on the firing range.'

After lunch we were told about our syllabus and were given a schedule. The lieutenant finished by saying, 'For the first month of your training you are confined to barracks except for supervised exercise. Next week you will start guard duties. Most of the time you will be in the watchtowers but occasionally you'll be on duty by the small gate on the path which leads to the ammunition store. If you are there at night and you hear anything to alarm you or if you see an intruder, don't stop to ask any questions, just fire. There are plenty of warning notices around that area. There is no excuse for anyone to stray into it. We cannot afford a break-in to the store so the rule is, 'Fire'.' I had reason to remember this instruction later.

I will never forget my first day on the firing range. We had been taught the theory, now was the time to put it into practice. We took up our firing positions three at a time and, on the order, fired at the targets. We took it in turns to record the efforts of each marksman and, in order to do this, we sat in a bunker behind the targets, about 20 metres to the right of them. When each set of three had finished firing our job was to run from the bunker, make a note of where each bullet had hit the target and then retreat once more to the dug-out where we were safe behind a big pile of soil and gravel. I had just taken shelter and firing had started when the petty officer next to me swore. 'My God, a bullet has just hit my hat'.

Before I could say anything, I heard a whistle and my hat flew off too. A bullet was embedded in the front – just above where my head had been.

'Telephone!' screamed the petty officer. 'Cease fire!'

I grabbed the field telephone which was next to me and shouted into it, 'Cease fire!'

The order was given at the other end of the field and for a moment there was silence. Then an officer came running to find out the problem. Firing practice was halted and an investigation followed. It transpired that one of the rifles had a damaged barrel which accounted for the angle at which its bullets travelled. The petty officer and I had had a lucky escape.

I had another escape a few weeks later, again connected with a firearm. We were on a joint exercise with the army. The army post was about half a kilometre ahead of us and our task was to capture it, hiding in bushes and crawling through long grass. We had been issued with blank bullets and were making good headway when some members of the army team started firing.

We retaliated and amidst the noise of the dummy bullets, there was suddenly a different sound. Something whizzed past me, a few inches to my right, and disappeared into the ground. I looked at the grass next to me and could see a trail scored through it. I was sure a live bullet had been fired. I didn't hesitate. We had been told that, in an emergency, we should fire in the air and I did, several times. There were shouts of 'Cease fire' from both posts and, as before, there was that uncanny silence.

An officer was soon by my side. 'What do you think you're doing? You'd better have a damned good excuse.'

'I was almost hit by a live bullet, sir,' I said.

'Are you sure?'

'Yes, sir.'

'Where is it?' I showed him the scoring. 'You could be right,' he said. 'See if you can find it.'

I pulled out my bayonet and dug around at the end of the scoring. The point struck metal and I was able to gouge the bullet out. I handed it to the officer.

'Good God!' he exclaimed and handed it to the sergeant who had come to see what was wrong. He turned back to me. 'Are you all right?'

'Yes thank you, sir.' I felt surprisingly cool, considering what had happened.

An enquiry into the bullet incident took place immediately while we were still on the 'battle field'. We were ordered to stand in line and empty our bullet pouches.

Live bullets were found in the possession of a member of the army – a Kosovan. He was marched away and the rest of us were dismissed. I often wonder whether he used live bullets on purpose or whether the quartermaster had handed them to him by mistake.

Afterwards, Milan teased me about having a charmed life and later, as I lay in bed, the full impact of my two close brushes with death hit me. I'd certainly been lucky. I smiled at the thought that some sort of guardian angel had followed me from Bol Monastery. I hoped he or she would continue to look out for me. I said a quick, silent prayer of thanks for my escapes.

Our training in Morse code, was soon underway. We learned to recognise which signals were urgent and Milan and I passed the Morse examination at the end of two months. After that we were taught how to operate the radio system and practised sending and receiving Morse messages by radio. We were also shown how to send Morse signals by Aldis lamp and by using the light at the top of a mast. Our next challenge was learning the semaphore system and, finally, we had a course on interpreting radar signals. It was not long before we could detect the height, distance and speed of ships which appeared on the radar screen. I was happy to be studying once more. I worked hard and passed all the tests. I was very eager to put my newly acquired knowledge into action on a ship.

Ivan practising semaphore

Although I'd written to Ostoja a couple of times, giving my address, there had been no reply. I often thought about him and wrote again but nothing came back from him. I never heard from Ostoja again. Through the years I've wondered why and speculated on what could have happened to him. We had been such good friends, had so many experiences together and he had been determined to stay in touch. His silence remains a sad mystery.

At the end of our first month, with just 100 dinars wages in our pockets, Milan and I polished our boots, showered and put on our whites.

'I hate this uniform,' Milan groaned, not for the first time. 'I feel like a bride, dressed all in white.' It's not manly. I wish I'd been recruited to the army. Now that *has* got a manly uniform.'

Ivan and Milan who is in a borrowed army uniform

I laughed at him and called him vain as we went to pick up our passes from the petty officer. We were going out for the evening. Our only sight of girls for four long weeks had been from the watchtowers when we were on duty. We saw the young women as they passed the camp on the way to or from a nearby sardine factory. They took pleasure in teasing us. 'Hello Sailor,' they'd call. 'You're very handsome. How would you like a date?' We couldn't respond in any way at all but had to stare fixedly to the front, not allowing even a smile.

'Hands!' barked the petty officer. We held out our hands for his inspection. When he was satisfied that they were clean, he checked behind our ears. 'You'll do' he said. 'Remember to be back by 22.00 hours.'

We caught a bus to Opatija, the resort where a former Austro-Hungarian Emperor had had his summer retreat. It was a fashionable holiday destination with expensive hotels and restaurants overlooking the sea. We sauntered along the prom, enjoying the admiring glances and comments from the groups of girls who were taking the air. We knew we looked good in our spotless whites.

'Let's buy a drink and watch the world go by,' I said and we selected one of the more modest bars facing the beach and sat outside under its awning. I felt a deep sense of contentment that I'd come this far in my ambition to go to sea. 'Only five more months and we'll be off,' I said. We ordered beers and drank them very slowly, talking about all we'd learned so far and about our fellow trainees. We began to realise that being in the navy was an enormous social asset. Hardly anyone passed by without exchanging a remark or a smile with us. Young women, particularly, hung back to talk and flirt.

'I'm glad I chose the navy after all, if only for the girls,' laughed Milan.

The time sped by and when I looked at my watch, it was 21.40. 'Milan, we've only got twenty minutes to get back to camp!' I cried, leaping up from the table. I couldn't believe we'd been so stupid. I'd been determined to have a spotless naval record and now we'd be in trouble after our very first outing. 'Come on, we might do it if we get a bus straight away.'

We sprinted to the bus stop but no bus was due for half an hour. We started to run in the direction of camp although we knew it was hopeless as we could never cover the distance in time.

'Let's try to hitch a lift as we run,' I said. 'It's our only hope.' Several vehicles passed us but then, miraculously, a smart little red, open-topped, sports car pulled up just ahead.

'Where to boys?' an American voice called. In the car, two beautiful young women had turned to watch as we ran up to them.

'Lovran Naval College, five kilometres ahead,' I gasped.

'We've got to be back by ten,' Milan added.

The driver laughed. 'We'll do it easy. Hop in the back. It'll be a bit of a squash. Hold on to your hats!'

Unable to believe our luck, we squashed into the luggage space, took off our hats and then we were away.

I had never been in a sports car, never travelled so fast. It was thrilling, it felt dangerous. 'I'll have one of these some day,' I shouted to Milan against the rush of wind and the roar of the engine.

At the camp, we leapt from the car and shouted our thanks to the girls. They waved and laughed. Replacing our hats, we raced through the gate with exactly one minute to spare.

'You lucky beggars!' said the guard. 'Your first time out and you meet a couple of gorgeous girls with a sports car. Some people get all the luck.'

We were turning away, laughing at our adventure, when the officer on duty called us back. 'Who were those girls?' Milan opened his mouth to answer but I broke in first.

'Just a couple of wealthy Croatians we met in a café,' I lied. I'd remembered we'd been forbidden to fraternise with foreigners. This, however, had been an emergency,

After that we didn't go as far afield during our time off. We made do with a couple of pleasant local parks. There we met a variety of girls, some of whom worked at the sardine factor. They brought tins of sardines to supplement our rations. Neither Milan nor I wanted any sort of serious relationship at this point. We simply made friends with some of the girls, drinking a beer or two with them and occasionally visiting local discos.

One night in January 1961, I was alone on guard duty near the ammunition store. It was a clear, cold, black night. There was a scattering of snow and I was standing in the sentry box, sheltering from the bitter wind. Suddenly I heard a noise among the trees at the edge of the forest which bordered the path. 'It's just the wind,' I told myself although my heart pumped hard.

The faint rustle became louder, dead leaves crunched underfoot and a shape loomed out of the darkness a few meters from me. I remembered my instructions and my stomach lurched. 'It's him or me,' I thought and fired. There was a crash and I saw an upward spray of snow as my victim fell with a thump. He made no other sound. I couldn't move. It seemed as if my feet had frozen into the snow.

Almost immediately two officers and a relief guard were by my side. One of them shouted the password. 'Don't look,' he said to me, realising I was a raw recruit. 'Go to the guardroom, warm yourself up, have a drink and a rest. I'll be in to see you directly.'

Gratefully I obeyed and as I walked away one of the officers, who had been to look at my victim, called to me, 'It's a donkey, lad. No need to worry. It was a good shot. It's dead.'

My knees went weak with relief. I was sorry to kill a donkey but glad, beyond measure, that it wasn't a man.

That morning, as we ran out of camp for exercise, we were halted by our instructor. An old farmer was blocking the gateway. 'My donkey! What am I going to do without my donkey? I demand compensation,' he shouted. 'I need compensation now or I'll sue the lot of you.'

The instructor spoke calmly to him and left one of the guards to look after him. I heard later that the farmer had been given the cost of two donkeys so he did very well out of my first shot, fired in earnest. I did, however, feel guilty about the poor donkey.

As the end of our communications training approached there was much discussion, between ourselves, about where we would be posted. Everyone wanted to go to a ship but we knew that many of us would be sent to land bases. We asked one of the leading seamen when we would know our fate.

'You'll have to wait until the last day,' he said. 'You'll be told at the time your new uniform is issued. I'll give you a clue. You'll know as soon as you see your allocation of uniform items. If you're given shoes and a belt with an anchor buckle, you'll be off to sea. If it's boots and a plain buckle then you'll be working on land.'

'Whatever happens, we'll keep in touch,' I said to Milan.

On the last morning we were marched into the stores. Our names were called in turn. Milan went to the issuing table before me. I saw the warrant officer hand him his new kit topped by two pairs of boots. He turned to me, disappointed. 'Land posting – to the island of Vis.'

'I've heard it's beautiful there,' I tried to cheer him up.

'It may be beautiful,' he replied, 'but I joined the navy to go to sea.'

'Vesligaj!' I heard my name. I snapped to attention and marched forward. I saw two pairs of black shoes with my uniform. My spirit soared. I was bound for a ship!

'Your posting is to M143,' the warrant officer told me. 'You leave this afternoon at 15.00 hours.'

I felt a slight dip in my delight. My posting was to a mine sweeper, a small ship, I had hoped for a gloriously big destroyer. I knew I was fortunate, though. It could have been a lot worse.

Milan and I went to our room to pack. We had been shown how to pack our belongings into the kitbag in a cuboid shape. If we got it right, our uniforms would arrive at our destinations uncreased. As we struggled with the technique, I said to Milan, 'I'm sorry you're going to a land base. Why don't you give it a month or two on Vis and then ask for a transfer to a ship?'

'Do you think they'd consider it?'

'It's worth a try.'

Milan was to travel part of the way with me. At 15.00 hours and accompanied by a petty officer, we left camp by jeep. We three were dropped off at Rijeka. From there we travelled by boat to Zadar and on to Šibenik, arriving at 03.00 hours. Milan was to stay on the boat so we said our goodbyes on board. As we shook hands, he said, 'I'll do what you suggested. I'll ask for a transfer in a bit. Perhaps we'll meet again soon.'

A lieutenant from the mine sweeper squadron came on board to collect me and I gave Milan a last wave. It was a forty five minute walk from the harbour to the minesweeper base but excitement blotted out tiredness. At last I was really on my way to join a ship.

Minesweeper: M143

'Straight to bed for you, lad,' the night duty officer said when we arrived on M143. 'Follow me.'

He took me down steps, along a short corridor and into a dimly lit cabin. There were eight bunks, ranged along two sides. Sounds of snores and deep breathing met me as I stood at the door. The bottom bunk, nearest the door, was empty except for a blanket and pillow. 'Hop in there,' said the officer. 'Get some kip before you have to get up again.'

He disappeared and I pulled off my outer clothes, pushed my kitbag under the bunk and lay down. I could feel the movement of the ship in the water and lay listening to the strange noises, clicks and creaks and the roar of the sea. I felt sure I was too excited to sleep... I knew no more until a shout of 'Everybody out!' woke me with a start.

I struggled to sit up and noticed that the other men were pulling on shorts. One of them, realising I was new, called to me, 'Exercise time. We go on shore.'

Within a few minutes, everyone was ready. The bunks converted easily into bench seats and kitbags were stowed under them. We trooped on deck and were led down the gangplank to the dock-side. The officer lined us up, making sure new members of the crew were at the back.

'Just follow the men in front,' he instructed and we were off. It was a long circuit, going inland, up and down a steep hill and finally doubling back to the ship. After breakfast I joined other new arrivals on deck for our orders of the day.

A leading seaman spoke to us first. 'To you new men,' he barked, 'I want you to know that while you are on this ship I am your father, your mother, your sister and your brother. If you have any questions or find yourself in trouble of any kind, you come to me. Understand?'

A few of us nodded and mumbled, 'Yes, sir.' Secretly, I hoped I would never have resort to going to him for anything.

A pleasant-faced lieutenant had come on deck and called my name. I stepped forward and, to my surprise, he shook my hand and introduced himself as Lieutenant Ćiril. 'I am the chief communications officer aboard,' he said. 'You will be working for me. We are a team of two.'

Now the captain appeared and introduced himself as Captain Dušan Račić, commander of the squadron of minesweepers moored at Šibenik. Lieutenant Ćiril saluted and said, 'This is Seaman Ivan Vesligaj. He arrived from Lovran at 03.00 hours. He will be working as my communications officer, sir.' The captain and I exchanged salutes and the lieutenant turned to me. 'Come with me now and I'll show you the ropes.' He was a softly spoken man and I knew I would like working for him.

He showed me where the Aldis lamp and semaphore flags were stored then he took me to the tiny radio and radar cabins. 'You'll be working mainly in one of these two cabins,' he said. 'There's heating when it's cold and if you want to leave any of your gear in here, you're welcome. It will be quite safe as only you and I are allowed in. I want you to put into practice all the techniques you have learned and to listen in to the radio as often as you can. Learn the codes of the ships, gather all the news, make notes of everything you hear and pass them to me. You'll join the rest of the crew for exercise ashore each morning and, twice a week, while we are in Šibenik, you will do a shift there.' (He pointed to our neighbouring minesweeper.) 'M142 is bigger than we are. She has a higher bridge and more sophisticated communication equipment.'

I couldn't wait to start work and did so immediately. It was thrilling for me to use my radio skills on a real ship but my officer had other plans for the afternoon. He called me out of the radio room and pointed to a large concrete building alongside the docks. 'I'm taking you there now to meet some officers who work for counter intelligence. Their headquarters is in Split but they're here in Šibenik at the moment. They visit each of the intelligence outposts from time to time. I won't say any more.'

We walked briskly to the building and were obviously expected for we were shown to an office straight away. The lieutenant knocked on the door. 'Come in,' someone called and we entered.

Three men rose as we walked through the door and salutes were exchanged. Lieutenant Ćiril introduced me and an officer called Jože Polajžar, who seemed to be in charge, invited us to sit down.

'Vesligaj,' he said, 'you are in an excellent position to eavesdrop when you listen in on the radio. You'll hear conversations and signals. Our radio room here gets a great deal of interference so we will rely on you to make a note of everything you hear – even if it seems insignificant to you. Make a note and then radio it to us.' What he said was simply endorsing what my lieutenant had already told me but it carried more weight, seemed more serious, here in the counter intelligence building.

On our way back to the ship, Lieutenant Ćiril asked, 'Well, what do you think of them?'

'They seem all right,' I said guardedly.

'Just be careful what you say to them,' he laughed. 'You can never trust a spy.'

I enjoyed my work very much and, for the first time, I was able to listen to western music. I loved it. I particularly liked *The Beatles, The Who* and *Pink Floyd*. I also listened to the BBC World Service. I was fascinated to hear about world affairs from a 'free' broadcasting station – one unaffected by communist censorship and propaganda.

Each evening, after tea, we gathered on deck with the political education officer. He would tell us what he knew of the latest news and we were allowed to ask questions. One evening, the subject was the war in Algeria. We were told about the ongoing struggle between France and the Algerian rebels who wanted independence for their country. One of the sailors asked, 'Who's leading the rebels?'

There was a pause and then the PEO admitted he didn't know. 'I'll find out for you,' he promised.

As it happened I had heard a programme about the Algerian war that morning and, unable to restrain myself, I said, 'I know who one of the leaders is, sir.'

'Do you? Who?'

'Ahmed Ben Bella, sir.'

'What do you know about him?' I was embarrassed. Suddenly I was afraid that everybody would think I was showing off. I hesitated. 'Go on Vesligaj,' the PEO said encouragingly.

'Well, sir, I think there is more than one group of rebels in Algeria but Ben Bella leads the most important one, the National Liberation Front. He was arrested by the French in 1956 and is still in prison.'

'How do you know all this?'

I thought quickly. I didn't want to admit I'd been listening to western news broadcasts in case I was stopped. 'I saw it in a newspaper in a pub, sir,' I lied.

Half an hour after the end of the lesson, the PEO came to find me. 'The captain wants to speak to you. Come with me to his cabin.'

'Sit down, Vesligaj,' the captain said. His cabin was tiny and there was barely room for the three of us. I noticed, at once, that my files were open on the captain's desk. 'I see from your records that you have had a good education also I understand that you are abreast of current affairs.'

'Of some of them, sir,' I said, feeling awkward.

'Well, I've decided to make you the new PEO, Vesligaj. Every evening you will be responsible for bringing the crew up to date with the latest news.' I was astonished and looked at the man who until now had had the job.

He was smiling and said, 'Don't worry about me. I suggested this to the captain.'

'I'll do my best, sir' was all I could say as the captain dismissed me. From now on, listening to the World Service was going to be very important.

On our fifth day in Šibenik, the captain gave orders for the mine sweeper squadron to sail to Split on an exercise. I had a chance to use the Morse code and semaphore to ensure our safe passage out of the harbour and into Split. We saw Marshal Tito's luxurious liner there. I heard that he had an elite naval crew but that he, himself, was not on board at that time. We stayed in Split for two days and I gazed for some time at the Island of Brač. I couldn't see the monastery, it was on the far side of the island, but I could imagine the quiet monks bent over the ancient biblical texts, in prayer or instructing the boys. In my mind's eye I could see the boys, themselves, working at Latin and ingesting bromide with their soup.

Leaving Split, we went to Zadar via Šibenik. Ćiril came up behind me as I was looking at the incredible view from the deck. A string of islands seemed to shimmer in front of me, washed round by a crystal clear, aqua sea.

'There are over three hundred islands, mostly uninhabited,' he said. 'They are the remains of what was a mountain chain.'

We were given shore leave so, after swimming and sunbathing, I decided to use the rest of the leisure time to sharpen my semaphore skills and Lieutenant Ćiril offered to help me. Soon I was able to send and receive signals very fast – too fast for some communication officers.

I was surprised and pleased to get my first promotion at about this time. I became Leading Seaman Vesligaj. I think the captain was impressed by the record of my education and pleased that I had agreed to be PEO. My new rank brought with it the responsibility for the ship's canteen. This was a cupboard which contained alcohol, and cigarettes. I had the key and officers came to me when they wished to buy goods. I took the money and kept a careful record of everything I sold. Seamen and NCOs had an allowance of rum and cigarettes daily. I usually sold my   rum – or gave it away and did the same with my surplus cigarettes.

One evening I was leaning on the rail of the deck looking at a particularly dramatic sunset, when I saw a soldier approach the guard on the gangway. 'Vesligaj!' bawled the guard. 'There's a man here, asking for you.'

It was Leopold, nicknamed Poldi, who was distantly related to me, and lived in my village. His family owned the vineyard next to ours. It was good to see him and we shook hands. 'I heard you were on a minesweeper,' he said. 'I thought I'd ask the guard about you, on the off chance. Will you come for a drink?'

'I'd like to. I'll see if I can get an evening pass from the officer.' I went to see Lieutenant Ćiril and explained. 'Make it until midnight, sir,' I pleaded, 'not 22.00.' He obliged with a smile.

We sat over a beer and talked about the village. Poldi told me the news of our old school friends and we swapped stories about our military training. After a while we realised that a disco was about to begin in the adjoining room and we decided to go and try our luck with the girls.

That evening I became aware of a phenomenon which I was to see again and again during my time in the navy. Girls did not like dancing with soldiers but they loved to dance with sailors. I never discovered whether this was because of the colour or texture of the army uniforms, whether it was to do with the romance of a life at sea or whether sailors are just better looking than soldiers. I only know that girls clamoured to dance with me that evening. The next night they were just as keen to dance with my shipmates whereas Poldi and his army colleagues were continually turned down by the fair maidens of Zadar.

A couple of days later we sailed out of the harbour bound for Šibenik. I was in the radio cabin when I picked up an urgent message. A mine had been sighted by the crew of a leisure cruiser. It was off one of the Kornati islands and as Ćiril wasn't around, I wrote down the co-ordinates and ran on to the bridge to tell the captain. He sounded the alarm and gave directions for a change of course. He instructed the men who operated the guns to be ready to fire at the mine. As we approached the Kornati islands, a group of us were on deck scanning the area with binoculars.

'I see it!' someone shouted and soon it was just visible to the naked eye.

'It's a strange mine,' the captain said, 'where are its "horns"?' He was right. The top of the object was smooth with no sign of the characteristic chargers.

'Fire!' the order was given.

After the thunder of the guns, there was an eerie silence and then, a short distance from where the 'mine' had been, pieces of wood floated to the surface and we could see that they were parts of a barrel. There was general laughter and the captain said, 'It doesn't matter. It's been good practice. Vesligaj, send a radio message to the tour company saying that the object they reported has been dealt with.' He turned away to issue orders for our swift return to Šibenik.

Lifeguard

While I was learning my trade, at Lovran, I had taken the opportunity to train as a lifeguard. The day after our return from the mine sweeping exercise, the crews of M143 and M144 were scheduled to swim at a beach set aside for naval personnel. I was tasked with assembling the sailors on the dockside and calling the roll. An officer, Lieutenant Kaufman, was to accompany us. He appointed me and a seaman, who also had lifeguard qualifications as official lifeguards for the afternoon. Just as I was about to report that everyone was present, one of my friends from M143, Marinko Peps, stepped forward to speak to me.

'Please may I be excused from swimming this afternoon?' he said.

I was surprised. He was our strongest swimmer and I'd never known him to miss a session before. 'Why don't you want to swim, Marinko?' I asked.

'I don't feel at all well.'

I looked at him. He didn't look pale and he had attended the exercise session that morning. On the other hand, I knew him to be honest and not one to shirk. 'I'm sorry, I can't make the decision,' I said. 'I'll ask Lieutenant Kaufman if you can be excused.'

'He's the best swimmer in the squadron,' Kaufman said sharply when I asked about Marinko. 'What's wrong with him?'

'He says he doesn't feel at all well, sir.'

The officer looked across at Marinko. 'He looks all right to me,' he said.

'I'm sure he's genuinely ill,' I insisted. 'It's not like him to lie.'

'I disagree, Vesligaj. The man will swim with the rest of the crews. Everyone will swim. Do you understand?'

'Yes sir.' I knew I'd said all I could and, unhappily, I reported my conversation to Marinko.

It was a glorious day and the sea reflected the deep blue of the sky. The water was glistening and clear. Soon everyone was in the water and I took a seat on a rock, a little out to sea, so that I could watch out for anyone in difficulties.

Before long I became aware of someone waving and then disappearing under water. I jumped into the sea immediately and swam quickly to where I had spotted the trouble. I was in time to catch hold of Marinko as he rose to the surface. I took him in the life-saving hold and started to swim for shore. 'What's wrong?' I asked.

'I suddenly got the most terrible pain in my chest. It was so bad that I couldn't swim,' he said. 'It's easing a bit now.'

When we reached the beach, I helped Marinko to a flat rock. 'Sit there and rest,' I said. 'Don't move. I'll be back in a few minutes. I need to tell Lieutenant Kaufman what has happened. Just stay there.'

I couldn't find Kaufman but I checked all was well with the swimmers and explained to the other lifeguard that I wouldn't be on duty for a while. I hurried back to where I'd left Marinko only to find that he had disappeared. I was angry and turned to a sailor who was standing nearby. 'Where did the man I left here go? Did you see?' I asked.

'No, sorry, I didn't. I heard you tell him to stay there but I didn't notice him going.' At that moment I saw Lieutenant Kaufman and hurried over to him. I explained what had happened.

He swore and said, 'We'd better have a roll call. I'll give the signal for it and if the wretched man doesn't turn up we'll spread out and search.' Marinko wasn't present at the roll call. Somehow I had known he wouldn't be. I also had a horrible feeling that our search would not end well. We found Marinko's pile of clothes but that was all. I said nothing to anyone but I thought that maybe he'd absconded.

Back on board, the captain informed the Military Police of the incident. They, in turn, contacted the police on the Dalmatian island of Mljet which was Marinko's home. The message came back that his parents knew nothing about their son's disappearance and that he had always seemed happy as a member of the navy. The captain reported all this to us, on deck. 'And now we have to consider the worst,' he said quietly. 'We must send frogmen into the water to search for the body of Marinko Peps. Vesligaj and Martin collect your diving equipment. A motor boat will take you to the bay immediately.'

As we came to the bay, I hoped fervently that we wouldn't find Marinko's body. There was a net stretched across the end of the swimming bay, fixed to the headlands which formed its sides. Its purpose was to stop sharks from getting into our swimming area. The boat stopped on the seaward side of the net, we flipped over it and swam to the shore.

We'd agreed to swim backwards and forwards across the bay, meeting half way and then turning back at a narrow angle so that the whole area would be thoroughly searched. This worked well and we'd almost reached the net when I saw a shape spread-eagled against it. At first I thought a shark or other large fish had been caught up in the mesh but, with a sickening lurch, I realised it was a man – Marinko. One hand reached up, tangled in the net as if he were trying to pull himself over. He was completely submerged, he wore a peaceful expression and his eyes were closed as if in sleep. I surfaced and signalled to Martin. He swam over and I warned him of what he was about to see. We didn't say much as we dived, released Marinko's body and tied one end of a rope to the belt of his trunks. Then we swam to the shore, pulling the rope as we went. We carried him on to the sand and laid him down gently. As we did so, he exhaled – a long breath – and then silence. An ambulance had been waiting on the road above the beach. Now the medics arrived with a stretcher and carried Marinko away. Our work was done. Numbly we re-entered the water and swam to the motor boat. I was exhausted and felt a great emptiness.

It was as I climbed aboard M143 that this empty space was filled with anger. Anger at the callous way Kaufman had refused Marinko's plea to be excused from swimming, at the way he had dismissed my intervention. Kaufman caused Marinko's death, I thought, and could not bring myself to look at him when we reached the ship. We went straight to the captain and told him what had happened. I also related Kaufman's refusal to allow Marinko to miss swimming, trying to keep my voice level.

The captain made no comment but said, 'You'll probably be needed at the inquest but there'll to be a post-mortem first. We'll know more after that. This is a very sad day for us all.' He looked at Martin and me, 'You must be tired. Have something to eat and then go and get a good night's rest.'

I wasn't hungry and I lay awake long into the night. I kept remembering things about Marinko – how he had often seemed extraordinarily tired after exercise sessions, how he was out of breath at the swimming survival course. Why hadn't I remembered all this earlier and told Kaufman? Perhaps I was partly responsible for his death. What had he died of, anyway? The biggest mystery of all was why he had re-entered the sea after my order to stay on the beach. Had he wanted to prove his fitness? Had his brain been affected by whatever caused him to almost drown the first time? In the early hours of the morning, I drifted in and out of sleep jolting awake with the pinioned figure of the drowned Marinko, grotesque, before my eyes.

At 10.00 hours, the captain assembled us on deck. 'I have just received the result of the post-mortem on Marinko Peps,' he said. 'The cause of his death was a heart attack. It is a tragedy that we all feel deeply. Our sympathy is, of course, with his parents and his family. We must immediately return Marinko to his home on the island of Mljet for burial. Six of the crew will accompany the body on a naval torpedo boat. My deputy will be in charge of the procedure. Vesligaj you will be in the group as it was you who found the body...' He named the rest of the funeral party but I had stopped listening. I didn't want to go. I was still shocked and I was shaky from lack of sleep. However, I had to obey orders.

A large group of people met us at the quay side. I immediately picked out the grieving parents; the weeping mother, supported on both sides, the father, pale and grim-faced. Please God Mama will never have to go through such a thing for me, I thought and tears sprang to my eyes as I heard the mother's sobs. The six of us lifted the coffin on to a trolley and slowly wheeled it down the gangway, a short way along the road and into the village church. The sorrowful procession followed. The priest conducted the service and our senior officer, a lieutenant, made a speech about what a fine sailor Marinko had been although I was pretty sure he'd hardly known him. I was in a bitter mood.

Outside the church, an argument broke out. The father was insisting on taking Marinko home for one night before the burial so that relatives, neighbours and friends could call at the house and pay their respects. 'That's not possible,' the lieutenant said firmly. 'Your son died while in service to the navy. In effect, he is naval property.' At this point the sobs of the mother grew louder and I looked at the ground and held my breath for a moment to stop myself joining in. 'The burial must be carried out now while members of the navy are present.' The officer had his way and the coffin was lowered into the ground. A volley of gunshots echoed round the small churchyard followed by the haunting and desperately sad 'Last Post'. Once more I struggled to remain calm but couldn't contain my tears when Marinko's father came to me and grasped my hand.

'Thank you lad, for finding my son and bringing him back to us,' he said. Then he turned round and, pointing at the open grave, addressed our officer in a loud, clear voice. 'When I gave my son to the navy he was a healthy man and look what the navy has sent back to me.' And for the first time, he began to cry – great rasping sobs which were still sounding in my ears as I boarded the boat.

The captain was waiting for us on our return. He shook hands with the six of us and thanked us for representing the ship. 'I'll need to speak to you again in the morning, Vesligaj,' he said. 'But now all of you must get something to eat and then rest. It's been a long and difficult day for you.'

I had another fitful night. This time it was the mother's tears and the sound of the father's sobs that haunted me. After morning exercise, the captain met me on the bridge as I was about to start work. He was talking to Kaufman and the sailor who had overheard the last order I had given to Marinko. 'Ah, Vesligaj,' he said, 'Both of you,' he indicated the other sailor and myself, 'and Lieutenant Kaufman have been summoned to the inquest for Marinko Peps. You have to report to the coroner's office immediately.'

I didn't look at Kaufman and we walked in uneasy silence until, 'What are you going to tell them?' he asked me.

'The truth,' I replied and none of us spoke another word.

I was called first. There were five naval officers sitting behind a long table. I saluted.

'Sit down Leading Seaman Vesligaj,' said one of the officers. 'You are here as a witness. Please tell us everything you know concerning Marinko Peps's death.'

I started at the beginning, from the moment Marinko had asked to be excused from swimming, finishing with his body being put in the ambulance. I left nothing out.

'It seems as if you did everything humanly possible, Vesligaj,' said the officer. 'Thank you for your full account.' He looked at his colleagues. 'Has anyone any questions?'

His four companions shook their heads and thanked me. I stood up, saluted and left the room.

The other witness was called next. 'How was it?' Kaufman said to me. 'How many officers are in there?'

I couldn't bring myself to tell him. I turned away, saying, 'You'll see when you get in there – sir.' After that, the silence lay heavily between us. Fortunately, the witness returned almost straight away and Kaufman was called.

He was away for about fifteen minutes and emerged white-faced and agitated. 'They tried to lay the blame on me,' he said. 'We know it was a heart attack. How could that be my fault? How dare they try to blame me…how dare they?' Neither of us answered and we returned to the ship in an even more uncomfortable silence. From that time on, Kaufman and I tried to avoid each other if at all possible. I carried out his orders when necessary and, if I needed to address him, I was unfailingly polite. I was determined he should have no cause for complaint about me. The verdict reached at the inquest, was 'accidental death'.

I was extremely pleased that there was a diversion the next day. We heard that a group of actors from *Narodno Kazaliste*, one of the best known theatres in Zagreb, had arrived in Šibenik and was performing a variety show especially for our naval squadron. It was my job to march the crew to the theatre. We were about half way there when suddenly I was aware that a German coach was being driven slowly alongside us and that its occupants were photographing us as we marched. Then I saw that cigarettes were being thrown through the open windows and landing at our feet. I called a halt and ordered the men to stand easy. The coach stopped too and still cigarettes were flying towards us. Forty or more faces peered at us through the windows to see what we would do. I remembered hearing that many stories were current, in the west, about the poverty in our country and how we were desperate for goods brought in by foreigners. I was determined not to give these gawping tourists the satisfaction of watching an undignified scramble. Slowly and deliberately I collected the cigarettes in my hat. When I had retrieved all I could, I mounted the steps of the coach. The driver opened the door, looking embarrassed. There was an empty seat next to him and I tipped the hatful of cigarettes on to it. The passengers watched, silent. I reached into my top pocket and pulled out a packet of cigarettes. I made as if to offer them to the man sitting closest to me.

'If we want to give someone a cigarette,' I said, in German, 'This is how we do it. We do not throw it at him.'

I smiled pleasantly and, as I turned to go down the steps, the tour leader apologised to me. 'I'm very sorry,' he said. 'We didn't mean to offend you.' I felt pleased with myself as I marched the men the rest of the way to the theatre to see what turned out to be an excellent show.

Ingrid

The next day, the captain mustered the crews of all the minesweepers for a briefing. He told us that, in four days time, we would put to sea on an acoustic minesweeping exercise. He finished by announcing my promotion to petty officer 2nd class. I was pleased, of course, as it meant more money as well as shore leave privileges. There was a shadow of sadness, however because I guessed that this early elevation had to do with my involvement in the story of Marinko.

I enjoyed the manoeuvres, which gave me plenty to do. At one point, we were anchored off the island of Viz. In the evening, I received a Morse message from a signals officer based there. 'What is your name?' he asked.

'Ivan. What is yours?'

'Milan,' came the reply.

'I'm Ivan Vesligaj,' I signalled. 'Do you remember me?'

'Of course. How are you?'

We exchanged news and he assured me that he was soon going to ask for a transfer. It was good to be in touch and we ended by saying we hoped to meet up in the not too distant future.

At the end of the manoeuvres, we anchored off the island of Rogoznica. We arrived in the early morning and I thought it was one of the most beautiful places I have ever seen. The islands of Dalmatia stretched out to the horizon. Each was surrounded by the dancing blue sea and glistened green in the sunshine. We were told that in the evenings we would be free to swim, dive, relax on deck or take the rowing boat on an excursion to Rogoznica. We were moored about 500 meters from the island and from the bridge, as the early sun warmed me, I noticed two bungalows set above a beach and thought it would be a wonderful spot for a holiday.

After breakfast we were allowed ashore. Rogoznica was covered with pine forests with a main path running round the perimeter and small paths leading from beaches to the interior. I wandered off by myself and came upon a restaurant full of Germans having breakfast. Two very pretty girls sat at a table outside and tried to engage me in conversation. They had a Croatian dictionary and I knew some German so we managed to discover each other's names.

Back in the rowing boat, I related my experience to my mate, Marko.

'Ingrid, the blond one's for me,' I said. 'The brunette's very pretty too. She's Gertude.'

'But I don't speak German,' complained Marko.

'They've got a dictionary. You'll manage.'

Marko still wasn't sure. 'Aren't we forbidden to fraternise with foreign tourists, Vesligaj? You're a petty officer, you should know. We could be sent to prison if we go out with these girls.'

I laughed, feeling grown up and reckless. 'You just wait till you see them. You won't mind being locked up for a date with one of them.' I liked Marko. A few weeks earlier, I'd chosen him to serve on M143, from a crowd of new trainees. He was younger than me and less experienced with women – or so I thought. It was a hot night and a few of us elected to sleep on deck. Marko's mattress was next to mine and we chatted softly about the prospect of meeting the two girls.

'What if they turn us down?' he said.

'No girl turns me down,' I laughed. 'You just let me do the talking.' And with that happy thought, I fell asleep.

The next morning Marko and I were working on the electric cables of one of the buoys a safe distance from the ship. We looked up as we heard the roar of a speed boat nearby. Ingrid and Gertude were on board. The engine cut and Ingrid shouted, in German, 'See you in the restaurant at 7 tonight?'

'OK,' I bellowed. The boat's engine re-started and it sped away. I translated and Marko and I grinned at each other. We'd got our dates without even asking.

After obtaining passes from Ćiril and discussing our financial situation, we realised we had only 200 dinars each – enough to buy drinks for ourselves and the girls but not to buy food. We would eat before we went out and hope that the girls would do the same. We took particular care over how we looked, donning our best whites and giving our shoes an extra polish.

The restaurant was half full when we arrived. We immediately noticed Ingrid and Gertrude sitting with, what we assumed were their families. We gave no sign of our assignations but tucked ourselves in a quiet corner away from tourists and ordered two beers.

'You're right,' whispered Marko. 'They're both gorgeous.' A couple of minutes later the girls came over, carrying their drinks.

'Good evening,' Ingrid said in Croatian.

Gertude added, 'Please may we sit down?'

'Of course. Can I get you drinks?' I asked in German.

'No thank you. We have these.' After this stilted beginning, I introduced Marko and, with the use of the dictionary and my rather limited German, conversation flowed. We discovered that the two girls' families were staying in the bungalows above the beach. Their homes were in Stuttgart and their holiday would last three weeks.

'Which are your parents?' I asked Ingrid.

'My father is the one who's nearly bald and my mother is next to him,' she replied and at that moment her parents turned to look at me. Our eyes met and the father gave a smile and a friendly wave.

'Have you got a boyfriend?' I asked.

'No. I've only just finished school. What about you. Girlfriend?'

'No.' Soft music was playing. A couple got up to dance. 'Would you like to dance?'

'Yes please.' She was wearing silk – a white blouse and pale blue skirt. I held her close as we danced but I was aware of her father's presence. After two dances, we returned to the table. A waiter was standing there, with a tray of glasses. There were two soft drinks, two beers and some cognac.

'I didn't order these,' I protested.

'Don't worry, they're a present from me,' Ingrid said soothingly. 'Drink up and enjoy.'

While we had been dancing, a crowd of people had arrived. With a lurch, I noticed that it was made up of officers from our ship, including the captain. I caught Marko's eye and nodded towards them.

Alarmed, he whispered, 'What shall we do?'

'Ignore them,' I hissed. 'Pretend we haven't seen them.'

A moment later, Ingrid's father joined us. He spoke Croatian fluently. I discovered that he'd been stationed in Zagreb where he'd served as a captain in the German army. He asked my name and where I lived. 'I hope you won't get into trouble for being friendly with Ingrid,' he said. 'I know that there are strict rules about mixing with foreigners.'

'There are but I think I should be free to talk to anyone I wish,' I said. 'I'm prepared to take the risk.'

He smiled at this, and as he rose to return to his wife, he said quietly, 'Look after my daughter Ivan Vesligaj. She's young and she's innocent.'

'I'll take good care of her,' I promised.

Ingrid suggested a walk by the sea and the four of us left the restaurant. The air was heavy with the scent of pine and the moon was reflected in the calm water. It was a night made for romance. Ingrid and I held hands and walked ahead. The others were slow and we hid behind some trees and waited for them. We were curious to know what they were doing. We smothered our laughter when we realised that they were studying the dictionary by the light of the lamps which were placed by benches at intervals along the path. They seemed to refer to it constantly so the action moved very slowly.

As they passed, I bent down to whisper in Ingrid's ear and she turned and kissed me on the lips. She hugged me tight and whispered that she was so pleased she'd met me. We walked away from the others, on to the beach, sat down on a flat rock and kissed each other in earnest. Suddenly I wondered what the time was. I looked at my watch – 11.40. I saw Marko and Gertrude in the distance, still looking in the dictionary.

'Time to get back to the ship,' I called. We had just time to walk the girls back to the bungalows. Ingrid gave me a last kiss.

'Good night my darling,' she said, 'Can you meet us at the same time tomorrow?'

'How about joining us for a swim during the day?' I asked. 'We plan to swim round the island in the afternoon when we go off duty. 'We'll be free by about two. Meet us just round that point.' I indicated a headland to the left of the beach. 'No one will be able to see us there from the ship or the path. Come ready to swim with us.' The two girls were enthusiastic about the plan and we left them, feeling pleased with ourselves.

'Glad you came with me?' I said to Marko.

'I certainly am,' he answered. 'But I think I need to buy a German dictionary.'

On deck, the next day, after our usual chores, Marko and I could talk of nothing but Ingrid and Gertrude. 'What does "*Ich liebe dich*" mean?' he asked me.

'It means "I love you", I laughed. Why?'

'Gertrude kept saying it to me,' he admitted. 'She was all over me. I know she wanted to make love.'

'Be careful,' I warned. 'You must let her take the lead. Don't assume anything. You could so easily be accused of rape if things go wrong.'

'How will I know she really wants to?' he said in a worried voice.

Once more, I felt as if I were the experienced one – a man instructing a boy. 'You'll know,' I said. 'She'll make you aware by how she kisses you, how she touches you.'

'What if I get carried away?'

'Just don't be,' I said sharply. 'Don't make a fool of yourself. If she says "No", stop immediately. Don't rush into anything.' And then I told him the things that Marica had taught me so long ago in the hay field and forest. Perhaps it was as well that the captain called us just then. He wanted us to row him and other officers to the beach. Several young women welcomed the men as we pulled the boat ashore. One, an attractive brunette, kissed the captain and I remembered hearing that he had a fiancée.

We hadn't been back on board long when I became aware that Lieutenant Ćiril was at the edge of the water, signalling to me, using semaphore. The officers had forgotten to take beers and wine. *Bring eight bottles of beer and a bottle of white wine. Don't forget the glasses*, ran the message. Within ten minutes I was back on the beach with the drinks. I'd forgotten the bottle opener but remembered a trick Adalbert had taught me.

'I'll go back for the opener, sir,' I said to the captain, 'or, if you're thirsty, I know a way to open the beer without one.'

'Vesligaj magic, is it?' laughed Ćiril.

'I'd like to see that, darling,' said the captain's fiancée.

'Then you shall, Vesna. Vesligaj?'

I picked up two bottles of beer and handed one to Vesna. 'Hold it horizontal and grip it tightly,' I said. I leant forward with my bottle, interlocked the two caps and gave a sharp twist. The caps came off, I righted my bottle immediately but Vesna was not fast enough and a little of the beer spilt down the front of her bikini. Everyone laughed but I was embarrassed. 'I'm so sorry,' I mumbled and produced a clean handkerchief from my pocket, holding it out to her.

Vesna was smiling but she didn't take the handkerchief. 'You should pay a forfeit for doing that,' she said. 'Take off your shirt. That's big enough to wipe all the beer away. I looked uneasily at the captain but he was still laughing so, even more embarrassed, I removed my tee shirt and held that out to Vesna.

Again, she shook her head. 'No, it's your fault the beer was spilt, you wipe me down.'

I leaned forward and wiped the drops of beer from Vesna's full breasts and then, hot all over, I replaced my shirt.

'I might not be happy if anyone else had done that,' I heard the captain whisper to Vesna, 'but Vesligaj spent two years training to be a priest. He's still a virgin and quite religious, I think.'

'Wait a moment,' Vesla said aloud, 'I saw this young man at the restaurant last night, drinking *and* he was dancing with a very pretty girl.' I wished myself anywhere but here, being talked about in this way. If only I hadn't been tempted to show off my bottle-opening skills.

'Nothing will have happened between them, though, rest assured. Vesligaj still crosses himself before he goes to bed, I've been told.'

'What was the girl's name?' his fiancée persisted, looking at me.

'I don't know, miss,' I lied.

The captain looked serious. 'That was faster work than I would have expected of you, Vesligaj. You can get back to the ship now.' Relieved, and not looking again at Vesna, I saluted the officers but then had a further thought.

'Shall I go back for a bottle opener for the wine and the other beers, sir?' I asked.

'No, I think you've suffered enough. We'll borrow an opener from the restaurant.'

Before he could change his mind, I turned and ran back to the boat where I related my experience to Marko. When he'd finished laughing he said, 'So the captain didn't seem to mind about us socialising with the girls?'

'He didn't seem to – but we'll be careful,' I said.

Just before 14.00 hours that afternoon, we climbed the mast and dived into the transparent, warm sea. As we swam past the beach, we could hear cheers and clapping from the captain's party which was watching us. We rounded the point and saw Ingrid and Gertrude waiting. They ran towards us as we emerged from the water. Ingrid threw her arms round me and kissed me on the mouth and, looking sideways, I saw that Marko was getting the same treatment from Gertrude.

We swam in twos, side by side. Although Ingrid was a strong swimmer, she couldn't talk and swim at the same time. After about twenty minutes, she tapped my shoulder and indicated that she was tired. We turned for the shore and the others followed. When we arrived on the deserted beach, Marko and Gertrude walked off together and Ingrid and I found a mossy rock and lay down to sunbathe.

Ingrid kissed me and as I put my arms round her, I realised she was shaking. 'I'm cold,' she said. I couldn't believe it. The sea was warm, the sun was scorching but I held her closer to try to warm her. 'I do love you,' she whispered. 'When can we make love? I want to so much.'

'Your father asked me to look after you. He said you are innocent.'

'I'm just 18. I'm a woman. I'm old enough to know what I want and I want you to make love to me.'

All sorts of things went through my head. I knew I could make her first experience of sex a good one and I thought she was old enough to know her own mind. I certainly wanted her but I was doubtful that there could be a future for the relationship. I also knew I'd be in terrible trouble if the Yugoslav authorities found out.

'Are you absolutely sure this is what you want?' I asked.

'Absolutely. Don't you?'

'Oh yes, I want to, can't you tell that? But...'

I knew that what I was going to say next would take the romance out of the situation but it had to be said. 'We can only make love if you can get hold of a Durex. I can't get to the chemist on the mainland and even if I could, I daren't be seen buying such a thing. You'll have to do it'

There was a moment's silence then Ingrid stood up, taking me by surprise. 'I'll get some. Don't worry, I'll borrow father's car and drive over the bridge. ' She called Gertrude and after a couple of words, they ran off together along the perimeter path, to the right.

As Marko was coming over to me, he halted and pointed to the left. Who should be walking along the path but Ingrid's mother and father. Fortunately, the girls were out of sight by now and Marko said, 'I'll see you back at the ship. You stay and speak German to these two.' And he sprinted off in the direction the girls had taken. I felt bound to stay and greet Ingrid's parents.

I stood up as they approached. Mr Gunther introduced his wife and I kissed her hand, Croatian fashion. 'It's nice to meet you,' she said. 'Let's sit on the bench for a while. I need a rest.' We sat down. 'I gather you come from Zagreb,' she went on. 'What did you do before you joined the navy?'

'I was a technician in a leather factory. I spent three years training at a polytechnic.'

She still hadn't finished her questioning 'What sort of education did you have before you went to the polytechnic?'

'I spent two years training for the priesthood.'

Mr Gunther laughed, 'Our Ingrid's safe with you then, Will you come to the bungalow and have lunch with us tomorrow, Ivan?'

'I'm sorry, sir, that's not possible. Imagine the trouble I'd be in if some busybody reported to my captain that I've been visiting foreign tourists.'

'Yes of course, how foolish of me. Have you arranged to see Ingrid again?'

'Yes, sir, tomorrow evening, with your permission.'

'You have it. I hope you'll allow me to buy you a drink if you're in the restaurant.'

'Yes, thank you, sir, but would it be possible to do it discreetly, please?'

'Don't worry. I'll sort it out.'

Mrs Gunther got up. 'Come on we'd better get back. It was nice to meet you, Ivan. We're sure to come across each other again.' I watched them out of sight and then followed. I wondered how Ingrid had got on at the chemist's shop and what her parents would have said if they'd known of her mission.

Back on the ship, I told Marko about the meeting with Ingrid's parents. 'I do feel a little guilty,' I confessed, 'but this is what the girls want, isn't it? They're the ones who have been so insistent. So, Marko, tomorrow night's the night!'

I spent the following morning diving and doing running repairs on the anchor-fixing. I'd arranged for Marko to pick me up in the boat afterwards because I wanted to scan the coastline of the island for a secluded place where I could be alone with Ingrid without fear of being overlooked.

On the south of the island, we saw two rocky bays, close but not too close to each other. Each was sheltered from the coastal path by the forest and large rocks gave concealment from anyone on the water. We landed to investigate and found the ground between the rocks dry and covered with moss and fallen leaves – ideal. 'Wonderfully soft,' I said. 'Marko, take the boat back to the ship and fetch two blankets, wrap them in small tarpaulins. We'll hide them under the rocks ready for tonight.'

Marko was back in twenty minutes with the blankets and with two bottles of beer. 'Thought we might need a drink tonight,' he grinned. 'I put it on your account. Well, you do earn more than I do.' I gave him a friendly slap on the back and then we hid the blankets and beer under rocks in our respective 'love coves'. Our preparations complete, we returned to the ship. On the way, we discussed our financial situation. We had only 190 dinars between us.

'It's enough for tonight,' said Marko, 'but if all goes well, we'll want to meet the girls again tomorrow.'

'Let's worry about that when tomorrow comes,' I said. 'I think something may turn up.'

I felt too excited and nervous about the prospect of love-making to eat much supper. It seemed a long time since I'd had such an assignation. Was I out of practice? What if Ingrid suddenly changed her mind and created a scene? What if we were discovered? This would not only be very embarrassing but would incur punishment for me. What if Mr Gunther found out and…? Stop this! I said to myself. It's a simple meeting between two young people who like each other. That's all. After supper I went to Lieutenant Ćiril's cabin to request a pass.

'Seeing the same girl again?' he asked casually as he signed the piece of paper.

'Yes, sir.'

'She must be nice. Is she on holiday here?'

Ćiril and I were on excellent terms, we were friends really, and I made a decision. 'Can I let you into a secret, sir?'

'Certainly.'

'Ingrid is German.'

'I did wonder, I won't say a word but you need to be careful. If the captain or Kaufman found out, you'd be in trouble.'

'I realise that. What would happen to me?'

Ćiril smiled. 'We're a bit far from any prison here so you'd be safe from that but you'd be confined to ship and probably lose at least one stripe which would be a shame. So, take care not to be caught.'

Marko and I were rowed ashore by the sailor on boat duty and we asked to be picked up at 22.50 hours. We went straight to the restaurant where we found Ingrid and Gertrude sitting at a table outside. They both leapt up and kissed us and Ingrid whispered to me, excitedly, 'We've got them.' She's certainly no shrinking violet, I thought. She showed no sign of nervousness – only barely suppressed excitement.

As we sipped the drinks sent out to us by Mr Gunther, several of the ship's officers, including the captain and Ćiril, arrived. Marko and I stood and saluted and Ćiril gave a knowing smile. Vesna was with the captain. She caught my eye, smiled and gave a little wave. Ingrid was impatient to move. I told her about the secluded cove I had found and she grabbed my hand. 'Come on,' she urged, 'Let's not waste time here. Let's go.'

'But I haven't finished my beer.'

'You can drink beer any time. Come on!' She got up and pulled at my arm. I laughed and said to Marko,

'It seems they can't wait. Are you ready? Oh, stop looking at that dictionary. It's time for action not words.'

Ingrid and I held hands as we walked, Ingrid very close to me. She was wearing extremely short shorts and a silk blouse. The others trailed behind, still dictionary-bound, and I forgot about them as soon as we reached the cove. I retrieved the blanket and we lay down.

I knew that Ingrid must take the lead this evening. She should have no reason to say I had forced myself on her if things did not turn out well. My only concern was that she'd be shy and unforthcoming but I needn't have worried. She was wearing nothing under her blouse. She slipped it off and pressed her firm breasts against me. 'Take off your uniform,' she whispered and bent over to help me. Her shorts were next to go. Under them, she wore red silk panties, edged in lace. Within a moment, she'd removed them and my swimming trunks, which were under my uniform. She clasped me tight and tried to pull me on top of her. 'I want you to make love to me *now,*' she insisted. Remembering that her father had called her 'innocent', I held back.

'Are you absolutely sure?'

'I'm sure, I'm sure.' I approached her softly, doing the things that Marica had told me women like so much.

'Now, now!' she was almost shouting as she thrust herself on me so I took her gently.

She cried afterwards. Alarmed, I asked if she was all right.

'I'm just so happy,' she sobbed and I held her close until she was still.

We shared the bottle of beer and then walked together into the sea. The moon and stars were bright overhead and the sea reflected their light. I knew then that, whatever happened to me or to our relationship, I would never forget the magic of this night. We made love twice more, slowly, almost languidly in the warm water. Afterwards we rubbed each other dry with a towel Ingrid had brought and she cried again because she was so happy and because the evening was almost over. 'You will be my proper boyfriend now, won't you?' she said.

'Ingrid, I can't promise you anything. I still have to do a long stretch in the navy.' Then, as I saw her despondency, 'I'm sure we can keep in touch. I'll give you my sister's address and she'll send your letters on to me. Any letter sent to me via the naval base would be opened by the naval security officers.'

She still looked worried. 'I love you so much. My father told me last night that we should be careful and not speak German when there are military personnel around. He said you'd be in big trouble if you were found to have fraternised with a foreigner.'

I didn't want to spoil the evening and I laughed and took her in my arms. 'Fraternised? Is that what you call it?'

Then she laughed too. 'We'll meet tomorrow evening, won't we?'

'I don't think I'll be able to see you tomorrow.'

She stopped kissing me. 'Why not? Don't you like me?'

'Of course I like you. Can I be honest with you?'

'Yes,' she said in a quavering voice.

'I simply don't have enough money to take you out and treat you as I want to.'

Ingrid started to laugh. 'Is that all?

'Ingrid, I'm a gentleman. I want to be able to buy you drinks and meals but, at the moment, I can't.'

She put her arms round my neck and hugged and kissed me again. 'Don't worry about money, my darling. I've got plenty. I work as a secretary at my father's chemical factory.'

'I can't take money from you, Ingrid.'

'Of course you can. I'll give you some tomorrow and you can spend it on me and on Gertrude. When you're rich you can pay me back if you like but just now, do please, please let me use my money. If I don't see you I'll be unhappy. You don't want that, do you?'

So I gave in, not imagining that this was the first of many times this would happen. She kissed me all over and we would have continued our love-making if I hadn't noticed the time.

'We must go and find the others now,' I said. 'It's time to walk you home and get back to the ship.'

We dressed and climbed slowly to the perimeter path, arms round each other. 'Thank you my darling,' Ingrid said. 'I love you so much.' She was happy, glowing.

Once on the path, I gave a long whistle and within a few moments, Marko and Gertrude appeared, arms wrapped round each other. 'Everything OK?' I asked Marko.

'Marvellous. You?'

'Marvellous.' And we all laughed.

As I undertook my duties the next day, I kept remembering the last evening, Ingrid's beauty and the joy of our love-making. I received a message saying that our sister ship, M141, would arrive at 09.00 hours the next day and then I took a seaman ashore to collect bread for the evening meal. He was gone for over two hours and, as I was responsible for collecting him from the quay, I scanned the mainland, searching for him.

I spotted him and called Marko over to look at him through the binoculars. We laughed so much that others came to see what was so funny. The seaman was sitting on a slope which ran down to the beach. Around him were dozens of gypsy children, reaching out to him and he was tearing loaves, *our* loaves, to pieces and handing them to the hungry youngsters.

'You'd better go and fetch him quickly,' Marko said, 'or we'll have no bread tonight.'

The seaman ran to the quay when he saw me. Before I could say anything, he told me that he'd bought a couple of extra loaves, with his own money, as he'd noticed the children on his way to the bakery. 'It wasn't our bread, don't worry,' he assured me, 'and by the way, I have a note for you. A German girl asked me to give it to you.' He handed me an envelope. 'Why are you getting a letter from a German?' he asked curiously.

I thought quickly. This was dangerous ground. 'She's my cousin,' I said. 'She's on holiday here from Zagreb.' He seemed satisfied but I waited until I was back on board before I opened Ingrid's letter. It was, of course, written in German.

My Darling, Meet me in the cove where we went last night. I'll be waiting for you at 7.30. Please come! URGENT XXXXXXXXXXX

I was concerned about the 'URGENT' and knew I must go. When I told Marko, he said he'd come too and try to meet up with Gertrude. As we walked along the perimeter path, approaching the coves, we saw the two girls just below the path. They saw us, ran up and embraced us. I looked round quickly. There was no-one in sight. Ingrid and I walked to our cove, found the blanket and sat down. 'What's so urgent?' I said. 'Is something the matter?'

Ingrid laughed. 'Of course not, silly.' I just *urgently* wanted to see you. I *needed* to see you. I love you so very much.' I was relieved and flattered and kissed her.

She clung to me. 'Let's make love,' she said.

'Ingrid, there's more to a relationship than making love time after time – although that is important, of course,' I added hurriedly.

She looked puzzled. 'Well, what do you want to do?'

'Tell me about yourself. What do you like to do, apart from making love. Where else have you been on holiday? Which music do you like?'

So she told me what I asked and ended by fishing in her bag and handing me 500 dinars. I shook my head and pushed the money away.

'Last night you said you'd take it,' she protested. 'You seemed to understand. You promised.' I kissed her again and accepted the 500 dinars. We made love again on the beach and in the sea. And once more it was sweet and I wondered if I were falling in love with her. She begged me to see her during day times. 'The days seem so long while I'm waiting to see you in the evenings,' she pleaded.

'I do come ashore regularly on errands or to bring my officer ashore. If you're around the beach area and I'm coming to the island, I'll take my hat off and wave and you can meet me on the footpath round the point. I won't be able to stay longer than about two hours.'

'It'll be better than nothing. I'll keep watching out for you.'

I signalled to her the next morning and she met me as planned. I rowed her to a tiny uninhabited island I'd noticed. It was flat and grassy and we lay, for a while, with our arms about each other. Small lizards shot across the warm rocks, the sky was unbroken blue, the waves creamed gently nearby. We could have been the only people in the world. 'We're going for a day out in Split, the day after tomorrow, Thursday,' Ingrid told me. 'My parents said you are welcome to come with us if it won't get you into trouble. Can you come?'

I thought for a moment. 'I'd love to come but I can't come in uniform. Would your father lend me a tee shirt and shorts, do you think? We're about the same size.'

'I'm sure he would. Is that the only problem?'

'I'll need to get a pass, just in case I'm stopped by the military police. It's unlikely but you can't be too careful. I can't see you tonight as I'm on boat duty but I will be bringing officers ashore. Watch out for me, go and sit on the bench by the quay when you see me rowing over and once the officers are out of earshot you can tell me if your father is happy to lend me the clothes and what the arrangements are for the trip.'

All went according to plan. That evening, I obtained a day's leave for Thursday and a pass to visit Split. I met Ingrid who said that her father was happy to lend me the clothes. 'He thinks it best for you to meet us just over the bridge, on the mainland,' she said. 'You can change in the car. Then, to my surprise, she pushed a thousand dinars note into my hand.

'I can't take...' I started

She put her finger to her lips. 'Don't say anything, Ivan, she whispered. It's my money and I'm giving it to you so that you'll have enough money to treat my parents and me to a meal tomorrow...Please.' How could I refuse?

I didn't see Ingrid on Wednesday. We were busy aboard ship. At 09.00 hours, I was on the bridge because we were expecting the arrival of M141. As she came into view, I went into the radio cabin and received a Morse message informing me that it would be anchoring for a few hours and that her captain and an important visitor would be coming on board M143.

Who is the important visitor? I asked.

God help your officers, came the reply. *It's the vice admiral. He's an expert on mine sweeping.*

As I was receiving the message, something was nagging at the back of my mind. I felt I knew this particular delivery style of Morse code. I recognised it from my training days and had heard it more recently too. As I went to deliver the message to the captain, it came to me – the radio officer on M141 was Milan.

Is that you, Milan? I signalled, when I was back in the radio cabin. *Veslagaj here.* For reply, a laugh echoed across the water which lay between our two ships. It was loud enough to startle the sailors on deck. Milan had decided to communicate his pleasure at my message, by using the megaphone. His message followed,

Nice to hear from you. I came to M141 a week ago from Vis. Took your advice. Can't go ashore as we're only here for a couple of hours. We'll be sailing around the Kornati Islands and you'll join us in 3 weeks. See you then.

It was good to hear from Milan again. I still often wondered about Ostoja and was very sorry to have lost touch with him. It was good to know this had not happened with Milan.

Within an hour, the captain of M141 and the vice admiral arrived by motor boat. I happened to be on deck as they arrived and saluted as they passed. The vice admiral, a wiry little man with a long face and rat's tail moustache, stopped. 'Who are you?' he said sharply.

'Vesligaj, sir. Radio officer.' He sniffed and walked off towards the captain's cabin.

A little later, I heard the captain's voice. 'Vesligaj, take the vice admiral to his cabin.'

The vice admiral held out his hat to me, 'Here, carry this.' When he saw the minute cabin, he turned to me, his face red. 'I'm not sleeping here,' he barked. 'There must be a bigger one.'

'I'm afraid there isn't sir,' I stammered.

He walked out on to the deck. 'Dušan!' he bellowed. Every sailor in sight turned to look at him and stood absolutely still. The captain appeared, looking flustered. 'Dušan, I am not going to sleep in that cupboard. This man says you haven't anything bigger to offer me. If that's the case, is there a hotel on this God-forsaken island?'

'Not on Rogoznica sir, but I believe there is one on the next island, Ciova,' he indicated the direction. 'But some people on Rogoznica offer accommodation in their own homes. Would you prefer that?'

'I don't care where I stay as long as it's not in a cupboard and there is a comfortable bed.'

'Vesligaj,' the captain turned to me. 'Fetch Lieutenant Ćiril and ask him to take the vice admiral ashore and find him somewhere to stay.' I fetched Ćiril and quietly suggested that he should take the vice admiral to the Rogoznica tourist office and let him choose somewhere from what was on offer.

'Good idea,' he said. 'Bring the boat round and you can row us ashore.'

I rowed Ćiril and the vice admiral back to our ship once arrangements had been made for the latter's overnight comfort. Ćiril climbed the ladder aboard first, while I kept the boat steady and close to the ship's side, using the paddles. The vice admiral stood up to follow him and grabbed the ladder which caused the boat to jerk away from the ship. 'Careful sir!' I shouted. 'Wait a moment and I'll take the boat close again.' He ignored me, tried to step on the ladder, missed and fell into the water. He didn't make a sound, he simply grasped the ladder again and mounted it. I rescued his hat before it could float away and handed it up to him. Everyone on the ship was watching, mesmerised.

The vice admiral, safely on deck, handed his sodden wallet to the captain. 'Dry this out,' he said. And, turning to look at me, he added, 'It's not his fault. It's mine. I didn't listen to his good advice.' Then he dripped his way towards the captain's cabin.

Ingrid 2: Manoeuvres

As planned, I met the Mercedes on the mainland side of the bridge the next morning and was greeted warmly by Urschula and Raulf Gunther. Ingrid's face was radiant as I climbed into the back of the car and sat next to her. She pressed herself against me by way of greeting and gave my hand a quick squeeze. Nothing more was possible, with her parents in the front seats.

As soon as we were on our way, I wriggled out of my uniform and into the bright Hawaiian shirt and grey shorts provided by Raulf. I'd taken the precaution of wearing swimming trunks so that the switch could be done with relative modesty. The garments fitted perfectly although Ingrid whispered that she preferred me in uniform.

It was about an hour's drive to Split. Urschula asked about my family and I regaled her with tales of my brothers and sisters and life at home on the farm.

'What's your job aboard your ship?' Raulf asked when I'd finished.

'Communications Officer.'

'What does that entail?'

'I'm afraid I can't say,' I answered awkwardly. 'I'm not permitted to talk about anything to do with the navy.'

'Of course not. Sorry for asking.' I was grateful he let the subject drop. A large part of my duty was to listen in to radio conversations, intercept signals and report anything unusual. I certainly shouldn't be talking about my work to a German, however friendly.

We separated when we arrived in Split, Ingrid and I wandered through the market and tourist shops which lay opposite the quay. She stopped outside a jewellery shop. 'Let's go inside and look properly,' she said.

'I haven't money to buy you anything, I'm afraid,' I said sorrowfully.

'I've got plenty of money so don't worry. I want to buy you a present.'

In spite of my protests, she bought me a gold ring, with a sovereign inset. 'Take it for my sake,' she pleaded. 'Please.' When she put it on my finger, she laughed, saying, 'There! Now we're engaged.'

Uncomfortable, I said, 'In my country the man buys a ring for the lady and puts it on *her* finger.'

She laughed again. 'Maybe we have different customs in Germany. Don't say another word about it. You don't want to upset me, do you?' And she kissed me.

My mind whirled. Engaged? I certainly wasn't ready for such a commitment. I was very fond of Ingrid – I could say I loved her but I wasn't 'in love' with her. As we walked out of the shop, I said, 'Ingrid, you do know that I can't…'

She reached up and put her finger on my lips. 'Sh, don't say anything. Don't spoil this perfect day.'

We met her parents for lunch and I remember I had the most delicious steak. I hadn't eaten steak for a long time and this one was cooked just the way I liked but Raulf swept away my attempt to pay the 800 dinar bill. 'Put your money away Ivan,' he said and Ingrid shot me a warning glance. I gathered she wanted me to let him pay and say nothing about the 1,000 dinar note in my pocket.

The four of us lazed on the beach in the afternoon. It was extremely hot so we swam and sunbathed. I liked Ingrid's parents very much. In the car on the way back, I thanked them for including me in their day trip. 'It's been a pleasure. You'd better change into your uniform,' Raulf said. I saw him wink at me in his driving mirror. 'You know what'll happen if the Yugoslavian naval officers find out that Ivan has a German girlfriend, don't you Ingrid?' he added.

'What?'

'They'll take him out at dawn, tie him to a post and shoot him.'

Ingrid and her mother screamed and Ingrid cried, 'Oh no!'

'Your father's only teasing,' I said and risked giving her a quick squeeze.

Laughing, Urschula asked me, 'When are you going back to your base?'

'In about four weeks,' I said.

'We'll be gone by then. Make sure you give us your address in Zagreb. It would be a pity to lose touch.' Ingrid was looking sad at the prospect of our parting and she suggested a walk before I returned to the ship.

We got out of the car at a safe distance from the harbour and, wandering over the bridge towards a small bar, I suddenly realised that there were no naval personnel about nor were there any in the restaurant they usually used.

'Something's up,' I said. 'I wonder what's happening to keep all officers and men away from their beer.'

'Do you need to go back now?' Ingrid asked.

'No, my pass is until midnight. I'll find out then.' We had a drink and walked to our special cove. That evening we didn't make love but lay, looking at the stars and telling each other more about our lives. Ingrid kept breaking off to tell me how much she loved me. At one point, she began to cry. 'I love you so much it hurts,' she sobbed. 'If you die, I'll die with you.'

I laughed at her gently and held her close. 'I'm not going to die,' I said. 'I'll see you tomorrow.'

But when I got back to the ship, I discovered that I would not be seeing Ingrid tomorrow. I'd noticed, as soon as I reached the harbour, that the buoys which indicated where the electric cable ran, had gone. Ćiril was waiting on deck for me.

'We're off on an exercise tomorrow,' he said. 'We leave at 02.00 hours. Go and get a couple of hours' sleep.'

As it was so hot, I slept on deck. Fleetingly I thought of Ingrid's surprise and disappointment when she woke to find M143 had gone. Then I was asleep and it seemed as if almost immediately I heard the call to get up.

After the usual bustle of departure, when I was busy receiving and sending signals, the captain gave me a sealed envelope. 'Our destination is inside,' he said. 'Read and then encode it and send the information to the rest of the squadron.'

'Primošten,' I said to Ćiril, who was nearby. 'We're going to Primošten,' It was one of the beautiful Kornati Islands.

We anchored to the west of Primošten. The other minesweepers anchored to the east, between Primošten and the island of Žut. We were given a few hours' leisure and Marko and I spent most of it swimming. The water was 23 degrees.

As we relaxed on deck afterwards, I asked him if he'd seen Gertrude the previous evening.

'No,' he said gloomily. 'She sent a message to say she wouldn't meet me as Ingrid wasn't around. Aren't girls strange?'

I told him a bit about the day in Split. 'I'm worried that Ingrid is getting too serious,' I said and showed him the ring.

When Lieutenant Ćiril noticed it he remarked, 'That looks expensive. Is it new?' Because I trusted him, I explained.

'I hope you didn't sell any secrets to get it,' he joked.

'I didn't, sir, but is anything really secret? With their advanced satellites, I expect NATO even knows what we have for breakfast.'

In the early evening it was my duty to take the captain, Ćiril and most of the other officers, in the motor boat, round the island of Žut to M144 for a meal and a conference. The vice captain was left in charge of M143.

I went to bed on deck soon after I returned but was woken at 23.00 hours by a scraping noise. I listened carefully and realised what it was. I woke the vice captain. 'Sir,' I said. 'The anchor is ploughing.' This was serious because it meant that the anchor was not doing its job. It was moving backwards and forwards along the seabed, jeopardising the stability of the ship. I saw panic on the officer's face and remembered something I'd learnt during my training. 'Isn't the best strategy to start the engine and reverse away from the island into deeper water, sir?'

'I can't start the engine without the captain's permission except in exceptional circumstances,' he said. 'Send a signal to *M144* and ask the captain to return immediately.'

I went into the radio cabin but could get no reception. I knew that there was a ridge of high hills running down the centre of Zut. The beam of the Aldis lamp would carry no further than the first hill. The ploughing sound was getting louder as I reported my failure to the officer. Even as I spoke to him and saw the panic return, I had another idea. I fetched the lamp and pointed it to the sky. I sent the message and within a couple of minutes, I received a reply. The captain was on his way back. When he arrived, he did exactly as I had suggested and the anchor was once more secure.

'Good idea to signal into the sky. Congratulations,' he said to his deputy who had the grace to say, 'It wasn't my idea, sir. You have Petty Officer Vesligaj to thank for that.'

The exercise lasted for three days. We arrived back at our mooring, off Rogoznica, at night. I was thinking about Ingrid as we were anchoring. I imagined her delight in the morning. We had reappeared as if by magic. I realised I was really looking forward to seeing her again. The next morning, Marko and I were on deck chatting and looking towards the beach. Suddenly we saw two figures running down to the sea and madly waving. Then they walked up to the top of the beach and sat on a seat. I looked at them through the binoculars and they were laughing and staring at us as if they could not believe their eyes. They were, of course, Ingrid and Gertrude.

Suddenly Ingrid got up and ran to the edge of the sea. She was shouting something that, at first, I couldn't understand. Then I heard it.

'Ivan, Ivan! Can we meet tonight?' She was shouting in German.

'She's mad,' I muttered to Marko, 'What does she think she's doing? If anyone on this ship didn't know I have a German girlfriend, they certainly will now. After all her father and I have told her about being discreet.'

I ran to the radio cabin, stripped down to my trunks and dived into the water. I swam to within easy reach of the shore. 'Seven tonight,' I called. 'Now go away and no more shouting!'

Ingrid waved and I returned to the ship.

Farewell Ingrid

The girls were waiting for us round the bend in the footpath although I thought the precaution rather wasted after Ingrid's earlier performance. She flung herself on me, crying and laughing. 'I was frightened you wouldn't come back in time to see me again. When I saw your ship this morning, I thought I was seeing things.'

I kissed her and said, 'When I heard you shouting this morning, I thought I was hearing things.'

'Sorry, sorry, sorry.' She sounded repentant. 'Don't be cross. I couldn't bear it.' I kissed her again and we walked slowly to our usual cove. As soon as we were settled on the blanket, she produced a box from her bag. 'I've bought you a present my darling,' she said.

'Another one?' I felt awkward about all the money Ingrid was spending on me.

'To show how much I love you. Open it.' It was a beautiful Swiss watch – an Omega.

'This is too much, Ingrid,' I protested. 'It's a lovely thought but you've already bought me a ring. I can't take this as well.'

I handed the watch back to her but she pushed it at me, crying again. 'If you love me you'll take it and wear it for me. We go home the day after tomorrow. This is my parting gift to you so you'll remember how much I love you. Every time you look at it, you'll have to think of me.'

Perhaps I should have been firm with her but I gave in and allowed her to fasten it round my wrist. I had grown to love Ingrid but not with the same intensity as she seemed to love me. I pushed to the back of my mind a gnawing awareness that Ingrid was manipulative and would probably prove to be possessive. It was a beautiful evening; we hadn't seen each other for a while so we made love and swam together in our own small paradise.

As we parted later, Ingrid said that her parents would like to see me before leaving so we arranged to meet the next day, at the usual time, in a bar just over the bridge on the mainland.

I was on general duties on board the next day. The vice admiral was in a rowing boat with a couple of the engineers attending to the cables. Suddenly there was the roar of an engine as a speed boat came towards the ship. A man was driving and two girls sat behind. I couldn't see their faces. The boat was heading for the cable.

'Ivan, shoot!' shouted the vice admiral. I picked up the flare gun and fired. The flare landed about six feet in front of the boat which was lifted right up and out of the water. I'd never seen such a thing before. Fortunately it landed safely and then, as if in slow motion, the boat turned and sped back to land.

'Well done Vesligaj!' shouted the vice admiral.

About twenty minutes later three figures appeared on the slipway opposite the ship. The man was shouting and gesticulating angrily. The two girls who followed him were Ingrid and Gertrude. I realised immediately that the man was the speedboat driver and the girls had been his passengers. 'Vesligaj!' called one of the officers. 'Go and sort that idiot out. Take someone else with you and go armed.'

As Marko and I got out of the boat, the man was still shouting. 'How dare you fire at my boat. We could have been killed.'

'Indeed you could, sir,' I said. 'Another minute and your boat would have cut the ship's cables and you and everyone with you would have been fried alive.'

'That doesn't give you the right to fire at me. I would have turned before I got to the cable.'

'You gave no sign of turning,' I said. 'You were in the danger zone. Couldn't you see the huge *DANGER* notices and the lightning signs which denote electric current?'

'You'll hear more about this.' The man was still angry. 'My father's a judge in Belgrade. He'll sue the navy for endangering my life.'

Marko took a notebook and pencil from his pocket. 'Please give me your father's name and address,' he said politely. 'I'm happy to write to him and explain what has happened and why the flare gun was used. Come to think of it, the vice admiral saw everything too. I'll request that he writes the letter.' The man was silent and, behind him, Ingrid gave me a big smile and a wink. Marko went on. 'I think the vice admiral may suggest sending the information to the civil police to ask them to take action against you.'

'Is that really necessary?' the man said sullenly.

'It may be. Now, your father's name and address please.' In the event, of course, no action was taken by anyone but we'd done what the officer had asked and sorted 'that idiot out'.

In the evening, Ćiril asked me to take him and a French girl he'd met, to the uninhabited small island Ingrid and I had once visited. 'You're not the only one with a forbidden foreign girlfriend,' he grinned. 'Good job we can keep each others' secrets.'

Ingrid and her parents were waiting for me at the bar and my beer was already on the table. 'We wanted to say a proper farewell,' Raulf said 'and to make sure we have your contact details.' I wrote down the addresses of my mother and my sister, Dragica, who had recently moved to a larger apartment.

'You'll be able to contact me through either of these,' I said. Raulf gave me their address and Ingrid started crying softly at the realisation of our imminent parting.

'Let's go,' she whispered to me and she stood up. 'Ivan and I need some time to say a proper goodbye,' she said. Her parents stood too. Urschula kissed me and Raulf shook my hand.

'What have you done to our daughter?' Urschula said.

She was smiling so I didn't feel alarmed and asked. 'What do you mean?'

'She used to be a difficult, argumentative girl. She seems to have grown up and calmed down a lot.' Ingrid was tugging at my arm so I just laughed and said goodbye once more.

As we were going through the door, Raulf called, 'Come and wave us off in the morning if you can. We're leaving at 10.'

'Will you do that? Will you come and wave us goodbye?' Ingrid pleaded as we walked towards the cove.

'I will if possible but I can't promise,' I said. 'If you park by the bar, I'll do my best to be there.'

That last evening together should have held the same magic as before but was overshadowed by Ingrid's despair at our parting. She kept asking if I loved her. 'Don't ever love anyone else,' she said again and again. Although I knew I couldn't promise this, I murmured as many reassurances as I felt able. I was fairly sure Ćiril would allow me to go ashore in the morning but said nothing to Ingrid in case of problems. She bade me a final sorrowful farewell on her doorstep.

I picked up Ćiril and his girlfriend from the island, deposited the latter on the quay and, as I rowed Ćiril back to the ship, obtained his permission to 'go and buy a paper' just before 10.00 hours the next morning. In bed, I thought of Ingrid. I knew I had to be careful. What had started as a casual holiday romance had turned into an obsession on Ingrid's part. I didn't want to hurt her and I'd tried to warn her at various stages of our relationship that I was not ready for the commitment she wanted. I liked her very much. I loved her, even, but I did not at the moment see her as a possible life companion. I knew that she had used her money to gain power over me. She was probably not really aware of this herself. I made up my mind that, although I would keep in touch with her and probably see her when I had my next leave, I would put off any decision about whether to continue the relationship long term. Who knew what was ahead?

Ingrid leapt out of the car as soon as she saw me the next morning. 'Thank you for coming,' she said. And she held me to her, tears running down her cheeks. She started gabbling in German, too fast for me to understand.

Raulf laughed and translated. 'She says you must never have another girlfriend while you're in the navy and that when you get back to Zagreb, she'll come to see you often and fulfil all your needs.'

I laughed with embarrassment. 'Sorry,' I said to Raulf.

'What for? You've changed my daughter into a woman. We should be thanking you.' We shook hands through the open window.

Urschula got out of the car and embraced me. 'Thank you, Ivan. Good luck,'

'Time to go, Ingrid,' said Raulf.

Ingrid and I kissed once more and, sobbing, she got into the car. She waved out of the back window until they were out of sight and I turned away. Life would be very different for the rest of our time here. I bought a newspaper and returned to the ship. As I handed the paper to Ćiril he said, 'The captain's gone to Split to get married. He'll be back on Sunday.'

'Split? Then he'll have gone across the bridge?'

'Yes, about fifteen minutes ago.'

I dimly remembered seeing a military car pass us as I was kissing Ingrid. It would be very annoying if I were in trouble about her just as she had gone.

'Don't worry about it,' Ćiril laughed when I told him. 'Would you notice anything, if you were on your way to be married?'

I picked the captain up on the Sunday. As I deposited his suitcase in his cabin, he said, 'I need to speak to you Vesligaj. Come back in an hour.'

'Is it true that you've had a German girlfriend for three weeks?' the captain asked as I stood opposite him in his tiny cabin.

'Yes, sir.'

'Do you know the rule forbidding fraternisation with foreigners?'

'Yes, sir. But I assure you I didn't reveal any military secrets. Our relationship was purely sexual '

I could see he was trying not to smile. 'So you never spoke about what you do on the ship?'

'No, sir.'

'I'm pleased to hear it and I believe you. However, I have to issue a punishment. You will be confined to ship for seven days.'

'Yes, sir.' I felt enormous relief. He was giving me the lightest possible punishment.

'You are allowed to swim and do boat duty but you must not go further than the quay.'

I was surprised to see Marko standing outside the cabin. 'You too?' I said. 'Tell the truth and you'll get seven days confined to ship.' He grinned and I went to report to Ćiril.

'You know who this is, don't you?' he said angrily. 'It's that bastard Kaufman. He's been dying for an opportunity to pay you back for the Marinko affair.'

The vice admiral came on to the bridge a few minutes later. 'Heard you've had a bollocking,' he said, his eyes twinkling with laughter.

'Yes, sir.'

'You've been spending time with a German girl, have you?'

'Yes, sir.'

He laughed outright. 'Good for you! We all break rules sometimes. Why aren't you a petty officer 1st class, Ivan Vesligaj?'

I was astonished at the question. 'It's up to the captain,' I stammered.

'Leave him to me,' he said and departed.

A few days later, the vice admiral was on board and the captain ordered an inspection. We assembled on deck and the captain thanked us for the work we had carried out and said we would be returning to base in two days. As he finished I stepped forward and, on behalf of the crew, congratulated him on his marriage. It was the first time we had all been together since the happy event.

'Thank you, Petty Officer Vesligaj,' he said.

The vice admiral, who was standing behind him, tapped him on the shoulder.

'Haven't you forgotten something?' he said sharply.

'Oh yes.' He took a piece of paper from his pocket. 'Petty Officer Ivan Vesligaj, I have received notification of your promotion to petty officer class 1 as from now. Your pay will rise to 500 dinars a month. Congratulations.'

'Thank you, sir,' I said, absolutely delighted. I looked at the vice admiral who gave me a barely perceptible wink.

A Bouquet

Back in Šibenik life settled down on *M143*. We carried out routine maintenance and exercises and, in September, I had a short leave and visited my sister and mother. I didn't have enough time to meet Ingrid but we continued to correspond and soon I had a collection of love letters any man would be proud to possess.

In Spring 1962, a conference for chief naval officers was held on the island of Hvar. We sailed to the north western corner of the long island and dropped anchor. Ćiril joined me on deck once the captain and first officer had disembarked.

'Are you keeping in touch with the lovely Ingrid?' he asked.

'Yes, sir.' I felt myself blushing.

Ćiril laughed. 'I thought you would. Too good to let go, eh?'

'Yes, I…'

'No need to explain to me. The other officers and I are going ashore this evening. You'll be duty officer – in charge of the ship. Just make sure the guard is changed every two hours. You don't need to keep going to look. Just check in the log book.' He wandered off and I felt a surge of pride. At last I'd made it in the navy and I didn't intend to let anything go wrong.

A couple of minutes later Marko arrived. I handed him a cigarette and we sat companionably for a few moments. 'It's ages since you saw Ingrid,' he said. 'Do you miss her?

'Yes I do. I'm planning to see her during my next leave. What about you and Gertrude?'

He looked uncomfortable. 'We've lost touch now. It was never the same between us as between you and Ingrid. Gertrude was all right for a bit of fun but I should never have got involved with her really. Actually I'm married.'

I almost choked on my cigarette. 'Married?' I gasped.

He nodded his head. 'And I've got a son.'

For once I was speechless.

174

Marko went on, 'I had to tell you because my wife and son are coming to Šibenik to visit me next week.'

I didn't know what to say. I still had rather conventional ideas and felt that you should be faithful to your partner if you were married. (I conveniently forgot about Marica.) I was shocked on two counts. First, on moral grounds and secondly, I realised I didn't know Marko as well as I had thought. I felt rather foolish as I remembered the advice I'd given him on the techniques of love-making.

'If I had known you were married, I think I would have told Gertrude,' I said slowly. 'You weren't fair to her. Suppose she had really fallen in love with you?'

'She wasn't in love with me. She wasn't anything like as crazy about me as Ingrid is about you. Still, I probably shouldn't have done it.' I left it there but over the next few weeks I had reason to reflect on this conversation.

As the officers went ashore and I watched the crimson sun sink behind the horizon, I felt elated. I'm in charge here. Really in charge, I thought. Everyone on board the ship has to obey my orders. This is what I had dreamed of – having the entire responsibility of a ship with no-one to answer to but myself.

At 20.00 hours, I found Isaac, the guard, signing on in the logbook. I walked with him to the guard post. Half an hour later, I went to check on him. I couldn't see him at first but I guessed he was under the canvas shelter, erected to make a sort of sentry box. I was right but when I looked inside he was standing, barefoot, reading. He jumped to attention and saluted me. I put my hand out for the book and he gave it to me, blushing. It was a copy of the Jewish Scriptures, in Croatian, open at the story of Cain and Abel. 'Put your shoes on,' I said quietly. He obeyed. I handed him back his book. 'Now take this to your locker.'

'Yes, sir. Sorry, sir.'

He was back in a moment and I spoke seriously, feeling old and experienced. 'As this is your first offence, I shall take no further action. Just promise me that you'll never take your shoes off again while you are on guard duty. You are representing the ship when you're here. What would passers-by think of us if they saw you without shoes? And if there was a problem, you would be very vulnerable if you were barefoot. Also I want you to promise that you will give your whole attention to your duty when you are at this post. You must not read – even a holy book. Do that in your own time. Do you understand?'

Isaac was embarrassed. 'Yes, sir. I promise. Thank you, sir.'

I accompanied the next guard to his post at 22.00 hours. He was Ely, another young Jew and great friend of Isaac's. We found the latter, standing bolt upright, bayonet at the ready. I thought he had learned his lesson. I filled in the logbook, noting weather and sea conditions but not mentioning Isaac's misdemeanour. A few minutes later he came on to the bridge and asked if he could speak to me. 'Of course, sit down.' I said

He sat and said quickly, 'I just want to say that I'm very, very sorry for what happened this evening. I was thoughtless and foolish. I promise such a thing will never happen again. Thank you for your understanding.'

'I have your promise and I believe you. Thank you for coming to see me. Now forget it happened and go to bed. There's just one word of warning – Of course it's all right to read your scriptures but always try to do so when you're on your own. There are a lot of members of the communist party on this ship and you know the communist view of religion, so be careful.' How wise I felt that evening. Little did I know my wisdom was to be short-lived.

Isaac and Ely received regular parcels of food from home. From that evening on, they never failed to share the contents with me. They introduced me to all sorts of new food including Jewish cake and bread and to a delicacy which, they said, was made of wheat dipped in honey. Of course I had to make it clear that, whereas I was delighted with their generosity, I could show them no favours. They simply smiled and I understood that sharing the goodies was their way of saying thank you.

Shortly after this the captain sent for me. He was holding a pot plant. 'Vesligaj,' he said, 'do you think a lady would be pleased to receive this?'

'It would depend on the lady, sir,' I was taken aback by his question.

'My wife. I'm asking you because you seem to have a way with the ladies. Do you think my wife will like this?'

I was doubtful that the small, unattractive pot plant would appeal to the lovely Vesna, of the spilt beer and beautiful figure, but I said, 'It would look all right on a windowsill.'

'We've got pot plants on the window sills. I asked the chef to buy some flowers for my wife when he went to the market this morning and this is what he brought back. He said he couldn't find any cut flowers. Honestly, what do you think?'

'I think she'd like a bouquet of flowers better than the plant.'

'So do I. Will you do me a favour? If I give you the money, will you take the boat to the quay, find a flower shop and buy some flowers. I'll give you a pass in case the MPs stop you. It's a favour, not an order. I just haven't time to go at the moment.'

I walked out of the flower shop with a luxurious bouquet of roses and chrysanthemums with greenery. I had spent only half the money the captain had given me and he was so delighted that he gave me 50 dinars for my trouble.

Within an hour he called me back once more. 'Sorry to bother you again,' he said. 'I've heard you can knot a tie in the modern way. Could you show me?'

I demonstrated how to make a triangular knot in his tie – the very latest fashion – and he left the ship to see his new wife, carrying the bouquet and looking pleased with himself.

I was puzzled about why he had chosen me to advise him on flowers and fashion and even more surprised when he summoned me to his cabin later in the week. 'You've shown me what a trustworthy chap you are,' he said, 'so I have a job for you. One I wouldn't ask anyone else to do. Will you please accompany my wife to the market? I'd promised to take her today but I just don't have the time.' He wrote a short note to Vesna and put his address on the envelope. 'Pick up a dozen bottles of beer too, please, and leave them at the flat.' He handed me some money and I went to explain to Ćiril why I would be absent from the ship for a few hours.

He stared at me for a moment then laughed. 'Talk about sending a lion to look after the sheep! He must be mad.'

I felt myself blushing. 'What do you mean? The captain trusts me.'

'I know he does but just be careful. I mean it. *Be careful*!'

I felt quite hurt by the implications of what Ćiril said. I had no intention of betraying the captain.

Vesna

I pressed the buzzer on the flat door. There was a short pause then Vesna's voice, 'Come right up, darling, I'm ready for you.'

I felt very awkward. 'It's Petty Officer Vesligaj, ma'am, from M143,' I called. 'I have a letter from the captain.'

A longer pause and then she was at the door, lovely in a thin, deep turquoise cotton dress. She was laughing. 'Sorry about that. I've been expecting Dušan for the last half hour.' I handed her the letter. 'Come in,' she said. 'Perhaps you'll kindly carry the beer up for me.' As we climbed the stairs to the first floor, she went on, 'I remember you now, Petty Officer Vesligaj. You're the man who spilt beer over me at the beach party.'

'Yes, ma'am. I'm sorry about that.'

'No harm done.' We'd reached the neat, stylish flat and I put the beer in a cupboard as she asked. When she'd read the letter she laughed again. 'Dušan says you are happy to accompany me to the market and the shops. Is that right? Are you sure you don't mind?'

'It will be my pleasure, ma'am,' I said gallantly.

'Don't call me ma'am. My name is Vesna and may I call you ...?' She hesitated.

'My name is Ivan.'

We chatted as we wandered round the meat market. It was noisy, each person, in the jostling crowd, eager for a bargain. Vesna had to raise her voice so I could hear. 'What do you advise me to buy for dinner tonight?'

I was surprised. Surely it wasn't part of my brief to supply a menu. 'Buy something you both like.'

'Steak then, we both like steak. Have you a favourite way of cooking steak?'

'I like Vienna steak.'

'Will you tell me how to make it?'

'Of course.' Now she was asking me for a recipe. I found it hard to believe.

I helped Vesna select the steaks and then took her to the herb and vegetable stalls to buy the necessary ingredients. On the way back to the flat, I gave her precise instructions on how to cook the dish. It was one of Dragica's specialities and I'd seen her prepare it many times.

Vesna seemed very interested in me and my background. 'I suppose you've had plenty of girlfriends?' she said.

'A few,' I answered guardedly.

'What about the girl I saw you with at the restaurant?'

This was tricky ground and, anyway, none of her business. 'She was just an acquaintance,' I lied once more.

'I met Dušan on holiday,' she mused. 'I had a boyfriend at home but Dušan swept me off my feet.' Suddenly an image of the captain flashed into my mind – a good deal older than Vesna, pale, stocky, with thinning black hair and an unprepossessing black moustache. And he'd swept her off her feet? I could only conclude that he had hidden depths – or was it his money and the prestige of being married to a high ranking officer that attracted her? Vesna was still talking. 'By the way, congratulations on your promotion to petty officer 1st class. You're quite young to get that, I think. How old are you?'

'Twenty two.'

'I'm an old lady in comparison. I'm twenty six. Tell me honestly, have you got a girlfriend in Zagreb?'

'No. I've got friends who are girls but nothing serious.'

'Why?'

'I don't want to tie myself down while I'm in the navy. Time enough for that afterwards.'

She asked me about my interests and when I said I liked to read, she asked me about the books I liked.

'My favourites are about Greek and Roman history and the Ottoman Empire.' She seemed surprised.

'Did you always like history when you were at school?' she asked.

'Yes, and geography and science.'

'Ah geography,' she sighed, 'I'd love to travel outside Yugoslavia. That's the way to learn geography. To see places with your own eyes.'

By this time we were back at the flat and I carried the shopping up to the kitchen.

'Coffee or cognac?' Vesna asked.

'Coffee, please.'

'I'll bring it in to you in a few minutes. Go into the living room.' She indicated the room opposite the kitchen. I looked round the pleasant large room. It had a fitted grey carpet, blue velvet suite, polished sideboard and small tables. Photos and pictures adorned the walls including a big portrait of Marshal Tito in the uniform of an admiral.

Vesna arrived with the coffee and a small cognac each. I had to admit she was beautiful. Her cheeks were flushed from the fresh air and exercise, her long brunette hair shone and her figure was perfect. She told me that only naval officers and their families lived in the apartment block. 'I don't know anyone yet,' she said. 'I suppose I'll make friends in time but I'm a bit lonely and homesick at the moment when Dušan's not here.'

As we finished our refreshment, Vesna got up. 'Come and see the rest of the flat,' she said. 'I'm very proud of it. It's a home of my own at last. I've always lived with my parents before.' She showed me the modern bathroom and then led me into her bedroom. It was sumptuously furnished with a huge bed on which were cream silk sheets and quilt and a mass of small colourful, glossy cushions. There was an air of unreality about the scene. How had I, a petty officer, ended up in my captain's bedroom with his wife?

I didn't know what to say so I did a stupid thing. I sat on the bed and bounced gently. 'Mmm,' I murmured, 'it's comfortable. As soft as…' Before I could get any further, Vesna sat down beside me, took my head in her hands and kissed me on the mouth. I leapt up. 'I have to go.' I gabbled. 'It's 11.30 and I need to be back on board by midday.' I almost ran to the door. I can see myself out,'

Vesna laughed. 'Perhaps next time!' she called after me.

A lucky escape, I thought and then realised that I felt a sense of anti-climax, a vague disappointment. Vesna was certainly exciting but she was also dangerous. And what about Ingrid? Only last evening I had been missing her and wishing we could meet once more in our cove. But in comparison to Vesna, Ingrid was a child. There was something of Marica about the former, something alluring and altogether womanly.

My mind was still filled with the bedroom scene when the post arrived in the early afternoon. I had two letters. I recognised the handwriting on the envelopes of both. One was from my sister, the other from my brother, Lujzek. I opened my sister's first. There was another envelope enclosed. I guessed that it contained a letter from Ingrid. Dragica wrote that the Gunther family had paid her a surprise visit recently.

… Your girlfriend is certainly very beautiful, she said. *She and her parents spoke very highly of you…*

I opened Ingrid's envelope and 500 dinars fell out.

My Darling, Darling, she wrote, *I'm thinking about you all the time and missing you so much. I can't sleep or eat. I am hurting with love for you. Please accept this money and when you spend it, think how much I love you. Please phone me if you possibly can…*

She gave me her phone number and the one for her father's office. She described her visit to Dragica and finished the letter in the same way as it had started. As I walked into the radio cabin for duty, I felt a pang of guilt about Ingrid. How could I even think of Vesna when Ingrid was so passionate and faithful? That's it! I told myself. I shan't need to see Vesna on my own again. I'll stay out of temptation's way and concentrate on Ingrid. I'll phone to thank her for the money and to tell her that I love her.

Just then all thoughts of love were driven from my mind. A message came through in Morse code, not in Serbo Croat but in Russian and then in English which was most unusual. I couldn't understand it but I wrote it down and phoned Ćiril who was in the radar cabin. He was beside me immediately, listened to the recorded message and looked at what I'd written.

'It's something about a missile base in Cuba,' he said. 'It sounds serious. I'll phone Split HQ.' When he put the phone down, his face was grave. 'HQ already knows. You stand by for further information while I find the captain.' Almost straight away, a message came through. The captain was summoned to a meeting in Split on the following Friday.

In the afternoon two lorries drew up at the quay. Boxes were unloaded and carried on to all of the minesweepers. In the boxes were rubber suits with boots attached and gas masks. 'What are they for?' everyone was asking.

Ćiril explained to me that we would wear them if there were a threat of fall-out from a nuclear explosion. 'Get the men together and give them the news,' he said. 'We'll distribute the suits afterwards. They come with instruction booklets.'

The men listened quietly while I told them about the protective suits. As soon as I had finished, questions were fired at me, most of which I couldn't answer. Why had we received the suits now? Was there really a chance of a nuclear explosion within range of us? Everyone was anxious for self and for family. Finally I called for order and told the men where to pick up their suits. 'Please read the instructions carefully. Learn them so that if there is an emergency, you'll know exactly what to do.'

'We'll be having plenty of exercises to make sure of that.' It was the captain. He had come on to the deck without my noticing.

The men could talk of little else all evening. It was a relief to go to bed. Of course, I was as anxious as the next man about the possibility of a nuclear bomb but there was nothing we could do except to be as prepared as possible.

When the captain called for me to go to his cabin, the next morning, I thought he had some further information about Cuba but he was smiling warmly. 'I gather you gave my wife the recipe for Vienna steak when you took her to the market yesterday.'

'Yes, sir. I hope you enjoyed it.'

'It was the best steak I've ever tasted. In view of your success, can I ask you for another favour?'

'Of course sir.' I felt my heart quicken. Was I to see Vesna alone again? And if so…I left that thought unfinished.

'It's a favour, mind,' the captain said. 'It's the same as last time. It's not an order.'

'I understand.'

'Tomorrow morning, could you pick up some more beers and take them to my flat. Then, if my wife wants to go to the market, go with her and carry her shopping home. She's rather homesick and I've got a lot on at the moment. I won't see her for three days because of the conference in Split.'

'I'll do that, sir. Could I have a pass, please?' I couldn't help the thrill I felt at the thought of seeing Vesna. I knew I should make an excuse, say I couldn't go for some reason but it would have been difficult to explain and I didn't even try.

'Do you want a weekend pass too?' he asked.

'Yes please, sir.' As he handed me the papers, he asked curiously, 'What did you and Vesna find to talk about?'

My mind raced. 'History and geography,' I said

He laughed. 'Oh yes. She said you were very knowledgeable. I hadn't realised she was at all interested in history and geography.' He paused then went on, 'I want you to buy another bouquet of flowers for her – even bigger than the last. I've written a note to go with it and here's the money.' He's besotted with her, I thought, as I left the cabin. I did have a qualm of conscience but then brushed it aside. It may never happen, I told myself.

Vesna was expecting me. She buzzed me in straight away and the flat door was open. 'Come in, Ivan, coffee's ready,' she called. 'I asked Dušan to send you again because the beer is very heavy.' She was in the kitchen, dressed in a transparent nightdress, partly covered with a glossy embroidered red satin kimono. She was laughing.

I stood, foolishly for a moment and stammered, 'Your husband sent these flowers and a note.' She took the huge bouquet and envelope and tossed them on the table without looking at them. I put the beers beside them.

Before I could move, she had her arms round me and was kissing me hard on the mouth. 'Thank you, thank you for coming to see me.'

I certainly wanted her but I kept my head. 'Vesna, I have less than two hours before I must be back on the ship. Please get dressed and we'll go shopping. That's what I've come for.'

'Is it? Is that what you've come for, Ivan? Surely not! Don't worry about the shopping. I've already done it.' As she spoke, she loosened her kimono and it slid to the ground.'

I swallowed hard. 'Vesna, this is very dangerous.' I knew it was a weak remark.

'Don't you like me, Ivan?' she said softly, pressing against me.

'Of course I like you but you're married to the captain of my ship. He's my commanding officer and I'm only an unimportant little petty officer.'

'There's nothing little about you,' she said, smiling. 'Anyway, I like to think about you as a monk in that big monastery – that excites me.'

She took my hand and placed it on her breast and all was lost. She led me to the bedroom and slipped out of her nightdress. Then she undressed me and pushed me on to the bed. She crossed the room to draw the blinds.

'Suppose someone notices that and puts two and two together?' I asked anxiously.

'Don't worry, this room is at the back. There's no back garden so no-one can overlook us.' It flashed through my mind that her husband had given me permission to be there. If anyone happened to comment on my presence, he'd think nothing of it. With that thought, I gave myself up to Vesna.

She was an experienced and passionate lover and I allowed her to take the initiative. She had none of the gentleness of Marica or the soft sweetness of Ingrid. There was a hardness, almost ruthlessness to her love-making and we reached climax after climax until, at last, she suggested a shower.

We made love again under the cool spray and when I looked at my watch, the morning had gone and it was past the time I should have left. 'I wish I'd met you earlier – much earlier, before I'd met Dušan,' Vesna said, as I hurriedly struggled into my clothes.

'But I haven't any money,' I replied, searching her face.

She gave a short laugh. 'That's true but perhaps money's not everything.'

I had a feeling, though, that money was very important to Vesna and that sex without money would soon lose its glow.

She hung on to me as I tried to leave, saying, 'Will you meet me tomorrow evening? In the bar near the church? It's very quiet. No-one we know goes there Will you meet me between 7 and 7.30?'

'I'll try.' She kissed me again and then I ran out of the flat. I was going to be late getting back to the ship. Nevertheless, I felt light on my feet as I sprinted to the quay. What a morning I'd had. I didn't think about the consequences but simply gave myself up to memories of pleasure.

Two French girls, sitting by the quay, called out to me, *'Bonjour Sailor.'*

'Bonjour,' I shouted as I untied the boat.

'Je m'appelle Jeanette. Comment t'appelle?'

I didn't speak French but guessed the meaning. *'Je m'appelle Ivan.'* I pushed off, feeling as if I could conquer the world.

Ćiril was waiting for me on deck. 'You're twenty five minutes late. Where the hell have you been?'

'I'm sorry, sir,' I said humbly. 'I've been on an errand for the captain. I thought you knew. I'm sorry I didn't mention it to you.'

'The captain's on M144 at the moment. We have lots to do now. Radio signals have been coming thick and fast. Come and help me in the radio cabin.'

We intercepted a message from the American fleet. We couldn't decode all of it but it was clear that serious trouble was brewing over allegations that a USSR missile base was being built in Cuba. We forwarded the signals to Split headquarters for decoding. A reply was received straight away, confirming the subject. There had been rumours about the base and we had noticed Soviet trucks unloading unmarked crates on to Soviet ships. Now it seemed that the Americans had got themselves involved in some way too.

There was a knock on the cabin door. Ćiril opened it and the captain stood there. We updated him on the latest message and then he said, 'This is certainly a very serious world situation. For the moment, all we can do is listen for news and continue with the safety exercises. I'll know more after the conference.' He paused and then said something which made my heart lurch. 'Lieutenant, would you mind leaving Vesligaj and me alone for a few minutes, There's something I want to discuss with him.'

How has he discovered about Vesna and me so quickly? I thought. What can I say? I have no excuse. Ćiril looked at me curiously and left the cabin.

'I want to talk to you about my wife,' the captain said in a low voice. He didn't seem angry and I felt weak with relief when he went on, 'As you know, I have to go to Split for the weekend and Vesna wants to go out tomorrow evening with a new friend, Lucy, who lives in the same block as us. I'm worried about them going out unattended. Lucy's husband is a major in the army and will be at the conference too.'

I could hardly believe my ears. The captain seemed to be implying that he wanted me to go out with the two women. I decided to pretend I didn't understand. 'Couldn't they wait until you get back on Sunday, sir? You could all go out together then.'

'My wife is a very determined lady, Vesligaj,' he said with a certain measure of pride. 'If she's made up her mind to go out on Friday, she'll go, I'm afraid.'

'How can I help, sir?' I asked innocently.

'Will you take Vesna out on Friday and Saturday evenings? That way she won't be bored while I'm away and she'll be safe. I know I can trust you. As it happens, I'm not terribly keen on Lucy. She's quite a bit older than Vesna and…well, I'd be happier if she were with you.'

I felt sorry for the man. He knew Vesna was spoilt and stubborn but he loved her and desperately wanted to keep her happy. I was in an impossible situation. If I refused his request, he'd want to know why but if I complied with his wishes, I knew what would happen.

I prevaricated. 'I haven't a special pass for Friday, sir,' I said, 'and your wife won't be expecting me.'

'Leave all that to me. I'll contact her and you can have passes, for both nights, until 01.00hours. Anything else?'

Once more the figures of Marica and her unsuspecting husband flashed through my mind. There seemed to be a sort of inevitability about the Vesna affair. I had a sudden thought and, embarrassed, knew there was something I must say. 'I'm sorry to mention this but there is the matter of money. If you want me to take your wife to a good restaurant or bar – well, I just can't afford to do it, sir. I'm sorry.'

'Of course,' he fished a thousand dinar note out of his wallet and handed it to me. 'Get her whatever she wants. She's very fond of champagne. And look after her for me.' He turned back as he opened the door to go and added softly, 'Please don't chatter about what I've asked you to do. I'd rather it were confidential.'

A few moments later, Ćiril came in. 'What's going on, Ivan – or is it a secret?'

'It is but I'll tell you if you like because I know I can trust you.'

'It will go no further. I promise you that.'

So I told him, finishing with, 'if you advise me against it, I'll find some excuse. What do you think?'

Ćiril's eyes widened. 'Tell me the truth, did you make love to her yesterday when the captain sent you there with the flowers?'

I paused briefly then said, 'Yes.'

Ćiril gave a laugh. 'You're in deep, Ivan,' he said. 'The man's a bloody fool. You can't do anything but go along with what he's asked because if you raise an objection now he'll get suspicious. I mentioned to my girlfriend, yesterday, that the captain had sent you to look after his wife. She remarked that you are a young sailor and an affair with the captain's wife would be one big adventure.' I realised that his girlfriend was right. I didn't love Vesna, I didn't even particularly like her but she was beautiful and forbidden and making love with her was certainly an adventure. Perhaps it was guilt that made me ask for a pass for the next morning so that I could phone Ingrid.

At the post office, the following day, I told the woman that I wanted to phone my sister who was living in Germany. It was a necessary lie because she, anyone in her office or in the queue behind me could be a member of UDBa. I spoke to Raulf Gunther first, in his office. 'Ingrid's in the other room,' he said. I heard him call, 'Ingrid, Ivan's on the phone!' He and I barely had time to exchange pleasantries before it seemed as if the phone was snatched from his hand.

'My darling, darling,' Ingrid started to cry. 'It's been such a long time. I miss you so much,'

'Calm down Ingrid,' I said. 'It's lovely to speak to you. Thank you very much for the letter and the money. You really shouldn't.'

'I want to, I want to,' she cried. 'I think about you day and night.' Then I did feel guilty.

'I think about you too,' I said. 'I'm due for leave soon. When I have the dates I'll phone and let you know. Perhaps you could come to Zagreb and we can both stay at my sister's.'

'That would be wonderful. Of course I'll come.' She told me that Gertrude was to be married and that nothing interesting was happening in her own life. 'It's deadly boring and empty without you,' she sighed.

As I walked towards the ship I thought about Ingrid and my coming leave. It would be good to see her again. Love seemed simple with her. I had allowed myself to become embroiled in a dangerous web of deceit with Vesna. Yet, even as I was thinking this, I knew I would do nothing to free myself even though I didn't know what the outcome would be.

I heard a shout from behind and when I turned round, Marko was hurrying towards me. A woman, carrying a small child, and another man were following him. Marko had taken a couple of day's leave in order to spend time with his wife while she was visiting Šibenik. He caught up with me and, turning, held out his hand to a stunning blonde.

'Ivan, this is Ana, my wife and my son, little Marko.' Ana looked just like Bridget Bardot and gave a laugh as I lifted her hand and kissed it.

'Ana, this is my friend and superior, Ivan Vesligaj.'

'I'm pleased to meet you,' she said. I admired the baby. He was about nine months old, with a mass of black hair and a dark complexion, a healthy, smiling boy. Ana indicated the second man. 'This is my cousin from Belgrade,' she said. The cousin, a dark swarthy man, and I shook hands and after exchanging a few more pleasantries, I went on board, leaving Marko to say his farewells.

I went straight to see Ćiril when I reached the ship. I thanked him for allowing me ashore to make the phone call and went on to remind him that I was due for my annual leave.

'So you are,' he said, 'when the captain returns from the conference tomorrow, I'll talk to him about when we can spare you. Where are you taking his wife this evening, by the way?' He grinned as he asked the question.

'I'm not sure yet,' I replied. 'Probably to the theatre. The opera 'Othello' is on and I'd like to see it.'

Ćiril laughed. 'But will she? She doesn't strike me as particularly cultured.'

I turned to go into the radio cabin and Ćiril said, 'I almost forgot Ivan. You're on your first security patrol on Sunday evening.' This meant that I, along with two others, would go ashore and act in the capacity of military police. Ćiril went on, 'There's been trouble recently with an anti-Tito faction so the orders are that you go fully armed with side-guns and sub-machine guns,'

I groaned. I hated carrying a sub-machine gun. It was just too easy to have an accident, to fire in error or to misfire. 'Do I have to take a sub-machine gun?' I asked.

'You do, I'm afraid.'

'Can I empty the magazine, then? I'll frighten any wrong-doers simply by carrying it.'

'All right. Make sure you lock the bullets away safely and don't tell anyone – except Marko. He's on duty with you. Tell him he can do the same if he wants to but to keep mum about it.'

'Thank you very much. Which officer is on with us?'

'Lieutenant Kaufman.' I groaned again. 'I know you don't like him any more than I do,' Ćiril said softly. 'I don't trust him. Watch him carefully. Listen to what he says and note where he goes. He's a slippery customer.' I didn't have time to follow up this remark as someone came to say the captain wanted to see me.

'Where are you planning to take my wife this evening, Vesligaj?' the captain asked.

'I thought we'd go to the theatre, if that's all right, sir.'

'A splendid idea. Vesna could do with widening her horizons a little. The tickets maybe rather expensive though.'

'You gave me a thousand dinars. I'm sure that'll be enough, sir.'

'Just give her a good time. That's all I ask,' he said. 'I'm leaving in half an hour so I won't have a chance to talk to you again. Keep her happy for me Vesligaj.'

By that time, Marko was back on board. I sat next to him for the midday meal. 'You have a very beautiful wife,' I said.

I expected him to laugh but he said seriously, 'My advice is, never marry a beautiful woman. She might be your wife but she'll be everybody else's woman. That man who travelled with her isn't her cousin. She made that story up. I've never seen him before and I'm sure I've met all of her cousins. Apart from that, she'd already told me that he was just someone she'd met on the train so she changed her story. The man wasn't staying in our hotel but she kept talking about him, wondering what he was doing. She included him in most of our outings too. We had hardly any time on our own. What do you think I should do? Please tell me what you think. I shan't be offended.' Then he added, as an afterthought, 'And I know I'm not perfect.'

'You're certainly not,' I laughed, 'and I'm not going to give you advice. I'm going to remind you of something that happened a couple of months ago. Do you remember that seaman who came to me with a letter he'd had from his wife. He couldn't read very well and he asked me to read it to him. It was a bit embarrassing because she'd written him a love letter. There was a sheet of paper, with the letter, on which there was the outline of a baby's hand. "Look," the lad said to me, "My wife has drawn round my new son's hand. I'm a daddy!" Do you remember what I said to you afterwards?'

'Yes,' said Marko slowly. 'You said that the poor bloke's last leave had been eleven months before… Oh God! What shall I do?'

'It's completely up to you. I can't advise you but I will say that I don't think the man with your wife is her cousin.'

'I'll have to have a proper think about the whole thing,' Marko said miserably and he went off to be by himself.

As I was about to leave the ship at 19.20 hours, I saw Ćiril. 'Inspection time,' he said. 'Can't have you letting the side down. You're not going out with just anyone. The captain's wife is *someone.*' He looked me over carefully, including shoes and nails. 'You'll do,' he laughed. 'Have a good time and don't do anything I wouldn't do.'

I wasn't sure whether I should meet Vesna at the bar near the church, as we'd agreed, or whether I should go to the flat. I decided on the former. If Vesna didn't turn up, I could go to on the flat. I also wasn't sure if Lucy would be with her. A crowd of us left the ship together. 'Where shall we go?' Marko asked me. 'I've heard about a great bar just off the square. We could give it a try.'

'It will have to be another time, sorry. I've arranged to meet an acquaintance.'

The bar was very quiet. There were a few foreign tourists and no music. I ordered a beer and sat in a corner but didn't have long to wait before Vesna appeared. She was on her own. She looked wonderful, red lips, glossy hair to her shoulders, summery close-fitting dress. She looked round, saw me, gave her beautiful smile and came straight over. I stood up and we embraced.

'Hello darling,' she whispered. She smelt of flowers. She wanted a glass of white wine and, as she sipped it, her leg touched mine under the table. She smiled again and said, 'What plans have you for this evening?'

'I thought we'd go to the theatre. There's an opera on, "Othello". Is that all right for you?'

'Anywhere with you will be all right with me. You know that,' she said. 'Dušan told me that you and I will be going out together tomorrow evening too. Are you sure you don't mind? You won't be bored with me by then?' She was provocative, flirting.

'I'll have to see,' I teased.

She moved her leg gently up and down mine. 'We could go back to the flat now, of course,' she murmured. 'I'll make sure you're not bored there.'

It was very tempting but I stood up. 'No Vesna, I told your husband we'd go to the opera and that's what we'll do.'

We sat in the back row of the raked auditorium. The lighting was soft, the seating comfortable. I would have liked to lose myself in the sublime music, the singing, the story, but Vesna had other ideas. As we sat close, my arm round her, she did all she could to distract me.

Finally, before the opera was half way through, she whispered, 'I need to go to the *Ladies*. I'm not sure where it is. Do you remember? Come and show me.'
We slid out of the seats and I started to guide her towards the correct door but she pulled away and made for the exit which let on to the street. She took no

notice of my whispered instructions and we were soon outside in the square. 'I've never been to an opera before, Ivan,' she said, 'and I'll never go again. All that singing and standing about. It's not for me. I'd rather go to the boring war films Dušan drags me to. Come on, let's go back to the flat.' I wondered if she'd planned this from the start. The captain was right when he described her as 'a very determined lady'.

As we reached the flat, Vesna went ahead of me to check there was no-one about. She locked the door behind us and, snatching my hat, threw it on to the kitchen table. She pulled me into the living room, and we made love there on the thick carpeted floor. She seemed desperate with desire and I needed no second invitation. Then, in bed, we drank cognac and coffee and it happened all over again, Vesna always in charge, dominant. Fleetingly, I wondered what her sex life with the captain was like. Later she asked me about my plans for life after national service. Recently I had been thinking about these, myself. 'I might go back to the monastery to do further study if they'll have me,' I said.

'Is that likely, seeing that you've broken your vow of celibacy?'

'How do you know I made a vow?' I asked. 'You told me you're not a Roman Catholic.'

'Dušan brought your file home one evening and I had a look through it. I found out all about you including the celibacy.' I was shocked that the captain had removed my confidential file from the ship but I didn't say so. My suspicion that 'celibacy' was one reason that Vesna found me attractive was confirmed, however. She hung on to me when it was time for me to leave. 'Stay with me for the night, Ivan,' she begged. 'Let's wake up together in the morning.'

'Not possible,' I said. 'I'd be in dreadful trouble and we can't take any more risks than we have already – or someone will discover our secret.'

She kissed me and laughed. 'Just think, Ivan, we're secret lovers. Isn't that exciting? We'll meet in the same bar tomorrow, shall we?'

Back on board, Marko was awake on his mattress on deck. I fetched mine and put it down next to him.

'Have a good evening?' he whispered.

'Yes thanks. You?'

'It was OK but I still haven't decided what to do about Ana. Your friend, Milan, was here looking for you when I got back. He asked me to tell you he'll come again tomorrow.'

I was on the look-out for Milan the next morning and he arrived at about 10.00 hours. As soon as he saw me on the deck he hurried over to shake hands. When he saw my stripes, he drew back in exaggerated respect. 'Sorry to be so familiar, sir,' he grinned. 'I'd no idea.'

I took his hand and pumped it up and down. 'It's good to see you Milan. Where are your stripes?'

'Never was as clever as you, Vesligaj,' he said, good-naturedly. 'I came to see if we could meet up this evening – go for a drink together?'

'Sorry, not tonight, I'm meeting a friend.'

'Tomorrow?'

'I'm on shore duty. Be careful, I'll be on the look-out for trouble-makers like you.'

He laughed again. 'Who's your officer?'

'Kaufman,'

'I don't envy you. He's a rotten sod. He once caught me smoking outside the radio cabin. I won't tell you what he called me. He's a nasty piece of work.' I nodded. I didn't want to say anything when there were people around. I knew Kaufman was always on the look-out for an opportunity to get me into trouble. We arranged to meet on Monday evening and Milan left.

During the day I ascertained, from Ćiril, that there had been no change of plan with regard to the officers' return from the conference. They were still expected back on Sunday afternoon. Vesna and I were safe for another evening. We met at the same bar. She looked as beautiful as ever but I noticed she was wearing flat shoes. 'I thought we could go for a walk,' she said, after we'd kissed. 'There's a little park near here. Dušan and I went there once and didn't see a soul.'

We walked through the park. It was a warm, fragrant evening. We sat for a while and Vesna held me close. It should have been perfect but I quickly realised that she had very few topics of conversation. The only thing we had in common was sexual attraction. She said she never read books, just magazines. The only music she liked was 'something to dance to'. She had no real interest in history and little knowledge of current affairs. She was a shallow woman, interested only in herself and fulfilling her own desires but she was, indeed, very beautiful. Quite soon, she got up, saying, 'Let's go back to the flat.'

This time, we had coffee and cognac first and then went to the bedroom. It was very hot and we made love and showered alternately until it was midnight and time for me to leave. Lying back against the pillows, she sighed. 'I just wish that Dušan was staying away for a month.' I asked her about something which intrigued me. At the start of our affair, I had produced a condom but she had brushed it aside. 'You don't need that,' she'd said, 'I'll look after that side of things.'

Now I asked, 'How do you manage about contraception Vesna? I know it's not easy for a woman to find a doctor willing to help.'

'I can't have children,' she answered. 'That's handy for us, isn't it?' I couldn't tell how she really felt about it.

'Does your husband know?' I said.

'Yes. He's fine about it,' she said carelessly. 'He says that if we decide we want children, we can adopt.' She paused and then said, 'When can we see each other next?'

'I'm not sure,' I replied. I was surprised by a sudden feeling that I wouldn't mind if I never saw her again. The magic had disappeared. 'The officers will be back tomorrow and I'm on duty in the evening, anyway,'

'And we're going to a wedding reception tomorrow evening. I'll contact you in some way. I can't survive for very long without seeing you again.' She kissed me and I hurried back to the ship.

When the officers returned from the conference the captain sent for me almost immediately. I experienced the familiar shiver of fear. He was sitting behind his desk looking serious when I entered his cabin.

'Did everything go all right with my wife, Vesligaj?'

Warily, I said, 'Yes thank you, sir. We went to the opera on Friday, as I planned and on Saturday we went for a drink and then later for a walk. I'm sure your wife will be pleased you're back, though, sir.'

At last the captain smiled and I relaxed. 'Thank you Vesligaj. I rely on you. I trust you. Report to me here at 14.00 hours tomorrow, there's a matter we need to discuss. That's all for now.' I wasn't concerned as I assumed he wanted to talk to me about my leave. I went straight to the radio cabin.

'Ah, I wanted to see you,' Ćiril said,' 'there's something I want you to do for me this evening. Do you remember I said I'd like you to keep an eye on Kaufman while you're on duty with him?'

'Yes, sir. I did wonder what you meant.'

'I think Kaufman may be married although he hasn't had official permission. It's just a feeling I've got. You may pick up something this evening. You'll be together the whole time, of course. The three duty officers must never separate.'

I promised I'd be alert to all Kaufman said and did and then went to find Marko.

I had a key to the armoury so he and I collected our weapons. At 20.00 hours, we presented ourselves to Kaufman and passed his inspection. Then the three of us set off for the centre of Šibenik.

There were lots of sailors about, many with their girlfriends. 'There won't be any trouble yet,' Kaufman said. 'The bars are only just opening and the disco hasn't started. I'd like to see my young lady before we get too busy.'

He led us up a narrow cobbled street and knocked at a blue front door. An elderly lady answered, smiled broadly and hugged him by way of greeting. Kaufman introduced us and we trooped into the living room.

The girlfriend got up and kissed Kaufman. She had a plain but pleasant face. 'Come into the bedroom darling,' she said. 'I've bought some new records I want you to hear.' Without a backward glance, Kaufman followed her out of the room. An elderly man appeared with some coffee and we sat, making small talk. After about twenty five minutes, I looked at my watch.

The woman noticed. 'Don't worry,' she said, 'they *are* married.'

'That's nice,' I said. 'When did they marry?'

'About a month ago. Just a small affair. Family only.' I didn't say anything but I felt triumphant. I knew that Kaufman's disobeying of a military rule would probably mean the end of his naval career and I was pleased. He was an unpleasant and dishonest man who used his power to bully those below him. I still held him partly to blame for the death of Marinko.

Kaufman was re-arranging his uniform and a little red in the face when he emerged from the bedroom. 'Come on,' he said sharply, as if we had been keeping him waiting. 'It's time we were off.'

The square and park were empty of sailors but blaring music drew us to the disco. Kaufman stopped to talk to the doorkeepers. As soon as Marko and I went inside I sensed trouble. It was a familiar scene. The hall floor was swirling with white naval uniforms and colourfully dressed young women while local youths were grouped sullenly along one side, muttering together. They didn't stand a chance of dancing while there were sailors in the room. They looked at us angrily as we stood inside the door.

I spotted a leading seaman from M143 talking to one of the girls and I attracted his attention. He came across to me. 'Can I see your pass, please,' I said. It was for 23.00 hours. That was the usual time for sailors to return to ship. 'When you all leave the hall I think there could be trouble from these local lads,' I said. 'I want you to send the word round that all naval personnel must assemble outside at 22.45 hours. You will be responsible for marching them back to their ships. Is that clear?'

'Yes, sir.' This was a common tactic if there were any hint of trouble in the town.

Kaufman sauntered over to me. 'We should get our lot marched back before 23.00 hours' he said. 'There could be a spot of bother here later.'

'I've just arranged that, sir,' I said.

We left the disco and walked through the streets, checking bars and clubs for potential trouble but we found none. 'It's a quiet night,' Kaufman commented. 'Nothing for us to do. I'd like to call in at that hotel over there. An officer I know was married today and the reception is being held there. Come on.' I was appalled at the slipshod manner in which Kaufman was carrying out his duty but he was our senior officer so we trailed behind him. The ballroom of the hotel was full of dancing and laughter and I spotted Vesna immediately, standing next to the bride. She looked beautiful in a dark blue silk gown and she wore a white flower in her hair. I was sure she'd noticed me but she gave no sign.

'Sit there,' Kaufman said, pointing to a table in the corner. He went off to congratulate his friend and mingle with the other officers and their wives. I saw him salute the captain and ask one of the ladies for a dance. Marko and I sat, our machine guns held between our knees, feeling out of place and like poor relations. Eventually, the bride took pity on us and brought over two small beers.

'Thank you but we can't drink. We're on duty,' we said.

She went to the captain who looked over and put his thumbs up. The bride brought the beers back and we thanked her and sipped them slowly. Suddenly, Vesna was in front of me, 'Will you dance with me?' she asked. She was clearly tipsy.

'Sorry, ma'am,' I said, 'I'm on duty.

'What will you have to drink, then?'

'The captain has given permission for us to have these small beers.'

'Is that all? We'll soon remedy that.' She was carrying a large glass of brandy and, without warning, she pushed my head back and poured some at my mouth which I had to open as I didn't want liquid trickling down my chin. Marko was watching, in astonishment and she reached across and delivered a swig of brandy to him in the same way. 'Now I'm going to ask my husband if I can dance with you,' she said loudly and wove her way over to the captain. She whispered to him, he nodded and she beckoned me over.

I put my guns on the table. 'Look after these,' I muttered to Marko and went across to Vesna. The captain smiled indulgently as we took to the dance floor and I made sure I held her at arm's length for the whole of the dance.

'I miss you so much,' she whispered. 'When can I see you again?'

I tried to speak through my teeth, without moving my mouth. I was very nervous that the captain would lip-read our conversation. I knew he was watching. 'I don't know. It depends on your husband.' I ignored the rest of her loving comments and was extremely relieved when the dance was over and I could escort her back to the captain. 'Thank you, ma'am,' I said. I saluted the captain. 'Thank you, sir,'

'I enjoyed the dance,' Vesna said and, to her husband, 'He's a lovely dancer.'

I went back to Marko but refused to be drawn on the subject of Vesna. Another half an hour elapsed before Kaufman was ready to leave.

Once more we walked through the town and in and out of clubs and bars. There were no sailors around and, at the disco, I was pleased to see that the leading seaman had taken the ratings back to their ships. We spotted two seamen in a small park. They were clearly drunk and one was throwing up in the bushes. Kaufman used his walkie talkie to contact the local Military Police garrison. Within a few minutes, the black Maria arrived to take the offenders back to their ship where they would be dealt with by the duty officer. That was our only incident.

Kaufman decided to go back to his 'girlfriend'. This time we were not invited in but told to wait outside on a bench. It was 23.15 hours. A couple of policemen came by and asked if we could spare them each a cigarette. We obliged and then sat smoking and chatting. Two hours later, Kaufman emerged. 'We'll make one more sweep of the town,' he said, 'and then head back to the ship.'

After breakfast the next day, I went to the radio cabin as usual. Ćiril was there.

'How did it go last night?' he asked. 'Anything to report?'

'It was a quiet night, sir,' I replied, 'but I do have one thing to report. It may be better not to talk about it on the ship.'

He understood immediately. 'Shall we go for a stroll ashore,' he said. 'Stretch our legs.' We'd often done this before so no-one would think it strange. 'Well?' he said as soon as we were out of earshot of any naval personnel.

'You were right,' I said. 'Kaufman is married.' I told him about Kaufman's two visits to his wife's house last evening and about the mother's remark.

'Got him!' he said gleefully. 'He's a nasty piece of work and cocky with it. As I said, I had a feeling about this – or rather my girlfriend did. She said that Kaufman treats his girl as if he owns her. He doesn't try to please her but always expects her to do whatever he wants.'

'Your girlfriend is very perceptive,' I said, thinking of another remark she'd made about me in relation to Vesna.

He laughed and went on. 'Now, about Kaufman...'

'I'd be grateful if you wouldn't involve me please, sir. Don't say I told you. You could just report your suspicion to the captain and then he's bound to follow it up at the registry office.'

'I'll do that. Thanks, Ivan.' I saluted him and went straight back to the ship, leaving him to think about the downfall of his fellow officer.

Promptly at 14.00 hours, I knocked on the captain's door. He invited me to sit down. 'You know I have trusted you and am grateful to you for the way you have helped me, don't you Vesligaj?' he said. 'Which is why what I'm going to say next, is not good news as far as I'm concerned.' I couldn't imagine what was coming. My conscience certainly wasn't clear and I felt very uneasy. The captain took a large envelope from his desk drawer. 'This is your transfer to the destroyer, the *Split, R11* '

I was incredulous, exhilarated. I had always wanted to serve on a destroyer but hadn't thought I stood a chance. I'd reconciled myself to finishing my national service aboard the minesweeper. I welcomed the challenge of serving on a big ship with a diverse and, on the whole, more intelligent crew. Above all, I wanted to travel the world which is what the destroyers did – unlike minesweepers which spent most of their time at base except for moving out for a few days each month for exercises. I knew I was unlikely to find another boss as good as Ćiril whom I liked and respected but I was surprised that my overriding feeling was one of relief. Relief that now my affair with Vesna must end. It couldn't have gone on without detection and I knew she wouldn't let go easily. I was tired of her constant demands, her indiscretion and lack of interest with anything but sex.

While all this was racing through my mind, the captain was still talking. 'We'll be very sorry to lose you, Vesligaj, but *R11* is short of one communications officer and needs to fill the position as soon as possible. You can transfer when she calls at Šibenik on Monday. She'll be on her way to the destroyer base at Split. An officer will come for you at 10.00 hours. I'll inform her commander that you are due for your annual leave which will start on 11th October, by the way.' He paused and then asked, 'How do you feel about this news?' I assured him that I would be sorry to leave *M143* but would welcome the new challenge. He stood up and shook my hand. 'I'm grateful for what you have done for my wife and I have one more favour to ask. I'd like you to go to my flat again on Thursday morning. Buy some beers and take them to the flat and take Vesna to the market to choose some good steak so we can have that delicious Vienna steak again in the evening.'

He handed me some money and I made up my mind that, if at all possible, Thursday would be the last time I'd see Vesna, that I'd make it a short visit and that I wouldn't mention my move to her. A clean break would be best. Then I heard the captain say, 'Please don't tell Vesna about your transfer.'

I didn't query what he said and, to this day, I don't know why he asked that of me. I simply said, 'I won't, sir. Thank you, sir,' put the money in my pocket, saluted and left the cabin.

I went straight to see Ćiril. 'Did you know I'm to be transferred to the *R11*, sir?' I asked him.

He was shocked. 'No I didn't. Why? It's not because the captain's...?

'I don't think so. It appears *R11* is in need of a radio officer.'

'When?'

'Next week when she calls here.'

'But we need you too. I'm going to see the captain.' He was back after a couple of minutes, shaking his head. 'It's no good,' he said. 'Apparently the order came from "on high" so the captain can't do anything about it. He has to obey orders. I'll miss you. I've enjoyed working with you. I hope we'll come across each other again.'

'I hope so too sir – and we can keep in touch by radio.'

I wondered if the vice admiral had had a hand in this move but I'd never know. As soon as I had some free time I sorted out my locker and started to pack my kitbag. I knew there were days before my transfer but I've always liked to be organised in very good time. I had no idea what lay ahead of me. How would it feel if I were involved in a real war rather than simply in exercises and manoeuvres? I told myself that there was no point in worrying. I'd always wanted adventure and this might be it. I still had a strong belief in God and still imagined my guardian angel watching over me. Secretly, I prayed every night for the safety of my family and myself. I never mentioned my faith to anyone.

I took the motorboat to Šibenik the next morning. I wanted to get the visit to Vesna over quickly and to phone Ingrid to give her the date of my leave before I returned to the ship. Vesna opened the door as I arrived.

'Come in,' she said and burst into tears.

'What on earth is wrong?' I asked.

'Oh Ivan, I've fallen head over heels in love with you. Whatever shall I do? I love you very much.'

'Don't say that, Vesna. You know we can have no future together,' and I drew away a little. She sobbed more loudly and clung on to me. I spoke to her softly. 'Now be calm, Vesna. I haven't got long this morning. Don't waste the short time we have in crying. Your husband asked me to go with you to the market to buy some steak and some vegetables and beer, as usual. I'll carry everything back here but then I have to get straight back to the ship. We'll have to talk about this another time. Please stop crying.' My quiet manner seemed to soothe her, and although I felt bad about leading her to think there would be another time, I couldn't see an alternative. The captain had told me not to mention my transfer and I dreaded to think how she would react if I did. Vesna kissed me and applied some make-up to her tear-streaked face and we set off for the market.

An hour later, I put our purchases on the kitchen table, kissed Vesna and walked to the door. She kissed me again and squeezed me to her. 'Come again as soon as you can,' she begged.

'Goodbye,' I said quietly and walked away. I was to see her only once more in Šibenik. I was in turmoil as I hurried towards the post office. Guilt jostled with relief, excitement with regret. I really need a holiday! I thought.

Ingrid answered the phone this time. Once more she started to cry when she heard my voice. I was drowning in women's tears and it was my own fault!

'Ingrid,' I said, 'don't cry. I'm phoning with good news. My leave starts on 11th October. I have twenty one days due to me. Can you get to Zagreb on the 11th?'

'Of course I can,' she was shouting down the phone. 'Of course, of course!'

I laughed. 'Go to Dragica's apartment and wait for me there. I'll get there as early as I can.'

'Wonderful!' Ingrid cried. 'I've missed you so much. I love you.'

Milan was on the deck of *M141* when I returned. I was pleased to see him. 'What are you doing here?' I asked.

'Waiting for you, *sir*,' he grinned. He pointedly turned sideways so that I could see the new stripe on his sleeve.

'Congratulations Leading Seaman,' I said, shaking his hand.

'I'm going into town tomorrow night to celebrate. Will you come too, please? I'll ask a few friends from my ship.'

'I'd be delighted,' I replied.

I walked down the gang plank to see him off and he said softly, 'There's something I want to tell you.' We walked a bit away from the ship. 'I wanted you to be the first to hear my news. I'm leaving M143 on Monday. I'm transferring to the destroyer *Pula, R22*.'

I laughed and clapped him on the back. 'Congratulations again! That's really good news. I know you've always wanted to serve on a destroyer – as have I – so here's my news. I'm transferring on Monday too, to *Split, R11*. This means we'll still be in the same squadron.'

We laughed together, delighted at our mutual good fortune. 'We'll have a double celebration tomorrow,' Milan declared.

The next evening I met Milan and four of his friends on shore and we strolled into town. 'How much money have you got?' Milan asked.

'Plenty. Don't worry. I was, indeed, relatively wealthy. The captain had told me he didn't want any change from the money he had given me to take Vesna out and I still had some left from Ingrid's gift.

We selected a restaurant which had a dance platform and a veranda overlooking the beach. The weather was very warm but a welcome cool breeze came off the sea. We ordered drinks and settled to chat about life on a minesweeper and to watch the girls go by. I told Milan about Ingrid and our holiday romance. In return, I heard about a beautiful girl he had dated while on the island of Vis.

After a while a group of officers arrived and I saw my captain with Vesna on his arm. I was hidden from her view by the sailors sitting opposite me. Nevertheless, I drew back and slid down in my chair in order to be as inconspicuous as possible. Milan noticed and looked at me inquiringly. 'It's my captain and his wife,' I explained. 'I'd rather they didn't see me.'

'Why?'

'It's a long story. It started on the beach in Rogoznica when I accidentally spilt beer over her tee shirt.' Before Milan could reply, I saw that the captain and Vesna were on the dance floor and she was looking straight at me. I pretended I hadn't noticed and continued talking to Milan in a low voice. 'That's all I'm going to say and now can we talk about something else? – or maybe we should move on to another restaurant.' But it was too late. I saw Vesna say something to her husband. As they sat down at the end of the dance the captain called the waiter who came straight over to us.

'What would you gentlemen like to drink?'

'We have drinks, thank you,' I said.

'I know, but the officers want to buy you a round.'

Milan's friends ordered cognac. I felt I should keep a clear head. 'Just a beer for me, please,' I said. Milan followed my example. Almost immediately, a bottle of cognac with small glasses and two bottles of beer appeared on our table. I went over to where the captain and his party were sitting.

I didn't look at Vesna but saluted the captain. 'Thank you very much for the drinks, sir,' I said.

'A pleasure,' he smiled. 'Don't get drunk.'

'Of course not, sir.' I saluted again and on my way back, I noticed some unaccompanied girls at a nearby table. 'Let's dance,' I said to the others and in a few moments we were all on the dance floor to the strains of *The Blue Danube.*

Vesna and the captain were dancing again and when they came close to me, Vesna broke away and called, 'Change partners!' I was astounded at Vesna's audacity but the captain laughed and held out his hand to my partner, leaving me to finish the dance with his wife. Once again, I held her well away from me, resisting her effort to pull me close. 'Darling, I miss you,' she said. 'I'm so pleased you came here tonight. Are you celebrating something?'

'A good friend of mine is transferring to Split,' I said.

'Thank God it's not you.'

'Change partners!' The captain was by us, smiling as he took his wife in his arms again.

'Thank you, sir,' I said.

'You're welcome,' he answered. As I was sitting down, I caught a whiff of Vesna's floral perfume. She was passing behind me, hand in hand with the captain. She ran her free hand down my back. I didn't look round but felt myself redden.

'I saw that,' Milan said. 'What's going on?'

'Milan!' I said severely. 'What do you mean? She's my captain's wife.' I lifted the cognac bottle. Half of it had gone and Milan's four friends were looking decidedly flushed and merry. 'Hadn't you better persuade your mates to go back to the ship? They're just about all right at the moment but if they drink much more...' They were no trouble. They'd enjoyed the evening and happily went off in the direction of the naval docks.

Without looking at the captain's table again, I got up. 'Let's go somewhere else to eat,' I said and, picking up the cognac and handing it to Milan, 'it would be a pity to waste this.' We ate kebabs at a taverna and then walked into the park. We sat on a bench for a smoke.

'Come on, Ivan,' Milan urged. 'Tell me about the captain's wife.' So I did. It was a relief to pour it all out to my friend. I trusted him absolutely. When I'd finished, he gave a whistle. 'Good God, Ivan. What if you get caught?'

'It's over. I won't get caught because nothing more is going to happen. It was exciting at first but it's finished now. I'm sorry if Vesna is hurt but I am quite sure that, whatever she says, she doesn't truly love me. She is interested in the sex that's all. She's not interested in me as a person and I'm not rich enough to make her happy, anyway. Now what about you? How is your love life?'

'Not as exciting as yours, certainly,' Milan laughed and he told me more about the beautiful girl on the island of Vis.

Goodbye *M143:* Leave

I was on duty on *M144* the next day. I was on the deck when, out of the corner of my eye, I glimpsed a silver flash. Turning, I saw the massive shape of a destroyer. I hurried to the radio cabin and confirmed its identity. It was *R11* – my new ship. I called the squadron duty officer to alert him that he would need to direct the docking of the new arrival and then I went out on to the quay to watch the manoeuvre. I felt a thrill of anticipation. Soon I would be a part of the large crew who kept this magnificent vessel afloat.

Once *R11* was in place, I returned to M143 and was immediately called into the captain's cabin. An admiral was talking to him. He was about fifty, with greying hair and a pleasant smile which revealed two gold teeth. I saluted and the captain said to the newcomer, 'Here is Petty Officer Vesligaj, as you requested, sir.' He turned to me. 'This is your new commanding officer Vesligaj. He wants you to join his ship tomorrow and not wait until Monday.'

'Yes sir. Thank you, sir.' I said, delighted that my wait was almost over.

My new captain was the commander of the squadron of battle ships, one of the most important men in the navy. He was observing me narrowly then he smiled again. 'It will be good to have you aboard, Vesligaj.'

'Thank you, sir.'

'That's all, Vesligaj,' my captain said.

The first person I saw as I walked to the radio cabin was Ćiril and I told him the news. 'Yes, I've just spent half an hour with the captain and your new commander. He asked me all about you and combed through your files,' he said. 'He was particularly interested in your education and laughed when he saw you'd been in a monastery. "Just the sort of man we want," he said. "He'll be a moral man and a fast learner."'

I detected gentle sarcasm in his voice and smiled. 'You know, I haven't mentioned anything to anyone except Marko about my transfer, sir,' I said. 'Some people were a bit jealous when I got my promotions so I don't want to seem to brag about this.'

'Modest on top of all your other attributes, are you?' he said laughing.

It was time for to bed – the last time I would sleep on *M143*.

After breakfast the next day, the crew was assembled on deck for a briefing. Ćiril was in charge and he told everyone I was leaving the ship immediately.

'We'll miss you, Vesligaj,' he said, 'but I congratulate you on your posting to the destroyer *R11*. Don't let us down. We want to be proud of you as a communications officer who cut his teeth on our ship.'

The captain appeared and thanked me for my service on the ship, adding, in an undertone, '…and thank you for all you've done. You know what I mean.'

'Thank you, sir,' and picking up my kitbag, I asked, 'Permission to leave the ship, sir?'

'Permission granted.' I saluted the crew, and marched ashore. Once there, I turned, saluted the Yugoslav flag, and prepared to march the few hundred yards to *R11*.

'Wait, Vesligaj,' Ćiril sped down the gangplank, calling, 'I'll walk with you.' As we walked, he said, 'I'll miss your company. You'll do well, though. You'll find life very different on a big ship. You'll have to work much harder but I know you don't mind work. You're a lucky devil. You'll see the world.'

I thanked him for all he'd taught me and we shook hands as we drew level with my new ship. I watched him walk back and I felt a moment of apprehension but turned to find the *R11* duty officer regarding me.

'Permission to board *R11*, please sir?'

'Are you Petty Officer Vesligaj, our new communications officer?'

'Yes, sir.'

'Welcome aboard. Follow me. I'll show you to your sleeping quarters.' I did as he instructed and, as he strode in front of me along passages and down several sets of stairs, I felt sure I'd get lost on this huge ship. Finally we arrived at a four berth cabin. 'This is your accommodation,' said the officer. 'Top bunk, that side. Stow your bag in the locker above and I'll take you to the radio room to meet your boss.'

This turned out to be a pleasant-faced Slovenian, Lieutenant Lojze Cvek. 'Welcome to the communications team,' he said and, turning to the duty officer, 'I'll look after him from here, thank you.' Two more lieutenants entered as the duty officer left. Cvek introduced them to me as Jose Zjoze Novak and David Anzic. 'We do two hour shifts on duty when we're away from base. On base, the destroyers take turns to do duties so our duties come round less often,' Cvek explained. He looked at a rota on the wall of the cabin. 'You're on from 22.00 hours until midnight tonight and on again at 04.00 until 06.00 hundred hours tomorrow morning. In at the deep end, eh? You could get some sleep before you start your shift if you like.'

He showed me round the radio cabin which was much bigger than that on the minesweeper. There were two radio transmitters and receivers, Morse code equipment and a large radar screen.

'Why are the switches all labelled in English?' I asked.

'We're British built. We'll go to the bridge now and I'll show you where the Aldis lamps and flags are stowed. You'll do extra duty on the bridge when we sail tomorrow, We're leaving at 11.00 hours.'

He showed me round the ship. It was well fortified with two rotating turrets housing anti-aircraft guns, fixed heavy machine guns, torpedoes and depth charges. He also showed me the dining room which doubled up as sleeping quarters for the lower ranks and the washing facilities. 'Now you can have some free time to get your bearings on the ship and have a rest, if you wish. I'll see you in the radio cabin at 22.00.'

I went up on deck for a breath of air and, to my astonishment I saw the familiar figure of Milan, leaning on the rail. 'What are you doing here?' I said, clapping him on the back.

He jumped, turned and laughed aloud. 'I was hoping I'd run across you but it would have been easy to miss you on this enormous ship. You're giving me lift to Split so I can join *R22*.' We chatted for a while and went to the canteen together. 'What about that business we were discussing in the park? He asked. 'Any further developments?'

I shook my head. 'I told you it was ended. Now I have leave coming up and have arranged to meet Ingrid in Zagreb.'

'Some people get all the luck,' he grumbled good-naturedly.

As I was still on duty at 06.00 hours the next morning, it was my task to sound the klaxon which served as the signal for everyone to get up. The crew assembled on deck before going ashore for exercise. There were about two hundred of us. After breakfast, Lieutenant Cvek called me to the radio room. 'The captain has your leave pass. He'll give it to you tomorrow. Your real settling in period will start when you return. Meanwhile, you and I will see our ship safely into base between us.'

We left Šibenik on time and I performed all my tasks without difficulty. Similarly, there were no problems as we arrived at Split. I was fascinated to see how the captain deftly swung the huge bulk of R11 round to the quay side. In the excitement of docking, I didn't see Milan leave the ship. I knew, however, that we'd be in contact fairly soon if only by radio or Morse code.

I was off duty that night and, in spite of a niggling fear that I'd get lost in a case of emergency, I slept heavily. There was an alarm-call practice at 03.00 hours which meant that we all had to take up our battle stations. I was extremely relieved that I found my way to the radio cabin quickly. Cvek said that these exercises were a regular part of life aboard a destroyer and I began to appreciate that we'd had a relatively easy life on *M143*.

After physical exercise the next morning, the captain issued my travel and leave documents. I was to leave Split, for Zagreb, on the late train. I went to inform Cvek and found him talking to the other two lieutenants.

'We hear, from your last boss, that you are a wizard at semaphore,' Cvek said. 'Fast are you?'

'Fairly fast sir.'

'Well, we're going to test you. We're going ashore and we want you to send this message to us. It will be interesting to see how fast you can do it.' He passed me a piece of paper.

'Yes, sir,' I said. 'That shouldn't be a problem.'

Smiling confidently at each other, the three went ashore and lined up some distance away. Using the flags very slowly, Cvek semaphored 'Are you ready?'

Quick as a flash, I replied, 'Yes, sir. The message is: *We arrived in Split at 15.00 hours yesterday. Petty Officer Vesligaj is starting his leave this evening.'* I couldn't see the officers' faces but they conferred for a moment and then Cvek lifted his flags. *'Please repeat the message.'*

I grinned to myself and signalled again as fast as before. Instead of acknowledging, Cvek ran aboard. 'Where on earth did you learn such speed?' he asked.

'My boss, Lieutenant Ćiril, and I worked on it every day for some time when we were at Zadar not long after I joined *M143*,' I said, pleased I'd surprised them.

'It's certainly paid off,' Novak said as he and Anzic joined us. 'How about setting up a wager?' the former said. 'We'll take on the other ships in the squadron and put money on Vesligaj being the fastest?'

Cvek laughed. 'Good idea but it'll have to wait until he gets back from leave.'

I was on Split railway station in plenty of time for the train. I sat in the waiting room, remembering my first visit here with Father Josip. A military policeman came in and asked to see my documents. 'Going on leave? Lucky beggar,' he said, as he handed them back. And I did feel lucky. I'd had a fortunate escape from Vesna, I was serving on a destroyer and seemed very likely to be able to fulfil my long held ambition to 'see the world'. And I was on my way to see Ingrid.

The journey was uneventful. I chatted briefly with a lad just demobbed from the army, the pretty young girl, next to me, dozed and slumped against me. When she woke up she was embarrassed to find her head on my shoulder. Soon, the rhythm of the train lulled me too and I slept.

It was greying into morning when I started awake just after 05.30. Looking through the window, I saw the familiar countryside of forests and mountains. Shortly, I would be in Zagreb. Soon I recognised the bridges across the river and then the streets. We arrived in the station at 06.00 hours.

There weren't many people about. I jumped on a number 2 tram and was soon on my way to Dragica's. Her new, larger apartment was very close to her old one. As the tram carried me through Zagreb, I could hardly believe that nothing had changed while I'd been away. I had seen and learned so much. I was a different person but everything here was just the same, it seemed. The car park outside my sister's block of flats was empty except for one car – a red, German-registered Mercedes. Ingrid had arrived.

I looked up at Dragica's apartment and saw her at the window, laughing and waving. Then she put her finger to her lips and indicated that she would come to the front door to let me in. 'Ingrid's still asleep,' she said after we'd hugged. She held me at arm's length to inspect me. 'You look very well, Ivek. Come in quietly so as not to disturb Ingrid. She'll have such a lovely surprise when she wakes up.'

I had other ideas. I took off my shoes and tiptoed into the spare room where Ingrid lay, as beautiful as the Sleeping Beauty I had once seen in a children's book at school. Softly, I bent and kissed her. Her eyes flew open and she screamed with delight, throwing her arms round my neck and pulling me down to her. She was laughing, crying and telling me how much she loved me all at the same time. Dragica, ever practical, called 'Have you had breakfast, Ivek?'

'No.'

'I'll do eggs. We can all sit down together.'

Ingrid leapt out of bed. 'I'll have a quick shower and be with you,' she said and, picking up a towel gave me another kiss before running into the bathroom.

I chatted with Dragica while she prepared the breakfast. 'Ingrid's a lovely girl,' she said. 'She and Franz jabber in German all the time. You be good to her Ivek and I hope you're going to see Mama this leave.'

'Of course,' I said. 'Ingrid and I will have this evening here with you, if that's all right, and then we'll go to Mama's tomorrow.'

'Ingrid too?'

'Yes, I want her to meet Mama and Stara mama too.'

'She'll find life very different there. She's used to living in a big house in a city. What on earth will she make of the village and the cottage and the toilet facilities – or lack of them?'

'It'll be a test. If she really loves me, she'll love my village and my family. If she doesn't love them, if the way of life there is beneath her, then she's not for me.'

Dragica didn't have time to answer because Ingrid came into the kitchen, looking radiant and carrying two packages. The first contained records by my favourite groups, unobtainable in Yugoslavia. There were recordings of the *Beatles, Rolling Stones, Deep Purple* and *Brian Poole and the Tremolos*. I didn't know how to thank her so I enfolded her in my arms. 'Here's one other thing from me and then there's something in the car for you from my parents,' she said. The 'one other thing' from her was an expensive looking German camera, a *Zenit*. 'Thank me later at the hotel,' she whispered, laughing when I started once more to try to express gratitude. By then Dragica had put the eggs and coffee on the table so we ate before going to fetch the present from Ingrid's parents.

When we did go down, a crowd had gathered to admire the car and people were staring from their balconies. 'Bloody sailors get all the best girls,' a familiar voice called.

'Be quiet Zenko. That's Dragica's brother,' a second, older voice remonstrated.

'Sorry Ivan. I didn't recognise you in that outfit,' laughed Zenko who I knew very well. 'What a brilliant car. Has your girlfriend got a sister?'

Ingrid had reached into the boot and brought out what looked like a chunky suitcase. She handed it to me. 'Let's go in,' she said. 'You can open it indoors.'

I gave Zenko and the neighbours a wave and we went back to the flat. I could hardly believe my eyes when I opened the 'suitcase'. There was a compact record player and tape recorder inside. I stared at it, dumbfounded. 'Do you like it?' Ingrid asked anxiously.

'Like it? Ingrid, these presents are the best things I've ever been given. Thank you, thank you, thank you! You and your parents are *so* generous. I'll write to thank them but just come here and I'll show you how grateful I am.' I kissed her all over her face and her hair while Dragica stood by, arms folded, laughing.

Ingrid in the Village: Politics

I had agreed to show Ingrid the sights of Zagreb.

'Come back in time for supper,' Dragica urged. 'Franz and Nevenka are looking forward to seeing you.'

We promised we would and caught a tram into the centre of the city. I took Ingrid to see the old town and the cathedral. She took lots of photographs especially of St Mark's Church which she snapped from every angle. We ate lunch in a restaurant in the square and, as we drank our coffee, Ingrid said, 'I was talking to Dragica yesterday and I found out that you haven't any decent civilian clothes.'

'I don't need any. I have to wear naval uniform all the time even when I'm on leave.' I was a bit put out that my sister had thought fit to discuss my wardrobe with my girlfriend.

'But it's not very long before your demob,' Ingrid insisted. 'You'll want some nice clothes then and I've brought plenty of money with me. Please, let's buy them now so they'll be waiting for you when you need them. I want to be proud to walk down the road with you.'

I felt the familiar tussle between irritation that Ingrid wanted to take control and gratitude to her for her generosity. 'You've given me quite enough today,' I said. 'I'll save enough over the next year to buy new clothes after demob.'

Ingrid began to cry. 'Why won't you let me help you? I love you so much and by rejecting my gift you're rejecting my love.'

In the end, she got her way and we walked out of the largest outfitters in town with a suit, shoes, shirts, tee shirts and even underclothes.

'I'll never be able to repay you, Ingrid,' I said.

'I don't want repayment. All I want is your love.'

Ingrid had booked into the Hotel Esplanade. 'Let's go and look at the room now,' she said, 'then we can go back to Dragica's for supper and to fetch the car. We can spend the night together at the hotel.'

'I'd love to,' I answered, 'but it's a tourist hotel. It won't accept military personnel.'

Her chin went up. 'We'll see about that.' Several members of the hotel's staff stared as we entered the reception hall.

The manager hurried up. 'Good afternoon Miss Gunther,' he said.

'Good afternoon,' Ingrid replied. 'I'd like to introduce you to my fiancé, Ivan Vesligaj. He'll be spending the night here with me.'

'Well, er… that could be a bit difficult. The rules, you know.'

'I'm afraid that if he isn't allowed to stay I'll walk out now and certainly will not stay here on my way back to Germany, as I'd intended. In fact, I'll never stay here again and nor will any of my friends or family.'

'Well, in that case, er... well of course … we don't want to inconvenience you, Miss Gunther.' The manager turned to me. 'You're welcome to stay,' he said.

'I doubt if military police will swoop tonight,' I said, laughing.

He gave a strained smile. 'I certainly hope not.'

Giggling, we ran up the stairs to Ingrid's room and made love. It had been a long time and we had to drag ourselves away from each other to fulfil our promise to have supper at Dragica's.

Although the bed at the hotel was very comfortable, we had very little sleep that night. We talked and made love and talked some more. It must have been almost four before we dropped off. No MPs raid disturbed us, and after a late breakfast, we left the hotel.

I admired Ingrid's slim ankles and high heeled shoes as she descended the hotel steps but I had a sudden thought. 'Have you any flat shoes with you?' I asked.

'No. I hardly ever wear them.'

'You'll need them for the next few days. High heels are no good through forests and over mountains. There's no road to my village so we'll have to leave your car at my friends' place, on the border of Slovenia and walk the last part. You couldn't do it in those.'

We returned to Dragica's, complete with flat lace up shoes. After a quick farewell, we got into the car and drove towards my home.

As we drew near, Ingrid exclaimed at the beauty of the countryside. 'It gets even better,' I promised. We stopped at my friends' inn just inside the Slovenian border. Over a beer, they agreed that we could leave the car there and we set off, on foot, for the last part of our journey.

At a small store we passed, I bought some sugar, salt and olive oil for Mama. We crossed the River Sutla and started through the forest. The pines were fragrant and we held hands, not saying much but enjoying the shade, the birdsong and each other's company. Every so often we sat for a short rest and each time, Ingrid put the jacket she carried on the ground for me to sit on. 'We can't have your white trousers getting dirty before your mother sees you,' she said. We emerged from the forest and climbed the last hill.

Looking into the valley, I said, 'Ingrid, there's my village. That cottage there, the third one along, is my home.' I regarded, with pride, the beauty of the valley. We could see the vineyards, corn fields and the deep green forested hills behind.

Ingrid took a deep breath of the pure air. 'What a wonderful place to live,' she said softly. 'How can you bear to leave it?'

I told her about our neighbours. 'There are only a few households and most of them are related to us. Štef and Barbara live to the left of us. They have three sons. Barbara is a black marketeer. She buys eggs, milk, vegetables and corn from the local farmers and takes it to the market in Slovenia. The authorities know nothing about it. We call her *kulak*/capitalist. Ivan and Dragica are next to them, they've got four sons. Dominique and Ana live in the other cottage. They have seven children. I didn't mention Marica and Mirko.

'Does everyone earn a living from farming?' Ingrid asked.

'Yes. We all keep a few cows and chickens and grow corn and vegetables – and grapes, of course. The vineyards are a little way out of the village.'

By now we were almost up to the houses. My mother was in the kitchen which overlooked the path. She ran out wearing her headscarf and apron and flung her arms round my neck. 'Ivica! Son, how good to see you.'

I gave her a big hug and then disentangled myself. 'Mama, this is Ingrid. She comes from Germany.' My mother embraced Ingrid and there followed, between them, an animated conversation in German. By the time we got inside, Mama had found out where Ingrid lived, what her job was and where we had met. She served us fresh strudel and coffee and Ingrid asked her about the selection of photographs which hung on the wall. When, in answer to her question about a picture of an angelic small boy, my mother said, 'It's Ivica, on the day of his first communion.' Ingrid got up and kissed me on the top of my head.

'How sweet you were,' she laughed and Mama looked pleased.

Ingrid took photographs of almost everything inside the house and in the garden. While she was doing this, I told Mama that we planned to visit my grandmother that afternoon. 'I'll be here for the rest of my leave so you'll see plenty of me,' I said.

Ingrid came in and said that taking the photos had reminded her of one she had of us in Split. 'My mother took it secretly,' she said as she pulled it from her bag. And there we were, relaxed and happy, smiling at each other. It took me right back to those magical few weeks when we first met.

We went across country to Stara mama's cottage. She was overjoyed to see us. She admired my uniform. 'You look almost as handsome dressed like that as when you were your priestly robes,' she said a little regretfully. Then she smiled. 'But if you were still dressed in those you wouldn't be able to have a beautiful girlfriend, would you?'

Once more, conversation flowed easily for she, of course, spoke German. We drank some coffee and then it was time to go. We were both tired. It had been a long day and we'd had little sleep the previous night.

We walked home through our neighbouring villages. People called out greetings to me or stopped me to ask how I was. 'It's so different from my home,' Ingrid said. 'I can walk down the street and not meet anyone I know. Here, everyone knows everyone.'

By the time we got home, a small crowd of my friends had gathered outside our house all eager to meet Ingrid and find out how I liked serving in the navy. Once Ingrid had shaken hands all round, she went inside and Mama brought out some of our own wine. 'That girl of yours is gorgeous,' said Pepi. 'How do you do it, Ivek?' and the other lads made noises of agreement.

When we went in, Mama called me into the bedroom she shared with Stjepan. 'Stjepan and I will sleep in the kitchen while Ingrid is with us,' she said. 'You two can sleep in here.'

I'd been thinking about the sleeping accommodation and had come up with a plan. 'No Mama. Ingrid and I will sleep in the barn. There's no need for you to give up your room.'

'The barn?' my mother was shocked. 'Ingrid's a lady. She has refined ways and comes from a rich family. You can't ask her to sleep in the barn.'

I went back into the kitchen. 'Ingrid, how would you like to sleep in the barn with me tonight? We can sleep on the fresh hay. What do you think?' I asked her.

'I'd love to!' she exclaimed. 'It will be so romantic.'

Turning to Mama she said, 'May we? It would be such an adventure.'

My mother shrugged her shoulders and laughed. 'I'll make you a proper bed in the barn loft, if that's what you really want.'

'Yes please,' and Ingrid turned to me with shining eyes. She delighted in every aspect of our country living, helping to dig vegetables for supper, drawing water from the well and she didn't even seem to mind using our rudimentary bucket toilet.

When she asked where she could have a proper wash I laughed and handed her an enamel bowl. 'I'll heat some well water on the fire for you,' I said. 'You can wash in Mama's room. Sorry, Ingrid, but we Croatian farmers live Spartan lives compared with the life you have in Germany.'

'I love it,' she cried. 'You've made me see it's possible to be happy without a lot of the things that I've always thought were important. Thank you. This is an experience I'll never forget.'

We went to our bed in the barn straight after supper, exhausted with the day's activities. The bed was more comfortable than any I'd ever slept in and we fell asleep straight away in each other's arms.

For the next two days, we all worked in the vineyard. Ingrid helped to pick the grapes and then I showed her how to operate the wine press. Mama and Stjepan slept in the tiny stone building which adjoined the vineyard so we had the cottage to ourselves in the evenings. We played house, picnicking on salami, cheese, salad and homemade bread. On the third day, I decided to visit Father Josip and the sisters. On the way there, I called at the military district office because I had to register the address at which I'd be staying for the rest of my leave.

As we climbed the slope towards the priest's house, I pointed out the castle and told Ingrid about the picnic I'd once had there with the trainee nuns. I saw the church and *Faruh* – and there were the three sisters working in the garden.

They looked up but didn't recognise me when I called, 'Good morning'. We reached the gate and I gave the customary greeting, 'Let Jesus bless you.'

'And you soldier,' Kazimira answered.

I smiled and said, 'I'm not a soldier, I'm sailor Ivan Vesligaj.' The three threw down their tools and ran to embrace me. Franceska had tears running down her cheeks.

'How lovely to see you,' she whispered. 'I've so often wondered how you were getting on.'

'Stay and have a meal with us Ivan, Father will be pleased to see you,' invited Sebastijana. 'And please introduce us to this lovely young lady who's welcome to stay too, of course.' I introduced Ingrid and the nuns welcomed her.

'We're invited to lunch,' I told her. 'What do you think?'

'I'd love to stay,' she said.

Kazimira took us in. The familiarity of the dark wooden floors and furniture, the smell of disinfectant and polish and the quiet orderliness struck me almost like a physical blow. Suddenly I was a shabby, ignorant, nervous nine year old again.

Kazimira brought me back to the present with, 'Come and surprise Father, Ivan.' She led the way to Father Josip's study, knocked on the door and opened it a crack.

'Father, guess who's come to see us.' Before he had time to reply, she opened the door wide. The priest was at his desk.

'Good morning Father,' I said.

He got up, walked to the door, folded his arms and, with his head on one side, regarded me. 'Ivan!' he exclaimed and then, 'Bless you.' He made the sign of the cross. He looked inquiringly at Ingrid and, once more, I introduced her. He set her at ease immediately as he spoke German. 'Make sure you ask me to marry the two of you,' he said and Ingrid blushed.

Sebastijana called that the food was ready and we sat down to her speciality, goulash – just like the one we'd taken to Mestinje many years earlier.

We spoke a mixture of German and Croatian. Franceska asked how we had met and the priest wanted to know about life aboard a minesweeper. I heard news of the families in the parish and about the sad death of Pubi. My mother had already told me this news and when we'd finished eating, I slipped away for a few minutes to stand in the barn and remember the happy times we'd had together. I thought I caught a whiff of his special smell and stroked his saddle which still hung on hooks. Ingrid came to look for me and I told her about the time that Pubi had 'protected' me from Branko Meznar and how he had saved Father Josip from the armed robbers.

We heard the priest calling us. 'Shall we take a stroll through the village?' I was sad to hear that the Contessa had died and her house sold. The three of us were silent for a few minutes then Father said, 'You know Ivan, I was so very disappointed when you dropped out of Bol. I had high hopes for you. I think you would have made an excellent priest.' When I didn't answer, he went on, 'I couldn't be angry with you. I realised it was your mother's wish that you should leave. I never really understood why she felt that way.'

'You did a lot for me, Father,' I said. 'I don't know what made Mama change her mind either but I'll always be grateful for my education which you made possible. But,' and here, I put my arm round Ingrid, 'there are certainly compensations for living a secular life.' We all laughed and the talk turned to other things.

The three of us drank wine together when we returned to the house. Then Father Josip shook hands and the sisters hugged us. As we were leaving, the priest called to me, 'Stay in touch, Ivan. Write a few lines now and then.'

Ingrid and I walked back to the cottage hand in hand. 'I loved hearing about your time at the priest's house,' she said, 'Tell me some more.'

As the next day was Ingrid's last with us, I planned a long walk and a picnic. She put on a dark blue mini skirt and pale muslin blouse. She looked stylish, cool and extremely desirable. 'You'd better stay away from the village lads,' I laughed, 'or you'll cause a riot.'

'I'm not interested in what anyone else thinks,' she answered demurely. 'I dress like this only for you.'

After breakfast, Mama made us a picnic, placed it in a covered basket and we set off. Almost straight away we met Marica.

'I'd heard you had a special visitor, Ivan,' she said, giving Ingrid a long look. 'And you look lovely, my dear.' I introduced the two women and translated Marica's remark but she hadn't finished. With a bitter little smile she said to Ingrid, 'Good luck with that one my dear. He'll get tired of you and dump you just as he did with me.' Ingrid looked at me enquiringly.

'She says she hopes we have a nice day,' I improvised and taking Ingrid's hand, I said a sharp 'Goodbye' to Marica and, blissfully ignorant, Ingrid smiled at her and said

'*Auf wiedersehen.*'

When I looked back, the older woman was watching us. I didn't feel anything for her now except a measure of gratitude for all she'd taught me. But, I reasoned, she had sought me out, had used a raw, inexperienced boy to fulfil her own needs. I owed her nothing. Nevertheless, I felt her still watching. I felt the whole village watching us and was relieved to leave the path and swing up the hillside with its sheltering shrubs.

I stopped in front of a small beech tree, known locally as a 'gaj bush' because the species grew in such abundance in an area we knew as Gaj – which was made up of the flat valley and slopes of the forest in front and to the right of my village. 'Ingrid,' I said solemnly, 'this is a very special and important bush.'

She looked at it carefully. 'Why? It looks the same as all the others.'

'I was born under this bush.'

She began to laugh and then realised I was serious. 'Born under a bush …why? ... how?'

'I told you we were a Spartan people,' I said, putting my arms round her. 'My parents had been working in the vineyard and suddenly Mama's labour pains started. My father was helping her home but she didn't make it in time. My father delivered me right here by this bush. He cut the cord, wrapped me in his coat and then, when Mama felt strong enough, they walked home.' There was silence and then I realised that Ingrid was crying softly. I held her close, puzzled. 'What's wrong?' I said.

'It's such a wonderful story,' she sobbed. 'It makes me love you even more. Where I live everyone goes into hospital to have a baby. Things are so different here – so much simpler.'

'It can be tough too.' I didn't want her to get too romantic a view of our lives. 'Not everyone survives the hardships.'

But she wasn't listening. She was too busy photographing the gaj bush from every angle. 'I want to show this special bush to my parents. I want them to know all about you. They already like you very much. They are pleased you make me so happy and I haven't one single regret about anything. You took my virginity and it was the most wonderful thing that ever happened to me.'

We wandered on and up into the forest. We rested for a while in a shady clearing where sun filtered through the fresh green leaves. I picked Ingrid a bouquet of wild cyclamen and she kissed me and called me 'romantic' and we lay on the moss and stared up at the jewelled sky. Then we walked further on and when we were hungry, found a green cave under a huge beech tree. I put the blanket down and we sat for a few moments, face to face with the picnic basket between us. We could hear the forest birds trying to out-sing each other and Ingrid leant forward and kissed me.

I drew back the white cloth which covered the basket. There was cheese, salami, hard boiled eggs, home baked bread, sweet grapes and, at the bottom, a bottle of our own white wine. I remembered reading about the Garden of Eden and thought it must have been just like this. 'Shall we eat and drink, Eve my darling,' I said. When I explained my fantasy, Ingrid laughed and said,

'In that case we should make love now just like Adam and Eve did.'

'I'd very much like to but it's not safe. The serpent may be about,' I joked and, right on cue, I heard a soft sound and saw a familiar shape through the canopy of green. It was Marica.

She ducked under the low branches and I saw she was carrying a basket full of fungi. I wondered if she had followed us, using the basket excuse of old.

'Well, fancy coming across you two,' she said breezily. 'Just about to eat I see.'

'Yes,' I answered but I didn't ask her to join us. I just wanted her to go away.

'Don't mind me. It's time I was getting home anyway,' she said. She selected three very large white fungi and held them out to me. 'Take these home for your supper, Ivan.'

A ridiculous thought raced through my mind. I knew the proffered *vrganji* were harmless and good to eat but what if Marica had rubbed them against the poisonous death cap which grew in profusion in the forest? Suppose she was so bitter about my rejection of her that she wanted to kill both Ingrid and myself. 'That's very kind of you,' I said hurriedly, 'but my mother has already prepared our supper so we wouldn't be able to use them. Thank you all the same.'

She put the fungi slowly back in her basket, took one more look at us and said, 'I'll leave you to it then. You must have so many memories of this forest, Ivan. Don't forget to share them with your girlfriend.' And she was gone.

Although we enjoyed the picnic, Marica had spoilt the magic of the place for me and I suggested moving on so that I could show Ingrid some more of my childhood haunts. We sat under another of my favourite trees, quite still, side by side, looking up through the leaves. Two squirrels played just above us. Ingrid carefully withdrew her camera and photographed them. 'My parents will be so impressed,' she whispered. When the squirrels had jumped to the next tree Ingrid went on. 'My family is very rich, Ivan. My father owns several factories and I realise I've never had to go without anything. I've been to the best school and college and yet, until I came here, I'd taken everything for granted, believing it was my right. You have shown me what real life is like.'

I was touched by her sincerity. 'I'm glad you feel that way. I consider myself wealthy because I have a loving family and all this,' I waved my arms to indicate the forest, the mountains, the village, the farm and the vineyard – everything which meant home to me. On top of all this, I am healthy. What more could I ask? These are things no amount of money can buy.' I saw that tears were running down her cheeks. I put my arm round her. 'What's wrong? Have I made you unhappy?'

'Just the opposite.' She gave a watery smile. 'I love it when you get philosophical. And there is one other thing I want to say. In all, we have spent only about three weeks together. They have been the very best weeks of my life. Thank you. I don't want to go back tomorrow. I don't ever want to go back.' She turned and kissed me.

'I've only a few days leave left,' I said. 'I've had a lovely time too – and there will be many more, I'm sure.' We got up and walked towards home, arm in arm in companionable silence. I was thinking that Ingrid had certainly passed the test concerning my humble home and family. I felt we'd really got to know each other over the last few days. I loved so many things about her. Was I actually 'in love'? I still wasn't sure.

We had a farewell supper of roast chicken and vegetables. I went outside for a cigarette and, from the fallen tree trunk, on which I sat, I could hear Ingrid and Mama chattering and laughing. I was pleased they liked each other. My cousin Pepi wandered over and we chatted a while.

Soon other village friends drifted along and Pepi began to play softly on his harmonica. We started to sing our country songs. Ingrid came running out 'Are we having a party?' she asked.

'Yes, especially for you,' I laughed.

By now almost all the neighbours had joined us. Mama brought us some trays of strudel and someone arrived with a demijohn of wine. Ingrid grabbed my brother, Stjepan. 'Let's dance,' she cried and whirled him away.

There was a light touch on my shoulder. 'Will you dance with me, Ivan?' It was Marica.

'Won't your husband mind?'

'He suggested I should ask you.' We danced together. I held her away from me and thought how I'd done the same with Vesna. I felt nothing for either of them now. Marica must have felt my coolness for she said no more and walked away as soon as the dance was over.

Ingrid was taking photographs of everyone, thrilled with the impromptu party. Then we danced together, holding each other close. I made a whispered request to Pepi and he played the German song, *Lily Marlene*. Once more, I saw tears in Ingrid's eyes as we danced to the haunting tune. 'Thank you so much, my darling. I just want this evening to last for ever.'

It couldn't, of course, and early the next morning, we were sitting at the kitchen table eating a cooked breakfast of eggs, sausage and fungi. As we finished

Mama said, 'Guess where the fungi came from. Marica kindly gave them to me last evening especially for you and Ingrid.'

We were soon on our way to collect the car from my friends in Cvetka. My mother and Ingrid had embraced and cried on our departure but, as we walked, I discovered the latter had a plan which meant we would spend a few extra hours together.

'You know, I never actually checked out of the hotel,' she said. I left some of my luggage there. Come back with me to Zagreb now and we can spend the afternoon in bed together. I can say goodbye to Dragica, Franz and Nevenka after that and then I'll take you back to Cvetka and drive from there towards home. I'll find a hotel on the way to stay the night.'

I was astonished. She must have planned this all along. In spite of her soft heart and easy tears, I realised, anew, that Ingrid was a very determined young woman – and also somewhat manipulative. However, I had nothing else I must do and no inclination to refuse an intimate afternoon with her.

We slept after our love-making and when I awoke Ingrid was packing the last of her clothes. The manager saw us off with a flourish, begging us to return as soon as possible. After a quick visit to my sister, we drove swiftly to Cvetka. Ingrid was crying most of the way and when she parked to drop me off, she hung on to me and sobbed,

'Phone me whenever you can and please, please don't fall in love with anyone else.' I kissed her, promised faithfulness and got out of the car.

'Don't drive too far before you find a hotel,' I said.

She started the engine, 'Look in your breast pocket,' she shouted. 'I love you' and she drove quickly away. I fished in my top pocket and pulled out my navy documents. Tucked inside them were 1,600 deutsch marks.

My friends, at the inn, were solicitous over my parting from Ingrid. I drank a beer with them and stared gloomily into my glass. They urged me to stay until the next day but I had only three days of my leave left and felt I should spend them with Mama. On my walk home, I stopped at the spot where Ingrid and I had picnicked. Perhaps I am really in love after all, I thought, as a pleasant sort of nostalgic sadness crept over me.

At home, Mama was anxious to know why I'd been away for so long. When I explained she said, 'Ingrid insisted on giving me 100 deutsch marks towards her keep. She gave Stjepan 50 as a present. She is so generous.' Then I pulled out the 1,600 deutsch marks she'd left in my pocket and told Mama about the clothes Ingrid had bought me for after my demob. 'She's certainly a lovely girl, Ivek,' my mother said. 'Make sure you treat her well. She's very serious about you. Don't break her heart.'

'I know she's serious about me Mama, but I can't commit myself to her at the moment. I have a year to do in the navy and anything could happen during that time.'

Just then Stjepan came in. 'What a golden girl you've got in Ingrid,' he said, clapping me on the back. 'Everybody in the village says so.'

'How have you got on at the vineyard today?' I asked, keen to change the subject. 'Have you finished bottling?'

'Not quite. I've bottled five thousand litres. I've two thousand more to do. Will you give me a hand tomorrow?'

'Of course.'

Some of our neighbours gathered outside to talk to me after supper. Pepi said, 'Stjepan told me that you know a lot about what is going on in the world, Ivek. Will you tell us?' So I told them about what I'd seen on and around the Dalmatian islands and went on to some of the things I'd heard about on the BBC World Service – the war between France and Algeria, the thalidomide tragedy in Britain and the new independence of the former British Colonies of Trinidad and Tobago. I didn't mention the Cuban crisis because the little I knew had come from naval sources.

My audience was transfixed, full of questions. I have to admit I felt a sense of importance. These simple people had no access to newspapers or radios and here was I, a fatherless boy from a large family, looked down upon by some, holding forth in front of the villagers, many of whom were much older than I. The power went to my head and I decided to deliver some political education. 'Who knows the difference between communism and the capitalism?' I asked. Various suggestions were made about communism standing for equality and capitalists being greedy but I brushed these aside. 'If I gave you the real answer I'd be arrested and put in jail,' I said. 'It is true that Yugoslavian communism is not as harsh as that of Soviet Russia but let me tell you one difference between any sort of communist regime and the capitalist west. In the west, men and women vote freely to choose who governs them.'

'We have elections here too,' said Ignac Kruslin, a man who lived just outside the village. I knew he was under-secretary of the local communist branch.

'Elections are held in Yugoslavia, that's true,' I answered, 'but I'm 22 and I've never had a vote. You have to belong to the Party to get a vote so, of course, the communists stay in power. I bet most of the people here have never voted either.'

A muted murmur of agreement came from the group. No-one wanted to say anything which might get him into trouble.

'Well, as you know, I'm a member of the communist party,' Ignac said. 'I've got a branch meeting tomorrow and I'll ask the comrades there if what you've said is true, Ivan. I'll also pass on the world news you've told us. I'll see if other people have heard it.'

I realised, then, that I may have said too much and was relieved to see Mama by my side with a demijohn of our wine and glasses. 'Enough of politics,' I said as lightly as I could. 'Long life and happiness to us all.'

Ignac came across to me as the drinking got underway. 'Don't worry Ivan,' he said quietly. 'Tomorrow I will raise what you've said but I won't mention your name.'

'Thank you.'

'Stjepan told me you are going to help in the vineyard tomorrow.'

'Yes. We'll finish the bottling.'

'Don't worry about it, mine is finished. I've told Stjepan that I'll lend him the man who works for me. I'll give a hand too, after the meeting. You enjoy your last couple of days of leave. Please yourself about what you do.'

I thanked him and we shook hands. 'Let me know what the officials say at your meeting,' I said.

As I lay in bed that night I thought about Ingrid. I wondered what she was doing. Her face was before me as I drifted off to sleep.

I took the cows to their pasture early the next morning, enjoying the freshness of fields and forest. I walked on for a while, revisiting the places to which I'd taken Ingrid. I stood under the same favourite tree but there were no squirrels to see this morning. After lunch I went into the garden to gather the succulent walnuts from our trees and had just spread a net under the first tree when I saw Ignac outside our house. He shouted to me as he came down the path. 'Sorry to disturb you.'

'What did the officials say?' I asked.

'They called what you said about communism, "capitalist propaganda",' he replied, 'but some of them knew about Algeria. I have to say, I think you talked a lot of sense yesterday but I was careful what I said. I don't want to get into trouble and I didn't want anyone questioning me about where I picked up the information.'

Ignac went off to help Stjepan in the vineyard and I continued with nut-picking. I was disturbed again a few minutes later. My elderly Uncle Francek, who had been present at my public tirade yesterday, joined me in the garden. 'Ivek,' he said, 'I was very impressed by all you said last evening. I've not heard anyone say stuff like that for a long time. You are certainly knowledgeable about world affairs.'

I was flattered. 'Thank you Uncle.'

'But you must be more careful. Remember, we are in *communist* Yugoslavia not democratic Germany where your beautiful girlfriend lives. Don't trust anyone, Ivek. Talk as freely as you like about girls, the crops, the local news but never, never talk about politics.'

I was chastened. 'You're right of course. It was stupid. I'll be more careful in future.'

'I speak from personal experience,' my uncle went on. 'Some years ago the government proudly launched a Five Year Plan. It covered everything, transport, industry, agriculture. It was going to change Yugoslavia into a successful industrial state. A few of us were discussing it in the pub one evening and one of my friends laughed and said, "They'll never succeed with this plan. They're always boasting about what they can achieve and nothing ever comes of it." Well Ivek, that friend of mine was arrested the very next day and sentenced to five years hard labour.' Our talk was interrupted by the shouts of a small boy.

'There's police coming! I just seen two of 'em coming into the village.'

Recall

My first inclination was to run away. I felt sure Ignac or someone else had reported my anti-communist talk. My second thought was that running would only make things worse. I was bound to be caught and trying to escape would add 'being absent from the navy without leave' to any other charge brought against me. I cursed myself for my self-important posturing yesterday and, with a rueful smile at Uncle Francek, I walked out to the path to join a group of neighbours who had gathered to watch the excitement. My mother came out too. It seemed as if my worst fears were realised when I saw the little boy point the policeman in our direction.

They smiled in a friendly manner and one of them said to Mama, 'Good afternoon Mrs Vesligaj. Could you tell us where we can find your son, Ivan, please?'

Normally they would have picked me out immediately because of my uniform but, on this one occasion, I was wearing trousers and a shirt of Stjepan's because Mama had just laundered my naval uniform. My chest felt tight with anxiety but Mama answered calmly.

'Why do you want him? He's on leave from the navy and I know he hasn't been up to any mischief.'

To my enormous relief the policemen gave a kindly laugh. 'We know that, Mrs Vesligaj. He's not in any trouble at all. We have an urgent telegram for him – from the Ministry of Defence.' As he spoke, the second policeman pulled a telegram from his map bag.

I stepped forward and held out my hand. 'I'm Ivan Vesligaj.'

On the top right of the envelope was written *URGENT* and a large *DD* which meant that the contents were secret. Inside, I read the words,

ALL LEAVE CANCELLED. RETURN TO BASE IMMEDIATELY.

'I have to go back to the ship straight away,' I said quietly to Mama but several people overheard and soon everyone knew – so much for *DD*!

'Has war broken out?' some of the neighbours asked the policeman.

'We don't know,' they said. 'All we know is that Ivan Vesligaj must come with us. Transport has been laid on at Pregrada Town Hall for him and other local men who are doing military service.'

'How long have I got?' I asked.

'As long as it takes you to change and pack your kit.'

As I changed into my uniform, I remembered that during training we'd been told that if we were called back from leave in this way it was because there was either a yellow or red alert. Perhaps, at last, I was about to see some real action.

Mama had packed my kitbag while I was changing. She came out of the house with me, carrying a bag of food which she'd hurriedly put together.

'What's that?' asked one of the policemen.

'Food for the journey.'

'He won't need that. Food will be provided.'

I kissed Mama and shook hands with the group of neighbours and I saw Marica watching from her garden. Suddenly the policemen noticed my rank. Their attitudes changed immediately. They saluted and from that moment treated me with the utmost respect.

The town hall was full of soldiers. I was the only sailor. An army major walked into the hall. He looked round and picked me out.

'I'll deal with you first,' he said. 'Come over to the table.' He looked at my telegram and checked my travel documents which he signed and stamped. 'Good, everything seems to be in order. Wait here for a moment while I make a quick phone call.' He was back in a couple of minutes. 'There is a police car outside which will take you to Zagreb,' he said. 'You will catch the train to Split at 21.00 hours. But first you must have something to eat. The police officers will take you to a restaurant and then you'll come back here before leaving for Zagreb.' I saluted and followed the policemen out of the hall.

On our way back, after our meal, I noticed two military coaches full of soldiers, ready to leave. I was glad I was travelling in style but wasn't quite sure why. It became clear when we re-entered the hall. The major beckoned me over. 'Sit down,' he said. I sat opposite him and he produced a leather briefcase. 'Are you trained to use a luger?' he asked.

'Yes, sir.'

'Good. I want you to take this letter to Colonel Nikola Hum in Zagreb and this briefcase to Military Intelligence in Split. Is that clear?'

'Yes, sir.' I was extremely surprised. Why use me rather than the official military courier service? I put the letter in my top pocket and reached for the case.

'Wait a moment,' the major commanded. 'This first.' He handed me a luger in a holster. I stood and, as I was clipping it on to my belt, he walked round the table and, without a word, handcuffed my left hand to the briefcase then said, 'Guard this case with your life. Now it's time you were off.' I felt uncomfortable as I walked out of the hall, the major at my heels.

One of the police officers noticed the gun immediately. 'My God, he's armed. He must be very important,' he said. 'That's why we're taking him to Zagreb and he's not going on the coach with everyone else.' Before I could answer, I saw two familiar figures at the edge of the crowded town square. They were Father Josip and Sister Kazimira.

'There are two good friends of mine coming this way,' I said. 'Could you wait a moment while I speak to them please?' The policeman looked at the major who gave a brief nod.

'All right don't be long,'

As soon as Father Josip saw me, he hurried forward and put his hand on my shoulder. I knelt in front of him as he said, 'Bless you my son. May God be with you always,' and, looking around at the crowded square, went on, 'and with all of you here today.'

As I kissed the priest's hand, Kazimira whispered, 'God love you, Ivan. The other sisters and I think about you and pray for you every day.' I saw she had tears running down her cheeks. It was strange to be blessed by a priest when I was carrying a gun, more so because a large number of the people in the square were kneeling and crossing themselves.

'Vesligaj, time to go.' I was jerked back to reality by the sharp voice of the major and, with a quick farewell to Father and Kazimira, I saluted him and got into the police car.

We drove away at speed. It was clear that the more talkative of the two police officers was intrigued by what had happened. 'First of all we find you're important enough to be an armed military courier and then a priest blesses you in front of everyone in the town square. What was that all about?' he asked.

'If I told you, you wouldn't believe me,' I replied. 'I know you probably don't approve of priests and blessings because you're a member of the communist party. Well, I'm not. Did you notice how many people in the square knelt when Father Josip gave his blessing? Almost a hundred, I'd say, and the few who didn't are probably members of the Party, like you.' I was surprised at how strongly I felt about the officer's implied criticism of my religion. I went on, 'The priest was blessing everyone there, soldiers, sailors, bystanders and probably even you. There's nothing wrong with that, is there? As far as I know we do have freedom to worship as we wish in communist Yugoslavia.'

I paused for breath and the police officer said hastily, 'I didn't mean to offend you. I was curious, that's all. I don't know much about Catholicism. I was born into the Russian Orthodox faith.'

'It's the same God whether you're Catholic or Orthodox.'

'I hadn't thought of it like that,' he said and was quiet for a while.

In Zagreb, we pulled up outside a military office next to the railway station. An MP appeared immediately beside the car, with the words, 'Is this man under arrest?' Before anyone could answer, I opened the car door so that the MP could see the briefcase. I noticed that he was a corporal.

'I am not under arrest,' I said, getting out of the car. 'I am Petty Officer Ivan Vesligaj, acting as special military courier. Please take me to your CO.'

The corporal saluted. 'Come this way, sir,' he said. I gave the police officers a wave and followed him.

'I am Petty Officer Ivan Vesligaj and I have a letter for Colonel Nikola Hum,' I said to the CO.

'I am Colonel Hum,' he said and I handed him the letter. 'Sit down Petty Officer,' and to the MP, 'you are dismissed Corporal.' He put on his spectacles and perused the letter.

'Plans have changed, Vesligaj,' he said. 'I've just been on the telephone to Split and it has been agreed that you should leave the briefcase here.' He produced a key and unlocked the handcuffs. I rubbed my wrist. It was a relief to be free. I started to unclip the luger. 'Keep the gun,' he instructed. 'Here is a permit which entitles you to carry it. I am assigning you as support for the MPs on the train. There will be a lot of servicemen on it and I don't want any trouble.'

'Thank you, sir.' I paused and then asked the question which was puzzling me. 'I hope you don't mind my asking but why was I chosen to carry an important message, sir?'

'There have been a few problems with the courier service lately and I had your details faxed to me. I sent orders to Pregrada that you should be entrusted with the case. I reckoned, from what I'd read about your education in a monastery, that you'd be an intelligent and reliable messenger.'

'Thank you, sir,' I said, pleased that once more my time at Bol had made me stand out from the crowd.

The MP, whose name I discovered was Daren, was waiting for me outside the CO's office and we walked to the station together. Extra coaches for military use had been added to the train and a compartment reserved for MPs. 'The train stops three times,' Daren explained. 'First stop, Knin. Some sailors will be joining the train there.' All was peaceful in the military coaches and I dropped off to sleep once the train got underway. I woke when we stopped at Knin. Looking out of the window, I could hardly believe what I saw.

Several MPs, armed with submachine guns, were pushing a group of soldiers and six sailors roughly towards the train. They were using the rifle butts to hit out at anyone who seemed to lag behind. I could hear the shouts and curses of the MPs even from inside the compartment. As a blow landed on one of the sailors, I leapt out of my seat. 'Don't go out, sir. You'll be in trouble yourself,' cried Daren.

'I'm going,' I retorted. 'They're not going to treat sailors in that way.'

'Take this then.' Daren pulled off his MP armband. Pushing it on hurriedly, I thanked him and was on the platform in a trice.

'Leave that man alone!' I bellowed to a towering individual who was dragging one of the sailors by his collar.

'Who says so?' the man snarled. He was a lance corporal.

'I say so.' I indicated the armband and my rank and, reluctantly, he let go of the sailor. Taking advantage of the momentary lull as everyone turned to look in our direction, I shouted, 'Will all naval personnel come here to me now.' Gratefully the six sailors pushed their way towards me and I ushered them on to the train.

Once I'd settled the men and checked their papers, I went back to the compartment and returned Daren's armband. 'Thank you, it really helped,' I told him.

'You're welcome. I have to admit we do have some thugs and bullies in our ranks, sir, but we're not all bad.'

I dozed again until Daren woke me. 'We're going to check the soldiers' papers now, sir. Will you come and do the checks for the sailors, please? As a favour, strictly speaking it's our job?' I willingly complied.

There were no real problems. I found a few seamen in one of the civilian compartments with their girlfriends. They weren't causing any trouble so I let it pass. One pretty girl with dimpled rosy cheeks and curly hair, stood up and kissed me on the cheek. 'What a kind officer you are,' she said.

One lad was nervous as he passed me his papers. 'I'm sorry they weren't stamped at the station. I was at the back of the queue and I would have missed the train if I'd waited.' I told him not to worry and signed the papers for him.

When we arrived at Split, I said goodbye to Daren and handed the luger in to the base commander who checked my papers. '*R11* isn't in base at the moment,' he said. 'It's moored off the island of Jabuka. Go and have some breakfast and come back afterwards. I'll lay on a boat to take you to your ship.'

Within an hour I was aboard a torpedo boat, speeding towards Jabuka which lay south of Vis. The sun was on my face, the brilliant sea, jewelled by Dalmatia's islands was all around. Joy and excitement surged through me. I was on my way to the real start of my life on a destroyer. I couldn't wait.

R11 again

Lieutenant Cvek was on deck to meet me. 'Am I glad to see you Vesligaj!' were his first words. 'We've just intercepted a message coded in Latin. None of us understands Latin so it's up to you.' It felt good to be needed but Cvek hadn't finished. 'But first the captain wants to see you – "as soon as he arrives," he said. What have you been up to?'

'Nothing illegal,' I replied. It was good to have a clear conscience…unless, of course, I was in trouble for having a German girlfriend. But how would anyone have found out? By this time we were outside the captain's door. Cvek stood to the side while I knocked and entered.

The captain was smiling. Nothing to do with Ingrid, then. 'Well, Vesligaj,' he said, 'I gather you've had an interesting journey, acting as courier and MP.'

'Yes, sir.'

'I just wanted to say well done but also to remind you that you must come right down to earth now. This is the proper start to your career as a crew member of a destroyer. You'll have to work hard, sometimes for long hours. I expect you to do your best.'

'Of course, sir.'

'Good. That's all for now.

'What was that all about?' Cvek asked when I emerged from the cabin.

'It was a pep talk,' I said. Later I would tell him about my journey but my priority, now, was the mysterious code.

Cvek had intercepted a message between 'NSK' in the USSR and 'JFK' in the USA. The Russians were demanding the removal of an American base in Turkey as a condition for dismantling some nuclear missiles in Cuba. I could understand how the use of Latin had made it impossible for the other communication officers to decode the message but I was surprised that they hadn't guessed the names of Premier Nikita Khrushchev and President John F. Kennedy, from their initials.

Almost before I'd finished explaining the message to Cvek, a Morse code message came through.

Cuban crisis over. Agreement reached between USSR and USA. Green Light for R11 to return to base.

The other two communication officers entered the cabin. We passed on the good news and then Novak said, 'Sit down Vesligaj. We've got some news for *you* too. In about two weeks, you and I are to transfer temporarily to, *Galeb*,

Marshal Tito's ship, for about three months. What do you think of that? We'll be going somewhere hot.'

'*R11* will be one of the battle ships which will escort *Galeb*,' added Cvek, 'so you'll see us and we'll be in radio contact but you will be living in luxury on the best of all our Yugoslav ships.'

'Galeb', Marshal Tito's ship

I could hardly take it in. Not so long ago I'd seen *Galeb* for the first time and been told that Tito took only the cream of the navy to man his ship. Was I now 'the cream'? Excitement swept over me, flooded me. I was speechless.

'Are you all right?' I heard Novak say. I nodded my head.

'Turn in Ivan,' advised Cvek. 'You're not on duty until tomorrow which will be a very busy day. You probably didn't get much sleep on the train last night. You look exhausted.' I was grateful for his thoughtfulness and, leaving the three men laughing indulgently at my reaction to the news, I hurried to my cabin.

I was on the bridge next morning, on semaphore and lamp duty, as we sailed away from Jabuka. We had received fresh orders and were bound for Tivat in Montenegro where *R11* would be cleaned and repainted before accompanying *Galeb* on its voyage. The captain wandered along to speak to me.

'Well, Vesligaj, this is your first full day of real work aboard although you'll be temporarily transferring to *Galeb* in a couple of weeks. You've been told that, have you?'

'Yes thank you, sir.'

'Sorry your leave was shortened, by the way, but I'm sure you realise that no-one knew how this Cuban trouble would end.'

'I understand, sir.'

About three hours later, we entered the Boka Kotorska Bay and slid into the dry dock at Tivat. The ship was lifted so that the barnacles could be scraped off, preparatory to the repainting.

The captain called us on deck for a briefing. 'You will receive meals in the army barracks which are five minutes walk away from the dock,' he said. 'You will be detailed to scrape the hull, fumigate the living areas (against cockroaches) or paint the deck. Work starts tomorrow.'

'We stay on communications,' Cvek told me. 'No scraping for us, thank goodness.'

As I stood inside the army canteen the next morning, a soldier, standing to one side and with his back to me was talking to a sailor. I heard a voice I recognised, asking,

'Do you happen to know a sailor called Vesligaj, Ivan Vesligaj?'

'Yes, he's a petty officer on my ship.'

'That can't be him. He's not an officer, he's just an ordinary seaman like you.'

I walked up behind him, laughing. 'Hello Lujzek,' I said.

My brother spun round and, astonished, he embraced me, stood back and took in my stripes. 'A petty officer eh? Congratulations. It's great to see you. Shall we have breakfast together?'

'Of course.'

Lujzek had to queue for porridge, two slices of black bread, marmalade and unsweetened coffee whereas I, as an officer, was served with fried eggs, smoked sausage, white bread, jam and sweetened coffee. Lujzek looked longingly at my plate and I handed it to him. 'You have this. I'll eat yours just this once,' I said, 'but I'll keep my own coffee if you don't mind.' I quite enjoyed the porridge and we chatted as we ate. Lujzek was a Border Guard. He was serving on the Albanian border, a dangerous posting. He was currently half way through four day's R and R and he was very envious of my next posting on *Galeb*.

I'd noticed Cvek having his breakfast a few tables away. When we'd finished ours, I took Lujzek across to him. 'This is my brother, sir,' I said. 'He'll be here for two days before returning to the Albanian border. I haven't seen him for some time. Would you give me permission to spend a little time with him?'

'You had your shore leave shortened, didn't you? Yes, we owe you a couple of days. I'll cover your duties for you. Off you go. Have a good time.'

Proudly I showed Lujzek over *R11*. I was pleased that he was suitably impressed. 'Let's go into Budva,' I said, when we'd finished. 'It's a tourist resort. Let's be tourists for a day.'

'I haven't any money,' admitted Lujzek ruefully.

'Don't worry, I've got enough for both of us. When we get to Budva the first thing I want to do is to go to the post office. I want to call Ingrid and let her know I'll be out of contact for three months or so.'

'Mama told me all about your capitalist German girlfriend,' he laughed.

I joined in his laughter. 'Have you got swimming trunks with you?' He hadn't so I lent him some and we went ashore to catch a bus to Budva.

At the post office, I had a brief telephone conversation with Ingrid. She said her parents had been fascinated with all the photos she'd taken when staying at my house. She promised me copies and then cried a little when I said I probably wouldn't be in touch for about three months as I was off to sea. She cheered up when a thought struck her. 'At least there won't be any girls at sea to tempt you,' she said.

First we made for the old town. It reminded me of Dubrovnik although it was on a smaller scale. I loved the way its marbled streets and Venetian walls rose from the clear sea below. Later we swam then lay on the beach. We finished up at a smart restaurant. I could tell by the look the patron gave Lujzek that soldiers were not welcome but when he saw that I was a naval officer, he smiled and ushered us to a table on the balcony, overlooking the beach.

In the bus, on the way back, we reminisced about our childhood. I reminded Lujzek of an argument between an aunt and uncle of ours. At one point Auntie, a large woman in height and girth, picked our smaller uncle up by his belt, carried him to the garden rubbish dump and dropped him right into it. We laughed so much at the recollection that people on the bus turned to look at us and smiled indulgently.

As we walked back to the barracks together, Lujzek said, 'I wish I'd joined the navy. You're so lucky to be going on a long voyage. Do you know where you're going?'

'Somewhere hot. Perhaps Africa.'

'Africa? Fantastic! Think of me, in danger every day from the Albanian snipers.'

'If they shoot at you, you can retaliate, can't you?'

'No. We have orders not to return fire.'

That seemed insane to me. 'Sod the orders,' I said. 'You have a right to protect yourself.'

'Orders are orders. You know that I can't ignore them, Ivek. As an officer in the navy, you must realise that.'

'Well just take care,' I said lamely. We arrived at the barracks and saw ranks of soldiers in battle dress and fully armed. A lieutenant hurried across to us and addressed Lujzek. 'Hurry up Vesligaj. Change into battle dress and collect your weapon. Your rest is over.'

'What's going on?' I asked but he'd already turned away. I gave my brother a quick hug and slipped 2,000 dinar into his hand. 'Take this and take care,' I said and watched as he sprinted off to obey orders.

We stayed in dry dock for ten days. Then, clean, repainted and glistening in the sunshine, we sailed back to our base in Split. As we approached, we saw *Galeb,* prominent in the harbour.

'There's our ship,' Novak called to me. 'In a few days, you and I will be aboard.'

'I can't wait,' I called back. And I really meant it.

Galeb – the start

At last my wait was over. Lieutenant Novak and I were aboard *Galeb* and I was surveying our two-berth cabin with satisfaction. '

'What luxury!' I exclaimed 'We've got a porthole.'

Novak laughed at my delight. 'And a telephone with a direct line to the bridge.'

There was a knock at the door and I opened it. A seaman was standing outside. 'Muster on deck at 15.00 hours,' he said.

At the appointed time, we joined the rest of the crew to await the arrival of our commanding officer. After looking us over, he told us to stand at ease and addressed us. 'We will be leaving here in four days,' he said. 'We will sail to Alexandria in Egypt and then on to Ethiopia. We will be carrying Marshal Tito and some government ministers. So, crew of *Galeb*, you will have a chance to put all your training into practice. We have some new crew members from destroyers who will undertake security and guard-of-honour duties. Those men have been trained in readiness. Two officers only are exempt from security guard duties. They are Lieutenant Novak and Petty Officer Vesligaj. They will have plenty to do as communication officers. They will, however, form part of the guard-of-honour. If at any time Marshal Tito or any of his guests ask you a question you must answer politely, of course, but keep it short. Don't allow yourself to become involved in a long conversation. Finally, wherever Marshal Tito goes, journalists follow. Radio, television and film crew will be coming on board as well as newspaper reporters. Do *not* answer questions or get drawn into discussions or conversations with these people. I don't trust them. Do you all understand?'

'Yes sir,' we chorused.

'The next few days will be very busy as we get ready to receive our guests.' The CO dismissed us and Novak and I were free to go back to our cabin.

'This is going to be even more interesting than serving on *R11*,' I enthused on our way back. 'Seeing Tito and all those other well known people and having photographers and journalists aboard and going to Egypt and Ethiopia. I can't believe my luck.'

Novak laughed at me again but in a kindly way. 'It will mean plenty of hard work and long duties,' he warned. But I didn't care. All I knew was that the real adventure, the one I'd been hoping for all my life, was about to begin.

Messages poured in over the next two days and while we were fully occupied in the radio cabin, almost all the rest of the crew were carrying provisions aboard from dozens of trucks. 'I bet they're bringing caviar aboard for the guests,' sighed Novak. 'It's my very favourite food.'

On the third day, at 10.00 hours, I was on the bridge when four coaches drew up on the quay, parallel to *Galeb*. I called Novak. 'Who do you think this lot are?'

'Journalists. Could be trouble.'

'What sort of trouble?'

'We're communications officers. We're the first to get any news aren't we? When we're far out to sea, we'll be the obvious people for them to approach for information. Come into the cabin. I've got something for you.' Curious, I followed him in. He unlocked a drawer and took out two pistols. 'One each,' he said, handing me mine. 'The CO arranged for us to have them just in case of any difficulties.'

I was amazed and rather thrilled at the importance the CO gave to my job. However, I meant it when I said, 'I hope I'll never have to use it.'

Final goods were loaded the next morning. After lunch, the order came for all members of the guard of honour to change into specially provided new uniforms, pick up from the store, rifles (unloaded) and white gloves and assemble on deck. A large crowd had gathered on the quay and police were holding it back. A chant rose as the first police motor bike approached – 'Tito, Tito, long live the communist party of Yugoslavia.'

Guard of Honour

221

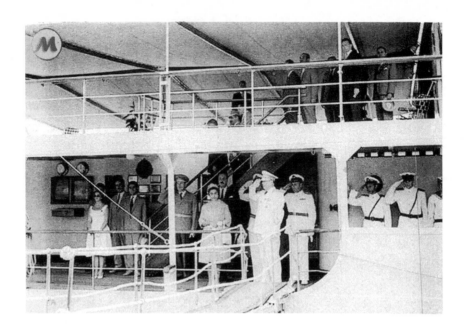

Guard of Honour

A duty officer ordered us into our positions for the parade and then told us to stand at ease. I saw more motorcycles and then several jeeps full of MPs. Next came a line of limousines which drew up adjacent to the ship. Marshal Tito, in a civilian suit of purist white, stepped out of the first. Tense with nerves and excitement I gave a sharp intake of breath.

'What's wrong?' whispered Novak who was next to me.

'I'm nervous,' I whispered back.

'Just take a few deep breaths and try to relax,' he advised. 'You know the drill.'

'Attention!' shouted the officer as Marshal Tito, his wife Jovanka, with a several dignitaries behind, walked slowly up the red carpeted gangway. Cameras were clicking and flashing and a film crew was recording everything. The sailors, not part of our guard of honour were chanting, 'Tito, Tito' so that when the Marshal stopped to speak to each of us in the guard of honour, I couldn't hear what he was saying to the others. He was shorter than I'd imagined, stocky and muscular. I thought he looked younger than his 66 years although his dark hair was receding. He had a lively intelligent expression and suddenly he was in front of me.

'Where do you come from, son?' he asked.

I swallowed hard and tried to keep my voice steady as I found myself face to face with the President of Yugoslavia. 'I am one of the *zagorac*/people from behind the mountain, sir,' I managed to say.

'Well, there's a coincidence. So am I.' Of course, I knew exactly where Marshal Tito had been born.

'Yes, sir,' I said.

'Which town are you from?'

I caught the duty officer's eye over Tito's shoulder. He was shaking his head as a signal that I should stop talking but what could I do? I had to answer. 'Near Pregrada, sir.' I was gaining in confidence and may even have smiled at him. 'Not far from Kumrovec.'

He was delighted at this and laughed. 'Why, that's my birthplace. Did you know?'

'Yes Comrade Marshal Tito.' He laughed again and moved on to speak to Novak.

I watched Jovanka as she passed me. She was fat and wobbled on high heels. Her jet black hair hid some of the rolls of flab which made up her chins. She was smiling just as she smiled in every single photograph of her that I'd ever seen. The common term for such a perpetual smile, a phony smile, was *Yugoslavenski smjesak* / the Yugoslav smile.

Once Marshal Tito had reached the end of the line, the CO accompanied him and his entourage to their quarters. The CO soon returned. 'Thank you for an excellent guard of honour,' he said. Then he asked each of us, in turn, what Marshal Tito had said to us. When he got to me, he frowned. 'What was that long conversation about, Vesligaj?' he asked. 'Marshal Tito spent more time with you than with anyone else.' When I told him, he tutted. 'We do have schedules to keep to you know.'

'Yes, sir,' I said although I really didn't see how I could have shortened the conversation.

Novak and I walked together to return our rifles and gloves. 'Looking at Jovanka, you can see why Tito has so many affairs, can't you,' I said softly. Rumours were always circulating about his latest girlfriends although, of course, we knew nothing for certain.

'Why do you think there are beautiful opera singers aboard?' laughed Novak.

That evening, members of the crew crowded into the assembly hall to watch the newsreel report of Marshal Tito arriving on Galeb. And there I was, next to Novak, on the news for the whole world to see. There was even a shot of my conversation with Marshal Tito.

We were busy in the radio cabin when word came that the four destroyers, *R11, R6, R18* and *R22* were waiting off the island of Vis to accompany *Galeb* to Africa. Taking a short break on deck, I was astonished to see one of the sailors walking a white poodle. I ran back to Novak. 'There's a dog on board,' I said. 'Isn't it forbidden to bring animals on to the ship?'

'It's forbidden to everyone except Marshal Tito,' replied Novak. 'Rules don't apply to the president.' He went on to say that throughout the voyage, we would take it in turns to do four hour shifts in the radio cabin during daytime. 'There are rarely radio messages at night,' he explained, 'but we will have to do night shifts on the bridge, looking out for Morse signals.'

'There's plenty of room in here,' I observed, looking round the radio cabin. 'Why don't we bring our mattresses up? It's close to the bridge and one of us can sleep while the other does signal duty. If by any chance a radio message does come, it would wake up whoever was sleeping, wouldn't it?'

'It would. Good idea,' he agreed.

Just then a lieutenant knocked at the cabin door. 'I've come to let you know that I have three seamen who can understand Morse but are not qualified to use lamps or the radio. Would they be any use to you?'

'What do you think?' Novak asked me.

I had an idea which would enable us to get more sleep. 'How about the men doing the signal duty shifts at night?' I suggested. 'As soon as they see a signal, they can come and wake one of us to deal with it.'

'Excellent!' said Novak. 'Is that all right with you, lieutenant?'

'Absolutely,' he replied. 'I'll send the men to you for their orders.'

Next morning there was an early call for all of us to assemble on deck for a photograph with Marshal Tito. We were amused by the fact that he sat in our midst with the poodle on his knee. I knew the picture would appear in the national newspapers and grinned to myself at the thought of how jealous lieutenants Cvek and Anzic on *R11* and Ćiril on *M143* would be.

Marshal Tito and his poodle

At 11.00 hours *Galeb* started to move out of the harbour. Once more crowds had gathered, lining the edge of the quay. 'Tito! Tito! Long live Tito,' they cried and their voices were carried to us on the breeze as we slipped away. Marshal Tito stood on deck, waving graciously at his loyal people until they were out of sight, A flotilla of small boats accompanied us for some distance, horns hooting, passengers cheering. At last they, too, were left behind. We were on our way to Africa.

Marshal Tito came up to the bridge while I was on signal duty. Almost at once, I spotted the four destroyers lined up close to Vis. We established contact and then, as we sailed past, their crews in identical formations, cheered Tito in unison. Delighted, he saluted each ship. It was an impressive display of Yugoslavian naval discipline and drill and I felt proud to witness it.

The destroyers now took up their positions as escort ships, one in front, one behind and one on either side of *Galeb*. I had a chat on the radio with Cvek who told me he missed Novak and me because he and Anzic had more duties to do. 'I wish I was on that plush ship,' he said. 'I can't understand why you were chosen and not me.' But he said it with good humour.

As I went off duty just before supper, Novak asked me to fetch some food from the galley. The chef put a pile of roast beef sandwiches on a tray and I suddenly remembered Novak's favourite food. 'You wouldn't happen to have any caviar, would you?'

'Sure I have,' he said obligingly and added a dish of caviar and a plate of biscuits.

'Am I glad you're here!' Novak exclaimed delightedly. 'I'd never have dared to ask. Well done.'

Marshal Tito and several of his guests joined us on deck for exercise the next morning. The Marshal's shorts exposed very white legs and varicose veins. However, for his age, he was fit and acquitted himself well.

I was on the bridge on signal duty later in the day and, scanning through binoculars, I realised that I could see no land at all. We were in the Mediterranean Sea and, for the first time ever, I was truly 'at sea'. Exhilarated, I drew a deep breath. At that moment, I felt as if I wanted to spend the rest of my life afloat.

My train of thought was interrupted by the arrival of Marshal Tito and senior officers including our CO who was, of course, also captain of *Galeb*. Tito took photographs of everything and everybody. Journalists and film crews took photographs of him taking photographs. I continued scanning and suddenly I realised there was no sign of *R22* although I could see the other three destroyers. Before I could ask Novak about this, the CO came over to me. He handed me a note. 'Vesligaj, send this message to *R11* immediately and ask the communications officer to pass it on to the other destroyers.' I didn't like to ask him about the whereabouts of *R22* so I fetched the lamps. I read the message, preparatory to signalling.

As from 03.00 hours today, when we crossed Yugoslavian boundary, every sailor participating in this expedition, will receive his salary in USA dollars, according to his rank. By order of Marshal Tito.

As I sent the signal, I thought that this was good news because of the advantageous exchange rate. (Later, information posted on the notice board was even better. Overnight, my pay leapt from 1,000 dinars a month to the equivalent of 7,000 dinars a day). When I'd finished signalling, I hurried to the radio cabin and told Novak about the message.

'We'll be rich men,' he laughed.

'We do have one problem, though,' I said. '*R22* seems to have disappeared. Did it get lost in the night?'

Novak laughed again. 'Lost on a clear, calm, starry night? I should hope not! Do you remember saying that a radio message would wake us if it came at night?'

'Yes.'

'Well, the one that came at 23.00 hours last night didn't wake you! Fortunately I'm a lighter sleeper.'

'Sorry,' I mumbled.

'No matter. Perhaps you'll be the one to wake next time. Anyway, the message was that *R22* had been ordered to divert and to meet the Yugoslav hospital ship which is anchored in international waters off the coast of Algeria.'

'What's our hospital ship doing in that part of the world?'

'You know there's been a war between France and Algeria, don't you?'

'Of course.'

'Well, apparently there's an agreement between Marshal Tito and Ben Bella, leader of the National Liberation Front and now also Premier of Algeria. The Yugoslavian hospital ship is taking wounded fighters to hospitals in Yugoslavia. *R22* is required as an escort until the hospital ship is safely in Yugoslavian waters.'

As I returned to the bridge, I thought about the evening, soon after I'd arrived on M143, when I'd explained to the crew about the Algerian conflict and been rewarded by my appointment as Political Education Officer. I didn't really know why but I felt pleased that Ben Bella was out of prison and was now in charge of Algeria.

Marshal Tito was still on the bridge when I resumed my duty. He took a photograph of me as I was receiving a message. 'How are you doing son?' he asked when I'd finished.

'Fine, thank you, sir.'

'Now, where did you say you were from? Oh yes, you're from the same part of the country as I am, aren't you?'

'Yes, sir.'

'What does your father do?'

'He was killed in the war, sir?'

'I'm sorry. Which side was he on?'

I hesitated but decided on honesty. 'He was in the German army, sir.'

Tito smiled. 'Well those were turbulent times. They set brother against brother and son against father.'

I thought of Milan and Josip. 'Yes, sir,' I said.

As if he could read my thoughts he asked, 'How many brothers have you got?'

'I'm one of ten. Seven brothers and two sisters.'

'I'm one of fourteen,' he said, 'but I'm the only one who has survived.'

'I'm sorry about that, sir.'

He sighed. 'Ah well that's fate I suppose. Are any of your brothers in the armed forces?'

'My brother, Milan, was among your very first naval recruits,' I said, not mentioning that he had been forced to join after serving in the German army. 'And my brother Lujzek is doing national service in the army at the moment, sir.'

'I'd better let you get on with your job,' he said. 'I think I'll sit in the shade for a bit.' He wandered away to the canvas chair which had been placed for him under a canopy.

I had my camera with me – the one that Ingrid had bought me. 'Please, Comrade Marshal Tito, may I take a photograph of you?' I asked boldly.

'Certainly you can, son,' he said, smiling. 'After all we are almost neighbours.'

Is this really happening? I asked myself as I pressed the button on my camera. I was tempted to pinch myself to make sure. As I lay in my bunk that evening, I tried to reconcile my intense dislike for the communist regime with my instinctive liking for Marshal Tito, its leader. I fell asleep before I had found a satisfactory answer.

Photo of Marshal Tito taken by Ivan

Alexandria and Beyond

An Egyptian destroyer escorted us into the harbour at Alexandria. Once more Novak and I formed part of the guard-of-honour. This time it was for President Nasser of Egypt. He was escorted on to *Galeb,* by Marshal Tito and the captain.

We were able to relax once the visitors had retired for refreshments although we knew they would be leaving *Galeb* shortly. I retrieved my camera from the radio cabin and gave it to one of the cameramen.

'Please take some photos of Marshal Tito and any other important people when they go ashore,' I begged and handed him several rolls of film.

'I'll do my best, I'll be following them wherever they go,' he laughed. 'You'll be the envy of the navy when you flash my photographs about.'

After an hour or so we stood to attention once more while Nasser, Tito, Jovanka , the CO and government officials went ashore, cheered by the large crowd which had gathered at the quay-side. They were driven away in limousines. I found out later that they were taken to Cairo to attend a conference of some of the heads of non-aligned states. Marshal Tito was the Chairman.

Alexandria. Ivan on right

A sightseeing trip for some of the crew had been arranged and the next morning we boarded coaches at 09.00 hours. It was already very warm as we drove through Alexandria and on into Cairo. I couldn't help thinking that city's piles of rubbish, multitude of ragged beggars and tumbledown shacks contrasted sharply with its magnificent gilded buildings, colourful bazaars and expensive cars.

By the time we arrived at Luxor we were extremely hot and uncomfortable but grateful that we had been issued with salt tablets and instructed to carry water. It was hard to take in the statues, obelisks and tombs. I felt so insignificant and small against their massive antiquity.

I had thought I'd known about pyramids because I'd seen the pictures in the library books at Bol but nothing had prepared me for their enormity. I could only marvel at how such sophisticated structures had been conceived and built without the advantage of modern technology. I thought of the thousands of men and women who had died, labouring in this relentless sun. In spite of the heat and the sightseers, I shivered. I bitterly regretted not having my camera with me.

Instead of going straight back to *Galeb,* we crossed the Suez Canal and, stopped at a UN camp which was on the edge of the Sinai Desert. It was manned by the Yugoslavian army and we were greeted warmly, not least because we brought a bag of post for them. Vodnik, a WO 1, took us into the canteen for a meal.

'What do you actually do here?' I asked him.

'We keep an eye on the Israelis. They are camped about 500 meters away and eager to encroach on Egyptian territory. Would you like to see their camp?' He took a few of us out to one of the observation posts, which sported the UN flag. I could see movement in the distance. We climbed into the tower and he handed me some binoculars. I focussed them and got a shock.

'Good Lord, they're women,' I gasped. But that wasn't all. 'They're washing themselves – stripped to the waist.' I lowered the binoculars, red and strangely embarrassed.

'They can't have realised they were being observed,' said one of our lads, innocently.

'They certainly did realise,' I retorted. 'They were all waving.'

I regaled Novak with this story in our cabin that evening. He was eager to hear about the trip as he was to join a similar one the next day. We hadn't any duties because *R11* was close by to attend to messages. We lay on our bunks, enjoying the chance to relax. We'd been so busy since our arrival on *Galeb,* that we'd had little time to talk about anything but work.

Now, suddenly Novak asked, 'Have you got a girlfriend, Vesligaj?'

'Yes. Have you?'

'I'm married to a beautiful girl, Marija, and I've a son of two months old, Branko.'

'That's wonderful,' I said. 'You must be longing to get home and see them again.'

'Yes I am. Now tell me about your girl. What's she called?'

'Ingrid.'

'Ingrid? Is that the German girl who was the cause of your seven days confinement to ship in Rogoznica?'

'How do you know...?' I began.

'Oh, I know all about you my lad. I know about your unusual education and your reputation for high moral values. All the communication officers, on *R11*, read your records before you arrived.'

I laughed. 'Fortunately not all of my secrets were in the records.' I said. When I wouldn't explain further, Novak asked me how I first met Ingrid and I told him a little of our whirlwind romance on Rogoznica. I was too tired to say more and the next morning he told me that I'd fallen asleep mid-sentence.

Four days later, I was in the guard-of-honour again as President Nasser waved Marshal Tito off amidst military music and much saluting.

This time, the Marshal was accompanied on to *Galeb* by the Ethiopian Emperor, Haile Selassie. He was even shorter than Tito, wore an army uniform and a hat sporting feathers. His wide smile displayed brilliantly white teeth. He stayed on board while we cruised along the Suez Canal, the Red Sea and then down the east coast of Africa. At Djibouti, he and Marshal Tito, with their entourages, disembarked and we continued south to Madagascar where we dropped off some businessmen and then turned back, stopping at Mogadishu for Marshal Tito. Prince Sihanouk, Prince of Cambodia was with him. Apart from the world leaders I have already mentioned, I saw others at various stages of that memorable voyage. I saw King Hassan II of Morocco, Kwame Nkrumah, Prime Minister of Ghana, Julius Nyerere, first President of Tanganika, President Nehru of India, Fidel Castro, Prime Minister of Cuba, and President Keita of Mali.

Next we crossed the Arabian Sea, and rounded India to Calcutta. The prince left us there and Marshal Tito went ashore to meet Mother Theresa. The crew had the chance of an hour's coach tour of Calcutta and my overriding memory of that is of noise, dust, and cows. I'm sure Calcutta had much more to offer but we weren't given the chance to find out. Ahmed Sukharno, first president of Indonesia joined us at Calcutta. Novak joked that we were a taxi service because we now sailed south east, through the Bay of Bengal to drop him off at Djakarta.

From left, Pres. Nehro (India) Pres. Keita(Mali) Pres.
Nasser(Egypt) King Hassan(Morocco) Marshal Tito

From left. Jovanka, Fidel Castro, Marshal Tito

Our return journey was fast and direct. We refuelled at Port Said and, on the
Mediterranean Sea, encountered a mighty storm. It seemed to me that all the
officials who were accompanying Marshal Tito and all the dancers and singers

who provided entertainment aboard were seasick. They leaned along the length of the deck rails, putting themselves in danger of being swept overboard. We were ordered to secure them with ropes and stand by to help in any way we could.

I came upon one of the young opera singers, Silva, clinging to the rail. 'Are you all right?' I asked. As she turned her sickly greenish face to me, I realised what a stupid question that was. 'What you need is dry bread.' I accompanied her down to the kitchen and secured two pieces of bread. 'Eat them slowly, Chew them well.' She did as I asked and began to look a little better. 'Come back on deck now. You need fresh air.'

On deck, I filled a bucket with water and prepared to swill the boards. Then I remembered a trick we'd been taught early in our training. I passed the bucket to the young singer. 'I want you to carry this for me,' I said. 'Carry it round this deck and use the water to swill if necessary. Then refill it at that tap and carry on with the job until the storm is passed.'

She looked surprised. 'Why?'

'Just do it, please. You'll understand why later,' I said.

'I don't think I can manage to do it.'

'You can manage it. I have a good reason for asking. Trust me.' Reluctantly she picked up the bucket and did as I asked. I followed her to make sure she was safe, attending to others on the way.

Half an hour later, the storm had blown itself out and Silva turned to me, pink-cheeked with the effort of her labours, all signs of sickness gone. 'Is there magic in the water?' she asked. 'How could carrying a bucket make me feel so much better?'

'It's all a matter of concentration,' I explained. 'If you are focussed on something other than feeling ill then the "feeling ill" disappears. Easy!'

Each week we broadcast a music request programme throughout the ship. It came from Radio Zagreb and was very popular. One day I was on duty on the bridge when I heard my name through the loud speaker

'This song is for Petty Officer Ivan Vesligaj,' the disc jockey announced. 'The sender wishes to remain anonymous.' A cheer went up from the crew as the song began. I can't remember the precise words but the sentiments were;

Dear Sailor, I send greetings and wish for your safe return.
You may be in a distant country but you're close to me because you are in my heart.

I knew immediately that the request came from Ingrid. Novak came over and clapped me on the back. 'Well done Vesligaj. That girlfriend of yours certainly loves you.' I was touched by Ingrid's gesture but, for the next few days, had to put up with members of the crew whistling or humming the song whenever they saw me.

I was in the radio cabin when I picked up a BBC World News bulletin. It reported that Aleksander Ranković, Yugoslavia's Minister of the Interior and head of UDBa, was in London. There was nothing alarming about that but the report continued with the information that Ranković was holding meetings with King Petar, the former monarch of Yugoslavia. The topics under discussion at the meetings were not known. I realised that this news could be significant. King Petar had escaped to England in 1941 taking with him, it was rumoured, a considerable amount of Yugoslavian gold. Just then, a coded message came through from civilian intelligence. It also indicated that Ranković had met King Petar. I took the decoded message to Novak who immediately encrypted it in a naval code and sent it to naval intelligence. The acknowledgement of receipt of the message came straight away and was followed by one which said that certain members of UDBa were being watched.

'What do you think is going on?' I asked Novak.

'I'm not sure. We'll find out soon enough. I gather that there is a rift between Ranković and Marshal Tito. Ranković is head of UDBa, remember. If he can count on the loyalty of all its members, he might try to topple Tito from power.'

I was aghast. Although Marshal Tito was the head of a communist state, with all its restrictions, he was Croatian, as opposed to the Serbian Aleksander Ranković and he was known to be more liberal than Ranković. Rumour had it that Marshal Tito did all he could to hold the hated UDBa in check.

Tito and his entourage left *Galeb* at Split. Before going ashore, he thanked us all for looking after him so well and raised his hat in a farewell. There was a strong police presence on the quay and we cheered him as he was driven off in his limousine, giving us a final wave. 'Thank goodness that's over,' Novak sighed as we briefly relaxed on our bunks.

'What an experience, though,' I said. 'I'm sure I'll never have the chance of another conversation with the President.' I couldn't have been more wrong.

Aleksander Rancović

Keeping Marshal Tito Safe

In Split and back on *R11*, Novak and I were the envy of everyone. Only those of us on *Galeb* had been allowed ashore to see the sights of Egypt. The sailors aboard the destroyers had spent the whole voyage on their ships. There was a pile of letters waiting for me and I slipped away to read them.

Dragica wrote that she had seen me on the newsreel when I was in the guard of honour for Tito and also when he spoke to me.

I've never been so proud, her letter ran. *There was my little brother, so smart...and talking to our president. Nevenka jumped up and down and pointed at the screen, shouting 'That's my uncle!' We could hardly believe our eyes.*

As the newsreel was shown at all cinemas for some time, other members of my family and many of my friends had seen it too. It was a long time before they stopped teasing me about what they laughingly called my 'stardom'. Even Ingrid, in Germany, saw the film. She wrote,

I went to see the newsreel every night for a week. My mother and father were also very impressed.

Communication duties resumed and life was settling into a comparatively boring routine when some unwelcome visitors arrived. I was on the bridge and able to hear the exchange between the duty officer and four men in dark civilian clothes who had arrived in a large car.

'These are our passes,' said the first. 'They entitle us to come aboard.'

'UDBa passes?' The duty officer said sharply. 'This is a naval vessel. UDBa has no authority here.'

'Be careful what you say to us,' a second man snapped. 'We want to see your captain.'

'Why?'

'That's no concern of yours.'

Sensing trouble, a second armed guard had joined the duty officer who now said to him. 'Stay with these men. Keep them where they are. I'm going to talk to the captain.'

The guard stood watch over the civilians while the duty officer sprinted off to find the admiral. The UDBa group muttered angrily among themselves. After about ten minutes, two jeeps screeched to a halt on the quay. In no time, eight naval MPs were out of the jeeps, had handcuffed the civilians, bundled them into the vehicles and driven away.

Novak came on to the bridge and called to me, 'What excitement!'

'What was it about?'

'UDBa came to arrest the captain, apparently. They're arresting officers and people of influence all over the country.'

'Why?'

'I can only guess that they want Ranković to be president and are trying to get rid of some of Marshal Tito's supporters. Naval Intelligence has arrested Tito in Belgrade, flown him to Pula and taken him by boat to the island of Brijoni.'

'Arrested Marshal Tito?' I was so shocked that I struggled with my words.

'Only for his safety. Brijoni is his own island, remember. It's his estate.'

I was still digesting this astonishing news when orders came through that *R11*, along with the other three battleships, should prepare to sail to Brijoni. It would be our task to defend President Tito.

Within two days we were in position to the south of Brijoni. The other ships were anchored to the north, west and east. Patrol boats continually circled the island outside the ring of destroyers and also moved up and down the coast of the mainland. Small boats from each of the destroyers circled Brijoni, itself in the waters between the island and the destroyers.

'How long do you think we'll be here?' I asked Novak.

'Until Ranković has been dealt with,' was his answer.

On the fourth day it was my turn to lead the patrol. On *R11*'s small boat, with me, were Petty Officer (2nd Class) Štef Kruslin and Leading Seaman Oto Rebič. We had just started our circuit of Brijoni when I heard a shout and saw a man in one of the island's sheltered coves. He was waving a stick. I couldn't hear what he was shouting but, when I looked through the binoculars, I saw that it was Marshal Tito.

Amazed, I stopped the engine, I still couldn't catch his words but his frantic gesticulations unmistakably meant that I should take the boat to the cove. The three of us looked at each other. 'There was nothing about this in our orders,' I said. 'What do you think we should do?'

The others looked at me helplessly. 'You'd better decide, sir,' Kruslin said and I knew he was right. I was the senior officer. Tito was still beckoning and shouting so I switched on the engine and made for land.

We jumped ashore and I went over to him while the others held on to the boat. He recognised me immediately. 'Why, it's my fellow countryman. That's good.'

'What can we do for you, sir?' I asked.

'You can take me to somewhere I can meet my people. I can't stay shut up on this island for ever. I need to get away and meet my people.'

My mind raced. Marshal Tito was here for his safety. Could I take it upon myself to remove him from that safety and put him at risk among the general public? I knew I couldn't quite do that but I could hardly ignore a request of the president. I had the beginning of an idea so I stalled for time.

'Where would you like to go, sir?' I asked.

'Anywhere, anywhere!' he said impatiently. 'Anywhere to meet my people.'

Still playing for time, I turned to my companions. 'Have you any suggestions about where we could go?' Looking nervous, they shook their heads but I had decided exactly what we would do.

There were numerous little islands to shelter us from the patrol boats and twenty minutes later we were tying up at the quay of a small, remote fishing village south of Pula. I had been here several times before and knew that the *Barba Jura,* its small restaurant, was owned by a loyal Partizan leader and that every one of the men in the village had fought by Tito's side in his struggle for power.

Some fishermen were mending their nets and had spotted their leader. They let out a cheer and came running towards us but I wouldn't let them approach him. I couldn't be too careful. In my anxiety, I left the walkie talkie in the boat. When I realised this later I wasn't in a position to fetch it. I told the other sailors to have their machine guns at the ready and I kept a finger on the safety catch of mine. I looked at my watch. It was 14.00 hours.

As we approached, we heard loud chatter and laughter from inside *Barba Jura.* 'Excuse me sir,' I said as we reached the door. I stepped in front of him and pushed it open and, as I entered, there was sudden quiet. I looked round the room quickly. Just fishermen. I stepped aside to allow Marshal Tito to enter.

Still silence for a moment and then Josip Barba, the owner, ran from behind the bar and embraced Tito. 'Comrade Broz!' he cried. 'Welcome to my restaurant!'

'Thank you Joza,' Tito said softly and I thought I saw the glint of tears.

There followed much handshaking and clapping on backs during which time I instructed my two shipmates to stand guard outside the door. I bolted it from the inside and took my position against it, still ready to shoot anyone who looked like a threat to Marshal Tito.

'Drinks on the house,' bellowed Josip. 'What will you have Broz?'

'What is your house wine?'

'Reisling, white and fruity.'

'A glass of that please.' Marshal Tito sat down, in his element. He and his friends swapped stories and reminisced and, finally, started to sing Partizan songs.

Time passed and suddenly there was a knock on the door. Cautiously I opened it a little. I could hear sirens and police klaxons.

Kruslin spoke through the crack. 'Please would you come out for a moment, sir.'

I went outside. Alarms were sounding from Pula and from Brijoni. Patrol boats were hugging the coast lines of the island and mainland. Lights were flashing on boats and on land. Clearly Marshal Tito had been missed.

I looked at my watch. It was 17.00 hours. By now, my party would have been missed too. I looked into the restaurant. Tito was singing and laughing, rocking to the music and more relaxed than I'd ever seen him. How could I spoil his afternoon? I decided to leave him until forced to do otherwise. I was almost certain to be in trouble anyway. A little while longer wouldn't make any difference. I went back into the restaurant but left the door ajar.

Ten minutes went by and I heard police sirens very close. They stopped and there was a slamming of doors. I stepped outside to see jeeps and several cars. There were naval MPs and behind them several journalists and cameramen.

'Halt!' One of my sailors had his machine gun levelled at the crowd, making sure no-one came any closer.

'Who's in charge here?' asked one of the MPs, an officer.

'I am,' I said.

'Who are you?'

'I'm Petty Officer Ivan Vesligaj.'

The MP held up his ID card, saying, 'Have you got Marshal Tito inside that building.'

'Yes, sir.'

'Is he safe?'

'Yes, sir.'

'Can I see him?'

I was concerned that if the officer went in waving his pistol, there might be serious trouble, perhaps even fatalities so I said, 'You may see him, sir, but go in unarmed. Give me your pistol.'

As I was pointing my machine gun at him, he handed me the pistol with a shrug. 'You'll pay for this latter,' he growled. I didn't doubt it.

He went inside and came out with Marshal Tito. Cameras were flashing and I thought fleetingly that once more I'd be in the newspapers.

'Hand over your arms,' the officer barked at us. We obeyed meekly. Now that Tito was safe we didn't need them. Then three of the MPs came across to us with handcuffs.

Marshal Tito had turned as he was getting into a police car. 'No!' he exclaimed. 'They don't need handcuffs.' The handcuffs disappeared, he got into the car and we were bundled into a jeep.

'We're for the high jump,' I said ruefully.

'We were just following orders, sir,' Rebič said. 'Orders from the president.'

We sped to the Military Police barracks in Pula and were taken to the duty officer. We identified ourselves and the accompanying MP handed our machine guns to the officer.

'I'll take care of these,' the duty officer said. 'These three won't need them.'

The words chilled me. Did he mean we wouldn't need guns because we were being locked up? The seriousness of what I'd done suddenly hit me as if someone had landed a hefty punch in my stomach. Could we be accused of abducting Marshal Tito. I had certainly absented us without means of communication and without permission. I could be shot for the first offence, spend time in a military prison for the second. At the very least, I felt sure I'd be demoted.

'Empty your pockets.' The order broke my train of thought. 'You can keep your cigarettes.' Then, to a military police officer who had been leaning against the wall and watching us, 'Take them up to 116, please, sir.'

Cell 116, I thought miserably, fearing the worst.

We went up to the first floor and I noticed that there were rifle racks outside each room. Perhaps this wasn't a prison after all. 116 turned out to be a three bedded room – just a normal room in a barracks and not the cell I'd dreaded. I allowed myself to feel a little more cheerful.

I was surprised when, instead of leaving us in the room, the officer leant against the door frame, grinning widely. 'Well you three have some nerve, I must say,' he remarked. He came forward and shook hands with us. 'How the hell did you manage it? You'd better tell me all about it because I'm representing the three of you at your court martial tomorrow.'

Court Martial

I'd been lulled by his relaxed manner. Now the room seemed to spin. 'Court martial?' I croaked.

'Yes but don't worry. I'll see you come out of this all right. My office is on the ground floor, Room 5. Come and see me after supper. You haven't eaten have you?'

'No,' I said although food was the last thing on my mind. I couldn't eat much and I don't remember what we were given. Whatever had possessed me to take Marshal Tito off the island, to ignore orders and to lose contact with *R11*? I should have pretended I hadn't noticed the president.

The officer called us into his room one at a time. I was last. I told him exactly what had happened from the moment we set off from *R11*. I had almost finished when his phone rang. He answered it.

'No I didn't know,' he said. 'When did it happen?' I couldn't hear the reply but the officer laughed. 'Heads will roll now. Thanks for letting me know.' He put down the receiver and looked at me. 'Ranković was detained when he got off the plane. He's being questioned now about his meeting with King Petar and what he knew about UDBa's actions while he was away. Some UDBa members have been arrested along with the guards on Brijoni who were negligent in their duty of protecting Marshal Tito. After all, you could have been kidnappers. The naval military police are taking over his protection.' I felt immediate relief but the officer continued, 'However, there will still be a court martial tomorrow. Try not to worry though. I feel sure it will come to nothing and you will be vindicated. I wouldn't be surprised if you are decorated. You did guard Marshal Tito in an exemplary fashion.'

'Who will be the judge tomorrow?' I asked weakly. I wouldn't allow myself to hope for a good outcome.

'There will be a panel of three judges, an admiral, vice admiral and a lieutenant colonel from the army. There will, of course, be a prosecuting council and I will lead the defence. You will plead not guilty to all charges of breaking rules, disobeying orders and endangering Marshal Tito's life. Don't look so terrified. Here, have a cigarette.'

The three of us tossed and turned all night, sometimes discussing the possible outcomes in low voices, sometimes dozing. Several times I jumped awake with a jolt of dread. It was a relief when 06.00 hours arrived and we could join the MPs in the courtyard for physical exercise as we'd been instructed.

As we were about to go down for breakfast, I noticed that Štef Kruslin seemed upset. He got out his handkerchief and kept blowing his nose. I put my hand on his shoulder. 'Try not to worry too much,' I said. 'What Oto said yesterday was correct. We were following the president's orders. We couldn't disobey them could we?' I spoke with more confidence than I felt. 'This isn't the Soviet Union,' I continued. 'We won't be shot. Prison is the worst that can happen.'

I felt a pang of guilt as I saw the white faces of my two colleagues. After all, I had got them into this mess. However, Kruslin looked a little less anxious but none of us could face any breakfast.

At 09.30 hours we were escorted to Room 5 for a final meeting with our defence council. He ran through the procedure of a court martial and checked we hadn't missed anything out when we had spoken to him the previous evening. 'Leave me to answer any tricky questions you are asked by the prosecution,' he said. 'You may have to answer direct questions from the judges. If you do, keep your answers short and if you are not sure what to say, leave it to me.'

At 10.00 hours we were marched along the corridor by three MPs. A number of our shipmates had come to support us and they put their thumbs up or shouted 'Good luck' as we passed.

Novak was there. He gave me a big grin and mouthed the words 'Character reference.' We entered a large hall with ranks of chairs. At the front was a table behind which were three large chairs. I felt cold all over, trembly and I was pleased to sit down. Our defence council sat nearby. The prosecuting council's chair was to the right of the judge's table.

The three MPs, who had escorted us, stood directly behind us and I noticed they carried side arms. Surprisingly, they whispered encouragement. 'You were obeying the orders of the most important man in the land,' one said.

'You did a good job of keeping Marshal Tito safe,' added another. I felt a bit better especially when I looked over at Novak and he winked at me and put up his thumb but my confidence seeped away again when we were ordered to stand and the three judges walked in, carrying brief cases.

I tried to steady my voice as I gave my name, date of birth and rank but I thought my response came out weak and wobbly. Then the vice admiral read a list of the crimes of which we were accused. 'First, you are all accused of ignoring the regulations and breaking the rules of the Yugoslav army. Secondly, you are all accused of disobeying the orders of the day. Finally, you are all accused of endangering the life of Comrade Marshal Tito, Supreme Chief of the Yugoslav navy.'

'Ivan Vesligaj, how do you plead on the first count?'

'Not guilty, sir.'

'How do you plead on the she second count?'

'Not guilty, sir.'

'How do you plead on the third count?'

'Not guilty, sir.'

Kruslin and Rebič entered the same pleas.

The council for the prosecution spoke first. He read the orders of the previous day and went on to show how we had disregarded them. 'By your own admission, you took Comrade Marshal Tito from a place of safety and, not knowing who would be in the restaurant *Barba Jura*, you allowed him to go inside without his bodyguards. You risked the life of our president. You are all culpable but I contend that Petty Officer Ivan Vesligaj is mainly responsible for this outrage.' He turned to address me. 'You were the senior officer, you were in charge. You made a wrong decision, one which not only put Marshal Tito in danger but also caused grave anxiety and confusion within the security services and further afield.' He said a lot more about my irresponsible behaviour and, while admitting my good record, said this action wiped out all that had come before.

That was my lowest moment. I saw the lieutenant colonel nodding in agreement and I thought the other judges regarded me with considerable disfavour. I felt faint with anxiety and lack of sleep and food. I gripped the side of my chair until my knuckles were white but then it was time for our defence council to speak.

First he told the judges exactly what had happened – the facts we had told him the previous day, from the time we left *R11* to the time when we were arrested by the MPs.

'These men did not set out to break any rules or laws,' he went on. 'They intended to do exactly what they had been told to do and would have done so if it had not been for the extraordinary circumstance of their noticing Comrade Marshal Tito signalling from Brijoni. Could they ignore him? Of course they couldn't and when they went to see what he wanted, he gave them an order. That order was, "Take me to my people." That was an order from the president of our country, the Supreme Chief of the Yogoslav Navy and superseded any previous order. I contend that these men, far from disobeying orders, obeyed them in an exemplary manner. I have been a military policeman for twenty years. I am in charge of general security both military and civil. I speak, therefore, from a position of knowledge and experience. I do not believe these men are guilty of jeopardising Marshal Tito's safety. Where were his personal bodyguards? Where was the chief of security on Brijoni when this incident happened? Why was Marshal Tito alone on the quay? A sniper could have killed him from a boat or from one of the small islands off the coast of Brijoni. He could have been snatched by kidnappers. These three men removed Marshal Tito from possible danger and took him to a place of safety where they guarded him with their lives.

'The men have excellent records. All recently accompanied President Tito on his much acclaimed tour of Africa. They have served the president well and rubbed shoulders with him and with many other important people. Do you think such men would risk his life? They showed initiative, presence of mind and courage. Remember they were confronted with armed MPs but stood their ground, removed one MP's arms to prevent any misunderstanding inside the restaurant and so enabled Marshal Tito to be escorted away safely. No blood was shed.'

Our council said a lot more in the same vein and when he'd finished, the admiral announced that it was time to adjourn for lunch.

'Will the men be taken to the cells, sir?' asked the prosecution council hopefully.

'Where did they spend last night?'

'In a bedroom in MPs' barracks, sir,' said our man.

'I don't think they pose a threat or will run away,' said the admiral. 'They can eat in the canteen.'

We couldn't eat. We drank coffee and smoked, sitting for the most part, in gloomy silence in spite of our council trying to cheer us by saying he thought it was going well.

After the break, Lieutenant Novak was called to give me a character reference. He talked about my time on the minesweeper, my attempt to rescue Marinko Peps, and my service aboard *R11* and *Galeb*. 'He had his last leave shortened by three days,' he said. 'On his way back to base, he was asked to be a special military courier. He carried a top secret letter to Colonel Nikola Hum in Zagreb.'

'A military courier?' queried the vice admiral.

'Yes sir,'

The three judges looked at each other. I heard the admiral say to the lieutenant colonel, 'Did you know about that?' He shook his head.

'Tell us more about this,' the admiral said so Novak explained that I had been chosen because of my excellent record and reputation for integrity and how I had been handcuffed to the briefcase and armed. 'And on the train from Zagreb to Split, he acted as MP, helping to supervise soldiers and sailors on the train,' he concluded. I thought – I hoped – that the judges looked impressed.

By the time character references for the other two had been given, it was almost 16.00 hours. Two of the judges said they had no comment to make at this stage but the lieutenant colonel said, 'These references are very impressive but, nevertheless, I think these men are guilty and should be punished...'

The admiral interrupted. 'We need to take into consideration everything that was said today. This we will do this evening. Our verdict will be delivered tomorrow.'

Our council stood up. 'May I respectfully suggest that you investigate what happened to security on Brijoni. Why was Marshal Tito on a beach on his own?'

'Rest assured we will consider everything,' the admiral replied. 'This court is now adjourned until 10.00 hours tomorrow.'

As we stood, our council whispered to me, 'That lieutenant colonel and I have often crossed swords. He is in overall charge of security on Brijoni. He's got a lot to lose.'

Another troubled night. I finally fell asleep in the early hours and dreamed that I was shut up in a tiny room with no window. I awoke sweating and shaking and lay listening to my thumping heart.

When everyone was assembled in court the next morning, the admiral told us, the three accused, to stand. *This is it!* I thought. He addressed us.

'We have discussed at length all we have heard about this case. We have taken into consideration your records and the circumstances in which you found yourselves. We find you guilty on the first two counts. One, you all broke the rules and regulations of the navy. Two, you all disobeyed the orders of the day in your duty as patrol crew. However, on count three, that of endangering the life of Comrade Marshal Tito, we find you not guilty.' I experienced a surge of hope. We'd been found 'not guilty' of the most serious of the three charges. The first two verdicts might mean prison but perhaps not for too long.

'Your punishments are as follows;' I heard him say. 'Petty Officer Vesligaj, you are demoted to petty officer 2nd class, Petty Officer Kruslin, you are demoted to leading seaman and Leading Seaman Rebič, you lose the rank you have.' My knees almost gave way with relief. Demotion by only one rank – it was a better result than I could have hoped.

At that moment, a side door in the hall opened and a naval officer hurried in, holding a white envelope. The admiral looked cross at the interruption but the officer went straight to him and saluted.

'Sir, I'm sorry to interrupt the court proceedings but this letter is important. It is imperative that you read it immediately please, sir.'

Puzzled, the admiral drew the letter from the envelope, read it and then, with raised eyebrows, surprised everyone. 'This court will adjourn for ten minutes,' he said. He rose and indicated that his fellow judges should follow him out. I was still so relieved that I hardly noticed our council congratulating us on the light sentences and an MP removing one of my stripes with a small sharp knife.

The judges returned. 'Will the accused stand,' demanded the admiral. Dreading what might follow, I stood up. 'New evidence on this case has been brought to light,' he said. 'It is extremely rare for judges to overturn their own verdicts but that is what we are doing now. The judgement of this court is that we find each one of the accused *not* guilty on all three counts.' There were exclamations of surprise from all around but the admiral called for silence and for our stripes to be returned to us. 'Petty Officers Vesligaj and Kruslin and Leading Seaman Rebic, we ask you to accept our deepest apologies for any distress you have been caused. Please be clear that all charges are dropped and will not appear on your records.' The vice admiral looked directly at me. 'Petty Officer Vesligaj, we now know that you were telling the truth.'

'Thank you, sir,' I managed to say.

'We are sorry for doubting your word.'

Then the admiral said, 'I want to see the three of you in my room immediately, please. I declare that this case is now closed.' The three judges swept out of the room.

My head whirled as I sank back on the chair. What was the new evidence? Who had sent the letter? Everywhere in the hall people were asking the same questions. The noise was immense.

Our council was grinning as he clapped us on our backs. 'Who cares who wrote it and what it said?' he laughed. 'You're off the hook, that's all that matters. Come on, we'd better go and see the admiral.' Everything was dream-like. My colleagues and I left the noisy hall as if in a daze, people congratulating us all the way.

'Come!' called the admiral when we knocked on his door. 'There's no need for you to be here, thank you,' he said to the defence council who shook hands with us, once again, brushed aside our thanks and left. We were invited to sit down and coffee was brought in for the four of us.

'Now tell me once more, in your own words, what happened.' Again we went through the story. The admiral smiled when I reached the part about Tito's reception in the restaurant.

'What did Marshal Tito drink?'

'Reisling, the house wine,' I said and he laughed.

When we'd finished, he had one more question about our adventure. 'We were very worried about the whereabouts of Marshal Tito and about what had happened to you. Why didn't you report what was happening on the walkie talkie?

'I should have done sir, I'm sorry. There were fishermen on the quay as we arrived. They ran over to us and I was so concerned for Marshal Tito's safety that I forgot to pick up the walkie talkie. I'm afraid I left it in the boat.' He seemed satisfied and went on to ask us about our families and where we came from.

When we'd finished the coffee, the admiral stood up and we followed suit. 'If I had my way, I'd promote you all,' he said. 'Goodbye and good luck.' Salutes were exchanged and we went out.

We stood and looked at each other in disbelief. How could everything have turned out so well? We shook hands, laughing and at that moment an MP arrived and, after congratulating us said, 'The duty MP has arranged for you to be collected by *R11's* small boat. It will soon be here. Come with me to the quay.' We followed him out and soon we saw the small boat approaching. When it arrived, the sailors leapt out and hugged us, shouting that we were heroes.

A huge tiredness gripped me as we sped towards *R11*. I felt as if I would not have the energy to climb aboard. I had no choice, however, and had to face virtually the whole crew who were on deck, cheering and shouting. It was good to be greeted in such a manner but I still felt as if I were sleep-walking.

Cvek, Novak and Anzic gave us a special welcome. 'The lost sailors return,' Anzic laughed and then said that the captain wanted to see us immediately. Could this be the real trouble? I wondered wearily.

Anzic knocked on the door of the captain's cabin and on the 'Come in,' he put his head round the door. 'Three lost sailors for you,' he said and we went inside. The smile on the captain's face set my mind at rest.

'Sit down the three of you and tell me all about it,' he said. When we'd finished, he stood up and shook our hands. 'I'm proud of all of you,' he said. He fetched a bottle of cognac from a cupboard, poured some for each of us and we stood together and toasted Marshal Tito. 'There's something else I want to say to you,' the captain went on when we sat down again. 'You've been at sea for three months and had quite an ordeal over the court martial. I have decided that you can all have fifteen days extra shore leave, to take when you wish. Vesligaj, as your last leave was cut by three days, you can add that to the fifteen to make eighteen. When you've had time to think, let me know when you want to take the leave. That's all for now and again congratulations.'

My three communication colleagues were waiting for me on deck and together we went to our cabin. I flopped on my bunk, my eyes heavy.

'Come on then,' urged Novak, 'what really happened?' So again and for the last time that day, I told the story.

Cvek started to ask me a question but then he stopped. 'The poor lad is almost asleep,' he said to the others. 'Let's leave him in peace. We'll call him at supper time.'

'There's just one thing you might like to know Ivan,' Anzic turned back as he spoke. 'The deputy of your defence council is a friend of mine. We trained together. When he phoned me to give me the good news, he let some information slip. He told me who that letter was from – the one that saved all your skins.'

'An officer brought it in. I didn't know him.'

'He was just the courier. The letter was from Marshal Tito.'

The image of Tito turning back from the car as we were arrested flashed into my mind. 'No handcuffs,' he had said. He must have realised we'd be in trouble. Doubtless he knew about the court martial. What a man – to think of us in the midst of all his other problems and affairs of state. I closed my eyes, still thinking of Marshal Tito and promptly fell asleep.

I was teased a good deal over the next few days but, at the same time, I noticed that I was treated with a certain amount of respect too. I wasn't given another patrol duty but, instead, became co-ordinating officer, in charge of all of the patrol boats which went out from the destroyers.

Four days later, crisis over, Marshal Tito left Brijoni and returned to Belgrade. Our work of protecting him was over.

Special Lunch: Special Leave

Back in Split, we were allowed time ashore to stretch our legs after so long at sea. On the Saturday afternoon, the captain summoned me. When I arrived outside his cabin, I found Štef Kruslin and Oto Rebič already there, looking nervous.

'What do you think he wants?' whispered Oto. I felt anxious but tried not to show it. I shrugged.

'Only one way to find out.' I knocked on the door.

'Come in.' We trooped in and saluted. 'Don't look so worried,' smiled the captain, 'you're not in any trouble.' He was positively beaming and I relaxed. 'I want to ask you a favour. Would the three of you be kind enough to come to my flat tomorrow, for Sunday lunch? My wife and daughter would like to meet you, having read all about your exploits in the newspaper.' We were all extremely surprised at the invitation but managed to say we'd be delighted to go.

Next day saw us taking great care over our appearance. I suggested buying a bouquet for our hostess and we duly presented ourselves at the apartment. The captain's wife greeted us at the door and seemed pleased with the flowers. She was a pleasant looking woman with short grey hair and a wide smile. Her daughter, Mira, was about nineteen or twenty, a very attractive brunette, with large dark eyes and a shapely figure. She came forward to meet us and, instead of shaking hands, kissed each of us on the cheek. 'I've so much to ask you,' she said.

'Let the poor men have a drink first,' laughed her mother. The captain was in the living room and he introduced us by name and invited us to sit down. We had agreed that we'd drink nothing stronger than beer so that we would keep clear heads. We stuck to our resolve although the excellent quality cognac was tempting.

Mira was holding a notebook and pencil. 'I'm a member of *Omladina* / the Young Communists,' she said. Will you tell me all about what happened when you were protecting Comrade Marshal Tito please? I want to be able to give a report on it at *Omladina!* and at university.'

'After lunch,' said the captain said firmly. 'There will be time then.'

The meal was delicious; homemade soup with pasta, *kremenatle* / lamb chops, roast potatoes and vegetables, with fruit to follow. We all relaxed as we ate and conversation ranged wide. Mira told us about her university course and asked what we'd done before our national service. The captain's wife was interested in our families and which parts of the country we came from. When we'd finished eating, I offered to help with the washing up and picked up some dishes to carry into the kitchen but Mira stopped me. 'No *Druze* / Comrade. You are our guest. We'll do it later. Come into the living room and drink some coffee while you tell me about Brijoni.'

'Ask Petty Officer Vesligaj if he minds your writing down what he tells you,' said the captain.

'I don't mind,' I said. So, once more, I recounted the story, aided by my fellow sailors.

When we'd finished, Mira closed her notebook. 'It's a disgrace that you were court martialled. You should have been decorated!' We smiled but said nothing.

'They are getting extra leave,' said her father.

'What do you like to do in your spare time?' I asked Mira as Štef and Oto drifted into conversation with the captain and his wife.

'I like music, discos, theatre and I love going to see the ballet.'

'Have you got a boyfriend?' I asked boldly.

'Several.' She laughed. 'Do you like ballet?'

'I haven't much experience of it.'

'*Swan Lake* is coming to the theatre soon. Will you come and see it with me?'

Be careful, I warned myself. I really didn't want any complications in my life – however attractive I was finding Mira. 'With your father's permission, I would like to,' I said demurely.

'Daddy, would you allow me to go to see *Swan Lake* with Petty Officer Vesligaj?' Mira called to her father.

He looked at me seriously. 'Yes, providing he promises to look after you.' Then, to me, he said. 'Look after her carefully. She can be a bit wild.'

We all laughed and I said, 'Thank you, sir.' And after many thanks and compliments to the chef it was time to go.

I did accompany Mira to the ballet a couple of weeks later. I met her outside the theatre and she wouldn't let me pay for the tickets. 'Daddy's treat,' she said. We had a pleasant evening. I saw her home afterwards and kissed her hand in farewell. I'd kept my silent vow to avoid further entanglement.

On 25th April, I left Split for my unexpected and special leave. In my pocket I had an extra 3,000 dinars which was paid to me as part of my 'reward'. At Zagreb I phoned Ingrid.

As usual, she cried with delight at hearing my voice and screamed her pleasure when I invited her to come to my home while I was on leave. 'I'll be there in two days,' she shouted. 'I can stay for ten days if that's all right.' We arranged to meet at Lupinjak. I spent the night at Dragica's and then caught the train to Lupinjak and visited my friends who owned the inn near there.

After a cold beer, I walked through the forest and, at the crest of the last hill, saw my village below. As ever, I was elated by the sight of home. I'd travelled a long way and seen a great deal since last I was here. I ran down the hill and, coming to the village, saw old friends working in fields and gardens.

Suddenly Mama was on the path in front of me. 'Ivica!' she cried, 'What a surprise.' And we were embracing and she was crying. I was home. She fried eggs for me, made coffee and showed me a newspaper Stjepan had bought from Pregrada. 'Look at you,' she said. 'My little Ivica holding a great big gun!' And there I was, aggressively pointing a machine gun at a member of the security forces outside *Barba Jura.* I looked extremely fierce, frowning and angry.

'I'll tell you all about it later – when Stjepan comes home. Where is he?'

'At the vineyard.'

'I'll go and help him now, and again tomorrow. Ingrid is coming the day after, to stay for ten days. Is that all right? She'll lend a hand in the vineyard too.'

'Of course it's all right. It'll be lovely to see her. Stjepan and I will sleep in here. You two can have the bedroom.'

I worked with Stjepan for the rest of the day and the next, pruning and tying the vines. August, my father's cousin, whose vineyard was near ours, saw us and came over to greet me. He asked if I could spare him a cigarette. I gave him a packet and, in return, when he had finished work in his vineyard, he and his hired hand came and helped us in ours. During my first evening home, the neighbours gathered outside, clambering to hear the story behind my photograph in the paper which Stjepan had shown them. I told them about my voyage on *Galeb* and my adventure concerning Brijoni but I steered clear of any talk of politics.

I met Ingrid, as arranged, and once more we left the car at the inn and walked through the forest and over the hill to my village. How sweet it was to be together and how glad her reunion with Mama. These were my thoughts at the start of the holiday but during the ensuing ten days I found myself irritated by Ingrid's clinginess. She wouldn't let me out of her sight for a moment. She kept questioning me about any girl I might have met since we were last together. It's true, the love-making was still wonderful and I tried to dismiss my feelings of dissatisfaction as a reaction from all that had happened to me over the last weeks.

The ten days went quickly. We worked in the vineyard, visited Stara mama and spent some time revisiting our favourite haunts of last year. But for me, nothing was quite the same.

One day, we went to see Father Josip and the sisters at Faruh. There, I had my first sight of a television set. 'We saw you on television, Ivan,' Franceska said.

'Twice,' added Father Josip. 'Once in the guard of honour for Marshal Tito and once when you were holding a gun.'

'That was frightening, Ivan,' said Sebastijana. 'It was a big gun and you looked so fierce.'

Kazimira was staring at me. 'Ivan, would you ever have used that gun – would you have shot someone?'

I looked at her kindly, anxious face. 'No, of course not,' I lied. And then I had to tell them the whole of the Brijoni story.

In bed, on our last night, Ingrid had some news for me. 'I've been saving this to tell you at the end of our holiday,' she said. 'It'll make it easier to say goodbye. My father does regular business with the leather factory where you used to work and he knows the director quite well. When you leave the navy, Father will put in a good word for you so that you can return there to work.' I started to speak but she had more to say. 'There is an exchange scheme in operation which enables skilled workers from Yugoslavia to swap jobs with German workers for six months or so. Father says that he'll arrange for you to take part in the scheme and come to Germany. Then we can be together for a whole six months. Isn't it a marvellous idea?'

I didn't know what to think or what to say. The plan certainly opened up new possibilities for me. 'It's very kind of your father to offer to help me,' I said guardedly. 'We'll talk about it more after I've been demobbed and am working at Almeria. I'm pretty sure they'll take me back without your father's intervention, but I am very grateful for the offer.'

'But you will come and work in Germany, won't you?' she persisted.

'I can't promise anything now Ingrid,' I said, 'but I'll certainly give it a great deal of thought.' She wasn't satisfied but I'd say no more even when she cried a little.

'Come on, let's make the most of this last night,' I said. So we did.

As I walked home, through the forest the next day, after waving Ingrid off, I had time to think about what she had suggested. I knew that she often tried to control me – by her tears, her regular gifts of expensive items and money and by her constant questions about my love for her and my faithfulness. I also knew that I was partly to blame. I had gone along with everything. Her obsession with me was flattering, the money had been useful and she was a very beautiful young woman. I was fond of her but, in my heart, I knew I was not in love with her. If I went to Germany, would this be interpreted as my wishing to spend the rest of my life with her? I did want to get away from the restrictions imposed by the communist regime and I did need a job to go to, in order to be allowed to leave the country, so Mr Gunther's offer was very attractive.

I was still pondering when I reached home. 'What a lovely girl Ingrid is,' was Mama's greeting. 'You seem so well suited. You should be thinking about settling down Ivica. Just imagine, if you marry her, you'll be rich. She's the only child and will inherit her father's factories and money.'

I turned away from her. 'Not now Mama,' I said. 'I'm not ready to make such a big decision. Once I'm out of the navy and have found a job with a good salary, I'll be in a position to think whether or not I want to get married.' And, in spite of my mother's pleas on Ingrid's behalf, I refused to say anything more on the matter. I was determined to act on what I had just said to Mama and defer any life-changing decisions until my naval days were over.

Voyage to USSR

Back on board *R11*, after my leave, I was greeted with enthusiasm because I brought with me a large torte made by my mother and some of Dragica's cakes. In the canteen, they disappeared in record time. I sensed, however, that the cakes were not the only reason for a change in attitude to me particularly among the officers. They started to call me 'Ivan' and most of them told me to dispense with addressing them as 'sir' and saluting every time we met.

'You're a hero,' laughed Novak when I mentioned this to him. 'You did what you thought was right, took the consequences of a court martial and then came out of the whole thing with Tito's blessing. It's the perfect story!'

After two weeks in Split, Cvek came to speak to me while I was on duty.

'We're off on a voyage,' he said, 'in about two weeks.'

My heart lifted. I had thought we might be stuck in base until my demob. 'Where to?' I asked.

'The USSR.'

'USSR? Why?'

'The navy is thinking of buying some new metal torpedo boats from the Soviets. We're taking the naval inspectors who will make the decision about them. I gather the navy wants to buy all the parts from the Soviets but to assemble them in the shipyards in Pula and Split to give employment to our ship-builders. I should think there'll be some delicate negotiations.' As Cvek was talking, I was looking at a map. He leant over me. 'Look, we'll go round Greece, through the Bosporus into the Black Sea and finish up at Odessa.' As he traced the route with his finger I felt my excitement rise. It would be fantastic to be properly at sea again and to visit strange places. I hoped we would be allowed ashore.

I will never forget passing through the Bosporus. As we moved through that strip of water which connects the Sea of Marmara with the Black Sea, we were sailing along the border between the Eastern and the Western Worlds. To the east, it seemed to me, lay waste land while to the west, there were hills, trees and farmland. The strait itself was very busy with ships travelling up and down and, at some points across it, in both directions. It is 37 kilometres long and, at its narrowest, only 700 metres wide. Flowing down its centre, from the Black Sea into the Sea of Marmara, is a dangerous and rapid current. The view along the strait is obstructed because of the rough and uneven nature of the coastline on each side. I was very impressed by the adroit navigation of our Turkish pilot. We saw, at last, the vast city of Istanbul, which straddles the Bosporus via a long bridge. We were now in the Black Sea.

For a while we followed the western coastline, passing Bulgaria and then we came to the delta of the mighty River Danube in southern Romania. Many of us went up on deck with our binoculars. We could see that reeds and small willows grew almost into the sea. Little streams and channels glistened as they found their way between the vegetation. Over all this lushness there were hundreds of birds: Birds flying, taking off, landing, paddling, feeding and swimming. Novak had told me that over 300 species of birds inhabited the Danube's wetlands and I felt sure I was seeing them all. I didn't know the names of many of them but I recognised pelicans, spoonbills and stilts and I saw ducks of many types, small cormorants and egrets. How I wished I had a bird book with me and I promised myself I'd buy one at the next possible opportunity.

Once past the delta, we were soon sailing northwest, making for our destination, Odessa, with its Soviet naval base. We were escorted into the harbour by four torpedo boats of the type our naval inspectors were to consider buying.

A brass band and a welcoming committee met us at the quay and the captain, senior officers and inspectors went ashore. When they returned, we were told that the whole crew, except for the unfortunate men on guard duty, were invited to a special dinner the next evening.

As we entered the huge canteen which was close to the docks, I noticed there were dishes of caviar, biscuits and bottles of vodka on every table. Almost before we had time to enjoy this aperitif, sauerkraut was served with more vodka. Spit-roasted lamb or beef followed with vegetables and vodka.

The Russian officer opposite me broke wind noisily and then belched. Novak, next to me, noticed my surprise and whispered, 'It's usual in Russia.'

The officer concerned saw Novak whispering and said belligerently, in Russian, 'There's nothing wrong in that. It's healthy.' I understood Russian but couldn't really speak it and, embarrassed, I looked the other way.

A young female member of the Soviet naval staff was sitting beside me and gave me a sympathetic smile. 'How long did your voyage take?' she asked. I stuttered some sort of answer. 'Well done,' she said. 'You understand Russian.' She was an attractive blond girl with extremely long, thick plaits. I smiled gratefully at her and imagined how beautiful she would look with her hair loose and flowing.

I had become aware that the Yugoslav naval personnel around me were succumbing to the effects of the vodka. I had drunk little but Novak was very merry. Suddenly the belching Russian officer leaned across the table and gripped my left arm hard. 'How much do you want for your watch?' he demanded loudly in German.

It was the one Ingrid had bought me. 'I don't want to sell it,' I said.

He stood up, leaned further over and, with two hands, undid the buckle on the strap and removed my watch. He sat down, holding it tightly.

'How much?' he repeated.

'No!' I said.

He pulled out a fist full of roubles. 'Here,' he said, 'Is this enough?'

'No thank you. I don't want to sell it.'

'Here!' he shouted. 'Take this as well.' He added to the pile of notes and threw them down in front of me then he put the watch in his pocket. There was nothing I could do but pick up the money and put it away. I didn't want to start a fight or provoke an international incident. I discovered, subsequently, that he had paid me about twice as much as the watch was worth.

At this point we were served more vodka and a space in the middle of the room was cleared. Russian music filled the hall and Kossak dancers entered. They wore baggy red trousers, high red boots, spotless white shirts, sashes and black hats. Their amazingly energetic dance was accompanied by rhythmic shouts. Finally they leapt on to tables which had been pushed together and finished with their famous 'bent knees' routine.

After the applause, I turned to talk to Novak and saw that he was slumped almost under the table. I looked round and realised that most of our crew was in a similar condition while the Russians seemed none the worse for all the vodka. Clearly they were in practice. They were even calling for more.

'Come on, drink up, drink, drink!' urged the belching officer.

I looked at Novak's watch. It was almost 03.00 hours. I'd had enough of the company and managed to rouse him. 'Come on, time to get back to the ship.' He staggered to his feet and allowed me to guide him through the door and along the quay. The duty officer laughed as I helped Novak aboard.

'He's not the first to come back in that condition,' he said, 'and I'm sure he won't be the last.'

Surprisingly, no-one seemed too hung over the next morning. 'I can't remember how I got back,' Novak confided.

'Don't worry, I saw you safely into your bunk,' I answered and he clapped me on the back.

'Our little priest,' he grinned. 'So pure!'

I laughed, 'Not always.'

'We've been invited to look at the radio cabin on one of the Russian destroyers. We're due there in half an hour,' Novak said.

The communications room on the destroyer was enormous – about twice the size of ours. I was pleased and surprised to find the blond, plaited girl inside and it was her job to show us round. Everything was on a larger scale than on *R11* but the room had the same components with one addition.

'What's this panel for?' asked Novak, pointing to an impressive and unfamiliar bank of switches.

'We control the position of the guns from here,' the girl said. We looked at each other in surprise. We had nothing to do with guns in our cabin. I was pleased this was the case. 'Would you like to go on deck now and watch the demonstration of the torpedo boats?' she asked.

The boats were fast, efficient and impressive. We learned later that the inspectors had approved their purchase and had obtained agreement that they could be built in Split and Pula. Our trip had proved successful.

The next day we sailed to the Crimea where we were able to visit some of the sites of the Crimean War. We saw remains of the trenches and the valley famous for the charge of the British Light Brigade. At a small museum, we were shown horrific photographs of the mutilated bodies of men and horses and also some of Florence Nightingale and her nurses. I was interested in the old medical instruments and the methods of healing that had been used. We were shown some large leaves of a plant that grew locally. I can't remember its name. 'If a wound became infected it was washed in vodka,' the guide told us, 'then these leaves were bound to the wound. They drew the poison out and, if the soldier was lucky, the injury would begin to heal.' I felt grateful I was living in the 1960s and not the 1850s.

Within two days we were on our way back to Split. We stopped at Istanbul and were given time to go ashore. It is a magnificent city with shining domes and minarets. I remembered, from my study of the Byzantine history that in 532 Justinian 3rd had allowed the building of a church called St Sophia. I made a point of visiting it only to find it had been converted to a mosque by Sultan Bayezid 2nd in the 15th century when he added four minarets. Then, in 1935, under Mustafa Ataturk, it had been secularised and turned into a museum. Inside, it was breathtaking, massive. Its walls were lined with marble of many different colours and decorated with fine Byzantine mosaics. Its great dome soared overhead. I saw, in the guide book, that this dome is even larger than the dome of the US Capitol.

We walked past the exterior of the impressive Topkapi Palace which was the home of Ottoman sultans for 400 years. A guide told us that at one time over 4,000 people had lived within its walls. He pointed out the section which had housed the harem. This sent a wave of excitement through our group. Perhaps men don't change very much, I thought.

Finally, after so much culture, we visited the Grand Bazaar. There has been an enormous covered market on the site since the 15th century. Colourful crowds thronged round every stall. The noise echoed off the roof as merchants proclaimed the benefits of buying their particular goods. Everyone haggled over the price of everything. There were displays of jewellery, gold, richly hued carpets, bright clothes, delicate fabrics, fine furniture and, what drew my attention, leather goods.

I examined these critically and turned to Novak who was with me. 'This isn't as good as we made when I was a leather technician.' I grinned and suddenly the smell of leather transported me back to Almeria. After all, I had been happy there, working with Ostoja. We'd had lots of good times.

Novak nudged me. 'Stop daydreaming,' he said. 'It's time to get back to the ship.'

Semaphore: Demob

We hadn't been back in Split long before Cvek called me into the radio cabin. Novak and Anzik were already there. 'We've been wondering about the semaphore competition we suggested just after you joined us,' Cvek said. 'If we don't do it soon, you will have left the navy.'

'Are you still willing?' Novak asked.

'I certainly am,' I had no fear of being beaten. I had never seen anyone signal as fast as I could and, anyway, a competition would be a welcome diversion from the routine of life at the base.

The more the officers talked about the competition, the more ambitious their plans became. In the end all the minesweepers and destroyers sent representatives to take part and there were four competitions.

Two in the daytime:
1. semaphore – using flags.
2. Morse code – using the light on the mast.

Two in the evening:
3. Morse – using Aldis lamps
4. Morse – using searchlights

Signals would pass between our ship and the top of the mountain in Maryan Park which lies just outside the city of Split. Competitors had to send and receive messages. There was a complicated marking system overseen by neutral 'inspectors'.

I thoroughly enjoyed the day of the event. Ćiril was there to watch and although a team from M143 was participating, he patted me on the shoulder and wished me luck.

It was late in the evening when we assembled on deck for the results. I had won the semaphore and mast light competitions and come second in the other two. A seaman who spoke fluent Italian had sprinkled his messages to me with Italian words when sending Morse by Aldis lamp and searchlight. I'd had to ask him to repeat a couple of sentences and so had lost points. I took his joke in good part and was quite happy with the result.

'Whoever taught you to signal so fast with flags?' asked an officer from *R22*.

'He did,' I answered and pointed to Ćiril who looked pleased. I was presented with a pennant and a trophy – a small model of a destroyer. I proudly displayed both in the radio cabin.

For some time I had been considering signing on as a regular member of the navy. I loved the life, the comraderie and the opportunities for travel. I spoke to Novak about it. 'I think you'd do very well,' he said. 'There are advantages – a fairly reasonable salary, travel and some disadvantages too. You'd have to do further training and you wouldn't be as free as you would be in civilian life – but you know that, of course. I'll fix a meeting between you and the captain, if you like. He'll tell you what is involved.'

'You'll have to pass a test and have an interview,' the captain told me when I saw him the next day. The written part will consist of an intelligence test and then you'll have to write about the history of the navy including the history of any ship you've served on. *R11* is fairly new so hasn't got much history but I should find out all about *Galeb* if I were you.

That held no fears for me. I had read up on the Yugoslavian navy before my national service and we'd had lectures on the subject during basic training. I also knew the background of *Galeb* and the minesweepers.

The exam papers were not difficult and I passed both and, within a few days, I was called for the interview on board *R21*. Four intelligence officers, three first lieutenants and a lieutenant commander, sat behind a table.

'Sit down,' said the chairman, the commander. I perched on a chair somewhat nervously. The faces were stern. I noticed that they had my naval records in front of them. The commander introduced himself and his fellow officers. It was an international panel. The boss was Serbian and the other three, Bosnian, Montenegrin and Macedonian. No Croatian, I noted. The commander opened the questioning.

'You want to make a career in the navy, do you Vesligaj?'

'Yes, sir.'

'Why?'

'I have enjoyed my national service in the navy, sir.'

'What have you enjoyed about it?'

I had rehearsed this answer. 'I've been able to travel and see places and people that I'd never have had a chance to see otherwise. I like the discipline, keeping fit, the comradeship and I love life at sea. I'm proud to be in the navy, sir, and to serve my country.' The commander seemed satisfied with my reply and one of the lieutenants took over the questioning. He asked about my family and where and when my brothers had done military service. He even asked about my father.

'That all matches with what we have on your records, Vesligaj,' one of the other lieutenants remarked. 'But now we come to 1960, not long before you joined the navy. I gather that you crossed the border into Italy illegally and then crossed back again. Tell us about that.'

This was the first time the Italian episode had been mentioned since I'd joined the navy. I drew a deep breath. 'Well, sir, I was young and immature and. I was desperate for adventure and the grass always seems greener on the other side. However, when I got to Italy, I found it wasn't greener so I came back.' For the first time, the officers exchanged smiles and then it was the third lieutenant's turn to ask a question.

'Tell us about the education you received in the Bol monastery.' That was easy and a couple of minutes later the interview was over.

'Thank you Vesligaj,' said the commander. 'You'll know the outcome of your application in three days time.' I stood up to leave but he had more to say. 'If you are accepted, you will do six months' training in Pula.' I had known that but hadn't been aware of what came next. 'A new ruling has been made, Vesligaj. If you complete the training successfully you will then have to serve on the island of St Ana, at the submarine base, for at least eighteen months, maybe more. Thank you, that is all.'

'Thank you, sir,' I said. I saluted and left the cabin.

'How did you get on?' Novak and Cvek asked when I got back to the radio cabin.

'All right, I think but I'm beginning to have second thoughts. I didn't realise I'd be stuck on land for two years. I joined the navy because I love the sea and life on board. There's not even a guarantee that I'll be posted to a ship when the two years is up.'

Three days later I was called to the captain's cabin. 'Congratulations, Vesligaj,' he smiled as he spoke. 'You have been accepted to go on the officers' training course.'

I had thought of little else since my interview and had made up my mind what to say. 'Thank you, sir, I am pleased to have been accepted but I have decided not to accept the place.'

The captain stopped smiling and looked puzzled. When I explained my reason, he shrugged. 'I have to respect your decision but I am disappointed. I think you would have made an excellent senior officer. Would you like more time to think about it?'

'No thank you, sir.'

I, too, was disappointed because I had enjoyed my years in the navy and had looked forward to many more. I knew, however, that I had a low boredom threshold and would hate a whole year in base on a small island, inhabited only by naval personnel. There would be no nightlife, no girls... No it would be better for me to get back into the real world and see what it had to offer. Once the decision was made, I started counting the days to my release from the navy.

A few days before my demob I was walking through Split when suddenly Vesna was standing in front of me – as beautiful as ever and she was smiling. 'Your thoughts were far away, Ivan. You didn't even hear me calling you.' For a moment I couldn't say anything but then I stammered out a greeting. 'Will you have a drink with me for old time's sake?' she asked.

We sat opposite each other outside a café and I said, 'I'm sorry I left without warning you, Vesna. I've often thought it was a shabby trick.'

'Dûsan told me that he'd asked you not to tell me. I was very upset at the time but I've got over it.'

'We couldn't have gone on as we were,' I said. 'Someone would have found out sooner or later and, anyway, there is another girl...'

'Ah, the German one.'

I didn't answer but asked, 'What are you doing in Split?'

'Dûsan and I have bought a flat here. What about you? How much longer have you left to serve in the navy?'

'Three days.' We finished our drinks, talking about nothing in particular and then it was time for me to return to the ship. I got up and extended my hand. 'Goodbye Vesna and good luck.'

Ignoring my hand, she jumped up and kissed me. 'Good luck to you too Ivan and thank you.' I walked away, feeling no regret that I was unlikely to see

Vesna again but glad that I'd had an opportunity to bring closure to an episode of which I was not particularly proud.

I phoned Ingrid on my way to the ship. She was delighted to hear that my demob day was so close. I didn't say anything to her about my plan to stay in the navy nor did I make arrangements to see her immediately. I needed time to get used to being a civilian again and to decide what I really wanted from life.

A large parcel was waiting for me when I got back. I had written to Dragica and asked her to send my civilian clothes. I spread them on my bunk, new underclothes, socks, shoes, a white shirt and a suit. They were, in the main, the clothes that Ingrid had bought me and I was relieved to find that everything still fitted.

On my last morning I had an interview with the captain. 'Remember that you are still under military discipline for 48 hours after you leave the ship,' he said. 'You will serve in the Naval Reserve for two weeks a year for three years. If there is an emergency you will be called up either to the navy or the army. In the Reserve you will have the higher rank of ensign in the navy or, if you are called to the army, it will be as a 2nd lieutenant.' He handed me my discharge papers, military paybook and travel document.

'Good luck Vesligaj.' He shook my hand.

'Thank you, sir. Permission to change into civilian clothes, sir.'

'Permission granted.' I saluted him for the last time and went down to my cabin.

I could hardly believe that my naval life was over. I would have many regrets. I'd miss the laughter, comradeship and the physical activities which had kept me so fit. Get a hold of yourself, I thought firmly. This is your choice…and you do look rather good in this suit.

Many of the crew were on deck to bid me farewell. I shook hands until my hand ached.

The three communication officers came to the top of the gangway with me, clapping me on the back and saying life wouldn't be the same without me.

'Permission to leave the ship,' I said to the duty officer.

'Permission granted.'

Novak walked ashore with me and, out of long habit, I turned and saluted the ship. Everyone on deck laughed and clapped, Novak shook hands with me and I walked away from *R11,* a free but strangely sad man.

I felt odd in my civilian clothes, aware that people would know I had just been demobbed because of my military haircut. I had a couple of hours before my train was due so I sat in a bar outside the station and reflected on my years in the navy. They're over, I said to myself firmly. They were good but they're over. No point in regrets. It's time to plan.

I decided I'd visit my sister and find some lodgings in Zagreb then give myself a week's holiday at home where I'd help with the harvest and visit Stara mama and Faruh. Then I'd go back to Zagreb and see if I could get work at Almeria. I felt better with a clear idea about what I was going to do. I finished my beer and walked into the station. I heard someone shout my name and, turning, I saw Novak and Anzic waving at me.

'Glad we've caught you,' Novak said. 'We've brought you some presents.'

Anzic handed me a parcel. Inside I found some framed photographs, of *R11,* of me participating in the signalling competition and one of me receiving the pennant and trophy. I was so moved by this act of friendship that I could hardly speak.

Sensing this Novak said, 'Don't go tonight. Come home with me and have a meal with us. Stay the night and catch an early train tomorrow. We'll make you very welcome.'

I knew it wouldn't be any easier to make the break the next day so I said, 'Thank you very much for the invitation but my ticket is valid only for today and, anyway, I need to get back to my family because it's harvest time.'

Novak accepted this and gave me a card with his address on and he and Anzic shook my hand again and gave me bear hugs. I thanked them once more and then went on to the platform for the train. I didn't look back and, although Novak called after me, 'Don't forget to look me up if ever you're in Split,' I knew I wouldn't. That part of my life was over. It was 'Goodbye Navy and goodbye Split.'

In 1960 Marshal Tito paid a high profile visit to NATO. There, he was becoming increasingly influential, particularly among the non-aligned member-states. Stalinists accused him of betraying socialist principles. He refuted this but, meanwhile, gave encouragement to market forces within the economy. He was elected chairman of a committee comprising the non-aligned group of nations, working closely with President Nehru, of India and Indonesia's President Sukharno. In 1962-3 he visited the non-aligned nations of Africa, in his ship 'Galeb', with Ivan as one of his two communications officers.

Shortly before the start of this trip, tensions between the USA and the USSR came to a head in, what became known as, the Cuban crisis. In April 1962 Premier Nikita Khrushchev, of the USSR, began to establish a base, on Cuba, for the launching of ballistic nuclear missiles, transporting the components there to assemble on site. His aim was to protect Cuba while placing missiles within striking range of the USA.

On October 16th President John F Kennedy, of the USA, appointed advisors to devise a plan to counteract Khrushchev's actions. A week later he published photographs, taken by a surveillance team, proving that the Russian installation was in progress. He imposed a blockade to prevent missile parts reaching Cuba and warned Khrushchev that building the missiles would be regarded as an act of aggression against the USA and would result in an attack on the Soviet Union. Tension heightened when Kennedy ordered 2 hourly reconnaissance flights over Cuba.

On October 26th Khrushchev offered to remove the missiles on receiving a promise that Cuba would not be attacked but the next day, an American U2 aircraft was shot down. War seemed inevitable. On October 28th, however, as a result of secret negotiations between the two heads of state, an agreement was reached. Khrushchev would remove the missiles and dismantle the launch pad and Kennedy would withdraw missiles from Turkey and promise not to attack Cuba.

Information about the Russian nuclear missile base in Cuba trickled slowly into Yugoslavia via intercepted radio messages. John explained to me that most of the population, particularly those in rural areas, knew nothing about the crisis but those in the military, who did, were extremely concerned and took the drills using the anti-pollution suits very seriously.

Internal affairs in Yugoslavia were disrupted when, in the early 1960s a rift developed between Marshal Tito and his heir apparent, Aleksander Ranković. Rancović, a Serbian, was one of the most important men in Yugoslavia during and after the Second World War. He became minister for the interior and, in 1946, head of UDBa (Uprava Drzavne Bezbednosti) which was called the national security service but was, in reality, a secret police force.

Rancović was a hard-line communist, a firm believer in centralization. He was often at odds with Marshal Tito, accusing him of allowing too much power to the nation states. He resisted the introduction of market forces, seeing them as a betrayal of the communist ideal.

It was into the struggle between the two most powerful men in the country that Ivan and his colleagues unwittingly stumbled when they removed Marshal Tito from Brjoni in their patrol boat. The result was the court martial.

In April 1963, Yugoslavia was yet again re-named. It became, 'The Socialist Federal Republic of Yugoslavia.'

Ivan Vesligaj
1963-1966: 23-26 years

Almeria Again

I dozed during the train journey and arrived in Zagreb at 6 am. I had breakfast at a café near the station and then caught a tram to Dragica's apartment.

I rang the bell and heard my niece's voice, 'Who's there, please?' When she realised it was me, I heard her shout, 'It's Uncle, Uncle Ivan,' as she ran down the stairs to let me in. She flung herself on me, chattering excitedly and running ahead to the apartment. It was a lovely welcome and that from Dragica and Franz was equally warm.

When my sister and brother in law had gone to work and Nevenka to school, I flopped on the bed and slept until Dragica returned then I told her my plans.

'If you're hoping to work at Almeria, try to get accommodation in the city centre,' she advised. 'You'll be able to get a tram from there to a stop outside the factory and you'll be near the theatres, clubs and bars.' She had an evening newspaper with her and I found advertisements for several possible lodgings.

The one I chose, the next morning, was at Tkalčićeva 54. The elderly landlady and her husband lived in the basement flat and let the rest of their house. Apart from me, there was an Albanian family in the cake and ice cream trade and a young, newly wed couple. My room took up the whole of the ground floor and contained a bed, wardrobe, table, chair and easy chair. It was fairly Spartan but clean. I decided not to take meals with the landlady, preferring to be independent. We settled the deal over coffee. I paid the rent for a couple of weeks and explained I was going to be away for about seven days, visiting my mother.

Back at Dragica's, Nevenka and I played records on the record player Ingrid had given me. 'Are you taking this with you now, uncle?' she asked. I looked at her troubled face and realised how much the player meant to her.

'No,' I replied. 'I couldn't play it at Auntie Hanika's because she hasn't got electricity and I don't expect I'll have much time once I'm working. Why don't you look after it for me? I shall be visiting you often when I move to my new lodging so I can hear the records whenever I come.' Nevenka was thrilled and gave me a dozen kisses.

'You're definitely my favourite uncle,' she declared.

By 2 pm, the next day, I was at back home with Mama. She fussed round me with coffee and strudel, delighted that my time in the navy was over. 'I could never really rest easy, knowing you had nothing but water underneath you,' she declared.

I had left some of the money I'd earned on Galeb with her for safe keeping and was pleased she hadn't spent it all while I was away. 'I did need some stuff for the vineyard,' she said. 'I hope you don't mind. The rest of it's here.' There was enough to pay my rent and for food for two to three months if, by any chance, I had a problem getting a job. This gave me a feeling of security.

Lujzek was due home in a couple of days, having finished his national service. Stjepan was now doing his, in Marshal Tito's Guards in Belgrade.

Neighbours and cousins had been helping Mama on the farm since Stjepan had gone but now it was my turn to be the dutiful son and I was looking forward to it. I couldn't get into any of my working clothes from pre-naval days so put on some old overalls I found in a cupboard. I harnessed the cow to the cart and went off to start harvesting our corn.

When Lujzek arrived, we finished the corn between us and made a good start on the grape harvest. On my last afternoon we went to the forest, collected fallen branches and chopped them into firewood for the winter. Lujzek would have a few more days at home and, with some help from neighbours, would be able to complete the work at the vineyard. He had found a government job as an electrician in Zagreb. This meant we would be able to see each other regularly.

On the train to Zagreb, I surveyed my worldly goods on the luggage rack. There was a rucksack full of clothes and a case of books. I felt a familiar surge of excitement. Once more, I was going into the unknown. Anything could happen. At my lodging, I arranged my few belongings in my room, had a meal in a nearby restaurant and slept well. It was my first night of complete independence for a long time.

'What can I do for you?' said the guard at the gate of Almeria, the next morning.

'I'm looking for a job. Please may I see the personnel officer?'

'There aren't any jobs going.'

I had a feeling of déjà vu. 'That's not for you to say,' I said firmly. 'Please let the personnel officer know I am here.'

Mumbling something, he made a telephone call. 'He'll see you now. Someone's coming to take you up to him.' A young woman appeared, and as we walked to the office, I asked her if Josip Puskar still worked at Almeria.

'No, he escaped into Germany,' she said. 'We've got three new technicians.' I could hardly believe that the rather dull Josip had succeeded where I had failed.

The mention of Germany made me think of Ingrid. I'd need to get in touch with her again soon. The personnel officer's door was open and I recognised the man inside as the one who had turned Ostoja and me away after our escape attempt and imprisonment. I didn't feel hopeful. The man didn't recognise me straight away.

'Come in,' he said. 'You're after a job, I gather.'

'Yes. I'm a qualified leather technician.'

'What's your name?'

'Ivan Vesligaj.'

He looked up sharply from the list of vacant positions in front of him. 'Vesligaj? Didn't you used to work here?'

'Yes I did, almost three and a half years ago.'

'Oh yes, you blotted your copybook, didn't you? He opened a big leather-bound book and found my name in it. 'You were sacked from here, weren't you?' I didn't answer and he looked at me again. 'Have you changed?'

'Well, I've grown up. I've just finished three years in the navy.'

'I remember now.' He said. 'The director pointed out an article about you in the paper. There was a picture too. Didn't you help Marshal Tito in some way?'

'Something like that,' I said guardedly.

At this point, the young woman arrived with two cups of coffee. She handed me one and I put it on a side table. I didn't want to sit drinking coffee if there was no prospect of a job. 'Have you a vacancy for a technician?' I asked.

'We have. We can never get enough technicians.'

'In that case, will you consider employing me?'

There was a pause and I held my breath. 'Yes, I'll give you a job providing you pass our medical. It will cost you 10,000 dinars. Would you like a loan from the firm?'

'No thank you,' I said, pleased that I didn't have to put myself in debt before I'd even started work.

'The clinic is open now. Here's a note for the receptionist. Go straight away and then come back to see me.'

I breathed out. 'Thank you very much. I don't think there will be a problem with a medical. I passed a stringent naval one before my demob'.'

An hour later, I was back in the personnel office with my medical certificate.

'Very good,' the personnel officer said after looking at it. 'Start work at 6 am on Monday morning. You'll be responsible for mixing the chemicals for all stages of the leather production. You'll work shifts. One week, 6 am – 2 pm and the next, 12 noon – 8 pm. You'll work with a young lady, Bozica, one of our newest technicians.

'You haven't mentioned salary,' I said cautiously.

'You'll start at 70,000 new dinars a month. Fill in this form now, please. We need all your details.' I did as he asked although I wasn't too thrilled with my starting salary – still, at least I had a job. I handed back the form and rose to leave. 'See you on Monday,' he said cheerily, his attitude had completely changed.

As I walked along the corridor I realised I'd forgotten to ask if Drago were still the director of the firm. Then I saw the door with his name on it so I knocked softly.

'Come in.' It was Drago's voice. I opened the door and saw the director and another man who turned to face me. It was Zdravko Ćorluka who had been in the year above me at college. We'd played in the orchestra together and recognised each other instantly but Drago was talking and shaking my hand.

'Ivan Vesligaj! I didn't expect to see you again. Welcome. Have you come for a job?'

'Yes, sir. I start on Monday.'

'Excellent.' Turning to his companion he said, 'Zdravko, this is Ivan. He has a chequered history here but he was always a good worker and he was responsible for updating many of our processes. Ivan, Zdravko is my deputy.'

'You've done well for yourself,' I said to Zdravko, laughing.

He laughed too. 'I have, haven't I? It must be because I went to such a good college.'

Having looked rather shocked by my opening words to Zdravko, Drago suddenly realised our connection and he grinned and invited me to sit down.

'Is the Matija Gubec Group still going strong?' I asked Drago.

'No, I'm afraid not. It kept going for a while after you and Ostoja left but no-one wanted to give up time to run it so it folded.'

I felt disappointed. 'Have you still got the instruments?'

He looked at me in mock alarm. 'Yes but surely you're not thinking of starting the group up again? You'd better not!'

I just smiled. I knew he didn't mean it and I knew I would re-activate Matija Gubec if I possibly could. This wasn't the time to pursue the topic, however.

'You made a name for yourself in the navy, didn't you Ivan?' Drago said. He pulled from a drawer an old newspaper and there I was, on the front page, pointing a gun at a military policeman. So I had to relate the whole story to the two of them. 'No heroic stunts here please,' Drago, smiled. 'Just good, solid work.'

'Certainly sir,' I replied primly.

Later, as Zdravko was walking to the gate with me, I said, 'I think my salary of 70,000 is rather low. I'm very grateful to be given a job here but, as you know, I'm well qualified and an experienced technician.'

'That's the starting salary,' Zdravko replied, 'but we'll review it after everyone's seen what you can do. I can't do anything about it at this stage, I'm afraid.' I had to be satisfied with that but I was curious to know how someone only a year my senior had obtained such a good position in Almeria.

'I went to night school and took business studies,' he said in answer to my question. You should do the same, Ivan, if you want to get on. Immediately I decided I'd follow his advice. Zdravko pointed to some new flats that were being built nearby 'Those are for Almeria's workers. They have to work here for five years to qualify.' Fleetingly I wondered if I would still be there in five years' time.

I spent the weekend re-acquainting myself with old friends. I met my distant cousin and childhood friend, Branko Vesligaj who lived in my village, (the one whose mother was a black marketeer). He was working in a big Zagreb office and told me where to find the best, new and cheapest restaurants. I phoned Ingrid to give her my news.

'I'll come to Zagreb for ten days over Christmas and New Year, if that's all right,' she said.

I had forgotten how crowded the trams were at 5.30 am. On the first morning I couldn't get inside – just hung on to the door and travelled through the darkness, clinging on because my life depended on it.

Zdravko was waiting for me at the factory and showed into the smart new changing rooms and showers. I knew a lot of the men who were there, changing into work clothes. They greeted me cheerfully, a couple shouted that they'd seen my picture in the paper. When I was ready, Zdravko took me to my laboratory.

'You'll spend the first two weeks training Bozica in the mixing of chemicals. After that I want you to take over the testing station for a special task. More of that later.'

I slotted back into work almost as if I'd never been away. I found it satisfying to work out precisely the right mixtures needed to obtain the best results for each batch of skins. I liked training Bozica, a pleasant but unnaturally thin young woman. I enjoyed being in charge of a team of workers and helping them with some of the heavy lifting of pelts. I was much stronger than I had been the last time I'd worked here and felt that this heavy work would keep me in trim. I was particularly pleased to see that the drying system I had suggested several years ago was still working well.

After a fortnight, I moved into the testing station to work with Poldi, a chemist. Our task was to develop a new method of removing hair from raw skins without having to put them through the labour intensive procedure of immersing them in tanks of chemicals. In the four weeks we worked together we discovered, through trial and error, a system which involved spreading a mixture of fat and chemicals between layers of skins. We worked out the precise proportion of each component needed in the mixture and the time required. It was a breakthrough and I later learned that Poldi patented the method. It was reward enough for me when, in my second month at Almeria, my salary rose to 105,000 new dinars a month.

When the experiments were over, I went back to the glass-sided office Ostoja and I had shared and supervised the mixing of chemicals for curing and dying, working with a team of labourers. I wished he were still working with me but I liked being boss of my own little domain.

About that time, I put up notices announcing that I intended to re-start Matija Gubec. There was a lot of interest, I held auditions, started rehearsals and even persuaded Drago to invest in some electric guitars.

Away from work, I went to the cinema, theatre and to discos. I had short flings with a nurse and a hairdresser – nothing serious, of course, because Ingrid was always in the background. We wrote to each other and I knew that, at some time, I'd have to make up my mind where our relationship was going.

By now Lujzek was working in Zagreb and one weekend we went to Rogaska Slatina, a small spa town in Slovenia. On the train, we met a couple of pretty girls, office workers from Zagreb and we fell into conversation with them. They told us where they worked. It was at the same place as my cousin, Branko so I asked if they knew him.

'He's our boss,' one of them replied.

'He's our cousin,' we said.

We spent a lot of time with the two girls over the weekend. We swam in the lido, sunbathed, went for walks in the surrounding countryside and ate out together. It was the first proper holiday I'd had for a long time and, although it was short, I thoroughly enjoyed it.

I followed Zdravko's advice and enrolled on the business studies course at Mosha Pijade College. He was pleased. 'Just think,' he said, 'when Drago retires, I'll become a director and you can slip very nicely into my current role as deputy director. It sounded a good idea but I hated the two evenings every week at the college. I found them utterly boring. I realised that being in business was not for me and after six months I left much to my relief and to the disappointment of Zdravko and Drago.

Just before Christmas, Ingrid arrived. We stayed at Dragica's and all was well with us for a while. We enjoyed the Christmas celebrations but Ingrid became increasingly possessive, resenting any conversation I had with other girls and monopolising me when we were in the company of my friends.

When a group of us went to a restaurant for dinner, she loudly insisted on paying the bill for everybody. She told the waiter again and again, in German, 'I'm paying,' and thrust a huge handful of notes at him.

I was embarrassed, not only by her domineering attitude but also because, at that time, it was seen as correct for the man to pay. I felt diminished in front of my friends who teased me a good deal. When I remonstrated with Ingrid afterwards, she cried and said she was only trying to be generous and thoughtful. Although I had been angry, I couldn't stay that way for long.

However, things came to a head on New Year's Eve. My brother in law, Franz worked for a bus company which owned a large hall close to the railway station. The firm organised a big New Year's party there, for employees and their families. When we arrived, there were already lots of people dancing or chatting. Initially, Ingrid held on to my arm tightly. I guessed that this was to prevent me getting into conversation with anyone or, heaven forbid, dancing with another girl. Of course, I had to translate everything for her, anyway, which I didn't mind but it did rather get in the way of the normal easy social interchanges. About half way through the festivities, Ingrid went to the ladies' room.

I noticed a girl I'd known for a long time and I went across to her for a chat. 'How about a dance?' she said. I was doubtful and she laughed at me. 'Oh come on, It's only a dance! Surely your girlfriend won't mind, will she? You're not frightened of her, are you?'

'Of course not.'

We had just started the dance when Ingrid returned. She took one look, strode across the dance floor, stopped in front of me and slapped my face hard. 'Schwein hund /Swine hound,' she screamed.

My partner broke away, shocked, and all heads turned in our direction. I don't know what would have happened if Dragica hadn't suddenly appeared beside Ingrid. She took her arm and marched her off to the bar.

My cheek was stinging, my face was scarlet but I managed to say to my partner, 'Shall we finish the dance?' And we did.

I was furious and, after escorting my partner back to her friends, I went outside and walked up and down, trying to calm myself. I had never felt so humiliated, not even when Ostoja and I had been caught after re-crossing the border. I felt as if I never wanted to see Ingrid again but I knew I was responsible for her while she was in Zagreb. I couldn't just wash my hands of her.

I heard a noise behind me. It was Ingrid. 'I'm sorry, I'm so sorry,' she sobbed. 'I don't know what came over me. It's just that I love you so much. Please forgive me. Please, please.' She flung herself on me, her face wet with tears. My anger drained away as I held her. She did love me, I knew. I'd have to talk quietly to her about her possessiveness but not now. Now we would simply go home.

The rest of Ingrid's stay passed without incident. She was quiet and gentle and, as usual, cried when we parted.

'Please don't go off me, darling, because of what happened at the party,' she said tearfully as I saw her on to the train. 'I'll never behave like that again, I promise.' I kissed her and reassured her but I knew that a rift had opened between us over the past ten days and I wasn't sure it would ever be completely healed.

During the summer of 1965 Ingrid came to Zagreb again. This time she drove and we went, for a week, to the resort of Opatija, which had once been the summer retreat of the Austrian royal family. It started well. I had money in my pocket and Ingrid submitted to my paying for some of our meals and entertainments. We went diving, swam and sunbathed.

Towards the end of the week, however, the old arguments recurred. 'Let me pay, let me pay,' she insisted. She was cross when I spoke to a girl who was staying in our hotel but she was sorry afterwards and held me close and told me how much she loved me.

Ana: Germany

My brother, Milan and his wife, Sylvia, lived in Ljubljana in Slovenia. I had been meaning to visit them for some time so, one bank holiday weekend, Nevenka, now fourteen years old, and I travelled by train to see them. I can't remember details of the visit, but I must have been having a good time because I decided not to return to Zagreb on the Monday, as planned, but to leave on Tuesday. I knew Dragica wouldn't worry, would guess we'd opted to stay for the extra day which was also a bank holiday. I couldn't get in touch with her because she had no phone.

'No, let's go home on Monday,' Nevenka said. 'That's what we said we'd do and I've got things I want to do in Zagreb.'

'You've got the rest of the week off to do them,' I laughed. 'We've come a long way. Let's make the most of it.' She was easily persuaded and we enjoyed our extra day. That evening, Sylvia switched on the television for the news. We heard that the very train on which we were to have travelled had crashed. Eighteen people had been killed, all from the first class compartment where we would have been sitting. Shocked, we stared at each other.

Nevenka dashed across the room to me. 'Thank you uncle, thank you for changing the day'. And she burst into tears.

The rail was clear by the next day and I could only think of the victims of the crash as we sped safely to Zagreb.

When we reached Dragica's flat, she flung the door open and caught Nevenka up in her arms. 'Thank God you're safe my darling,' she cried. 'We couldn't get any news about the names of the dead and injured. I'm never letting you go anywhere without me again. Thank God, thank God.' And sobbing, she pulled her daughter indoors.

A few months later, a group of German engineers came to Almeria to install a new heating system. They were men who worked for Ingrid's father. One of them asked to see me. 'I have a letter for you from Raulf Gunther,' he said, handing me an envelope.

After the usual greetings, the letter ran,

... I hope that next year I will be able to organise an exchange visit for you. A friend will send a leather technician to take your place at Almeria and, if you like the plan, you can come to work in my factory. You will gain experience in engineering and in the galvanising process. Please let me know what you think of this arrangement...

I could think of little else for a while. I knew I needed a work permit to get out of Yugoslavia. Was this an opportunity too good to miss? Eventually I decided it was and I wrote to Raulf, accepting his offer with thanks. I closed my mind to any thought that I was entering on a dangerous venture as far as my relationship with Ingrid was concerned. I also ignored my conscience which whispered that I wasn't being fair to her.

I said nothing to anyone about the possibility of going to Germany but in January 1966, Drago called me into his office. 'Ivan,' he said, 'you need to get yourself a passport.' He didn't explain why and I didn't ask but, of course, I guessed.

Mićo, my sister Marija's husband who had studied law, countersigned the form and photos for me. When I took them back to the passport office, the official noticed Mićo's signature and the fact that he was a member of the dreaded UDBa. 'There'll be no problem with this,' he said. 'Collect your passport in two weeks.'

It is certainly true that *who* you know is important, I thought and, not for the first time, wondered at the fact that so kind and gentle a man as Mićo should belong to UDBa.

Ivan's sister, Maria and husband Mićo

As soon as I collected my passport, I took it to show Drago. He pulled a folder of papers from a drawer. 'Arrangements have been made for you to go on an exchange visit to Germany,' he said. My stomach flipped with excitement. 'You'll go on 1ˢᵗ June and stay for six months. You will work at Mr Gunther's factory in Stuttgart and he says he and his wife can accommodate you in their home. We'll miss you but it is a great opportunity. You'll need visas to enable you to pass through Austria and stay in Germany.' There was no discussion. Drago didn't ask how I felt about the arrangements. As I walked away from his office, I reflected that, in a communist country, you were expected to do as you were told. I couldn't wait to get out.

I phoned Ingrid and told her the news. It was the first she'd heard of the development as her father had wanted to surprise her. He certainly did that. She was almost hysterical with delight. 'Don't buy a train ticket,' she cried. 'I'll drive down and fetch you.'

In early May, I went home to my mother's. Stjepan had just been demobbed and was planning to start an apprenticeship with General Motors in Zagreb. I visited

268

Stara mama and Father Josip and the sisters. Everyone promised to pray for me as I ventured abroad once more.

As May drew to a close, I was very excited at the prospect of a new challenge and fresh experiences. I worked my last day at Almeria, had a last drink with my mates and then Ingrid arrived in the Mercedes.

We spent the night at Dragica's and set off early the next morning, driving all day and stopping for the night in Vilah, Austria. We arrived at Ingrid's home in the late morning the next day. The Gunthers were on the look-out for us. Urschula ran down the steps and hugged us both to her, planting a big kiss on my cheek. Raulf shook hands warmly and led us indoors.

'It's so lovely to see you Ivan,' Urschula exclaimed. 'Are you hungry?'

The house was massive, set back in an enormous garden. The hall was as big as our living room at home and the rooms which led off it were large and light with high ceilings. The wide oak staircase led to a spacious landing. I couldn't help comparing the luxury of the space and the rich décor with our humble cottage. It was to Ingrid's credit, I felt, that she had taken my home and my family to her heart. I determined to try to make a go of things with her. This would be a new start.

We sat down to a splendid meal of steak and roast vegetables. I discovered that the Gunthers employed a gardener and a cleaner but that Urschula loved to cook. After lunch, I was shown my room. It was next door to Ingrid's. Throughout my stay, Ingrid and I spent almost every night together but nothing was ever said about it by her parents although they must have known.

I spent my first week at the factory learning the chemistry involved in preparing the mixture of metallic powder and oil needed for galvanising the iron tanks produced there. I found it interesting at first but, once I was familiar with the process, I realised it was far less challenging than working with leather, with its different thicknesses and textures.

Boredom at work was compensated for by the fast and furious social life Ingrid and I enjoyed. There was hardly an evening we weren't out, dancing, visiting the theatre or cinema or eating in one of the many local restaurants. We had our differences – often over the same issues as of old – but we were always reconciled later in bed. She planned a long weekend in the millionaire's playground, Baden Baden, as a surprise for me. She turned up at work one Friday, with a case of my clothes.

'My father has said you can have a few days off,' she said. 'Have a shower and change. We're off on holiday.' We stayed at the Grand Hotel. Both inside and out it was whitewashed and beamed. Our room had its own luxurious bathroom and nearby was a Jacuzzi, the first I'd ever seen. We had a wonderful weekend. We played tennis, watched a volley ball match, scuba dived and, of course, sunbathed and swam.

There was a letter from my mother waiting for me when we returned. With Lujzek and now Stjepan working in Zagreb, she was having problems getting the grape harvest in. When I related this to Raulf, he suggested I should take seven days off to go home to help Mama. 'You've worked hard since you've been here,' he said. 'This will be paid leave.'

I travelled home by train and, in spite of the communist restrictions, it was good to be in my own country, speaking my own language again. Mama was delighted to see me and, between us and with the help of neighbours, we harvested the grapes. It was an excellent crop that year.

I spent a night with Dragica before returning to Germany. I contacted a couple of friends and in the evening we went to a disco. That was when I was introduced to a dance called *The Twist*. By now, western music was percolating into Yugoslavia.

However, something much more important than my learning a new dance occurred that evening. I asked a pretty girl to dance and, afterwards, as we sat down with our drinks, I asked her where she lived. 'My home is here in Zagreb,' she said, 'but I work in London.'

'London?' I was amazed. I had always longed to go to London – ever since the time I'd spent reading in the British Consulate. 'How did you manage to get work in London?'

'It was easy,' she replied. 'My mother is a cleaner for the British consul. He helped me. He arranged for me to become nanny to the children of the Spanish ambassador in London.'

'You're so lucky!' I said.

'Would you like to work in London?'

'I'd love to but there's no chance. I don't know anyone who could help me.'

'I'll give you an address in London. Write there and ask for a job and a work permit. You'll have to write in English, though.' Hurriedly, I'd taken my little notebook from my pocket. She took it from me and wrote,

Intercontinental Agency,
Crystal Palace,
England.

She handed the book back. 'Good luck,' she said. 'Shall we have another dance?'

I thought about that address on my way back to Germany although I didn't mention it to Ingrid or to anyone else.

The last part of my stay flew by. On one of our last times together, Ingrid became angry over a small incident which I can't remember. Then she said, 'We never move any further forward, do we? I've had enough boys sniffing round me here, you know. I could have my pick. Are we ever going to get married?'

I knew it was a fair question. We'd known each other for several years but I was also now absolutely certain that I didn't want to spend the rest of my life with Ingrid. We'd had some good times but I could not live, long term, with someone as possessive as she was, with someone who always had to be in control. I should have been honest and broken it off there and then but I'm sorry to say that I soothed her and said, 'Let's not talk about it now. I'm off in a day or two. Let's just make the most of the time we've got left.'

Everyone at Almeria seemed pleased to have me back but I was restless. I took my notebook out a couple of times and looked at the Crystal Palace address but I had to admit to myself that, although the idea of going to England was exciting, it also daunted me. It would be a jump into the unknown. I didn't speak the language, I didn't know any English people. I'd leave it a while and think about it further.

Ivan with his godfather 1966

Ivan's brothers. From left, Milan, Stjepan, Martin and his cousin, Pepi 1966

1963 – 1966

From 1963-64 Aleksander Rancović continued to use his powerful position, as head of UDBa to spy on and to remove many of his opponents. Finally, he seems to have over-reached himself by arranging for Marshal Tito's private residence to be bugged. Ranković was relieved of all his duties and removed from power in 1966.

In 1965 Marshal Tito held talks with the USSR in an effort to repair the relationship between the two states.

Within Yugoslavia, a measure of free speech was now tolerated although radio and television programmes were still government controlled.

By 1966 the economic system was failing, many businesses folded and the standard of living had dropped. Much grass-root support for the Party had evaporated and it is in this climate of hopelessness and depression that Ivan became obsessed, once more, with the idea of 'escape'.

John Baker
1966-1967: 26-27 years old

Mr and Mrs Baker

Ivan/John with his niece Nevenka

Early in 1967, Zagreb Theatre presented the ballet *Swan Lake*. I decided I'd like to see it again and went on my own. I found myself sitting next to an elderly couple who were conversing in English. As we walked towards the bar, in the interval, the lady spoke to me in Croatian.

'Are you enjoying the ballet?' she asked.

'Very much,' I said. 'Are you?'

'It's a brilliant production.' By now we were at the bar, we ordered our drinks and sat down at a small table.

The lady introduced her husband. 'This is John,' she said to me in Croatian. 'I'm Mari. I was born in Croatia but John is American. We're on holiday here at the moment. We live in Denver, Colorado, USA.'

I introduced myself and Mrs Baker translated everything to her husband who smiled and shook my hand. He was bald and had a pleasant face, sporting a goatee beard. Mrs Baker was short and plump with curly grey hair and twinkling brown eyes. We talked about what they'd seen while they were in Zagreb and then it was time to go back to our seats.

After the performance, there was a little hurried conversation between Mr and Mrs Baker and then the latter turned to me. 'Ivan, can you recommend somewhere that serves good food, please?' I took them to a small restaurant, tucked away down a side street. I knew it specialised in homemade Croatian cuisine. 'It looks perfect,' Mrs Baker said.

'Good night. It's been nice meeting you. Bon appetit.' I said. I turned to go but Mrs Baker grasped my arm. 'We'd like to get to know you better, Ivan. Will you stay and eat with us, be our guest? We'd really love you to.'

I was surprised but they seemed nice people and I hadn't had time to eat much before the ballet so I agreed. During the meal, Mrs Baker asked about my family and what I had done with my life so far. Somehow her questions weren't intrusive. She seemed genuinely interested in me as did her husband as she translated everything for him. By the time we'd finished eating and were drinking coffee, they knew a great deal about my home, mother, brothers sisters and even about Father Josip, Bol, the polytechnic, Almeria and my time in the navy. However, I didn't mention the 'escape' or Ingrid.

I was just thinking it was time for me to go when they dropped the bombshell. 'How would you like to go to the USA, Ivan?' Mrs Baker asked.

'I'd love to but it's impossible. The USA won't issue visas to people from communist countries.'

'That's true but there is a way round that. My husband owns a business and employs a considerable number of people. We have no children and for a long time we have talked about adopting a young man who could learn the business and carry it on when John retires and inherit it when we die. We think you are exactly the sort of young man we've been looking for with your monastery education and your service in the navy. What do you think? Would you be interested?'

I was astonished. I could hardly speak. 'Well, it's very kind…but you hardly know me.'

'We've learned enough about you this evening. Well, what do you say?'

My mind was racing. A whole new world opened up before me but I couldn't commit myself to something so huge. I needed time. 'I am very interested in your offer,' I said slowly, 'and thank you again but I need time to think about it and to talk to my mother and the rest of my family.'

Mrs Baker smiled. 'Of course you do. I would expect nothing less of you. How long do you need?'

'I can take a few days holiday next week and go home to see my mother. I need about seven days.'

'That's fine. Seven days it is. There is one more thing I must tell you. We would want you to change your name to John Baker if you agree to the adoption. Would you be prepared to do that?'

This was the biggest shock of all. My whole being seemed wrapped up in my name, *Ivan Vesligaj*. That is who I am, I thought. Could I ever be a *John Baker*? Again I spoke slowly, trying to find the right words. 'I'm not sure. I understand that if I agree to the adoption, I will have to change my name but, as I said, I need time before I give you my answer.'

'We'll wait with impatience but of course we understand. We're asking you to take a big step.' She passed me a piece of paper on which was the name and telephone number of the hotel at which they were staying. 'We'll expect you in seven days.'

I don't remember thanking them and saying goodnight but I suppose I must have done. I walked back to my flat in a daze and lay awake for a long time going over this strange turn of events. I'd never seen myself as a businessman. In fact I'd once decided it was not the life for me. But to go to America…and it would be to a business which would be my own one day…I fell asleep at last, my mind in turmoil.

'Go ahead, if you want to,' Mama said when I told her of the Bakers' proposal. 'You've always loved adventure. This is right up your street.'

'And you don't mind if I change my name?'

'You'll always be Ivan, my little Ivica to me,' she said and kissed me. She's right, I thought. Inside I'll still be the same man. The name I'm called by isn't important.

'I'll have money so I can send you plenty and I can come and see you. You, and anyone in the family, can come and visit me. I'll send the fare.'

'You come to see me, Ivica. I'm not sailing on water at my age, thank you,' Mama laughed then, suddenly serious, 'But what about Ingrid?'

I had conveniently not allowed myself to think about Ingrid. I couldn't conceive of telling her I was going to the USA. I'd have to write to her some time and break off our relationship but not now.

'Mama, Ingrid is beautiful and kind but I am not going to marry her. I don't think we would make each other happy.'

I was surprised that she didn't argue. 'Perhaps you're right. You'll meet a beautiful American girl and marry her, I expect.'

Everyone was encouraging about this new venture, even Stara mama. 'Write and tell me all about America,' she said. 'And come and see me when you're back home on holiday. You have the wanderlust. You'd never be happy settling down here.'

My brothers and sisters were enthusiastic too, imagining I think, luxurious holidays. No-one said a word to put me off the idea and by the end of the seven days I had decided to let the Bakers know I was willing for them to go ahead with the adoption.

I met them at their hotel. Mr Baker ordered drinks and his wife couldn't contain herself. 'Well?' she said. She seemed unable to say anything else.

I smiled. 'I feel honoured that you wish to adopt me. Thank you very much and…yes, if the offer is still open, I accept.' Mrs Baker gave a cry and, with tears running down her cheeks, embraced me. She translated to her husband and he clapped me on the shoulder and shook my hand.

'That's wonderful news. Your family doesn't mind?' Mrs Baker asked.

'They think I should take this opportunity,' I replied.

'We must be John and Mari to you now you're going to be one of the family,' Mrs Baker said, 'and John says the first thing is for you to change your name. We've found a local solicitor and will make an appointment with him to fit in with your shift work. Is that all right with you?'

I laughed and nodded.

Mr Baker leant forward and shook my hand again. 'John,' he said and I laughed again at the strangeness of it all.

The next afternoon we went to the solicitor's office and, surprisingly easily, I was changed from Ivan Vesligaj to John Baker. Then we went to the American consulate to apply for a visa and fill in the necessary forms. There was a four month waiting list. John and Mari saw to all the necessary legalities for the adoption and then, bidding me a fond and reluctant farewell, sailed for England and on to New York.

My friends were intrigued by the story of the Bakers which seemed, to them – and to me, like a fairy tale. They started to call me 'Johnnie' and put in their orders for what they'd like me to send them from the USA.

Three months passed, with letters back and forward between the Bakers and myself. Mari wrote that she had prepared my room and that John had bought me a desk. Just one month to go before my visa would arrive and I could set sail.

Then, at the beginning of March, a letter from Mari arrived. In it she wrote the terrible news that John had suffered a fatal heart attack. She was distraught and didn't feel she could go through with the adoption. She proposed selling the business and moving to be near her sister. She was full of apologies and grief.

I was shocked. I'd grown to like John very much. I felt immense sympathy for her and immediately wrote to her to express this. However, I couldn't help thinking about myself too. I was like a deflated balloon. Here I am, I thought, a man called *John Baker,* with nowhere to go. I realised just how much store I had set by the promise of a new free life in America. How could I tell everyone that all my plans had come to nothing?

I sat with Mari's letter in my hand for a long time then suddenly I remembered the English address that the girl at the dance had given me. I took out my notebook and stared at the page on which she had written the address. I knew what I was going to do.

England

I wrote a letter to the Intercontinental Agency straight away. I said that I was prepared to take on work of any kind and requested an English work permit. The next day I paid to have my letter translated then I posted it and waited, mentioning nothing about it to anyone.

Ten days later, I received a reply saying, that on receipt of £8 sterling, the agency would send me a permit and details of employment. I was pleased that there was the promise of a job but banks in Yugoslavia would not supply sterling unless you could produce a work permit. I wrote explaining this and saying that if they sent me the permit, I would pay the £8 once I was in England and earning.

They must have thought I sounded trustworthy for, within a couple of weeks, I received the work permit and a letter offering me a position as waiter at the *Ponsmere Hotel, Perranporth, Cornwall.* I would start work on 30th April. I was delighted. Now I could tell everyone that I was going to England instead of the USA. Later, I was to wish I'd looked at a map of England before I left. For some reason, I assumed that Cornwall was very close to London.

I decided that *John Baker* was a good name to go to England with and so it proved. When I went to the British consulate for a visa, the receptionist took one look at my name and moved me to the head of the queue. The consul, himself, called me into his office. 'That's an unusual name for a Croatian,' he said.

'Yes it is,' I replied but I didn't enlighten him about its origin. He simply smiled and stamped the visa and my passport. He probably thought my poor mother had had an affair with an Englishman. Next I went to a travel agent and booked my passage from Zagreb to London Victoria. Then I visited the bank and showed my passport and work permit. The bank clerk changed some of my dinas into just £8 sterling. That was all I could take out of the country – for use on the journey.

Now was the time to announce my change of plan to my friends and family. I handed in my notice to Drago who was not very pleased. 'We can't afford to lose an experienced technician, Ivan,' he said. 'Of course I'll give you a good reference and there will still be a job for you here if things don't work out in England.'

I had a few days leave owing so I went home to say goodbye to Mama, Stara mama, Father Josip and the sisters and my friends and neighbours. I was the first person from our village to venture to England and promised to come back and tell everyone what it was like. As I was saying my farewells, I was suddenly glad that I was going to England and not America. England wasn't nearly as far away as the USA and I could fairly easily return for holidays and to help with harvests. I was determined to work hard and earn good wages.

Back in Zagreb, I sat down to write the letter I'd put off for so long. I knew Ingrid would be devastated by my decision to end our relationship and I knew that it would have been fairer to tell her the news, face to face, during our last time together. Nevertheless, I was sure that she and I could never make each other happy, long term, and that it was better to break it off before my journey to England than let it drag on. Beyond thanking her for the good times we'd had together, I can't remember what I wrote but I do remember that, in spite of feeling guilty, I experienced an enormous sense of relief as I posted the letter. I was free to embark on my new adventure.

On my last day at work, Drago and Zdravka organised a farewell party for me. I had lots of friends, both at work and from polytechnic days. I was sorry to leave them but the pull of a new adventure was strong. I wished Ostoja was embarking on it with me. I wondered where he was and what he was doing. He was the closest friend I ever had.

I couldn't sleep on the night before my departure. I packed and repacked my two small suitcases. I felt sick with excitement and a little fearful too. I would be a foreigner in a strange land, knowing no-one, an outsider, unable to speak the language. I spoke firmly to myself. Adventure is what you've always wanted and adventure is what you are going to get. Enjoy it! I fell asleep just before it was time to get up at 5.30am.

Lujzek, Dragica, Franz and Nevenka saw me off on the train. Nevenka was crying but I cheered her by promising to send her something nice from England as soon as I could. At last the Orient Express drew away, I waved from the window until my family disappeared from view and then I sank into a seat, tired out with excitement, a mixture of emotions and lack of sleep. I looked out of the window and dozed alternately, until I had to change trains at Munich. There I boarded the Balkan Express to Ostende.

I arrived at the ferry port at 2 am the following morning. There was a long delay before the ferry was ready to leave but there was a cheerful air at the terminal. A group of English people started to sing. I didn't understand the words then but now I know they were singing, *Why are we waiting?* I don't think they received an answer to their question. I certainly didn't.

At last, as it began to get light, we were allowed on board. It was wonderful to be on a ship again, even a small ferry. As we got underway, I leant over the rail, breathed in the familiar salty air and felt the sea breeze on my face and in my hair. I decided to treat myself to a beer. At the bar, I saw the beer cost a mystifying 1/6d. I held out a coin to the barman. He took it and gave me the beer. Later, when I became familiar with English currency, I realised that I had given the wretched man half a crown and he hadn't given me any change.

I went back on deck to see the faint outline of land appear. The sun was shining and as we drew closer, I saw at last, the famous White Cliffs of Dover which seemed to shine in the early sun. I'm really nearly there, I thought.

Then I *was* there, on English soil – well, English concrete, and I was being pushed along in the tide of people to the port buildings. When we came to passport control an officer glanced at my passport and directed me to a section marked *ALIENS*. Another officer studied my visa and work permit and stamped them. He called to a third man who told me, in Serbian, that I must report to my nearest police station in seven days time.

'Go in there,' he said, pointing to a door with a red cross on it.

Inside the room, a nurse directed me to a cubicle where I stripped to the waist. A doctor tested my heart and lung capacity and then I had an eye test. 'You're OK,' he said and gave me a certificate. Relieved, I put my clothes back on, picked up my cases and followed the crowd on to the railway station.

And then I had the most enormous piece of luck.

As I stood on the platform, a lady turned to me and said something in English. I smiled foolishly and shook my head.

'I wonder how long we'll have to wait,' she said in Serbian. I could have kissed her. I can't explain the thrill of hearing a friendly remark in a familiar language just at a moment when I was feeling so foreign.

'Not long I hope,' I said, grinning.

'I hope not either. My brother is meeting me at Victoria Station. Poor thing, we're already running late.'

'Does your brother live in England?'

'Yes, he works in England. He's a secretary at the Yugoslavian embassy in London and I've come over for a holiday. It's my second time. I love London. What about you? Is this your first visit here?'

I started to explain but the train arrived. We found seats on it together and I completed my tale as we sped towards London. I finished by saying, 'I don't know where Perranporth, Cornwall is. I hope I can find someone on Victoria Station who will be able to direct me if I show them the address.'

'Don't worry about that,' the lady reassured me. 'My brother will know the way. He'll direct you.' Much happier, I was able to enjoy the rest of the journey. We chatted about our families and work and, in between, I looked out of the window at the unfamiliar landscape. We sped past neat farms, rolling green countryside, chalky slopes and towns full of houses which looked very different from those at home.

At Victoria Station, my new friend and I walked towards the platform exit. Loud echoing announcements, which made no sense to me, the chatter of foreign tongues and cold blasts of air combined to make me very glad she was with me.

'There he is,' she cried and ran forward to embrace a tall, dark man who stood at the barrier. Then she turned to me and introduced us. Quickly she explained my situation. Her brother, smiling at me, asked to see the address of the place I was bound for.

His eyebrows shot up as he looked at the piece of paper. 'My goodness, you've a very long way to go, I'm afraid. 'You need to get another train but not from here, from a station called Paddington.' I felt my heart hammering as panic started to rise inside me What if I didn't have enough money to pay the fare for an extra journey? How would I find my way to Paddington?

My dismay must have shown on my face because the man put his hand on my shoulder. 'Don't worry. I'll take you to Paddington, I'll help you buy your ticket and make sure you get on the right train. You'll travel to a city called Truro and then you can get a taxi. Just show the taxi driver this address and he'll take you right to the gate.' My heart resumed its normal rhythm as I stammered my thanks. He turned to his sister. 'You stay here. I shan't be very long. Have a coffee and something to eat over there in that bar and I'll come back for you as soon as I can. You'll be OK, won't you?'

'Of course I will. I'll buy a newspaper and practise my English.' She gave me a hug. 'Good luck. I hope everything works out well for you.'

'Thank you so much. You have been very kind,' I said and shook her hand.

Her brother and I now descended into what seemed to be a sort of hell. Escalators, which were easy to trip on, bursts of hot air, strange unearthly noises, dark tunnels and rushing, thundering trains. I had never travelled underground before. The inside of the carriage was stifling and crowded. No-one looked at anyone else even though we were all crushed together. I was relieved to emerge on to Paddington Station.

My benefactor discovered that a train left for Truro in half an hour and he bought my ticket with the money I gave him. It cost £6.10s. 'You're left with one pound, seven shillings and sixpence,' he said. 'That'll be enough for a taxi.' He kindly bought me a sandwich to eat on the train which had already arrived. He came on the platform with me and spoke to the guard.

'I've asked him to make sure you get out at Truro. Get into a carriage near the guard's van.' At the door of the carriage, he shook my hand and wished me luck. He handed me his card. 'Don't hesitate to contact me if you need help at any time,' and, cutting me off as I was thanking him, 'I'd better get back to that sister of mine, hadn't I?' Then he turned away and was gone.

As I walked along the corridor of the train, looking for a suitable compartment, I thought again about my childhood fancy – that of a guardian angel who looked after me. I smiled to myself as I thought that he or she had certainly had a very busy day.

I chose a compartment where a young lady was sitting on her own. She gave me a friendly glance but said nothing as I sat down.

Shortly after the train started, the guard arrived at the door of the compartment. He spoke to me in heavily accented German. 'Come on lad,' he said. 'You're not allowed to sit here. This is a ladies only compartment. I'll show you where to go.'

I pulled my cases from the luggage rack. 'I'm sorry, I didn't realise. Where did you learn to speak German?'

'I did my national service in West Germany.' He led me to another compartment where two elderly men were dozing. 'This will do. I'll know where you are so I can tell you when we get to Truro.' I thanked him and, knowing I wouldn't miss my station, I ate my sandwich and fell asleep.

'Wake up, we'll be in Truro in ten minutes.' The kindly guard shook me out of my deep sleep. I couldn't think where I was for a moment then I sat up quickly and thanked him. I was alone in the compartment. I'd slept the entire journey, had not woken even when the two elderly gentlemen had left the train. I looked at my watch. It was 7.15 am. I retrieved my cases from the rack and walked along the corridor to the door.

Fields gave way to roads and houses, the train slowed to a halt in the station. As I alighted, the guard, already on the platform, called to me, 'Taxi rank over there. Good luck!' He pointed the way.

I shouted my thanks and hurried in the direction he had indicated. There weren't many people about and I saw a taxi immediately. Once more my heart was beating fast. I was so nearly at my destination – I just needed to make myself understood this one last time and then I'd be there.

I smiled at the taxi driver and handed him the piece of paper on which the address of the hotel was written. 'OK,' he said and got out to help me with the cases. Then he said something in English.

I was embarrassed and spoke to him in German, '*Ich verstehe si nicht* / I don't understand.'

'Ah,' he nodded and signalled that I should get into the car.

We travelled in silence and I looked eagerly out of the window. Everywhere was green, rocky outcrops dotted the landscape, sheep and cows grazed and farmers went about their work using tractors and machines which were unfamiliar to me. At last, after about half an hour, as we reached the top of a hill, I saw the sea, deep blue in the sunshine – almost as blue as the sea around the Dalmatian islands. I saw the sign, *Perranporth* and soon we turned left and were driving alongside sand dunes. We drove past some cottages and, slowing, pulled into a carpark.

'Ponsmere Hotel,' said the driver slowly and clearly, pointing to a large white building. He got out and I followed. I held out my remaining money to him, desperately hoping I had enough. He took the pound note, pulled my cases from the boot and, giving a cheery wave, drove away.

I looked at what was to be my home, gleaming white in the morning sun, tubs of bright flowers outside. Then I crossed the car park. Steps led from the back of the hotel down to the sandy beach. I stood at the top of them and gazed towards the sea. The beach was clean and smooth, two or three people were braving the brisk breeze on an early walk. My heart lifted. I would be living so close to the ocean that I'd hear its roar day and night. In my free time, I'd be able to swim and dive and maybe even sail. Huge waves broke in front of me, foaming on to the shore.

I have arrived, I thought. I am here at last, far away from all the petty rules of communism. I grasped my cases tightly and turned towards the hotel. I was about to start my new life in a free land.

1967

With unemployment and poverty widespread throughout Yugoslavia, the level of emigration soared. Ivan was just one of the many who chose to seek a better life elsewhere

Appendix 1
List of Ivan's Brothers and Sisters

Milan born 1926
Josip born 1928
Adalbert born 1930
Dragica born 1932
Ignac born1934
Marija born1936
Martin born1938
Ivan born 1940
Alojz (Lujzek) born 1941
Stjepan born 1943

Appendix 2
Maps

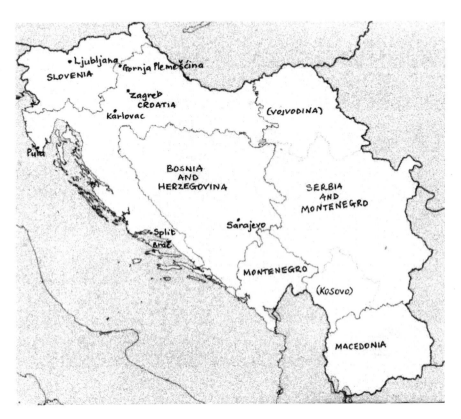

Map 1 The Nation States of Yugoslavia 1946 – 1990

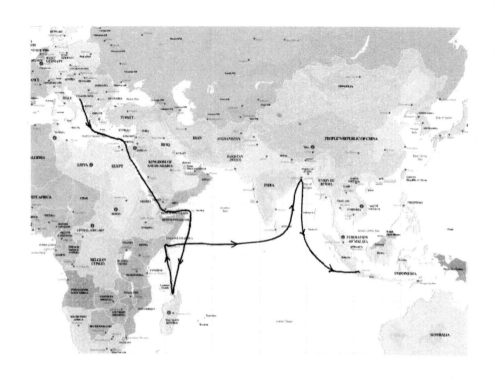

Map 2 Route of Ivan's outward journey, aboard Galeb, to Alexandria and beyond.

Bibliography

Books

Benson Leslie. Yugoslavia A Concise History (Basingstoke, Hampshire and New York: Palgrave Macmillan 2004).

Silber Laura and Little Allan. The Death of Yugoslavia (London: Penguin Books Ltd 1995 and 1996)

Websites

Aleksandar Ranković. en.wikipedia.org/wiki/Aleksandar_Rankovic

Cuban Missile Crisis. jfklibrary.org/JFK/JFK-in-History/Cuban-Missile-Crisis.aspx
Cuban Missile Crisis. en.wikipedia.org/wiki/Cuban_missile_crisis

Diocletian's Palace. whc.unesco.org/en/list/97 (Historical Complex of Split with Diocletian's Palace UNESCO)
Diocletian's Palace. en.wikipedia.org/wiki/Diocletians_Palace

Franciscans. www.newadvent.org7/cathen/06217a.htm. (Catholic Encyclopedia)

Hungarian Uprising. www.johndclare.net/cold_war14.htm - Hungarian Revolution 1956

Hungarian Uprising. www.britanicca.com/EBchecked/topic/276709/Hungarian-Revolution

Josip Broz Tito. www.britanicca.com/EBchecked/topic/597295/Josip-Broz-Tito
Josip Broz Tito. www.infoplease.com/encyclopedia/people/tito-josip-broz-tito-dictatorship.html

King Petar 2nd of Yugoslavia. en.wikipedia.org/wiki/Peter_11_of_Yugoslavia
King Petar 2nd of Yugoslavia
www.britanicca.com/EBchecked/topic/453727/Peter-11ahtm

Partizans. en.wikipedia.org/wiki/Yugoslav_Partisans

UDBa. www.slideshare.net/OWTF/udba-the-state-security-administration
UDBa.en.wikipedia.org/wiki/State_Security_Service_(Socialist_Federal_Republic_of_Yugoslavia)

Photograph 25

en.wikipedia.org/wiki/Aleksander_Ranković
(see http//creativecommons.org/licences/by-sa/3.0/ for direction to licence for use of this photograph)

Maps

Map 1. en.wikipedia.org/wiki/File:Yugoslavia_(1946-1990)_location_map.svg

Names of states and some towns have been added to original map (see http//creativecommons.org/licences/by-sa/3.0/ for direction to licence for use of this map.)

Map 2. is part of a map from the web page:
www.nationalarchives.gov.uk/cabinetpapers/themes/maps-interactive/maps-in-time.htm
The route of the voyage has been added to this map